Options
Third Edition

Options
Third Edition

Robert W. Kolb

First edition published in 1991 by Kolb Publishing.

Second edition published in 1994 by Kolb Publishing.

Third edition published in 1997 by Blackwell Publishers.

Blackwell Publishers Inc.
350 Main Street
Malden, MA
02148

Blackwell Publishers Ltd.
108 Cowley Road
Oxford OX4 1JF
UK

Library of Congress Cataloging-in-Publication Data

Kolb, Robert W.
  Options / Robert W. Kolb—3rd ed.
    p. cm.
  Includes index.
  ISBN 1-57718-064-X (hc)
  1. Options (Finance)—Prices—Mathematical models. I. Title.
HG6024.A3K65 1997
332.63′728—dc20   96-34107
                                                CIP

British Library of Congress Cataloging-in-Publication Data

Typeset by AM Marketing.

This book is printed on acid-free paper.

To Lori

*upon whom I exercised the call option I
held on her before she exercised the put
option she held on me*

CONTENTS

PREFACE

In this third edition of *Options,* we build our knowledge from the simple to the more complex. Chapter 1 introduces the essential institutional features of the U.S. options market. Chapter 2 begins the analytical portion of the book by exploring popular trading strategies and their payoffs at expiration. When an option is at expiration, there is no difference between an American and European option. (An American option can be exercised at any time; a European option can be exercised only at expiration.) Also, it is easy to specify what the price of an option must be when it is about to expire. Chapter 3 uses no-arbitrage arguments to place rational bounds on option prices. We assume that traders in option markets are money hungry and not foolish. Such traders will exploit any trading opportunity that offers a sure profit with no risk and no investment. By assuming that no such profit opportunities exist, we learn much about which option prices can rationally prevail. The bounds developed in Chapter 3 follow solely on our assumptions of greed and the absence of stupidity. These boundaries do not provide exact option prices, but they specify the range in which the exact price must lie.

To specify the exact price that an option should have requires a model of how stock prices can move. Chapter 4 develops formal pricing models for European options. The price of an option depends on the characteristics of the underlying instrument, notably upon the way in which the price of the underlying instrument can vary. We consider the binomial model and eventually elaborate this model into the Black-Scholes model. Chapter 4 also explores the Merton model. Thus, in Chapter 4 we begin by assuming that the stock price can change only once before the option expires and that the stock price can rise or fall only by a certain percentage. Next, we allow slightly more realism by allowing the stock price to change more frequently before the option expires. Finally, we allow the stock price to change continuously. Under each circumstance, we can say precisely what the option price should be. By following this building block approach, we come to understand the factors that affect option prices. In addition, we can understand the principles of option pricing without suffering mathematical fatigue. At the end of Chapter 4, we are able to specify prices for options that conform very closely to the prices we observe in the marketplace. Chapter 5 is a companion to Chapter 4 in that it explores the option sensitivities of the Black-Scholes and Merton models. These sensitivities (delta, theta, vega, gamma, and rho) are extremely important in using options to hedge or in controlling the risk of speculative strategies.

Chapter 6 develops an extensive treatment of American options. It includes coverage of American puts, the exact American call option pricing formula, the analytic approximation approach to pricing American options, and the binomial model as it applies to options with and without dividends. The coverage of the binomial model for American options with dividends includes continuous dividend yields, episodic dividend yields, and cash dividends.

Chapter 7 explores stock index options, foreign currency options, and options on futures. In doing so, it covers both European and American options. The chapter begins by focusing on European options and the application of the Black-Scholes and Merton models to these options. Soon the discussion shifts to American options, and the chapter applies the analytic approximation technique, the exact American call option pricing model, and the binomial model to pricing American options with and without dividends.

Chapter 8 shows that the principles of option pricing can be extended to analyze corporate securities. The chapter considers the option features of common stock, straight bonds, convertible bonds, callable bonds, and warrants. One of the most useful features of this chapter is to illustrate the power of the option approach to the world of finance.

Chapter 9, ''Exotic Options,'' considers an emerging class of options. As the name implies, these exotic options have features that make them more complex than the standard or ''plain vanilla'' options considered in the first eight chapters of the text. A chooser is one type of exotic option. Sometime after the purchase date, the owner of a chooser can choose whether the option should be treated as a call or put option. As a second example, a lookback call option has an exercise price that equals the minimum price observed over a period before expiration. These and other exotic options trade primarily in the over-the-counter market and are becoming increasingly popular as they give a way to tailor risk positions in the ever-changing real world.

OPTION! SOFTWARE

The text is accompanied by an IBM PC program called **OPTION!**. This program consists of nine modules; its procedures can compute virtually all of the model prices and examples in the text. Where applicable, the program can also graph option relationships. Some of the more prominent features of the software are the ability to compute payoffs from option strategies at and prior to expiration, Black-Scholes model prices and sensitivities, Merton model prices and sensitivities, implied volatilities in the Black-Scholes and Merton models, dividend adjustments for European option prices, the binomial model with known price movements, the binomial model as an approximation to the Black-Scholes model, simulation of stock prices consistent with the Black-Scholes model, exact American call option prices, the analytical approximation of American option prices, the binomial model for American option prices with a variety of dividend payment plans, as well as all of the exotic options studied in Chapter 9.

For stock index options, foreign exchange options, and options on futures, the program can compute Black-Scholes and Merton model prices and sensitivities, the analytic approximation for American option prices, and binomial model prices for European and American options with a variety of dividend payment plans. In addition, the program includes a utility for computing univariate and bivariate cumulative normal probabilities. Many of these modules allow extensive graphing of option pricing relationships, with the capability of saving graphs for printing. The program has been designed for easy use. The appendix to this text shows how to install and use **OPTION!**. Further, the text includes more than 50 exercises that can be completed using the software. It is an extremely powerful tool for learning option pricing and for exploring option pricing relationships.

CHANGES IN THE THIRD EDITION

For the third edition of *Options,* the text has been checked carefully for accuracy and revised where needed for enhanced readability and comprehension. The major new material in the third edition is a completely new chapter, Chapter 9, *Exotic Options.* This new chapter reflects the emergence of an important new class of options and considers these options in detail, including detailed pricing formulas and worked-out computational examples for each type of option. In addition, the **OPTION!** software that accompanies this book has been expanded to provide full coverage of all of the exotic options covered in the new Chapter 9.

ACKNOWLEDGMENTS

The preparation of this book has benefitted from the assistance of a number of people. Andrea Coens, Phil Rizika, Adam Carlin, Joe Rodriguez, Sandi Schroeder, and Evelyn Gosnell worked on earlier editions of this book.

I would like to express my gratitude to everyone at Blackwell, with special thanks to Rolf Janke, Editorial Director, Mary Beckwith, Assistant Editor, Jan Phillips, Production Manager, Megan Zuckerman, Graphic Designer, and Diane McCree, Production Editor. Of course, I alone am responsible for any remaining deficiencies.

Over the years, the students in my futures and option classes have used this book since the early page proofs of its first edition, giving me a chance to test it in the classroom before publication. A large number of scholars around the country contributed their time and effort to help improve the book. The following individuals commented on the book and made numerous suggestions for improvement. My profound thanks to them all:

Peter Alonzi	*Chicago Board of Trade*
Fernando Alvarez	*Babson College*
Michael Auster	*University of Nevada*
Ron Best	*University of South Alabama*
Laurence E. Blose	*University of North Carolina*
Gerald Buetow	*James Madison University*
Joe Brocato	*Tarleton State University*
Anthony Byrd	*Tulane University*
Alyce Rita Campbell	*University of Oregon*
Chao Chen	*California State University*
Ren-Raw Chen	*Rutgers University*
Jin Wook Choi	*Chicago Institute of Futures and Options*
Kewn Victor Chow	*West Virginia University*
Andreas Christofi	*Azusa Pacific University*
Dennis Debrecht	*Carroll College*

Karen Craft Denning	*West Virginia University*
David Ding	*Nanyang Technological University – Singapore*
Richard J. Dowen	*Northern Illinois University*
Don Fehrs	*University of Notre Dame*
James H. Filkins	*University of St. Thomas*
Hung Gay Fung	*University of Baltimore*
Dean Furbush	*Economists Incorporated*
Gerry Gay	*Georgia State University*
Nicolas Gressis	*Wright State University*
G. D'Anne Hancock	*University of Missouri*
T. Harikumar	*University of Alaska*
Delvin Hawley	*University of Mississippi*
Shantaram Hegde	*University of Connecticut*
Anthony Herbst	*University of Texas*
Joanne Hill	*Goldman Sachs*
Marcus Ingram	*Clark Atlanta University*
Ameeta Jaiswal	*University of St. Thomas*
Kurt R. Jesswein	*Laredo State University*
Joan Junkus	*DePaul University*
Kandice Kahl	*Clemson University*
Dongcheol Kim	*Rutgers University*
Dorothy Koehl	*University of Puget Sound*
Gary Koppenhaver	*Iowa State University*
William Kracaw	*Pennsylvania State University*
Paul Laux	*University of Texas – Austin*
C. Jevons Lee	*Tulane University*
Chun Lee	*Southern Illinois University*
Jae Ha Lee	*University of Oklahoma*
Jay Marchand	*Westminster College*
Michael B. Madaris	*University of Southern Mississippi*
A.G. Malliaris	*Loyola University of Chicago*
David Martin	*Davidson College*
Robert Mooradian	*University of Florida*
R. Charles Moyer	*Wake Forest University*
Dec Mullarkey	*Boston College*
Richard Osbourne	*American University*
Jayendu Patel	*Harvard University*
Ramon Rabinovitch	*University of Houston*
Sailesh Ramamurtie	*Georgia State University*
Cyrus Ramezani	*University of Wisconsin*
Dick Rendleman	*University of North Carolina*
Bruce Resnick	*Indiana University*
Tom Schneeweis	*University of Massachusetts*
Robert Schweitzer	*University of Delaware*
R. Stephen Sears	*Texas Tech University*

Bipin Shah	*University of Nebraska*
Kuldeep Shastri	*University of Pittsburgh*
Bruce Sherrick	*University of Illinois*
Sandeep Singh	*State University of New York*
William E. Stein	*Texas A & M University*
Hans R. Stoll	*Vanderbilt University*
Steve Swidler	*University of Texas*
Alex Tabarrok	*George Mason University*
Russ Taussig	*University of Hawaii*
Kashi Nath Tiwari	*Kennesaw State College*
Alex Triantis	*University of Wisconsin*
George Tsetskos	*Drexel University*
Anne Fremault Vila	*Boston University*
Joseph Vu	*DePaul University*
James Wansley	*University of Tennessee*
Brian Webb	*Indiana University*
Paul Weller	*University of Iowa*
Tony R. Wingler	*University of North Carolina*
John Yeoman	*University of Georgia*
Jin Zhenhu	*University of Houston*

<table>
<tr><td>CHAPTER
1</td><td></td></tr>
</table>

CHAPTER 1 — THE OPTIONS MARKET

INTRODUCTION

Everyone has options. When buying a car, we can add more equipment to the automobile that is "optional at extra cost." In this sense, an option is a choice. This book examines options in financial markets. These are a very specific type of option – an option created through a financial contract. This chapter defines the options created by these financial contracts and shows how participants in financial markets can use these special option contracts.

Options have played a role in security markets for many years, although no one can be certain how long. Initially, options were created by individualized contracts between two parties. However, until recently, there was no organized exchange for trading options. The development of option exchanges stimulated greater interest and more active trading of options. In many respects, the recent history of option trading can be regarded as an option revolution. This chapter considers the options exchanges and the well-defined options contracts that trade on these exchanges.

In modern options trading, an individual can contact a broker and trade an option on an exchange in a matter of moments. This chapter explains how orders flow from an individual to the exchange and shows how the order is executed and confirmed for the trader. At first, the options exchanges traded options only on stocks. Now exchanges trade options on a wide variety of underlying goods, such as bonds, futures contracts, and foreign currencies. The chapter concludes with a brief consideration of these diverse types of options.

The importance of options goes well beyond the profit-motivated trading that is most visible to the public. Today, sophisticated institutional traders use options to execute extremely complex strategies. For instance, large pension funds and investment banking firms trade options in conjunction with stock and bond portfolios to control risk and capture additional profits. Corporations use options to execute their financing strategies and to hedge unwanted risks that they could not avoid in any other way. Option research has advanced in step with the exploding option market. Scholars have found that there is an option way of thinking that allows many financial decisions to be analyzed using an option framework. Together, these developments constitute an options revolution.

WHAT IS AN OPTION?

Every exchange traded option is either a **call option** or a **put option**.[1] The owner of a call option has the right to purchase the underlying good at a specific price; this right lasts until a specific date. The owner of a put option has the right to sell the underlying good at a specific price; this right also lasts until a specific date. In short, the owner of a call option can call the underlying good away from someone else. Likewise, the owner of a put option can put the good to someone else by making the opposite party buy the good. To acquire these rights, owners of options buy them from other traders by paying the price, or premium, to a seller.

Options are created only by buying and selling. Therefore, for every owner of an option, there is a seller. The seller of an option is also known as an **option writer**. The seller receives payment for an option from the purchaser. In exchange for the payment received, the seller confers rights to the option owner. The seller of a call option receives payment and, in exchange, gives the owner of a call option the right to purchase the underlying good at a specific price with this right lasting for a specific time. The seller of a put option receives payment from the purchaser and promises to buy the underlying good at a specific price for a specific time, if the owner of the put option chooses.

In these agreements, all rights lie with the owner of the option. In purchasing an option, the buyer makes payments and receives rights to buy or sell the underlying good on specific terms. In selling an option, the seller receives payment and promises to sell or purchase the underlying good on specific terms – at the discretion of the option owner. With put and call options and buyers and sellers, four basic positions are possible. Notice that the owner of an option has all the rights. After all, that is what the owner purchases. The seller of an option has all the obligations because the seller undertakes obligations in exchange for payment.

Every option has an underlying good. Through most of this book, we will speak of a share of stock as the underlying good. However, all the principles that we will develop apply to options on different underlying goods. The call writer gives the purchaser the right to demand the underlying good from the writer. However, the writer of a call need not own the underlying good when he or she writes the option. If a seller writes a call and does not own the underlying good, the call is a **naked call**. If the writer owns the underlying good, he has sold a **covered call**. When a trader writes a naked call, he undertakes the obligation of immediately securing the underlying good and delivering it if the purchaser of the call chooses to exercise the call.

AN OPTION EXAMPLE

Consider an option with a share of XYZ stock as the underlying good. Assume that today is March 1 and that XYZ shares trade at $110. The market, we assume, trades a call option to buy a share of XYZ at $100 with this right lasting until August 15 and the price of this option being $15. In this example, the owner of a call must pay $100 to acquire the stock. This $100 price is called the **exercise price** or the **striking price**. The price of the option, or the **option premium**, is $15. The option expires in 5.5 months, which gives 168 days until expiration.

If a trader buys the call option, he pays $15 and receives the right to purchase a share of XYZ stock by paying an additional $100, if he so chooses, by August 15. The seller of the option receives $15, and she promises to sell a share of XYZ for $100 if the owner of the call chooses to buy before August 15. Notice that the price of the option, the option premium, is paid when the option trades. The premium the seller receives is hers to keep whether or not the owner of the call decides to exercise the option. If the owner of the call exercises his option, he will pay $100 no matter what the current price of XYZ stock may be. If the owner of the option exercises his option, the seller of the option will receive the $100 exercise price when she delivers the stock as she promised.

At the same time, puts will trade on XYZ. Consider a put with a striking price of $100 trading on March 1 that also expires on August 15. Assume that the price of the put is $5. If a trader purchases a put, he pays $5. In exchange, he receives the right to sell a share of XYZ for $100 at any time until August 15. The seller of the put receives $5, and she promises to buy the share of XYZ for $100 if the owner of the put option chooses to sell before August 15.

In both the put and call example, the payment by the purchaser is gone forever at the time the option trades. The seller of the option receives the payment and keeps it, whatever the owner of the option decides to do. If the owner of the call exercises his option, then he pays the exercise price as an additional amount and receives a share. Likewise, if the owner of the put exercises his option, then he surrenders the share and receives the exercise price as an additional amount. The owner of the option may choose never to exercise. In that case, the option will expire on August 15. The payment the seller receives is hers to keep whether or not the owner exercises. If the owner chooses not to exercise, the seller has a profit equal to the premium received and does not have to perform under the terms of the option contract. Table 1.1 shows the disposition of stock options. It gives a good guide to the frequency with which options are disposed of by exercise, by sale, or by expiring worthless. Most are sold, while many others expire worthless. A relatively small percentage of options are exercised.

MONEYNESS

"Moneyness" is an option concept that is as important as the word is awkward. It refers to the potential profit or loss from the immediate exercise of an option. An option may be **in-the-money**, **out-of-the-money**, or **at-the-money**.

A call option is in-the-money if the stock price exceeds the exercise price. For example, a call option with an exercise price of $100 on a stock trading at $110 is $10 in-the-money. A call option is out-of-the-money if the stock price is less than the exercise price. For example, if the stock is at $110 and the exercise price on a call is $115, the call is $5 out-of-the-money. A call option is at-the-money if the stock price equals (or is very near to) the exercise price.

Disposition of Equity Options, 1995	Table 1.1	
	Percentage Disposition	
Disposition	**Calls**	**Puts**
Exercise	10.6	11.7
Sale	60.4	49.5
Long expired worthless	29.0	38.8

Source: From Chicago Board Options Exchange, *Market Statistics,* 1995. Reprinted by permission of the Chicago Board Options Exchange.

A put option is in-the-money if the stock price is below the exercise price. As an example, consider a put option with an exercise price of $70 on a stock that is worth $60. The put is $10 in-the-money because the immediate exercise of the put would give a $10 cash inflow. Similarly, if the put on the same stock had an exercise price of $55, the put would be $5 out-of-the-money. If the put had an exercise price equal to the stock price, the put would be at-the-money. Puts and calls can also be **deep-in-the-money** or **deep-out-of-the-money**, if the cash flows from an immediate exercise would be large.

AMERICAN AND EUROPEAN OPTIONS

There are two fundamental kinds of options: the **American option** and the **European option**. An American option permits the owner to exercise at any time before or at expiration. The owner of a European option can exercise only at expiration. Thus, the two kinds of options differ because the American option permits early exercise. To this point, we have considered option values only at expiration. If the option is at expiration, American and European options will have the same value. Both can be exercised immediately or be allowed to expire worthless. Prior to expiration, we will see that the two options are conceptually distinct. Further, they may have different values under certain circumstances. In this chapter, and through the remainder of the book, we will need to distinguish the principles that apply to each kind of option.

Consider any two options that are just alike, except one is an American option and the other is a European option. By saying that the two options are just alike, we mean that they have the same underlying stock, the same exercise price, and the same time remaining until expiration. The American option gives its owner all the rights and privileges that the owner of the European option possesses. However, the owner of the American option has the right to exercise the option before expiration if he desires. From these considerations, we can see that the American option must be worth at least as much as the European option.

The owner of an American option can treat the option as a European option by deciding not to exercise until expiration. Therefore, the American option cannot be worth less than the European option. However, the American option can be worth more. The American option will be worth more if it is desirable to exercise earlier. Under certain circumstances, which we will explore later, the right to exercise before expiration can be valuable. In this case, the American option will be worth more than the otherwise identical European option.

In some cases, the right to exercise before expiration will be worthless. For these situations, the American option will have the same value as the European option. In general, the European option is simpler and easier to analyze. However, in actual markets, most options are American. This is true both in the United States and throughout the world. We should not associate the names ''American'' and ''European'' with geographic locations. In the present context, the names simply refer to the time at which holders can exercise these options.

WHY TRADE OPTIONS?

Options trading today is more popular than ever before. For the investor, options serve a number of important roles. First, many investors trade options to speculate on the price movements of the underlying stock. However, investors could merely trade the stock itself. As we will see, trading the option instead of the underlying stock can offer a number of advantages. Call options are always cheaper than the underlying stock, so it takes less money to trade calls. Generally, but not universally, put options are also cheaper than the underlying goods. In relative terms, the option price is more volatile than the price of the underlying stock, so investors can get more price action per dollar of investment by investing in options instead of investing in the stock itself.

Options are extremely popular among sophisticated investors who hold large stock portfolios. Accordingly, institutional investors, such as mutual funds and pension funds, are prime users of the options market. By trading options in conjunction with their stock portfolios, investors can carefully adjust the risk and return characteristics of their entire investment. As we will see, a sophisticated trader can use options to increase or decrease the risk of an existing stock portfolio. For example, it is possible to combine a risky stock and a risky option to form a riskless combined position that performs like a risk-free bond.[2]

Many investors prefer to trade options rather than stocks in order to save transaction costs, avoid tax exposure, and avoid stock market restrictions.[3] We already mentioned that some investors trade options to achieve the same risk exposure with less capital. In many instances, traders can use options to take a particular risk position and pay lower transaction costs than stocks would require. Likewise, specific provisions of the tax code may favor option trading over trading the underlying stock. If different traders face different tax schedules, one may find advantage in buying options and another may find advantage in selling options, relative to trading stocks. Finally, the stock and option markets have their own institutional rules. Differences in these rules may stimulate option trading. For example, selling stock short is highly restricted.[4] By trading in the option market, it is possible to replicate a short sale of stock and avoid some stock market restrictions.[5]

THE OPTION CONTRACT

One of the major reasons for the success of options exchanges is that they offer standardized contracts. In a financial market, traders want to be able to trade a good quickly and at a fair price. They can do this if the market is **liquid**. A liquid market provides an efficient and cost-effective trading mechanism with a high volume of trading. Standardizing the options contract has helped promote liquidity. The standardized contract has a specific size and expiration date. Trading on the exchange occurs at certain well-publicized times, so traders know when they will be able to find other traders in the marketplace. The exchange standardizes the exercise prices at which options will trade. With fewer exercise prices, there will be more trading available at a given exercise price. This too promotes liquidity.

Each option contract is for 100 shares of the underlying stock. Exercise prices are specified at intervals of $10, $5, or $2.50, depending on the share price. For example, XYZ trades in the $100 range, and XYZ options have exercise prices spaced at $5 intervals. Every option has a specified expiration month. The option expires on the Saturday after the third Friday in the exercise month. Trading in the option ceases on the third Friday, but the owner may exercise the option on the final Saturday.

THE OPTIONS MARKET

In this section, we consider the most important facets of the options market in the United States. We begin by considering the exchanges where options trade. We then consider an extended example to see how to read option prices as they appear in *The Wall Street Journal*. We conclude this section by analyzing the market activity in the different types of options that are traded on the various exchanges.

Reading Option Prices

Table 1.2 shows typical price quotations for options on a common stock from a U.S. newspaper. Prices are for January 26 for trading options on the stock of XYZ corporation. On that day, XYZ closed at 96 7/8 per share. The table shows listings for XYZ options with striking prices of $90, $95, $100, and $105. It would not be unusual for other striking prices to be represented as well. Options expire in February, March, and April of the same year, and the table shows option prices for both puts and calls. An "r" indicates that the option was not traded on the day for which prices are reported, while an "s" shows that the specific option is not listed for trading.[6]

As an example, consider the call option with a striking price of $100 that expires in March. This option has a price of $1 7/8 or $1.875. This is the price of the call for a single share. However, each option contract is written for 100 shares. Therefore, to purchase this option, the buyer would pay $187.50 for one contract. Owning this call option would give the buyer the right to purchase 100 shares of XYZ at $100 per share until the option expires in March.

We can learn much from a careful consideration of the price relationships revealed in the table. First, notice that option prices are generally higher the longer the time until the option expires. This is true for both calls and puts. Other things being equal, the longer one has the option to buy or sell, the better. Thus, we expect options with longer terms to expiration to be worth more. Second, for a call, the lower the striking price, the more the call option is worth. For a call, the striking price is the amount the call holder must pay to secure the stock. The lower the amount one must pay, the better; therefore, the lower the exercise price, the more the call is worth. Third, for a put option, the higher the striking price, the more the put is worth. For a put, the striking price is the value the put holder receives when he exercises his option to sell the put. Therefore, the more the put entitles its owner to receive, the greater the value of the put. A moment's reflection shows that these simple relationships make sense. Following chapters explore these and similar relationships in detail.

Table 1.2	Option Price Quotations						
XYZ	**Strike Price**		**Calls**			**Puts**	
		FEB	MAR	APR	FEB	MAR	APR
96 7/8	$ 90	6 5/8	s	9 1/8	5/8	s	1 3/8
	95	2 7/8	4 3/8	5 1/2	1 5/8	2 5/8	3 1/8
	100	7/8	1 7/8	3 1/8	4 5/8	r	6 1/4
	105	1/4	13/16	1 5/8	9 1/2	r	11

Note: r indicates no trading on the day for which prices are reported; s indicates that the specific option is not listed for trading.

Option Exchanges

Trading options undoubtedly grew up with the development of financial markets. In the nineteenth century, investors traded options in an informal market; however, the market was subject to considerable corruption. For example, some sellers of options would refuse to perform as obligated. In the twentieth century, the United States developed a more orderly market called the Put and Call Broker and Dealers Association. Member firms acted to bring buyers and sellers of options together. However, this was an over-the-counter market. The market had no central exchange floor, and standardization of option contract terms was not complete. The lack of an exchange and imperfect standardization of the contracts kept this option market from flourishing.

In 1973, the Chicago Board of Trade, a large futures exchange, created the Chicago Board Options Exchange (CBOE). The CBOE is an organized options exchange that trades highly standardized option contracts. It opened to trade calls on April 26, 1973; put trading began in 1977. Since 1973, other exchanges have begun to trade options, with annual trading of about 300,000,000 options.

Trading of options on organized exchanges in the United States embraces a number of different underlying instruments. First among these is the stock option – an option on an individual share of common stock issued by a corporation. While we focus most closely on this type of option for the majority of this book, there are other important classes of options with very different underlying instruments. Options trade on various financial indexes. These indexes can measure the performance of groups of stocks, or precious metals, or any other good for which an index can be constructed as a measure of value. Options also trade on foreign currencies. In this case, the underlying good is a unit of a foreign currency, such as a Japanese yen, and traders buy and sell call and put options on the yen, as well as other currencies. Another major type of underlying good is a futures contract. An option on futures is also known as a futures option. As we will see, this is an important class of options. Futures contracts are written on a wide variety of goods, such as agricultural products, precious metals, petroleum products, stock indexes, foreign currency, and debt instruments. Therefore, futures options by themselves embrace a tremendous diversity of goods.

Table 1.3 lists the principal option exchanges in the United States and shows the kinds of options traded on each exchange. The exchanges in Table 1.3 may be classified into three groups depending upon whether the primary business of the exchange is the trading of options, stocks, or futures. The CBOE deals exclusively in options, although as the leading option exchange in the United States, it trades a wide variety of different kinds of options. The Philadelphia Stock Exchange (PHLX), the American Stock Exchange (AMEX), the Pacific Stock Exchange (PSE), and the New York Stock Exchange (NYSE) are principally stock markets that also trade options. The underlying instruments for the options at these exchanges go far beyond stocks as we will see. The third group consists of futures exchanges, such as the Chicago Board of Trade (CBOT), the Chicago Mercantile Exchange (CME), the Coffee, Sugar and Cocoa Exchange (CSCE), the Kansas City Board of Trade (KCBT), the MidAmerica Exchange (MIDAM), the New York Cotton Exchange (NYCE), the New York Futures Exchange (NYFE), and the New York Mercantile Exchange (NYME). These futures exchanges trade options on futures exclusively, and they tend to trade options on the futures contracts in which they specialize.

Exchange Diversity and Market Statistics

In this section, we consider the options market in more detail. Table 1.4 shows the volume of all exchange traded options in the United States by the type of option: stock option, index option, foreign

Table 1.3	Principal Option Exchanges in the United States
Chicago Board Options Exchange (CBOE)	Options on individual stocks, options on stock indexes, and options on Treasury securities
Philadelphia Stock Exchange (PHLX)	Stocks, futures, and options on individual stocks, currencies, and stock indexes
American Stock Exchange (AMEX)	Stocks, options on individual stocks and stock indexes
Pacific Stock Exchange (PSE)	Options on individual stocks and a stock index
New York Stock Exchange (NYSE)	Stocks and options on individual stocks and a stock index
Chicago Board of Trade (CBOT)	Futures, options on futures for agricultural goods, precious metals, stock indexes, and debt instruments
Chicago Mercantile Exchange (CME)	Futures, options on futures for agricultural goods, stock indexes, debt instruments, and currencies
Coffee, Sugar and Cocoa Exchange (CSCE)	Futures and options on agricultural futures
Kansas City Board of Trade (KCBT)	Futures and options on agricultural futures
MidAmerica Commodity Exchange (MIDAM)	Futures and options on futures for agricultural goods and precious metals
Minneapolis Grain Exchange (MGE)	Futures and options on agricultural futures
New York Cotton Exchange (NYCE)	Futures and options on agricultural, currency, and debt instrument futures
New York Futures Exchange (NYFE)	Futures and options on stock indexes
New York Mercantile Exchange (NYME)	Futures and options on energy futures

currency option, and options on futures. Stock options continue to lead in terms of volume, but they are followed closely by index options. Options on futures are also widely traded, but foreign currency options account for only 4 percent of all options traded.[7]

Stock Options. Options on individual stocks trade on the Chicago Board Options Exchange and four exchanges that principally trade stocks themselves. These same five exchanges trade all options in the United States, except options on futures, which trade on futures exchanges.

Option Volume in the United States by Type of Option		Table 1.4
	1995 Volume	
Type of Option	**Contracts**	**Percentage**
Stock Options	174,380,271	45.58
Index Options	107,810,490	28.18
Foreign Currency Options	4,978,519	1.30
Options on Futures	95,406,042	24.94
Total	382,575,322	100.00

Source: Chicago Board Options Exchange, *Market Statistics,* 1995; Commodity Futures Trading Commission, *Annual Report,* 1995; Philadelphia Stock Exchange. Data for options on futures are for the fiscal year ending September 30, 1995.

Table 1.5 shows the relative importance of these five exchanges (CBOE, AMEX, PHLX, PSE, and NYSE) in options trading. The CBOE clearly dominates the trading volume, which is mostly concentrated in options on stocks. Table 1.6 shows the distribution of trading volume in stock options among the exchanges.

Figure 1.1 shows a sample of the price quotations for options on individual stocks that appears each day in *The Wall Street Journal.* The first column lists the identifier for the stock and shows the closing stock price for the shares immediately beneath the identifier. The next two columns of data show the exercise price and the month the option expires. The option will expire on a specific date in the expiration month. For the call and the put separately, the quotations show the volume and the final price for the option. Options trade on hundreds of individual stocks.

Index Options. Table 1.7 shows the distribution of trading in index options by exchange. The lead of the CBOE is overwhelming. Most index options are based on various stock indexes. The most successful single index contract is based on the S&P 100 and trades at the CBOE. While the S&P 100 index captures the price movements of the largest stocks in the market, many index options are

Total Option Volume by Exchange, 1995		Table 1.5
Exchange	**Contract Volume**	**Percentage**
Chicago Board Options Exchange	178,533,465	62.27
American Stock Exchange	52,391,899	18.27
Philadelphia Stock Exchange	22,000,030	7.67
Pacific Stock Exchange	30,905,131	10.78
New York Stock Exchange	2,885,698	1.01
Total	286,716,223	100.00

Source: From Chicago Board Options Exchange, *Market Statistics,* 1995. Reprinted by permission of the Chicago Board Options Exchange.

Table 1.6	Equity Option Volume by Exchange, 1995	
Exchange	**1995 Volume**	**Percentage**
Chicago Board Options Exchange	77,040,466	44.18
American Stock Exchange	48,886,858	28.03
Philadelphia Stock Exchange	14,739,706	8.45
Pacific Stock Exchange	30,852,968	17.69
New York Stock Exchange	2,860,273	1.65
Total	174,380,271	100.00

Source: From Chicago Board Options Exchange, *Market Statistics,* 1995. Reprinted by permission of the Chicago Board Options Exchange.

based on more narrow stock market indexes. For example, the AMEX trades index options based on biotech stocks. Figure 1.2 shows a sample of the quotations for index options from *The Wall Street Journal.* It also indicates the wide variety of indexes that underlie various options. Notice that these include stock indexes for foreign stock markets. The quotations show the expiration month, the exercise price, whether the option is a call or a put, the volume, the closing price, the change since the previous day's close, and the open interest.

Foreign Currency Options. Option trading on individual foreign currencies is concentrated at the Philadelphia Stock Exchange (PHLX).[8] Each option contract is written for a specific number of units of the foreign currency. For example, a contract is written for DM62,500, £31,250, or ¥6,250,000. These different amounts of the foreign currencies place the U.S. dollar value of each contract in the range of $25,000 to $75,000. Prices for the options are quoted in U.S. dollars, and the exercise prices are also stated in U.S. dollars. The dominant currency is the German mark, with the Japanese yen being a distant second.[9]

Figure 1.3 shows price quotations for these options from *The Wall Street Journal*; the quotations are organized in the same fashion as the others we have already considered. The PHLX trades American and European style options and some options with expirations at the end of selected months. However, the American style options continue to be the dominant market.

Options on Futures. In the United States, options on futures trade only on futures exchanges, and futures exchanges trade options only on futures. In general, each futures exchange trades options on its own active futures contracts. Therefore, the variety of options on futures is almost as diverse as futures contracts themselves.

Because the futures market is dominated by two large exchanges, the Chicago Board of Trade and the Chicago Mercantile Exchange, these two exchanges have the largest share of trading of options on futures. Table 1.8 shows the relative volume of trading in options on futures by exchange. Together, the CBOT and CME have about 85 percent of all volume. Both of these exchanges trade options on agricultural commodities and financial instruments. The New York Mercantile Exchange is the third-largest exchange for trading options on futures, largely because of its successful oil-related products. The other exchanges have only minor volume.

Table 1.9 shows the volume of trading in futures options by the type of the underlying futures. Financial instruments account for the majority of futures options and include options on stock index

Price Quotations for Stock Options **Figure 1.1**

MOST ACTIVE CONTRACTS

Option/Strike				Vol	Exch	Last	Net Chg	a-Close	Open Int
Dig Eq	May	60		12,517	XC	3 1/4	+ 1 3/4	60 5/8	5,469
Cisco	Jul	50		6,486	XC	2 7/8	+ 1/8	48 5/8	13,451
Wlwrth	Jun	20		6,148	PB	1 3/16	+ 9/16	19 3/4	86
Compaq	May	45		5,943	PC	1 11/16	+ 11/16	43 7/8	10,639
Motrla	May	60		5,789	AM	2 15/16	+ 1 3/16	61 3/4	8,313
TelMex	May	35	p	5,487	XC	3/4	+ 1/8	36	11,636
BnkNwk	May	35		4,845	XC	1 3/16	+ 3/16	32 5/8	7,305
Iomega	May	45		4,354	XC	9 7/8	+ 7 1/8	51 7/8	1,572
Dig Eq	May	50		4,167	XC	10 1/2	+ 4	60 5/8	8,042
IntgDv	May	12 1/2		4,047	XC	2 1/4	+ 1 7/16	14 1/4	5,649
Iomega	May	40	p	3,674	XC	1 11/16	−1 13/16	51 7/8	1,279
MicrTc	May	35		3,650	XC	1 1/16	+ 1/8	33 1/4	11,056
TelMex	May	35		3,633	XC	1 15/16	− 7/8	36	28,369
SunMic	May	55		3,586	PC	2 3/8	+1 11/16	54 3/8	3,149
Iomega	May	40		3,508	XC	13 1/2	+ 8 1/2	51 7/8	6,755
BayNwk	May	25		3,332	XC	7 3/4	+ 1 1/2	32 5/8	3,992
Seagte	May	50	p	3,267	XC	1 1/16	− 5/16	54	647
SunMic	May	50		3,081	PC	5 1/2	+ 3 1/16	54 3/8	5,609
SunMic	Jul	40	p	3,022	PC	5/8	− 3/8	54 3/8	4,137
Dig Eq	May	50	p	2,980	XC	5/16	− 13/16	60 5/8	1,929

Option/Strike				Vol	Exch	Last	Net Chg	a-Close	Open Int
Cisco	Jun	50		2,965	XC	2 7/16	+ 7/16	48 5/8	8,634
Dig Eq	May	55		2,958	XC	6 3/8	+ 2 7/8	60 5/8	3,088
Cisco	May	50		2,952	XC	1 1/2	+ 3/8	48 5/8	6,824
Cisco	Jul	40	p	2,855	XC	1 7/16	− 1/2	48 5/8	8,299
Cisco	Jun	40	p	2,512	XC	15/16	− 7/16	48 5/8	3,836
StrlCh	Jul	12 1/2		2,511	XC	13/16	− 1/4	12 5/8	2,339
Seagte	May	55	p	2,460	XC	2 3/4	. . .	54	2,691
MicrTc	May	37 1/2		2,415	XC	7/16	+ 1/16	33 1/4	3,201
Iomega	May	45	p	2,373	XC	3 3/8	− 3 3/8	51 7/8	546
Intel	Jul	70		2,347	AM	3 3/8	+ 1/4	68 7/64	11,653
Intel	May	70		2,342	AM	1 1/4	+ 1/8	68 7/64	4,409
I B M	May	115		2,259	CB	1 1/4	− 5/16	107	18,339
L S I	Jul	40		2,194	CB	1 1/2	+ 1/4	34 3/4	2,415
Chase o	May	70		2,182	AM	1 7/8	− 1/8		250
AmerOn	May	65		2,181	XC	4 1/8	+ 1 7/16	65 1/8	2,882
I B M	May	110		2,153	CB	2 5/8	− 1/2	107	12,446
Seagte	May	60		2,136	XC	1 5/8	+ 1/16	54	2,806
CmpAsc	Oct	80		2,100	CB	6	+ 1	74 1/2	104
Dig Eq	May	65		2,093	XC	1 5/16	+ 13/16	60 5/8	2,237
K mart	May	10		2,081	CB	1/2	+ 1/16	10 1/8	5,383

			–Call–		–Put–	
Option/Strike		Exp.	Vol.	Last	Vol.	Last
ABR Inf	55	May	55	6 1/2	...	...
60 1/4	60	Jun	75	4 3/8	...	...
ADC Tel	40	May	143	2 3/4	...	...
41 1/4	40	Nov	65	6 5/8	...	...
ADT	17 1/2	Sep	100	1 1/4	...	...
AGCO	25	May	130	1 1/8	...	...
AMR	80	May	15	9 1/8	125	1/4
90	85	May	20	5	161	7/8
90	90	May	116	2 3/4	122	2 1/2
90	90	Nov	100	9 1/8	...	...
90	95	May	97	1 1/8	2	5 1/2
APACT	75	May	52	9 1/4	4	2 7/8
ASA	42 1/2	May	...	...	80	7/16
45	45	May	126	1 3/16	66	1 3/8
45	45	Aug	255	2 7/8	260	2 3/4
AT&T	60	May	172	1 7/8	591	3/4
60 5/8	60	Jun	...	...	125	1 1/4
60 5/8	65	May	440	3/16	5	4 1/4
60 5/8	65	Jun	293	9/16	...	...
60 5/8	65	Jul	236	13/16	...	...
60 5/8	65	Oct	91	1 11/16	...	...
AVX Cp	22 1/2	Nov	85	3 3/4	...	...
23 3/4	25	Jun	120	1	...	...
23 3/4	25	Aug	135	2 1/8	...	...
23 3/4	25	Nov	52	3	...	...
Aames	45	Jun	80	3 1/2	...	...
44 1/8	45	Sep	210	6	...	...
Abbt L	40	Jun	3	2 7/16	100	7/8
41 3/4	45	May	202	1/8	...	...
41 3/4	45	Aug	79	15/16	...	...
Aclaim	10	Jul	75	1 3/16	...	...
AccuStff	23 3/8	Jul	403	8 1/8	...	...
30	25	May	61	5 1/2	8	3/4
30	27 1/2	May	10	5	71	1 7/16
30	30	May	193	2 5/8	68	2 15/16
30	30	Jun	52	3 3/4	...	...
30	30	Jul	56	4 1/2	...	...
30	35	Oct	127	4 5/8	4	9
Actel	15	May	70	3 5/8	...	...
Adaptc	50	May	151	6 1/4	60	1 3/16
55	55	May	256	3 3/8	102	3 1/8
AdobeS	30	May	132	8 1/4	...	...
38 1/8	35	May	61	4	52	7/8
38 1/8	35	Jul	125	5 5/8	17	2 1/2
38 1/8	40	May	345	1 3/16	3	3 5/8
38 1/8	40	Jun	56	2 1/8	10	3 7/8
38 1/8	45	May	90	5/16	...	...
Adtran	45	Aug	...	...	70	2 7/8
59 3/4	60	May	100	4 1/8	...	...
A M D	15	Jul	...	...	158	5/8
17 3/8	17 1/2	May	248	5/8	38	3/4
17 3/8	17 1/2	Jul	328	1 7/16	172	1 3/8
17 3/8	20	Jul	266	1/2	2	3 1/2
17 3/8	20	Oct	70	1 1/4	...	...

			–Call–		–Put–	
Option/Strike		Exp.	Vol.	Last	Vol.	Last
Baan	65	May	182	1 15/16	...	...
BabySst	40	May	10	6 3/8	95	1
BakrHu	25	May	525	5 3/8	...	...
BallyEnt	15	Jul	111	6 5/8	...	...
21 7/8	17 1/2	Jul	...	...	425	13/16
21 7/8	20	May	1480	2 9/16	196	7/8
21 7/8	20	Jun	240	3	290	1 1/4
21 7/8	22 1/2	May	1001	1	27	1 7/8
21 7/8	22 1/2	Jun	546	1 7/8	300	2 9/16
21 7/8	22 1/2	Jul	55	2	...	...
21 7/8	25	May	1041	7/16	...	...
BancOne	35	May	158	7/8	2	1 1/16
BncoFrn	30	May	148	3/8	...	...
27 1/2	30	Jul	128	1 3/8	...	...
BkBost	42 1/2	Jun	1000	4 3/4	...	...
47 3/8	45	Jun	75	3 1/8	...	...
47 3/8	47 1/2	May	68	7/8	...	...
47 3/8	47 1/2	Jun	1000	1 5/16	...	...
BankNY	45	May	230	2 3/4	...	...
47 1/2	50	Jul	53	1 1/2	...	...
47 1/2	55	Oct	79	7/8	...	...
BankAm	75	May	170	1 3/8	...	...
BarNbl	40	Jun	102	13/16	...	...
BarickG	30	May	468	1 1/8	70	7/8
30 1/4	30	Jun	122	1 5/8	5	1 7/16
30 1/4	30	Jul	640	2	10	1 11/16
30 1/4	35	Jul	757	1/2	...	...
30 1/4	35	Oct	220	1 1/8	...	...
BattlM	10	Jul	104	7/16	...	...
8 7/8	10	Oct	1511	13/16	...	...
BausLm	40	May	10	5/8	70	13/16
BayNwk	25	May	3332	7 3/4	149	3/16
32 5/8	25	Jun	235	8 1/8	139	11/16
32 5/8	25	Sep	86	9 3/4	55	1 11/16
32 5/8	27 1/2	Jun	...	...	90	1 1/16
32 5/8	30	May	1088	3 1/2	335	7/8
32 5/8	35	May	4845	1 3/16	125	3 1/4
32 5/8	40	May	463	1/4	...	...
32 5/8	45	Jun	765	5/16	...	...
32 5/8	50	Sep	1660	1	...	...
BearSt	25	May	121	1 1/8	...	...
BedBth	45	May	94	8 1/8	...	...
52 1/4	50	May	67	4 3/4	20	3 1/8
52 1/4	55	May	85	2 1/8	...	...
BellAtl	60	Oct	2	8 3/4	60	1 5/16
66 1/4	65	May	60	2 3/8	170	7/8
66 1/4	70	Jun	82	1	...	...
BellSo	40	May	198	15/16	30	7/8
39 7/8	40	Jun	54	1 9/16	...	...
39 7/8	40	Jul	36	2	101	1 3/4
BestBuy	15	Jun	203	4 3/4	38	1/4
19 3/8	17 1/2	May	55	1 7/8	25	5/16
19 3/8	17 1/2	Jun	97	2 1/8	...	...
19 3/8	20	May	518	7/16	43	1 1/4
19 3/8	20	Jun	454	1	40	1 5/8

			–Call–		–Put–	
Option/Strike		Exp.	Vol.	Last	Vol.	Last
81	75	Jun	1	7 1/4	55	1 1/8
81	75	Aug	5	8 1/2	106	2
81	80	May	92	2 5/8	168	1 1/2
81	80	Jun	124	4	2	2 3/4
81	80	Aug	70	5 5/8	11	3 5/8
81	85	May	1064	1/2	2	5
81	85	Jun	74	1 1/2	...	...
81	85	Aug	180	3 1/2	...	...
CCFems	30	May	1000	5/16	...	...
Cognos	55	May	72	8 1/4	...	...
Cohrnt	45	May	211	7 1/4	...	...
52 5/16	50	May	103	3 1/8	...	...
ColgPl	85	May	...	...	150	8 1/8
ColData	20	May	...	...	150	3/4
21 3/8	25	Jun	120	1	...	...
ColHsp	55	May	188	3/4	...	...
52 3/8	55	Aug	113	2 5/8	...	...
ColLb	10	Jun	81	2	...	...
Comeric	40	May	305	4 1/8	...	...
43 3/4	45	Jul	63	1 11/16	...	...
CmpUSA	25	May	32	7 1/2	224	1/8
32 1/2	27 1/2	May	564	5	60	3/8
32 1/2	27 1/2	Aug	266	6 7/8	5	1 7/16
32 1/2	30	May	964	3 1/4	1145	5/8
32 1/2	30	Jun	285	4 1/8	20	1 13/16
32 1/2	30	Aug	63	5 1/8	200	2 3/8
32 1/2	32 1/2	May	145	1 11/16	228	1 5/8
32 1/2	32 1/2	Aug	142	3 3/4	190	3 1/4
ChileT	90	May	80	4	...	...
93 3/8	95	May	184	1 1/4	15	4 1/4
Compaq	32 1/2	May	20	12	100	1/16
43 7/8	35	May	58	9	221	3/16
43 7/8	37 1/2	May	63	6 3/4	53	5/16
43 7/8	37 1/2	Jul	76	7 3/4	46	7/8
43 7/8	40	May	835	5	1954	5/8
43 7/8	40	Jul	272	6 1/8	291	1 5/8
43 7/8	40	Oct	56	8	70	2 7/16
43 7/8	42 1/2	May	1159	3 1/8	644	1 1/4
43 7/8	42 1/2	Jun	31	3 7/8	185	2
43 7/8	42 1/2	Jul	67	4 1/2	15	2 1/4
43 7/8	45	May	5943	1 11/16	1439	2 3/8
43 7/8	45	Jun	552	2 1/2	15	3
43 7/8	45	Jul	831	3 1/4	42	3 1/2
43 7/8	45	Oct	979	5	10	4 3/4
43 7/8	47 1/2	May	422	15/16	...	...
43 7/8	47 1/2	Jun	288	1 5/8	...	...
43 7/8	47 1/2	Jul	299	2 3/8	10	5 5/8
43 7/8	50	May	472	7/16	...	...
43 7/8	50	Jun	169	7/8	...	...
43 7/8	50	Jul	1085	1 1/2	...	...
43 7/8	50	Oct	246	3	...	...
43 7/8	55	Jul	57	9/16	...	...
43 7/8	55	Oct	68	1 5/8	...	...
43 7/8	60	Oct	120	1	...	...

Source: From *The Wall Street Journal,* April 24, 1996, p. C12. Reprinted by permission of *The Wall Street Journal,*

Table 1.7	Index Option Contract Volume by Exchange. 1995	
Exchange	**Total Volume**	**Percentage**
Chicago Board Options Exchange	101,427,897	94.08
American Stock Exchange	3,505,041	3.25
Philadelphia Stock Exchange	2,799,964	2.60
Pacific Stock Exchange	52,163	0.05
New York Stock Exchange	25,425	0.02
Total	107,810,490	100.00

Source: From Chicago Board Options Exchange, *Market Statistics,* 1995. Reprinted by permission of the Chicago Board Options Exchange.

futures and interest rate futures. Options on foreign exchange futures, traded principally at the CME, come next. Options on energy and wood product futures constitute the third-largest category, and this volume stems mainly from options on oil-related futures traded primarily at the New York Mercantile Exchange. Options on traditional agricultural futures are much less important than options on financial instruments, currencies, and energy products. Figure 1.4 shows a sample of the quotations for options on futures.

OPTION TRADING PROCEDURES

Every options trader needs to be familiar with the basic features of the market. This section explores the action that takes place on the market floor and the ways in which traders away from the exchange can have their orders executed on the exchange. From its image in the popular press and on television, one gets the impression that the exchange floor is the scene of wild and chaotic action. While the action may become wild, it is never chaotic. Understanding the role of the different participants on the floor helps dispel the illusion of chaos. Essentially, there are three types of people on the exchange floor: traders, clerical personnel associated with the traders, and exchange officials. First, we describe the system that the CBOE uses. Later, we note some differences among exchanges.

Types of Traders

There are three kinds of traders on the floor of the exchange: market makers, floor brokers, and order book officials. A trader who trades for his own account is a market maker. A trader who executes orders for another is a floor broker. The order book official is an employee of the exchange who makes certain kinds of option trades and keeps the book of orders awaiting execution at specified prices.

The Market Maker. The typical market maker owns or leases a seat on the options exchange and trades for his or her own account to make a profit. However, as the name implies, the market maker has an obligation to make a market for the public by standing ready to buy or sell options. Typically, a market maker will concentrate on the options of just a few stocks. Focusing on a few issues allows

INDEX OPTIONS TRADING

Tuesday, April 23, 1996.

Volume, last, net change and open interest for all contracts. Volume figures are unofficial. Open interest reflects previous trading day. p-Put c-Call

CHICAGO

Strike		Vol.	Last	Net Chg.	Open Int.
CB MEXICO INDEX (MEX)					
Jun	70 c	10	19⁵/₈	+ 2	20
May	80 p	25	¹³/₁₆	+ ¹/₁₆	65
Jun	80 c	20	10³/₄	− ⁵/₈	248
Jun	85 c	30	8¹/₈	− 1	144
Dec	85 p	20	8³/₄	− 2⁵/₈	20
May	90 c	132	3¹/₈	− ⁵/₈	101
May	90 p	10	4	+ ¹/₈	110
Jun	95 c	10	3	− 2	190
Sep	95 c	10	6⁷/₈	− ³/₄	40
Dec	95 p	10	13¹/₂	+ 1³/₈	30
Call Vol.		**212**	Open Int.		**2,364**
Put Vol.		**65**	Open Int.		**2,685**
CB TECHNOLOGY (TXX)					
Jun	155 p	22	2³/₄	− 4¹/₂	20
May	160 p	2	2¹¹/₁₆	− 1³/₁₆	95
Jun	160 c	19	12¹/₂	+ 3	56
Jun	160 p	10	4¹/₂	− 1³/₈	77
May	170 c	2	3⁷/₈	+ 1¹/₂	17
Jun	170 c	55	6	+ 1	120
May	175 p	10	10¹/₂	...	...
Jun	175 c	15	4³/₈	+ 2³/₄	102
Jun	190 c	20	1¹/₄	− ³/₈	12
Call Vol.		**113**	Open Int.		**1,952**
Put Vol.		**46**	Open Int.		**3,278**
NASDAQ-100 (NDX)					
May	565 p	5	¹/₂	− 5³/₄	5
May	575 p	12,200	1	− ¹/₈	14,301
Jun	580 p	22	3¹/₄	− 5¹/₄	40
Jun	590 p	2	4¹/₄	− 12¹/₂	239
Jul	590 p	10	7¹/₂	...	...
May	600 p	7,866	2	− ³/₄	270
Jun	600 p	13	6¹/₈	− 1³/₄	250
Jun	600 p	33	6	− 1⁵/₈	126
May	605 c	6	53	+ 9¹/₈	38
May	605 p	5,006	2	− 1¹/₄	584
May	610 p	33	3	− 1	512
Jun	610 c	10	50	+ 10	15
Jun	610 p	600	8	...	1
May	615 p	1,220	3¹/₂	− 1³/₄	1,092
May	620 c	46	39³/₄	+ 8⁷/₈	564
May	620 p	26	3³/₄	− 2¹/₄	251
Jun	620 p	18	10¹/₈	− 1⁷/₈	58
May	625 p	28	4³/₄	− 3	86
May	630 p	2,221	6¹/₄	− 2³/₄	367
Jun	630 p	5	12	− 2⁷/₈	4
Jul	630 p	20	16¹/₈	...	...
May	635 p	43	7³/₄	− 4¹/...	28
May	640 c	46	24	+ 7³/₄	340
May	640 p	1,427	9	− 3¹/₄	351
Jun	640 p	5	16⁵/₈	− 3¹/₄	2
May	645 c	52	10	− 4³/₈	22
Jun	645 p	42	18¹/₄	− 1⁷/₈	5
May	650 c	4	15¹/₄	+ 4	150
May	650 p	55	12	− 5¹/₄	...
Jun	650 c	138	18⁷/₈	− 5¹/₈	10
Jun	650 p	36	18⁷/₈	...	3
Jul	650 p	10	27¹/₂	...	...
May	655 c	2	8³/₄	− ¹/₄	2,310
May	655 p	20	13³/₄	...	...
May	660 c	21	8³/₄	+ 2	398
May	660 p	20	13³/₄	...	...
Jun	660 c	51	17³/₄	...	...
Jun	660 c	25	17³/₄	+ 3	85
Jun	660 p	22	23³/₄	− 4³/₄	...
Jun	660 p	20	24³/₄	...	2
May	665 c	6,095	8³/₄	+ 3¹/₂	6,010
Jun	665 p	2	14	+ 3⁷/₈	10

RANGES FOR UNDERLYING INDEXES

Tuesday, April 23, 1996

	High	Low	Close	Net Chg.	From Dec. 31	% Chg.
S&P 100 (OEX)	628.77	624.97	628.62	+ 3.30	+ 42.70	+ 7.3
S&P 500 A.M.(SPX)	651.59	647.70	651.58	+ 3.69	+ 35.65	+ 5.8
S&P Banks (BIX)	358.11	355.92	356.94	+ 0.39	+ 26.44	+ 8.0
CB-Tech (TXX)	167.74	163.50	167.66	+ 4.15	+ 11.13	+ 7.1
CB-Mexico (MEX)	90.17	88.12	88.95	− 1.22	+ 17.21	+ 24.0
CB-Lps Mex (VEX)	9.02	8.81	8.89	− 0.13	+ 1.72	+ 24.0
Nasdaq 100 (NDX)	654.63	643.02	654.49	+ 10.20	+ 78.26	+ 13.6
Russell 2000 (RUT)	343.53	340.99	343.52	+ 2.53	+ 27.55	+ 8.7
Lps S&P 100 (OEX)	62.88	62.50	62.86	+ 0.33	+ 4.27	+ 7.3
Lps S&P 500 (SPX)	65.16	64.77	65.16	+ 0.37	+ 3.57	+ 5.8
S&P Midcap (MID)	234.55	232.65	234.34	+ 1.69	+ 16.50	+ 7.6
Major Mkt (XMI)	578.35	575.49	578.10	+ 1.69	+ 42.50	+ 7.9
Leaps MMkt (XLT)	57.84	57.55	57.81	+ 0.17	+ 4.25	+ 7.9
Hong Kong (HKO)			220.62	− 0.43	+ 17.71	+ 8.7
Leaps HK (HKL)			22.06	− 0.05	+ 1.77	+ 8.7
IW Internet (IIX)	243.77	234.84	243.73	+ 8.89	+ 10.53	+ 4.5
AM-Mexico (MXY)	103.86	101.20	102.06	− 1.80	+ 18.44	+ 22.1
Institutl A.M.(XII)	674.55	671.08	674.50	+ 2.86	+ 37.78	+ 5.9
Japan (JPN)			224.88	+ 0.04	+ 23.04	+ 11.4
MS Cyclical (CYC)	388.12	385.44	387.84	+ 2.30	+ 47.62	+ 14.0
MS Consumr (CMR)	291.45	289.87	290.88	− 0.21	+ 6.13	+ 2.2
MS Hi Tech (MSH)	339.39	331.82	339.29	+ 7.24	+ 23.52	+ 7.5
Pharma (DRG)	298.89	295.91	296.93	− 0.86	+ 0.98	+ 0.3
Biotech (BTK)	146.78	144.01	144.69	− 0.67	+ 10.92	+ 8.2
Comp Tech (XCI)	262.12	256.73	261.99	+ 4.84	+ 33.37	+ 14.6
NYSE (NYA)	349.60	347.74	349.60	+ 1.78	+ 20.09	+ 6.1
Gold/Silver (XAU)	141.47	139.81	141.47	+ 2.00	+ 21.05	+ 17.5
OTC (XOC)	472.97	465.23	472.97	+ 6.47	+ 48.27	+ 11.4
Utility (UTY)	247.54	246.26	247.16	− 0.02	− 30.44	− 11.0
Value Line (VLE)	618.51	614.52	618.47	+ 3.95	+ 48.57	+ 8.5
Bank (BKX)	425.86	423.12	424.35	+ 0.40	+ 30.50	+ 7.7
Semicond (SOX)	202.37	195.41	202.37	+ 6.38	+ 1.17	+ 0.9
Top 100 (TPX)	583.12	580.18	583.09	+ 2.45	+ 30.07	+ 5.4

Strike		Vol.	Last	Net Chg.	Open Int.
Jun	650 c	79	5⁵/₈	+ ³/₄	2,213
Jun	650 p	16	25³/₄	− ⁷/₈	262
Jul	650 c	100	8¹/₂	+ ¹/₄	203
Jul	650 p	6	27	− 4³/₄	367
May	655 c	1,461	³/₄	+ ³/₁₆	10,205
Jun	655 c	78	4¹/₈	+ ¹/₄	895
May	660 c	1,127	³/₈	...	9,785
May	660 p	1	35	− 16⁵/₈	61
Jun	660 c	241	2⁷/₈	+ ³/₈	4,111
Jun	660 p	1	34³/₄	− 4³/₄	15
Jul	660 c	53	5¹/₂	− ¹/₈	577
Aug	660 c	102	7³/₄	...	...
May	665 c	2,762	¹/₄	+ ¹/₈	8,778
Jun	665 c	1,421	1¹¹/₁₆	+ ¹/₁₆	2,349
May	670 c	218	¹/₈	− ¹/₁₆	4,577
Jun	670 c	385	1¹/₄	...	4,427
Jun	670 c	1,855	3¹/₄	+ ¹/₈	1,276
Call Vol.		**42,608**	Open Int.		**217,802**
Put Vol.		**44,657**	Open Int.		**201,543**

Strike		Vol.	Last	Net Chg.	Open Int.
May	100 c	10	4⁷/₈	...	...
Jun	100 p	10	5¹/₈	+ ⁷/₈	10
Call Vol.		**21**	Open Int.		**738**
Put Vol.		**10**	Open Int.		**717**
COMP TECH(XCI)					
May	225 p	5	⁷/₁₆	− 1¹/₁₆	44
Jun	240 p	5	4³/₈	− ³/₄	5
Jul	240 c	2	26⁵/₈	+ 2⁷/₈	2
May	245 p	5	2¹/₄	− 1	168
May	250 c	30	13¹/₈	+ 1³/₄	133
May	250 p	50	3¹/₂	− 1³/₈	160
May	255 c	25	11³/₄	+ 3¹/₄	98
May	255 p	42	5	− 1³/₈	51
May	260 c	36	7¹/₂	+ 2¹/₈	70
Jun	260 c	35	10¹/₄	...	...
Jun	270 c	5	6¹/₈	+ ⁵/₈	10
May	275 c	3	1⁷/₈	− ¹¹/₁₆	150
Jul	275 c	6	7³/₄	...	...

Source: From *The Wall Street Journal,* April 24, 1996, p. C14. Reprinted by permission of *The Wall Street Journal,* © 1996 Dow Jones & Company, Inc. All rights reserved worldwide.

Figure 1.3   Price Quotations for Foreign Currency Options

OPTIONS
PHILADELPHIA EXCHANGE

	Calls Vol.	Calls Last	Puts Vol.	Puts Last
JYen				**93.74**
6,250,000 Japanese Yen-100ths of a cent per unit.				
91 Jun	...	...	200	0.28
93 May	27	1.43	6	0.37
93 Jun	...	...	200	0.74
94 May	30	0.69	...	...
95 May	20	0.41	...	...
96 May	50	0.21	...	...
98 Jun	5	0.29	...	...
99 Jun	10	0.23	...	...
Australian Dollar				**79.03**
50,000 Australian Dollars-cents per unit.				
79 Jun	...	...	17	1.02
British Pound				**151.58**
31,250 British Pounds-European Style.				
150 Jun	...	...	3	0.67
British Pound-GMark				**230.51**
31,250 British Pound-German Mark cross.				
230 Sep	42	2.12	...	...
31,250 British Pound-German Mark EOM.				
228 Apr	10	1.94	...	...
Canadian Dollar				**73.40**
50,000 Canadian Dollars-cents per unit.				
77½ Jun	...	...	10	0.12
77 Jun	...	...	64	3.62
French Franc				**194.80**
250,000 French Francs-10ths of a cent per unit.				
19¾ May	50	0.34	...	...
GMark-JYen				**70.15**
62,500 German Mark-Japanese Yen cross EOM.				
70 Apr	...	...	32	0.19

	Calls Vol.	Calls Last	Puts Vol.	Puts Last
62,500 German Mark-Japanese Yen cross.				
71½ Jun	5	0.32	...	...
German Mark				**65.76**
62,500 German Marks EOM-cents per unit.				
60 May	...	...	10	0.39
64 May	...	...	10	0.16
65½ Apr	...	...	1550	0.11
66 Apr	350	0.21	...	...
66½ Apr	930	0.06	...	...
67 Apr	...	...	200	1.06
62,500 German Marks-European Style.				
66 Jun	200	0.94	...	...
66½ Jun	25	0.21	...	...
67½ Jun	16	0.36	...	...
62,500 German Marks-cents per unit.				
62 Jun	...	...	4	0.07
64 Sep	...	...	10	0.74
65 May	80	0.97	495	0.15
65 Jun	...	...	6	0.51
65½ May	...	...	25	0.35
66 May	...	...	350	0.47
66 Jun	5	0.95	147	0.88
66½ May	366	0.27	...	...
66½ Jun	325	0.73	...	...
67 Sep	...	...	33	1.98
67½ Jun	650	0.39	...	...
68 Jun	...	...	5	2.22
68 Sep	110	1.04	...	...
69 Sep	50	0.72	...	...

	Calls Vol.	Calls Last	Puts Vol.	Puts Last
70 Jun	...	...	600	4.18
71 Jun	...	...	310	5.19
73 Jun	...	...	960	7.19
Japanese Yen				**93.74**
92½ Apr	7	1.21	...	...
92½ May	...	...	8	0.17
93½ May	56	1.03	...	...
6,250,000 Japanese Yen EOM-100ths of a cent per unit.				
93 Apr	...	...	20	0.07
94 Apr	50	0.42	...	...
95 May	30	0.76	...	...
6,250,000 Japanese Yen-European Style.				
97 Jun	70	0.53	...	...
Swiss Franc				**81.24**
62,500 Swiss Franc EOM-cents per unit.				
82 Apr	40	0.09	...	...
62,500 Swiss Francs-European Style.				
78 Jun	10	4.00	...	...
81 May	...	...	20	0.40
82 Jun	10	1.18	...	...
85 May	...	...	5	3.43
88 Sep	10	0.59	...	...
62,500 Swiss Francs-cents per unit.				
75 Sep	...	...	164	0.26
80 Sep	...	...	8	1.24
81½ Jun	70	0.61	...	...
82 May	...	...	5	1.00
82 Sep	...	...	13	2.10
83½ May	18	0.15	...	...
85 Jun	80	0.28	...	...
Call Vol.	**7,873**	**Open Int.**	**153,290**	
Put Vol.	**8,386**	**Open Int.**	**163,609**	

Source: From *The Wall Street Journal,* April 24, 1996, p. C22. Reprinted by permission of *The Wall Street Journal,* © 1996 Dow Jones & Company, Inc. All rights reserved worldwide.

the market maker to become quite knowledgeable about the other traders who deal in options on those stocks.

Market makers follow different trading strategies and switch freely from one strategy to another. Some market makers are scalpers. The scalper follows the psychology of the trading crowd and tries to anticipate the direction of the market in the next few minutes. The scalper tries to buy if the price is about to rise and tries to sell just before it falls. Generally, the scalper holds a position for just a few minutes, trying to make a profit on moment-to-moment fluctuations in the option's price. By contrast, a position trader buys or sells options and holds a position for a longer period. This commitment typically rests on views about the underlying worth of the stock or movements in the economy. Both scalpers and position traders often trade option combinations. For example, they might buy a call at a striking price of $90 and sell a call with a striking price of $95. Such a combination is called a **spread**. A spread is any option position in two or more related options. In all such combination trades, the trader seeks to profit from a change in the price of one option relative to another.

The Floor Broker. Many option traders are located away from the trading floor. When an off-the-floor trader enters an order to buy or sell an option, the floor broker has the job of executing the order. Floor brokers typically represent brokerage firms, such as Merrill Lynch or Prudential Bache. They work for a salary or receive commissions, and their job is to obtain the best price on an order while executing it rapidly. Almost all brokers have support personnel that assist in completing trades. For example, major brokerage firms will have clerical staff that receive orders from beyond the

Futures Option Volume, by Exchange, 1995	Table 1.8	
	Contracts Traded (millions)	
Exchange	**Contracts**	**Percentage**
Chicago Board of Trade	42.90	44.93
Chicago Mercantile Exchange	38.33	40.14
New York Mercantile Exchange	6.50	6.81
Commodity Exchange	3.25	3.40
Coffee, Sugar & Cocoa Exchange	2.62	2.74
New York Cotton Exchange & Association	1.62	1.70
Kansas City Board of Trade	0.09	0.09
New York Futures Exchange	0.09	0.09
MidAmerica Commodity Exchange	0.03	0.03
Minneapolis Grain Exchange	0.05	0.05
Total	95.48	

Source: *Annual Report,* Commodity Futures Trading Commission, 1995. Data are for the fiscal year of the CFTC ending September 30, 1995. *Negligible

Futures Option Open Interest and Volume, 1995		Table 1.9	
	Average Open Interest		**Contracts Traded (millions)**	
Type of Underlying Good	**Contracts**	**Percentage**	**Contracts**	**Percentage**
Financial Instruments	3,287	60.45	65.5	68.73
Currencies	430	7.91	7.7	8.08
Energy/Wood Products	429	7.89	6.4	6.72
Grains	350	6.44	4.3	4.51
Other Agricultural	374	6.88	4.2	4.41
Metals	312	5.74	3.3	3.46
Oilseeds	183	3.37	3.1	3.25
Livestock	73	1.34	0.8	0.84
Total	5,438		95.3	

Source: *Annual Report,* Commodity Futures Trading Commission, 1995. Data are for the fiscal year of the CFTC ending September 30, 1995.

Figure 1.4　Price Quotations for Options on Futures

FUTURES OPTIONS PRICES

Tuesday, April 23, 1996.

AGRICULTURAL

CORN (CBT)
5,000 bu.; cents per bu.

Strike	Calls-Settle			Puts-Settle		
Price	Jly	Sep	Dec	Jly	Sep	Dec
440	36	17	10	16	....	....
450	31	....	....	21	....	....
460	26$^1/_2$	13	8$^1/_2$	25$^1/_2$	....	....
470	22	....	....	31	....	....
480	19$^1/_4$	11	....	....	....	....
490	16$^1/_2$	....	....	....	....	....

Est vol 30,000 Mn 14,064 calls 16,898 puts
Op int Mon 210,467 calls 220,267 puts

SOYBEANS (CBT)
5,000 bu.; cents per bu.

Strike	Calls-Settle			Puts-Settle		
Price	Jly	Aug	Sep	Jly	Aug	Sep
775	61	69$^1/_2$	66	14	25	37$^1/_2$
800	47$^1/_4$	58$^3/_4$	57	25$^1/_2$	39	53$^1/_8$
825	37	49	49	40	53$^7/_8$	....
850	29$^1/_4$	41$^3/_4$	42$^3/_8$	56$^3/_4$	71	88
875	23$^1/_2$	35	37$^1/_2$	75$^3/_4$	....	107
900	19$^1/_2$	30	32	96$^3/_4$	108$^1/_2$	....

Est vol 25,000 Mn 15,112 calls 9,366 puts
Op int Mon 134,896 calls 110,667 puts

SOYBEAN MEAL (CBT)
100 tons; $ per ton

Strike	Calls-Settle			Puts-Settle		
Price	Jly	Aug	Sep	Jly	Aug	Sep
240	24.10	27.50	27.50	3.75	6.75	9.75
250	18.00	22.00	22.75	7.50	11.00	15.00
260	13.50	18.00	19.00	12.75	17.00	....
270	10.50	14.50	16.50	....	....	....
280	8.00	12.00	14.00	....	....	....
290	6.50	10.50	12.25	....	....	....

Est vol 2,800 Mn 2,532 calls 1,252 puts
Op int Mon 24,818 calls 17,537 puts

SOYBEAN OIL (CBT)
60,000 lbs.; cents per lb.

Strike	Calls-Settle			Puts-Settle		
Price	Jly	Aug	Sep	Jly	Aug	Sep
2600	1.500	1.850	2.060	.450	.650	....
2650	1.230	1.620	1.770	.650	.880	....
2700	1.000	1.400	1.590	.920	....	....
2750	.800	1.250	1.400	....	....	....
2800	.680	....	1.250	....	....	....
2850	.550	....	1.100	....	....	....

Est vol 2,000 Mn 668 calls 146 puts
Op int Mon 13,758 calls 10,455 puts

WHEAT (CBT)
5,000 bu.; cents per bu.

Strike	Calls-Settle			Puts-Settle		
Price	Jly	Sep	Dec	Jly	Sep	Dec
590	49$^1/_2$	58	....	24$^3/_4$	....	....
600	46$^1/_2$	56	64$^3/_4$	31$^1/_2$	45	48
610	40	50$^1/_2$	57	35	....	....
620	34$^1/_2$	47	50	39$^1/_2$	....	....
630	32	43$^1/_2$	47$^1/_2$	....	....	....
640	29	42	43$^1/_2$	....	....	....

Est vol 20,000 Mn 13,673 calls 15,627 puts
Op int Mon 77,329 calls 62,412 puts

COTTON (CTN)
50,000 lbs.; cents per lb.

Strike	Calls-Settle			Puts-Settle		
Price	Jly	Oct	Dec	Jly	Oct	Dec
81	4.78	5.53	4.84	1.28	3.10	3.98
82	4.13	5.00	4.37	1.62	3.54	....
83	3.53	4.50	4.03	2.01	4.02	....
84	3.00	4.05	3.53	2.46	4.53	5.56
85	2.52	3.65	3.16	2.98	....	....
86	2.10	3.30	2.82	3.54	....	6.78

220	.151	.171	.181	.058	.072	.088
225	.120	.144	.157	.077	.094	....
230	.090	.120	.134	.097	.120	....
235	.070	.099	.115	.127	.149	....
240	.055	.082	.100	.161	....	....

Est vol 4,024 Mn 1,117 calls 795 puts
Op int Mon 49,154 calls 39,444 puts

BRENT CRUDE (IPE)
1,000 net bbls.; $ per bbl.

Strike	Calls-Settle			Puts-Settle		
Price	June	July	Aug	June	July	Aug
19.50	1.26	.80	.70	.53	1.08	1.61
20.00	.98	.61	.54	.75	1.39	1.95
20.50	.77	.46	.42	1.04	1.74	2.33
21.00	.59	.34	.32	1.36	2.12	2.73
21.50	.44	.25	.24	1.71	2.53	3.15
22.00	.32	.18	.18	2.09	2.96	3.59

Est vol 1,756 Mn 200 calls 1,760 puts
Op int Mon 13,230 calls 18,200 puts

GAS OIL (IPE)
100 metric tons; $ per ton

Strike	Calls-Settle			Puts-Settle		
Price	May	Jun	Jly	May	Jun	Jly
165	9.25	7.15	9.55	1.25	4.65	6.85
170	5.80	5.25	6.85	2.80	7.75	9.60
175	3.00	3.50	4.60	5.00	11.00	13.15
180	1.90	2.20	3.15	8.90	14.70	17.00
185	0.50	1.35	2.00	12.50	18.85	21.25
190	0.15	0.75	1.25	17.15	23.25	25.75

Est vol 495 Mn 100 calls 20 puts
Op int Mon 5,838 calls 4,144 puts

LIVESTOCK

CATTLE-FEEDER (CME)
50,000 lbs.; cents per lb.

Strike	Calls-Settle			Puts-Settle		
Price	Apr	May	Aug	Apr	May	Aug
50	....	1.25	....	0.10	1.50	1.82
51	0.05	....	....	0.50	....	....
52	0.00	0.47	....	1.42	2.65	2.65
53	0.00	....	....	2.45	....	....
54	....	0.00	1.95	3.45	4.40	3.75

Est vol 1,451 Mn 550 calls 693 puts
Op int Mon 12,167 calls 9,397 puts

CATTLE-LIVE (CME)
40,000 lbs.; cents per lb.

Strike	Calls-Settle			Puts-Settle		
Price	May	June	Aug	May	June	Aug
55	....	....	....	....	1.07	....
56	....	2.77	....	....	1.40	1.25
57	....	....	....	....	1.82	1.52
58	....	1.70	3.60	1.80	2.32	1.85
59	....	1.27	....	....	2.90	2.25
60	....	0.92	2.52	3.30	3.52	2.75

Est vol 4,538 Mn 1,881 calls 1,806 puts
Op int Mon 17,382 calls 20,149 puts

HOGS-LIVE (CME)
40,000 lbs.; cents per lb.

Strike	Calls-Settle			Puts-Settle		
Price	June	July	Aug	June	July	Aug
55	4.45	3.40	....	0.50	1.45	....
56	3.65	2.82	1.45	0.70	1.85	....
57	2.95	2.32	....	1.00	2.35	....
58	2.37	1.90	0.90	1.40	....	....
59	1.82	1.55	....	1.85	....	....
60	1.37	1.17	0.52	2.40	4.20	....

Est vol 612 Mn 416 calls 192 puts
Op int Mon 8,021 calls 16,245 puts

METALS

COPPER (CMX)
25,000 lbs.; cents per lb.

Strike	Calls-Settle	Puts-Settle

15500	0.02	0.20	....	....	3.54	....

Est vol 8,447 Mn 519 calls 841 puts
Op int Mon 57,801 calls 55,901 puts

SWISS FRANC (CME)
125,000 francs; cents per franc

Strike	Calls-Settle			Puts-Settle		
Price	May	June	July	May	June	July
8050	....	1.76	....	0.17	0.70	....
8100	....	1.46	....	0.29	0.89	0.97
8150	0.55	1.17	....	0.48	1.10	....
8200	0.32	0.94	....	0.75	1.37	....
8250	0.18	0.75	....	1.11	1.67	....
8300	0.11	0.58	....	1.54	2.00	1.92

Est vol 1,564 Mn 882 calls 893 puts
Op int Mon 17,558 calls 18,547 puts

INTEREST RATE

T-BONDS (CBT)
$100,000; points and 64ths of 100%

Strike	Calls-Settle			Puts-Settle		
Price	Jun	Sep	Dec	Jun	Sep	Dec
108	2-44	3-30	3-50	0-28	1-48	2-40
109	1-61	....	....	0-45	....	....
110	1-21	2-23	2-50	1-05	2-40	3-35
111	0-55	....	....	1-39	....	....
112	0-33	1-33	1-61	2-17	3-50	4-43
113	0-17	....	....	3-01	....	....

Est. vol. 75,000;
Mn vol. 39,361 calls; 66,549 puts
Op. int. Mon 440,897 calls; 278,074 puts

T-NOTES (CBT)
$100,000; points and 64ths of 100%

Strike	Calls-Settle			Puts-Settle		
Price	Jun	Sep	Dec	Jun	Sep	Dec
106	2-22	2-51	2-52	0-12	0-61	1-36
107	1-35	2-10	2-17	0-25	1-19	1-63
108	0-58	1-39	....	0-47	1-47	....
109	0-29	1-12	1-25	1-09	2-19	3-04
110	0-13	0-53	1-03	2-03	2-59	....
111	0-05	0-36	0-50	2-58	3-41	....

Est vol 30,000 Mn 24,662 calls 15,993 puts
Op int Mon 318,806 calls 245,463 puts

5 YR TREAS NOTES (CBT)
$100,000; points and 64ths of 100%

Strike	Calls-Settle			Puts-Settle		
Price	Jun	Sep	Dec	Jun	Sep	Dec
10500	1-36	1-53	....	0-10	0-46	....
10550	1-11	1-33	....	0-16	0-57	....
10600	0-51	1-15	....	0-25	1-06	....
10650	0-33	0-63	....	0-39	1-22	....
10700	0-19	0-50	....	0-57	1-40	....
10750	0-10	0-38	....	1-16	1-60	....

Est vol 5,000 Mn 1,583 calls 2,384 puts
Op int Mon 103,915 calls 88,711 puts

EURODOLLAR (CME)
$ million; pts. of 100%

Strike	Calls-Settle			Puts-Settle		
Price	May	Jun	Jly	May	Jun	Jly
9400	....	0.55	....	....	0.00	0.03
9425	....	0.31	0.21	0.00	0.01	0.08
9450	0.07	0.09	0.08	0.02	0.04	0.20
9475	0.01	0.01	0.02	0.21	0.21	0.39
9500	0.00	0.01	0.01	0.45	0.45	....
9525	0.00	0.00	....	....	0.70	....

Est. vol. 52,469;
Mn vol. 12,328 calls; 20,482 puts
Op. int. Mon 790,506 calls; 954,622 puts

2 YR. MID-CURVE EURODLR (CME)
$1,000,000 contract units; pts. of 100%

Strike	Calls-Settle		Puts-Settle	
Price	Jun	Sep	Jun	Sep
9300	0.48	....	0.08	....
9325	0.31	0.38	0.16	0.30

trading floor. These individuals deal with all of the record keeping necessary to execute an order and assist in transmitting information to and from the floor brokers. In addition, many brokerage firms engage in proprietary trading – trading for their own account. Therefore, they have a number of trained people on the floor of the exchange to seek trading opportunities and to execute transactions through a floor broker.

The Order Book Official. The order book official is an employee of the exchange who can also trade. However, the official cannot trade for his or her own account. Instead, the order book official primarily helps facilitate the flow of orders. The order book is a list of orders awaiting execution at a specific price. The order book official discloses the best limit orders (highest bid and lowest ask) awaiting execution. In essence, the order book official performs many of the functions of a specialist on a stock exchange. The order book official also has support personnel to help keep track of the order book and to log in new orders.

Exchange Officials. Exchange officials comprise the third group of floor participants. We have already noted that the order book official and assistants are exchange employees. However, there are other exchange employees on the floor, such as price reporting officials and surveillance officials. After every trade, price reporting officials enter the order into the exchange's price reporting system. The details of the trade immediately go out over a financial reporting system so that traders all over the world can obtain the information reflected in the trade. This process takes just a few seconds. Then traders and other interested parties around the world will know the price and quantity of a particular option that just traded. In addition to personnel involved with price reporting, the exchange has personnel on the floor to monitor floor activity. The exchange has the responsibility of providing an honest marketplace, so it strives to maintain an orderly market and ensure that brokers and market makers follow exchange rules.

Other Trading Systems

The alignment of personnel described here follows the practice at the CBOE and the Pacific Stock Exchange. Other exchanges, such as the American and Philadelphia Stock Exchanges, use a specialist instead of an order book official. In this system, the specialist keeps the limit order book but does not disclose the outstanding orders. Also, the specialist alone bears the responsibility of making a market, rather than relying on a group of market makers. In place of market makers, these exchanges have registered option traders who buy and sell for their own account or act as brokers for others.

One of the most important differences between the two systems is the role of the market makers and registered option traders. At the CBOE and the PSE, a market maker cannot act as a broker and trade for his account on the same day. The same individual can play different roles on different days, however. Restricting individuals from simultaneously acting as market makers and brokers helps avoid a conflict of interest between the role of market maker and broker. The system of allowing an individual simultaneously to trade for himself (as a market maker) and to execute orders for the public (a broker) is called dual trading. Many observers believe that dual trading involves inherent conflicts of interest between the role of broker and market maker. For example, consider a dual trader who holds an order to execute as a broker. If this dual trader suddenly confronts a very attractive trading opportunity, he may decide to take it for his own profit, rather than execute the order for his customer.

Types of Orders

Every option trade falls into one of four categories. It can be an order to:

1. open a position with a purchase (resulting in a long position);
2. open a position with a sale (resulting in a short position);
3. close a position with a purchase; or
4. close a position with a sale.

For example, a trader could open a position by buying a call and later close that position by selling the call. Alternatively, one could open a position by selling a put and close the position by buying a put. An order that closes an existing position is an **offsetting order**.

As in the stock market, there are numerous types of orders in the options market. The simplest order is a market order. A market order instructs the floor broker to transact at whatever price is currently available in the marketplace. For example, one might place an order to buy one call contract for a stock at the market. The floor broker will fill this order immediately at the best price currently available. As in the stock market, the alternative to a market order is a limit order. In a limit order, the trader instructs the broker to fill the order only if certain conditions are met. For example, assume an option trades for $5 1/8. In this situation, one might place a limit order to buy an option only if the price is $5 or less. In a limit order, the trader tells the broker how long to try to fill the order. If the limit order is a day order, the broker is to fill the order that day if it can be filled within the specified limit. If the order cannot be filled that day, the order expires. Alternatively, a trader can specify a limit order as being good-until-canceled. In this case, the order stays on the limit order book indefinitely.

Order Routing and Execution

To get a better idea of how an order is executed, let's trace an order from an individual trader. A college professor in Miami decides that today is the day to buy an option on XYZ. He calls his local broker and places a market order to buy a call. The broker takes the order and makes sure she has recorded the order correctly. The broker then transmits the order to the brokerage firm's representatives at the exchange. Usually this is done over a computerized system operated by the brokerage firm.

The brokerage firm's clerical staff on the floor of the exchange receives the order and gives it to a runner. The runner quickly moves to the trading area and finds the firm's floor broker who deals in XYZ options. The floor broker executes the order by trading with another floor broker, a market maker, or an order book official. Then the floor broker records the price obtained and information about the opposite trader. The runner takes this information from the floor broker back to the clerical staff on the exchange floor. The brokerage firm clerk confirms the order to the Miami broker, who tells the professor the result of the transaction. In the normal event, the entire process takes about two minutes, and the professor can reasonably expect to receive confirmation of his order in the same phone call used to place the order.

THE CLEARINGHOUSE

In executing the trade just described, the buyer of a call has the right to purchase 100 shares of XYZ at the exercise price. However, it might seem that the buyer of the call is in a somewhat dangerous position because the seller of the call may not want to fulfill his part of the bargain if the price of XYZ rises. For example, if XYZ sells for $120, the seller of the call may be unwilling to part with the share for $100. The purchaser of the call needs a mechanism to secure his position without having to force the seller to perform.

The clearinghouse, the Options Clearing Corporation (OCC), performs this role. After the day's trading, the OCC first attempts to match all trades. For the college professor's transaction, there is an opposite trading party. When the broker recorded the purchase for the professor, she traded with someone else who also recorded the trade. The clearinghouse must match the paperwork from both sides of the transaction. If the two records agree, the trade is a matched trade. This process of matching trades and tracking payments is called **clearing**. Every options trade must be cleared. If records by the two sides of the trade disagree, the trade is an **outtrade** and the exchange works to resolve the disagreement.

Assuming the trade matches, the OCC guarantees both sides of the transaction. The OCC becomes the seller to every buyer and the buyer to every seller. In essence, the OCC interposes its own credibility for that of the individual traders. This has great advantages. The college professor did not even know the name of the seller of the option. Instead of being worried about the credibility of the seller, the professor needs to be satisfied only with the credibility of the OCC. But the OCC is well capitalized and anxious to keep a smoothly functioning market. Therefore, the college professor can be assured that the other side of his option transaction will be honored. If an option trader fails to perform as promised, the OCC absorbs the loss and proceeds against the defaulting trader. Because the OCC is a buyer to every seller and a seller to every buyer, it has a zero net position in the market. It holds the same number of short and long positions. Therefore, the OCC has very little risk exposure from fluctuating prices.

MARGINS

Besides having a net zero position, the clearinghouse further limits its risk by requiring margin payments from its clearing members. A clearing member is a securities firm having an account with the clearinghouse. All option trades must be channeled through a clearing member to the clearinghouse. Most major brokerage firms are clearing members. However, individual market makers are not clearing members, and they must clear their trades through a clearing member. In effect, the clearing member represents all of the parties that it clears to the clearinghouse. By demanding margin payments from its clearing members, the clearinghouse further ensures its own financial integrity. Each clearing member in turn demands margin payments from the traders it clears. The margin payments are immediate cash payments that show the financial integrity of the traders and help to limit the risk of the clearing member and the clearinghouse.

To understand margins, we recall that there are four basic positions: long a call or long a put and short a call or short a put. The margin rules differ with the type of position. First, options cannot be bought on credit. The buyer of an option pays the full price of the option by the morning of the next business day. For example, the college professor in Miami who buys a call or put must pay his broker in full for the purchase. We may think of long option positions as requiring 100 percent margin in all cases.

For option sellers, margin rules become very important. The Federal Reserve Board sets minimum margin requirements for option traders. However, each exchange may impose additional margin requirements. Also, each broker may require margin payments beyond those required by the Federal

Reserve Board and the exchanges. A single broker may also impose different margin requirements on different customers. Further, options on different underlying instruments are subject to different margin requirements. Because these option requirements may differ so radically and because they are subject to frequent adjustment, this section illustrates the underlying principles of margin rules for options on stocks.[10]

The seller of a call option may be required to deliver the stock if the owner of a call exercises his option. Therefore, the maximum amount the seller can lose is the value of the share. If the seller keeps money on deposit with the broker equal to the share price, then the broker, clearing member, and clearinghouse are completely protected. This sets an upper bound on the reasonable amount of margin that could be required. Sometimes the seller of a call has the share itself on deposit with the broker. In this case, the seller has sold a **covered call** – the call is covered by the deposit of the shares with the broker. If the call is exercised against the seller of a covered call, the stock is immediately available to deliver. Therefore, there is no risk to the system in a covered call. Accordingly, the margin on a covered call is zero.

If the seller of a call does not have the underlying share on deposit with the broker, the seller has sold an **uncovered call** or a **naked call**. We have just seen that the maximum possible loss is the value of the share. For the writer of a put, the worst result is being forced to buy a worthless stock at the exercise price. This worst case gives a loss equal to the exercise price. Therefore, if the margin equaled the exercise price, the broker, clearing member, and clearinghouse would be fully protected. Instead of demanding complete protection, the seller of a call or put must deposit only a fraction of the potential loss as an **initial margin**.

For a seller of an option, the margin requirement depends on whether the option is in-the-money or out-of-the-money. If the option is in-the-money, the initial margin equals 100 percent of the proceeds from selling the option plus an amount equal to 20 percent of the value of the underlying stock. For example, assume a stock currently sells for $105 and a trader sells a call contract for 100 shares with a striking price of $100 on this stock for $6 per share. Ignoring brokerage fees, the proceeds from selling the call would be $600. To this we add 20 percent of the value of the underlying stock, or $2,100 for the 100 shares. Therefore, the initial margin requirement is $2,700.

If the option is out-of-the-money, the rule is slightly different. The initial margin equals the margin sale proceeds plus 20 percent of the value of the underlying stock minus the amount the option is out-of-the-money. However, this margin rule could result in a negative margin, so the initial margin must also equal 100 percent of the option proceeds plus 10 percent of the value of the underlying security. Consider a call on the stock trading at $15 per share and the option having an exercise price of $20 and trading for $1. Based on a 100-share contract and ignoring any brokerage commissions, the margin must be the proceeds from selling the option ($100), plus 20 percent of the value of the underlying stock ($.20 \times $15 \times 100 = 300), less the amount the option is out-of-the-money ($[$20 - $15] \times 100 = 500). This gives a margin requirement that is negative ($100 + $300 - $500 = -$100$). Therefore, the second part of the rule comes into play. The minimum margin must equal the sale proceeds from the option ($100) plus 10 percent of the value of the underlying stock ($.10 \times $15 \times 100 = 150). Therefore, the margin for this trade will be $250.

The margins we have been discussing are initial margin requirements. The trader must make these margin deposits when he or she first trades. If prices move against the trader, he or she will be required to make additional margin payments. As the stock price starts to rise and cause losses for the short trader, the broker requires additional margin payments, called a maintenance margin. By requiring maintenance margin payments, the margin system protects the broker, clearing member, and clearinghouse from default by traders. This system also benefits traders because they can be confident that payments due to them will be protected from default as well.

Many option traders trade option combinations. Margin rules apply to these transactions as well, but the margin requirements reflect the special risk characteristics of these positions. For many option combinations, the risk may be less than the risk of a single long or short position in a put or call.[11]

COMMISSIONS

As we have seen, the same brokerage system that trades stocks can execute option transactions. In stocks, commission charges depend on the number of shares and the dollar value of the transaction. A similar system applies for call option contracts. The following schedule shows a representative commission schedule from a discount broker. Full-service brokerage fees can be substantially higher.[12] In addition to these fees, each transaction can be subject to certain minimum and maximum fees. For instance, a broker might have a maximum fee per contract of $40.

Representative Discount Brokerage Commissions

Dollar Value of Transaction	Commission
$0–2,500	$29 + 1.6% of principal amount
$2,500–10,000	$49 + 0.8% of principal amount
$10,000 +	$99 + 0.3% of principal amount

As an example of commissions with this fee schedule, assume that you buy five contracts with a quoted price of $6.50. The cost of the option would be $650 per contract, for a total cost of $3,250. The commission would be: $49 + .008 × $3,250 = $75. For the same dollar value of a transaction in stocks, the commission tends to be lower. However, once the dollar amount of the transaction approaches $10,000, commissions on stocks and options tend to be similar.

Even though the commission per dollar of options traded may be higher than for stocks, there can be significant commission savings in trading options. In our example, the option price is $6.50 per share of stock. The share price might well be $100 or more. If it were $100, trading 500 shares would involve a transaction value of $50,000. Commissions on a stock transaction of $50,000 would be much higher than commissions on our option transaction. Trading the option on a stock and trading the stock itself can give positions with very similar price actions. Therefore, option trading can provide commission savings over stock trading.

Another way to see this principle is to realize that options inherently have more leverage than a share of stock. As an example, assume the stock price is $100 and the option on the stock trades for $6.50. If the stock price rises 3 percent to $103, the option price could easily rise 30 percent to $8.45. On a percentage basis, the option price moves more than the stock price. Unfortunately for option traders, this happens for price increases and decreases. With this greater leverage, the same dollar investment in an option will give a greater dollar price movement than investment in the stock.

TAXATION

Taxation of option transactions is no simple matter. We cannot hope to cover all of the nuances of the tax laws in this brief section. Therefore, this section attempts merely to illustrate the basic principles.

Disposition of an option, through either sale, exercise, or expiration, gives rise to a profit or loss. Profits and losses on options trading are treated as capital gains and losses. Therefore, option profits and losses are subject to the rules that pertain to capital gains and losses. Capital gains may be classified as long-term or short-term. A capital gain is a long-term gain if the instrument generating the gain has been held longer than one year, otherwise the gain or loss is short-term. In general, long-term capital gains qualify for favorable tax treatment.

Capital losses offset capital gains and thereby reduce taxable income. However, capital losses are deductible only up to the amount of capital gains plus $3,000. Any excess capital loss cannot be deducted but must be carried forward to offset capital gains in subsequent years. For example, assume that a trader has capital gains of $17,500 from securities trading. Unfortunately for the trader, he also has $25,000 in capital losses. Therefore, $17,500 of the losses completely offset the capital gains, freeing the trader from any taxes on those gains. This leaves $7,500 of capital losses to consider. The trader can then use $3,000 of this excess loss to offset other income, such as wages. In effect, this protects $3,000 of wages from taxation. The remaining $4,500 of losses must be carried forward to the next tax year, where it can be used to offset capital gains realized in that tax year.

Option transactions give rise to capital gains and losses, and the tax treatment differs for buyers and sellers of options. Further, the tax treatment becomes very complicated for combinations of options. Therefore, we consider only the four simplest stock option positions: long a call, short a call, long a put, or short a put.

Long a Call. If a call is exercised, the price of the option, the exercise price, and the brokerage commissions associated with purchasing and exercising the option are treated as the cost of the stock for tax purposes. The holding period for the stock begins on the day after the call is exercised, so the stock must be held for a year to qualify for treatment as a long-term capital gain. If the call expires worthless, it gives rise to a short-term or long-term capital loss equal to the purchase price of the option plus any associated brokerage fees incurred in purchasing the option. If the option is sold before expiration, the capital gain or loss is the sale price of the option minus the purchase price of the option minus any brokerage fees incurred.

Short a Call. When a trader sells a call, the premium that is received is not treated as immediate income. Instead, the treatment of this premium depends upon the disposition of the short call. If the call expires without being exercised, the gain on the transaction equals the prices of the option less any brokerage fees, and this gain is always treated as a short-term gain, no matter how long the position was held. If the trader offsets the position before expiration, the capital gain or loss equals the sale price minus the purchase price minus any commissions, and this gain or loss is considered a short-term gain or loss without regard to how long the position is held. If the call is exercised against the trader, the strike price plus the premium received minus any commissions becomes the sale price of the stock for determining the capital gain or loss. The gain or loss will be short-term or long-term depending upon how the stock that is delivered was acquired. For example, if the trader delivers stock that had been held for more than one year, the gain or loss would be a long-term gain or loss.

Long a Put. If a put is purchased and sold before expiration, the gain or loss equals the sale price minus the purchase price minus any brokerage commissions, and the gain or loss will be short-term or long-term depending on how long the put was held. If the put expires worthless, the loss equals the purchase price plus the brokerage commissions, and the loss can be either short-term or long-term. If the trader exercises the put, the cost of the put plus commission reduces the amount realized upon the sale of the stock delivered to satisfy the exercise. The resulting gain or loss can be either short-term or long-term depending upon how long the delivered stock was held.

Short a Put. The premium received for selling a put is not classified as income until the obligation from the sale of the put is completed. If the trader offsets the short put before expiration, the capital gain or loss equals the sale price minus the purchase price minus the brokerage commissions, and the resulting gain or loss is always a short-term gain or loss. If the put expires worthless, the capital gain equals the sale price less the brokerage commissions, and the capital gain is a short-term gain. If the put is exercised against the trader, the basis of the stock acquired in the exercise equals the strike price plus the commission minus the premium received when the put was sold. The holding period for determining a capital gain or loss begins for the stock on the day following the exercise.

There are other special and more complicated rules for taxing option transactions, so the account here is not definitive. Additional complications arise for some options on stock indexes, for example. Also, there are special tax rules designed to prevent option trading merely to manipulate taxes.

THE ORGANIZATION OF THE TEXT

The remainder of this text is organized as follows. Chapter 2 explores the payoffs from a variety of option strategies. As we will see, options can be held as individual investments or combined to provide very specific investment opportunities that pay only in certain circumstances. This flexibility makes options an extremely useful and powerful risk management tool.

Chapter 2 considers payoffs only when options expire because this special time is much easier to analyze than the value of options prior to expiration. Chapter 3 begins the analysis of options prior to expiration by using the idea of arbitrage. An **arbitrage opportunity** is a chance to make a riskless profit with no investment. Thus, arbitrage is akin to finding free money. Chapter 3 approaches option pricing by asking the question: What option prices are consistent with the absence of arbitrage opportunities? This key idea of no-arbitrage pricing turns out to be an extremely powerful analytical tool that we introduce in Chapter 3 and employ throughout the text.

Option pricing inescapably involves some rather complicated mathematics. But the mathematics are much simpler for European options. Chapter 4 extends the no-arbitrage approach to analyze the pricing of European options and explains the famous Black-Scholes option pricing model. The Black-Scholes model expresses the price of an option as a function of the price of the underlying stock, the exercise price, the time until expiration, the risk-free rate of interest, and the volatility of the underlying stock. As we will see, it gives extremely accurate results. Chapter 5 explores in detail the exact way in which option prices respond to the various parameters in the Black-Scholes model. These sensitivities can be used to shape the risk and return characteristics of option positions with great precision.

While European option pricing is simpler than American option pricing, most options traded in the actual market are American options. Therefore, Chapter 6 explores the pricing of American options. The principles of European option pricing still hold, but American option pricing involves some special considerations.

Chapter 7 applies the conceptual apparatus developed in earlier chapters to three special instruments: options on indexes, options on foreign currencies, and options on futures. The pricing of these instruments requires applying the concepts already developed to the particular institutional features of these underlying goods.

Chapter 8 shows the power of option pricing and analysis in a very different application. The concepts of option pricing can be used to analyze corporate securities as having option characteristics. Therefore, the option approach to corporate securities gives a totally new and very powerful way of thinking about common stock, bonds, convertible debt, and other corporate securities.

Chapter 9, "Exotic Options," is a completely new chapter in this edition. The chapter discusses a wide variety of exotic options, presents the pricing formula for each, and offers a detailed calculation example of each type of exotic option.

OPTION! SOFTWARE

As we have mentioned, option pricing is mathematically challenging. While it is critical to understand the formulas (and to compute each different formula by hand at least once!), it is not necessary or useful to compute the same formulas repeatedly. **OPTION!** software can compute virtually every option value discussed in this book. Further, **OPTION!** can graph many of the relationships among different option prices discussed in the chapters that follow, including all of the exotic options discussed in Chapter 9. Exploring the option concepts of the text with the software can greatly enhance an understanding of option pricing. Instructions for **OPTION!** are found in an appendix at the end of this text.

SUMMARY

This chapter has introduced the options market. In the short time since options started trading on the Chicago Board Options Exchange, options have helped to revolutionize finance. They permeate the world of speculative investing and portfolio management. Corporations use them in their financing decisions to control risk. Beyond their uses as trading vehicles, options provide a new way to analyze many financial transactions.

The chapters that follow build an understanding of the option revolution on several levels. Foremost, we seek to build an understanding of option trading and speculating as a topic that is interesting in its own right. However, by following the argument of this book, the reader will develop skills in financial thinking that will apply to many problem areas. After completing the book, the careful reader should even be able to analyze many financial problems using an option framework. At that point, the reader has become part of the option revolution.

QUESTIONS AND PROBLEMS

1. State the difference between a call and a put option.
2. How does a trader initiate a long call position, and what rights and obligations does such a position involve?
3. Can buying an option, whether a put or a call, result in any obligations for the option owner? Explain.
4. Describe all of the benefits that are associated with taking a short position in an option.
5. What is the difference between a short call and a long put position? Which has rights associated with it, and which involves obligations? Explain.
6. Consider the following information. A trader buys a call option for $5 that gives the right to purchase a share of stock for $100. In this situation, identify the exercise price, the premium, and the striking price.

7. Explain what happens to a short trader when the option he or she has sold expires worthless. What benefits and costs has the trader incurred?
8. Explain why an organized options exchange needs a clearinghouse.
9. What is the difference between an American and a European option?
10. Assume a trader does not want to continue holding an option position. Explain how this trader can fulfill his or her obligations, yet close out the option position.

NOTES

[1] There are also other more complicated types of options that are not traded on exchanges. For example, an **exchange option** is an option to exchange one asset for another. As we will see when we discuss options on futures, there is a **delivery option** that gives a trader the right to choose which of several assets to surrender. There are still other types of options, but the most important market for options is the option exchange, where just put and call options trade.

[2] Christopher K. Ma and Ramesh P. Rao, "Information Asymmetry and Options Trading," *Financial Review,* 23:1, February 1988, pp. 39–51, discuss the different roles that options can play for informed and uninformed traders. The informed trader is one with special knowledge about the underlying stock; the uninformed trader has no special knowledge. In their analysis, the informed trader tends to take an outright position in the option, while the uninformed trader is likely to use options to reduce the risk of an existing stock position. While these factors may benefit market participants, the same authors analyze the effect of a new listing of options on stock prices in "The Effect of Call-Option-Listing Announcement on Shareholder Wealth," *Journal of Business Research,* 15:5, October 1987, pp. 449–65. Ma and Rao show that the listing of an option on a stock that never had options before leads to stock price declines and thus to a loss of shareholder wealth. Apparently, this drop in stock prices reflects the market's view that new option trading is likely to make the stock more volatile. However, Ma and Rao also find that stock prices rebound when the option actually begins to trade.

[3] Consider an option position and a stock position designed to give the same profits and losses for a given movement in the stock price. If we consider a short-term investment horizon, the option strategy will almost always be cheaper and incur lower transaction costs. This is not necessarily true for a long-term investment horizon. All exchange-traded options are dated; that is, they expire within the next few months. Therefore, maintaining an option position in the long-term involves trading to replace expiring options. By contrast, taking the stock position requires only one transaction, and the stock can be held indefinitely. Therefore, the repeated transaction costs incurred with the option strategy can involve greater transaction costs in the long-term than the stock strategy.

[4] Selling stock short involves borrowing a share, selling it, repurchasing the share later, and returning it to its owner. The short seller hopes to profit from a price decline by selling before the decline and repurchasing after the price falls. Rules on the stock exchange restrict the timing of short selling and the use of short sale proceeds.

[5] Stephen A. Ross, "Options and Efficiency," *Quarterly Journal of Economics,* 90, February 1976, pp. 75–89, shows that options serve a useful economic role by completing markets. In a complete market, a trader can trade for any pattern of payoffs that he or she desires. The more nearly complete a market is, the greater is its likely efficiency. Thus, because options help to complete markets, they contribute to economic efficiency and thereby raise the welfare level of society as a whole.

[6] The "r" and "s" have no specific meaning. However, this is the convention used by *The Wall Street Journal* for its option price reports.

[7] However, some futures options are options on foreign currency futures, and these are traded on the CME.

[8] The Chicago Mercantile Exchange trades foreign currency futures and options on those futures in a robust market. However, the CME trades no options on the foreign currencies themselves.

[9] The table does not show statistics on very small market currencies, such as the French franc and the European Currency Unit (ECU).

[10] George Sofianos, ''Margin Requirements on Equity Instruments,'' *Federal Reserve Bank of New York Quarterly Review,* 13:2, Summer 1988, pp. 47–60, explains margin rules in more detail. Stephen Figlewski, ''Margins and Market Integrity: Margin Setting for Stock Index Futures and Options,'' *Journal of Futures Markets,* 4:3, Fall 1984, pp. 385–416, argues that margins on stocks are set too high relative to margins on options and futures. According to his analysis, the margin requirements give different levels of protection for different instruments.

[11] Margins can be devilishly complicated. Andrew Rudd and Mark Schroeder, ''The Calculation of Minimum Margin,'' *Management Science,* 28, December 1982, pp. 1368–79, present a linear program to compute minimum margin under a variety of scenarios.

[12] A discount broker executes unsolicited orders for its customers. It provides little or no research information but seeks to offer competitive order execution at reduced prices. Charles Schwab and Quick and Reilly are two leading discount brokerage firms. By contrast, full discount brokers typically have account executives that actively solicit orders from their customer base. The full discount broker also maintains a research department.

CHAPTER 2 | OPTION PAYOFFS AND STRATEGIES

INTRODUCTION

This chapter considers the factors that determine the value of an option at expiration and introduces the principal strategies used in options trading. When an option is about to expire, it is relatively easy to determine its value. Thus, we begin our analysis by considering option values at expiration. When we say that an option is at expiration, we mean that the owner has a simple choice: exercise the option immediately or allow it to expire as worthless. As we will see, the value of an option at expiration depends on only the stock price and the exercise price. We also give rules for whether an owner should exercise an option or allow it to expire.

With all assets, we consider either the value of the asset or the profit or loss incurred from trading the asset. The value of an asset equals its market price. As such, the value of an asset does not depend on the purchase price. However, the profit or loss on the purchase and sale of an asset depends critically on the purchase price. In considering options, we keep these two related ideas strictly distinct. We present graphs for both the value of options and the profits from trading options, but we want to be sure not to confuse the two. By graphing the value of options and the profits or losses from options at expiration, we develop our grasp of option pricing principles. To focus on the principles of pricing, we ignore commissions and other transaction costs in this chapter.

Option traders often trade options with other options and with other assets, particularly stocks and bonds. This chapter analyzes the payoffs from combining different options and from combining options with the underlying stock. Many of these combinations have colorful names such as spreads, straddles, and strangles. Beyond the terminology, these combinations offer special profit and loss characteristics. We also explore the particular payoff patterns that traders can create by trading options in conjunction with stocks and bonds.

We can use **OPTION!** to explore the concepts we develop in this chapter. The first module of **OPTION!** analyzes values, profits, and losses of options and option combinations at expiration. **OPTION!** can prepare reports of outcomes and can graph profit and losses of all the combinations in this chapter. Detailed instructions for using **OPTION!** appear at the end of this book.

STOCKS AND BONDS

We begin our analysis with the two most familiar securities – common stock and a default-free bond. Figure 2.1 presents the value of a share of stock and the value of a bond at a certain date. At any time, the value of a risk-free pure discount bond is just the present value of the par value. The graph expresses the value of a share of stock and the value of a bond as functions of stock price. In other words, we graph the stock price, or stock value, against the stock price. In the graph, a line runs from the bottom left to the upper right corner. Also, the graph has a horizontal line that intersects the Y-axis at $100.

The diagonal line shows the value of a single share of the stock. When the stock price on the X-axis is $100, the value of the stock is $100. The horizontal line reflects the value of a $100 face value default-free bond at maturity. The value of the bond does not depend on the price of the stock. Because it is default-free, the bond pays $100 when it matures, no matter what happens to the stock price. For convenience, we assume that the bond matures in one year, and we graph the value of the stock and bond on that future date. Notice that the value of these instruments does not depend in any way on the purchase price of the instruments.

We now consider possible profits and losses from the share of stock and the risk-free bond. Let us assume that the stock was purchased for $100 at time t and that the pure discount (zero-coupon) risk-free bond was purchased one year before maturity at $90.91. This implies an interest rate of 10 percent on the bond. Figure 2.2 graphs the profit and losses from a long and short position in the stock. The solid line running from the bottom left to the top right of Figure 2.2 shows the profits and losses for a long position of one share in the stock, assuming a purchase price of $100. When

Figure 2.1	The Value of a Stock and a Bond

Profit and Loss from a Stock | **Figure 2.2**

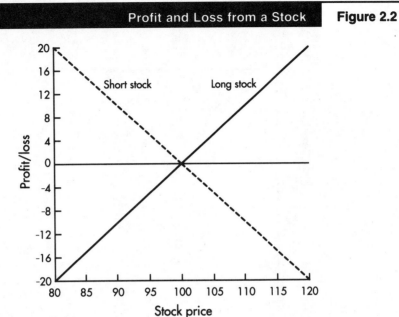

the stock price is $100, our graph shows a zero profit. If the stock price is $105, there is a $5 profit, which equals the stock price of $105 minus the purchase price of $100.

The dotted line in Figure 2.2 runs from the upper left corner to the bottom right corner and shows the profits or losses from a short position of one share, assuming that the stock was sold at $100. Throughout this book, we use dotted lines to indicate short positions in value and profit and loss graphs. If the stock is worth $105, the short position shows a loss of $5. The short trader loses $5 because he sold the stock for $100. Now with the higher stock price, the short trader must pay $105 to buy the stock and close the short trade. As Figure 2.2 shows, the short trader bets that the stock price will fall. For example, if the trader sold the stock short at a price of $100 and the stock price falls to $93, the short trader can buy the stock and repay the person from whom he borrowed the share, earning a $7 profit ($100 − $93).

As a final point on stock values and profits, consider the profit and loss profile for a position that is long one share and short one share. If the stock trades at $105, the long position has a profit of $5 and the short position has a loss of $5. Similarly, if the stock trades at $95, the long position has a loss of $5 and the short position has a profit of $5. No matter what stock price we consider, the profits and losses from the long and short positions cancel each other. The profit or loss is always zero.

Figure 2.3 graphs the profits from the bond that we considered. The purchase price of the bond is $90.91, and it matures in one year paying $100 with certainty. The profit equals the payoff of $100 minus the cost of $90.91. Thus, the owner of the bond has a sure profit of $9.09 at expiration. Figure 2.3 shows this profit with the solid line in the upper portion of the graph. Similarly, the issuer of the

Figure 2.3   Profit from a Bond

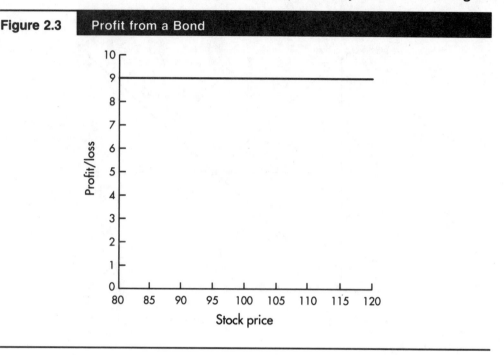

bond will lose $9.09. The issuer receives $90.91, but pays $100. Presumably, the issuer has some productive use for the bond proceeds during the year that will yield more than $9.09.

ARBITRAGE

To explain the value of options, we rely throughout the book on the concept of **arbitrage** – trading to make a riskless profit with no investment. Consider the following example of arbitrage, in which we ignore transaction costs. Some stocks trade on both the New York and Pacific Stock Exchanges at the same time. Suppose that IBM sells for $100 on the New York Stock Exchange and for $102 on the Pacific Stock Exchange. With these prices a trader can simultaneously buy a share in New York and sell the same share on the Pacific Exchange for a $2 profit.

This transaction provides an arbitrage profit. First, there is no investment, because the trader buys and sells the same good at the same time. Second, the profit is certain once the trader enters the two positions. Notice that we ignore transaction costs in this example. We also ignore other real-world problems, such as execution risk, the risk that we cannot execute both transactions simultaneously at the quoted prices. The trader who engages in such transactions is called an **arbitrageur**.

Properly functioning financial markets allow no such arbitrage opportunities. If the two prices of our example prevailed, arbitrageurs would trade exactly as we described. They would buy the cheap share and sell the expensive share. Of course, they would do this for as many shares as possible, not just the single share of our example. These transactions would generate a tremendous demand for IBM shares in New York and a tremendous supply of IBM shares on the Pacific Exchange. This high demand would raise the price of shares in New York, and the excess supply would cause prices on the Pacific Exchange to fall. The prices on the two exchanges would continue to adjust until they were equal, thus removing the arbitrage opportunity. If a financial market functions properly, there should be no such arbitrage opportunities in the market. In other words, in a smoothly functioning market, traders are alert and immediately compete away such opportunities as they arise. These reflections give rise to a **no-arbitrage principle**. Under the no-arbitrage pricing principle, we examine the prices of financial instruments under the assumption that the price of an instrument excludes any arbitrage possibility.

While we have assumed that there are no transaction costs, we can see their effect within the framework of our example. Assume that the transaction cost of monitoring the market and trading one share is $.10. In our example, a trader must trade two shares, buying a share in New York and selling it on the Pacific Exchange. Thus, the trader faces transaction costs of $.20. Now assume that the price of a share is $100 in New York and $100.15 on the Pacific Exchange. The trader cannot trade profitably on such a small discrepancy. If he tries, he will pay $100 for the New York share and incur $.20 in transaction costs trying to exploit the apparent arbitrage opportunity in an effort to get a share worth $100.15. Thus, the arbitrage attempt loses $.05. This example shows that small differences in prices can persist if the difference is less than the cost of trading to exploit the difference. We know that such small discrepancies in prices can persist in actual markets; however, we ignore these differences for the sake of simplicity in our examples, and we continue to assume that transaction costs are zero.

OPTION NOTATION

We now introduce some notation for referring to options. As we will see, in analyzing options we are often interested in the option price as a function of the stock price, the time until expiration, and the exercise price. The options may be either calls or puts, and the options may be either European or American. Therefore, we adopt the following notation:

S_t = price of the underlying stock at time t
X = the exercise price for the option
T = the expiration date of the option
c_t = the price of a European call at time t
C_t = the price of an American call at time t
p_t = the price of a European put at time t
P_t = the price of an American put at time t

We will often write the value of an option in the following form:

$$c_t(S_t, X, T - t)$$

which means the price of a European call at time t given a stock price at t of S_t, for a call with an exercise price of X, that expires at time T, which is an amount of time $T - t$ from now (time t). For convenience, we sometimes omit the "t" subscript, as in:

$$p(S, X, T)$$

In such a case, the reader may assume that the current time is time $t = 0$, and that the option expires T periods from now. In this chapter, we focus on the value of options at expiration, so we will be concerned with values such as:

$$C_T(S_T, X, T)$$

which indicates the price of an American call option at expiration, when the stock price is S_T, the exercise price is X, and the option expires at time T, which happens to be immediately.

EUROPEAN AND AMERICAN OPTION VALUES AT EXPIRATION

In general, the difference between an American and a European option concerns only the exercise privileges associated with the option. An American option can be exercised at any time, while a European option can be exercised only at expiration. At expiration, both European and American options have exactly the same exercise rights. Therefore, European and American options at expiration have identical values, assuming the same underlying good and the same exercise price:

$$C_T(S_T, X, T) = c_T(S_T, X, T) \text{ and } P_T(S_T, X, T) = p_T(S_T, X, T)$$

Throughout this chapter, we focus on option values and profits at expiration. Therefore, we use the notation for an American option throughout, but the results hold perfectly well for European options as well.

BUY OR SELL A CALL OPTION

We now consider the value of call options at expiration, along with the profits or losses that come from trading call options. At expiration, the owner of an option has an immediate choice: exercise the option or allow it to expire worthless. Therefore, the value of the option will either be zero, the **exercise value**, or the **intrinsic value** – the value of the option if it is exercised immediately. The value of a call at expiration (whether European or American) equals zero, or the stock price minus the exercise price, whichever is greater. For our discussion of option values and profits at expiration, we use the notation for American options (C_T or P_T), but the principles apply identically to European options as well.

$$C_T = \text{MAX}\{0, S_T - X\} \tag{2.1}$$

To understand this principle, consider a call option with an exercise price of $100 and assume that the underlying stock trades at $95. At expiration, the call owner may either exercise the option or allow it to expire worthless. With the prices we just specified, the call owner must allow the option to expire. If the owner of the call exercises the option, he pays $100 and receives a stock that is worth $95. This gives a loss of $5 on the exercise, so it is foolish to exercise. Instead of exercising, the owner of the call can merely allow the option to expire. If the option expires, there is no additional loss involved with the exercise. In our example:

$$S_T - X = \$95 - \$100 = -\$5$$

By allowing the option to expire, the option owner acknowledges the call is worthless. With our example numbers at expiration:

$$C_T = \text{MAX}\{0, S_T - X\} = \text{MAX}\{0, \$95 - \$100\} = \text{MAX}\{0, -\$5\} = 0$$

We can extend this example to any ending stock price we wish to consider. For any stock price less than the exercise price, the value of $S_T - X$ will be negative. Therefore, for any stock price less than the exercise price, the call will be worthless. If the stock price equals the exercise price, the value of $S_T - X$ equals zero, so the call will still be worthless. Therefore, for any stock price equal to or less than the exercise price at expiration, the call is worth zero.

If the stock price exceeds the exercise price, the call is worth the difference between the stock price and the exercise price. For example, assume that the stock price is $103 at expiration. The call option with an exercise price of $100 now allows the holder to exercise the option by paying the exercise price. Therefore, the owner of the call can acquire the stock worth $103 by paying $100. This gives an immediate payoff of $3 from exercising. Notice that this example conforms to our principle. Using these numbers we find:

$$C_T = \text{MAX}\{0, S_T - X\} = \text{MAX}\{0, \$103 - \$100\} = \text{MAX}\{0, \$3\} = \$3$$

Figure 2.4 graphs the value of our example call at expiration. Here the value of the call equals the maximum of zero or the stock price minus the exercise price. As the graph shows, the value of the call is unlimited, at least in principle. If the stock price were $1,000 at expiration, the call would

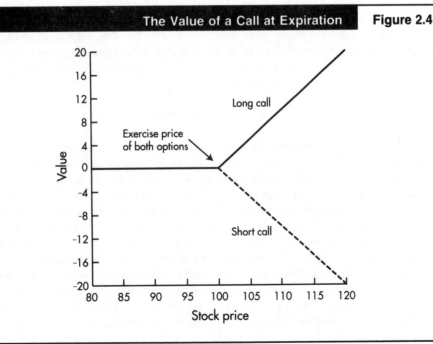

The Value of a Call at Expiration   **Figure 2.4**

be worth MAX{0, $S_T - X$} = $900. This graph shows the characteristic shape for a long position in a call option.

Figure 2.4 also shows the value of a short position in the same call option. The dotted line graphs the short position. (For stock prices between 0 and $100, both graphs lie on the same line.) Notice that the short position has a zero value for all stock prices equal to or less than the exercise price. If the stock price exceeds the exercise price, the short position is costly. Using our notation, the value of a short call position at expiration is:

$$-C_T = -\text{MAX}\{0, S_T - X\}$$

Assume that the stock price is $107 at expiration. In this case, the call owner will exercise the option. The seller of the call must then deliver a stock worth $107 and receive the exercise price of $100. This means that holding a short position in the call is worth −$7. The short position never has a value greater than zero, and when the stock price exceeds the exercise price, the short position is worse than worthless. From this consideration, it appears that no one would ever willingly take a short position in a call option. However, this leaves out the payments made from the buyer to the seller when the option first trades.

Continuing with our same example of a call option at expiration with a striking price of $100, we consider profit and loss results. We assume that the call option was purchased for $5. To profit, the holder of a long position in the call needs a stock price that will cover the exercise price and the cost of acquiring the option. For a long position in a call acquired at time $t < T$ the cost of the call is C_t. The profit or loss on the long call position held until expiration is:

$$C_T - C_t = \text{MAX}\{0, S_T - X\} - C_t$$

The seller of a call receives payment when the option first trades. The seller continues to hope for a stock price at expiration that does not exceed the exercise price. However, even if the stock price exceeds the exercise price, there may still be some profit left for the seller. The profit or loss on the sale of a call, with the position being held until expiration is:

$$C_t - C_T = C_t - \text{MAX}\{0, S_T - X\}$$

Figure 2.5 graphs the profit and loss for the call option positions under the assumptions we have been considering. Graphically, bringing profits and losses into consideration shifts the long call graph down by the $5 purchase price and shifts the short call graph up by the $5 purchase price.

We can understand Figure 2.5 for both the long and short positions by considering a few key stock values. We begin with the long position. To acquire a long position in the call option, the trader paid $5. If the stock price is $100 or less, the value of the option is zero at expiration, and the owner of the call lets it expire. Therefore, for any stock price equal to or less than the $100 exercise price, the call owner simply loses the entire purchase price of the option. If the stock price at expiration is above $100 but less than $105, the graph shows that the holder of the long call still loses, but loses less than the total $5 purchase price. For example, if the stock price at expiration is $103, the long call holder loses $2 in total. The call owner exercises, buying the $103 stock for $100 and makes $3 on the exercise. This $3 exercise value, coupled with the $5 paid for the option, gives a net loss of $2. As another example, if the stock price is $105 at expiration, the holder of the call makes $5 by

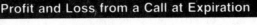

Profit and Loss from a Call at Expiration   **Figure 2.5**

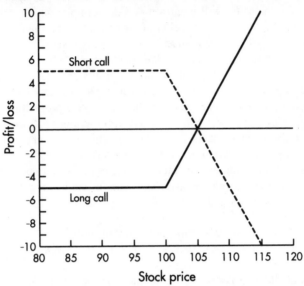

exercising, a profit that exactly offsets the purchase price of the option, so there is no profit or loss. From this example, we see that the holder of a call makes a zero profit if the stock price equals the exercise price plus the price paid for the call. To profit, the call holder needs a stock price that exceeds the exercise price plus the price paid for the call.

Figure 2.5 shows several important points. First, for the call buyer, the worst that can happen is losing the entire purchase price of the option. Comparing Figure 2.5 with Figure 2.2, we can see that the potential dollar loss is much greater if we hold the stock rather than the call. However, a small drop in the stock price can cause a complete loss of the option price. Second, potential profits from a long position in a call option are theoretically unlimited. The profits depend on only the price of the stock at expiration. Third, our discussion and graph show that the holder of a call option will exercise any time the stock price at expiration exceeds the exercise price. The call holder will exercise to reduce a loss or to capture a profit.

We now consider profit and losses on a short position in a call option. When the long trader bought a call, he paid $5 to the seller. As we noted in Chapter 1, the premium paid by the purchaser at the time of the initial trade belongs to the seller no matter what happens from that point forward. As Figure 2.5 shows, the greatest profit the seller of the call can achieve is $5. The seller attains this maximum profit when the holder of the call cannot exercise. In our example, the seller's profit is $5 for any stock price of $100 or less, because the call owner will allow the option to expire worthless for any stock price at expiration at or below the exercise price.

If the call owner can exercise, the seller's profits will be lower and the seller may incur a loss. For example, if the stock price is $105, the owner of the call will exercise. In this event, the seller will be forced to surrender a share worth $105 in exchange for the $100 exercise price. This represents a loss for the seller in the exercise of $5, which exactly offsets the price the seller received for the option. So with a stock price of $105, the seller makes a zero profit, as does the call owner. If the stock price exceeds $105, the seller will incur a loss. For example, with a stock price of $115, the call owner will exercise. At the exercise, the seller of the call delivers a share worth $115 and receives the $100 exercise price. The seller thereby loses $15 on the exercise. Coupled with the $5 the seller received when the option traded, the seller now has a net loss of $10.

In summary, we can note two key points about the profits and losses from selling a call. First, the best thing that can happen to the seller of a call is never to hear any more about the transaction after collecting the initial premium. As Figure 2.5 shows, the best profit for the seller of the call is to keep the initial purchase price. Second, potential losses from selling a call are theoretically unlimited. As the stock price rises, the losses for the seller of a call continue to mount. For example, if the stock price went to $1,000 at expiration, the seller of the call would lose $895.

Figure 2.5 also provides a dramatic illustration of one of the most important and sobering points about options trading. The profits from the buyer and seller of the call together are always zero. The buyer's gains are the seller's losses and vice versa.

$$\text{Long call profits} + \text{Short call profits} =$$
$$(C_T - C_t) + (C_t - C_T) = (\text{MAX}\{0, S_T - X\} - C_t) + (C_t - \text{MAX}\{0, S_T - X\}) = 0$$

Therefore, the options market is a **zero-sum game**; there are no net profits or losses in the market.[1] The trader who hopes to speculate successfully must be planning for someone else's losses to provide his profits. In other words, the options market is a competitive arena; profits come only at the expense of another trader.

CALL OPTIONS AT EXPIRATION AND ARBITRAGE

What happens if option values stray from the relationships we analyzed in the preceding section? In this section, we use the no-arbitrage pricing principle to show that call option prices must obey the rules we just developed.[2] If prices stray from these relationships, arbitrage opportunities arise. In the preceding section, we considered an example of a call option with an exercise price of $100. At expiration, with the stock trading at $103, the price of a call option must be $3. In this section, we show that any other price for the call option will create an arbitrage opportunity. If the price is too high, say $4, there is one arbitrage opportunity. If the call is too cheap, say $2, there is another arbitrage opportunity. To see why the call must trade for at least $3, consider the arbitrage opportunity that arises if the call is only $2. In this case, the arbitrageur would transact as follows.

Transaction	Cash Flow
Buy 1 call	−2
Exercise the call	−100
Sell the share	+103
Net Cash Flow	+$1

These transactions meet the conditions for arbitrage. First, there is no investment because all the transactions occur simultaneously. The only cash flow is a $1 cash inflow. Second, the profit is certain once the trader enters the transaction. Therefore, these transactions meet our conditions for arbitrage: they offer a riskless profit without investment. If the call were priced at $2, traders would follow our strategy mercilessly. They would madly buy options, exercise, and sell the share. These transactions would cause tremendous demand for the call and a tremendous supply of the share. These supply and demand forces would subside only after the call and share price adjust to prevent the arbitrage.

We now consider why the call cannot trade for more than $3 at expiration. If the call price exceeds $3, a different arbitrage opportunity arises. If the call were priced at $4, for example, arbitrageurs would simply sell the overpriced call. Then they would wait to see whether the purchaser of the call exercises. We consider transactions for both possibilities – the purchaser exercises or does not exercise.

If the purchaser exercises, the arbitrageur has already sold the call and received $4. Now to fulfill his exercise commitment, the seller acquires a share for $103 in the market and delivers the share. Upon delivery, the seller of the call receives the exercise price of $100. These three transactions yield a profit of $1. If the purchaser foolishly neglects to exercise, the situation is even better for the arbitrageur. The arbitrageur already sold the call and received $4. If the purchaser fails to exercise, the option expires and the arbitrageur makes a full $4 profit. The worst case scenario still provides the arbitrageur with a profit of $1. Therefore, these transactions represent an arbitrage transaction. First, there is no investment. Second, the transactions ensure a profit.

With a $4 call price, an exercise price of $100, and a stock price at expiration of $103, traders would madly sell call options. The excess supply of options at the $4 price would drive down the price of the option. The process would stop only when the price relationships offer no more arbitrage opportunities. This happens when the price of the call and stock conform to the relationships we developed in the preceding section. In other words, prices in financial markets must conform to our no-arbitrage principle by adjusting to eliminate any arbitrage opportunity.

The Purchaser Exercises

Transaction		Cash Flow
Sell 1 call		+4
Buy 1 share		−103
Deliver share and collect exercise price		+100
	Net Cash Flow	+$1

The Purchaser Does Not Exercise

Transaction		Cash Flow
Sell 1 call		+4
	Net Cash Flow	+$4

BUY OR SELL A PUT OPTION

This section deals with the value of put options and the profits and losses of buying and selling puts when the put is at expiration. Again, we use the notation for an American put (P_T), but all of the conclusions hold identically for European puts. In most respects, we can analyze put options in the same way we analyzed call options. At expiration, the holder of a put has two choices – exercise or allow the option to expire worthless. If the holder exercises, he surrenders the stock and receives the exercise price. Therefore, the holder of a put will exercise only if the exercise price exceeds the stock price. The value of a put option at expiration equals zero, or the exercise price minus the stock price, whichever is higher:

$$P_T = \text{MAX}\{0, X - S_T\} \tag{2.2}$$

We can illustrate this principle with an example. Consider a put option with an exercise price of $100 and assume that the underlying stock trades at $102. At expiration, the holder of the put can either exercise or allow the put to expire worthless. With an exercise price of $100 and a stock price of $102, the holder cannot exercise profitably. To exercise the put, the trader would surrender the stock worth $102 and receive the exercise price of $100, thereby losing $2 on the exercise. Consequently, if the stock price is above the exercise price at expiration, the put is worthless. With our example numbers we have:

$$P_T = \text{MAX}\{0, X - S_T\} = \text{MAX}\{0, \$100 - \$102\} = \text{MAX}\{0, -\$2\} = 0$$

Now consider the same put option with the stock trading at $100. Exercising the put requires surrendering the stock worth $100 and receiving the exercise price of $100. There is no profit in exercising, and the put is at expiration, so the put is still worthless. In general, if the stock price equals or exceeds the exercise price at expiration, the put is worthless.

When the stock price at expiration falls below the exercise price, the put has value. In this situation, the value of the put equals the exercise price minus the stock price. For example, assume the stock trades at $94 and consider the same put with an exercise price of $100. Now the put is worth $6 because it gives its owner the right to receive the $100 exercise price by surrendering a stock worth only $94. Using these numbers we find:

$$P_T = \text{MAX}\{0, X - S_T\} = \text{MAX}\{0, \$100 - \$94\} = \text{MAX}\{0, \$6\} = \$6$$

Figure 2.6 graphs the value of our example put option at expiration. For stock values equaling or exceeding the $100 exercise price, the put has a zero value. If the stock price is below the exercise price, however, the put is worth the exercise price minus the stock price. As our example showed, if the stock trades for $94, the put is worth $6. The graph reflects this valuation.

Figure 2.6 also shows the value of a short position in the put. For stock prices equaling or exceeding the exercise price, the put has a zero value. This zero value results from the fact that the holder of the long put will not exercise. However, when the stock price at expiration is less than the exercise price, a short position in the put has a negative value, which results from the opportunity that the long put holder has to exercise. For example, if the stock price is $94, the holder of a short position in the put must pay $100 for a stock worth only $94 when the long put holder exercises. In this situation, the short position in the put will be worth -$6.

Our analysis of put values parallels our results for call options in several ways. First, as we saw with the values of call options at expiration, the value of long and short positions in puts always sums to zero for any stock price. We noted in our discussion of call options that the option market is a zero-sum game. The same principle extends to put options with equal force. Second, we see for put options, as we noted for call options, that a short position can never have a positive value at

The Value of a Put at Expiration   **Figure 2.6**

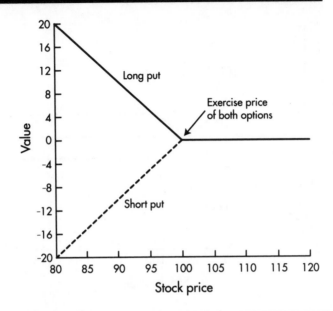

expiration. The seller of a call or put hopes that nothing happens after the initial transaction when he collects the option price. The best outcome for the seller of either a put or a call is that there will be no exercise and that the option will expire worthless. Third, noting that a short put position has a zero value at best, we might wonder why anyone would accept a short position. As we saw with a call option, the rationality of selling a put requires us to consider the sale price. This leads to a consideration of put option profits and losses.

We continue with our example of a put option with an exercise price of $100. Now we assume that this option was purchased for a price of $4. We consider how profits and losses on long and short put positions depend on the stock price at expiration. As we did for calls, we consider a few key stock prices.

First, we analyze the profits and losses for a long position in the put, where the purchase price is $4 and the exercise price is $100. If the stock price at expiration exceeds $100, the holder of the put cannot exercise profitably, and the option expires worthless. In this case, the put holder loses $4, the purchase price of the option. Likewise, if the stock price at expiration equals $100, there is no profitable exercise. Exercising in this situation would involve surrendering a stock worth $100 and receiving the $100 exercise price. Again, the buyer of the put option loses the purchase price of $4. Therefore, if the stock price at expiration equals or exceeds the exercise price, the buyer of a put loses the full purchase price. Figure 2.7 shows the profits and losses for long and short positions in the put.

If the stock price at expiration is less than the exercise price, there will be a benefit to exercising. For example, assume the stock price is $99 at expiration. Then, the owner of the put will exercise, surrendering the $99 stock and receiving the $100 exercise price. In this case, the exercise value of

Figure 2.7   Profit and Loss from a Put at Expiration

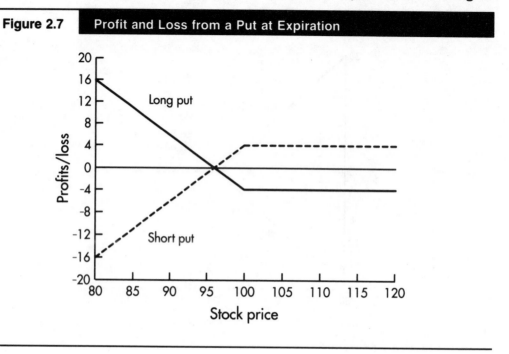

the put is $1. With the $99 stock price, the holder of the put makes $1 on the exercise but has already paid $4 to acquire the put. Therefore, the total loss is $3. If the stock price is $96 at expiration, the buyer of the put makes a zero profit. The $4 exercise value exactly offsets the price of the put. When the stock price is less than $96, the put buyer makes a profit. For example, if the stock price is $90 at expiration, the owner of a put exercises. In exercising, he surrenders a stock worth $90 and receives the $100 exercise price. This gives a $6 profit, after considering the $4 purchase price of the option.

MONEYNESS

In the preceding sections, we have explored the value of calls and puts at expiration. We noted that calls have a positive value at expiration if the stock price exceeds the exercise price, and puts have a positive value at expiration if the exercise price exceeds the stock price. We now introduce important terminology that applies to options both before and at expiration. Both calls and puts can be **in-the-money**, **at-the-money**, or **out-of-the-money**. The following table shows the conditions for puts and calls to meet these moneyness conditions for any time t.

	Calls	Puts
In-the-money	$S_t > X$	$S_t < X$
At-the-money	$S_t = X$	$S_t = X$
Out-of-the-money	$S_t < X$	$S_t > X$

In addition, options can be **near-the-money** if the stock price is close to the exercise price. Further, a call is **deep-in-the-money** if the stock price is considerably above the exercise price, and a put is deep-in-the-money if the stock price is considerably smaller than the exercise price.

OPTION COMBINATIONS

This section discusses some of the most important ways that traders can combine options. By trading option combinations, traders can shape the risk and return characteristics of their option positions, which allows more precise speculative strategies. For example, we will see how to use option combinations to profit when stock prices move a great deal or when they stagnate.

The Straddle

A **straddle** consists of a call and a put with the same exercise price and the same expiration. The buyer of a straddle buys the call and put, while the seller of a straddle sells the same two options.[3] Consider a call and put, both with $100 exercise prices. We assume the call costs $5 and the put trades for $4. Figure 2.8 shows the profits and losses from purchasing each of these options. The profit and losses for buying the straddle are the combined profits and losses from buying both options.

Profit and Loss at Expiration from the Options in a Straddle   **Figure 2.8**

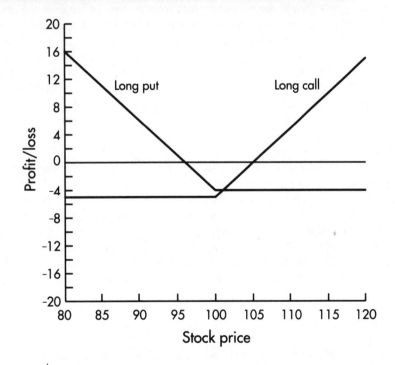

If we designate T as the expiration date of the option and let t be the present, then C_t is the current price of the option and C_T is the price of the option at expiration. Similarly, P_t is the present price of the put and P_T is the price of the put at expiration. Using this notation, the cost of the long straddle is:

$$C_t + P_t$$

and the value of the straddle at expiration will be:

$$C_T + P_T = \text{MAX}\{0,\, S_T - X\} + \text{MAX}\{0,\, X - S_T\} \tag{2.3}$$

Similarly, the short straddle position costs:

$$-C_t - P_t$$

so the short trader receives a payment for accepting the short straddle position. The value of the short straddle at expiration will be:

$$-C_T - P_T = -\text{MAX}\{0,\, S_T - X\} - \text{MAX}\{0,\, X - S_T\}$$

Because the options market is always a zero-sum game, the short trader's profits and losses mirror those of the long position. Figure 2.9 shows the profits and losses from buying and selling the straddle. As the graph shows, the maximum loss for the straddle buyer is the cost of the two options. Potential profits are almost unlimited for the buyer if the stock price rises or falls enough. As Figure 2.9 also shows, the maximum profit for the short straddle trader occurs when the stock price at expiration equals the exercise price. If the stock price equals the exercise price, the straddle owner cannot exercise either the call or the put profitably. Therefore, both options expire worthless and the short straddle trader keeps both option premiums for a total profit of $9. However, if the stock price diverges from the exercise price, the long straddle holder will exercise either the call or the put. Any exercise decreases the short trader's profits and may even generate a loss. If the stock price exceeds the exercise price, the owner will exercise the call, while if the stock price is less than the exercise price, the straddle owner will exercise the put.

Figure 2.9 shows that the short trader essentially bets that the stock price will not diverge too far from the exercise price, so the seller is betting that the stock price will not be too volatile. In making this bet, the straddle seller risks theoretically unlimited losses if the stock price goes too high. Likewise, the short trader's losses are almost unlimited if the stock price goes too low.[4] The short trader's cash inflows equal the sum of the two option prices. At expiration, the short trader's cash outflow equals the exercise result for the call and for the put. If the call is exercised against him at expiration, the short trader loses the difference between the stock price and the exercise price. If the put is exercised against him, the short trader loses the difference between the exercise price and the stock price.

The Strangle

Like a straddle, a **strangle** consists of a put and a call with the same expiration date and the same underlying good. In a strangle, the call has an exercise price above the stock price and the put has

| Profit and Loss at Expiration from a Straddle | Figure 2.9 |

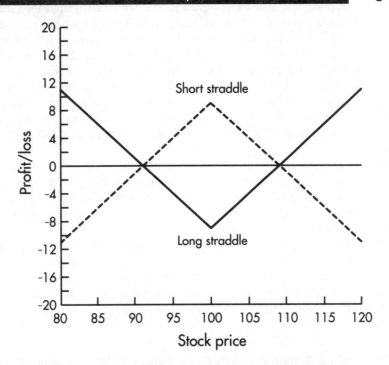

an exercise price below the stock price. Let X_1 and X_2 be the two exercise prices, such that $X_1 > X_2$. Therefore, a strangle is similar to a straddle, but the put and call have different exercise prices. Let $C_{t,1}$ denote the cost of the call with exercise price X_1 at time t, and let $P_{t,2}$ indicate the cost of the put with exercise price X_2. The long strangle trader buys the put and call, while the short trader sells the two options. The cost of the long strangle is:

$$C_t(S_t, X_1, T) + P_t(S_t, X_2, T)$$

Then the value of the strangle at expiration will be:

$$C_T(S_T, X_1, T) + P_T(S_T, X_2, T) = \text{MAX}\{0, S_T - X_1\} + \text{MAX}\{0, X_2 - S_T\} \tag{2.4}$$

The cost of the short strangle is:

$$-C_t(S_t, X_1, T) - P_t(S_t, X_2, T)$$

The value of the short strangle at expiration will be:

$$-C_T(S_T, X_1, T) - P_T(S_T, X_2, T) = -\text{MAX}\{0, S_T - X_1\} - \text{MAX}\{0, X_2 - S_T\}$$

To illustrate the strangle, we use a call with an exercise price of $85 and a put with an exercise price of $80. The call price is $3 and the put price is $4. Figure 2.10 graphs the profits and losses for long positions in these two options. The call has a profit for any stock price above $88, and the put has a profit for any stock price below $76. However, for the owner of a strangle to profit, the price of the stock must fall below $76 or rise above $88. Figure 2.11 shows the profits and losses from buying and selling the strangle based on these two options. The total outlay for the two options is $7. To break even, either the call or the put must give an exercise profit of $7. The call makes an exercise profit of $7 when the stock price is $7 above the exercise price of the call or $92. Similarly, the put has an exercise profit of $7 when the stock price is $73. Any stock price between $73 and $92 results in a loss on the strangle, while any stock price outside the $73–$92 range gives a profit on the strangle.

Figure 2.11 shows that buying a strangle is betting that the stock price will move significantly below the exercise price on the put or above the exercise price on the call. The buyer of the strangle has the chance for very large profits if the stock price moves dramatically away from the exercise prices. Theoretically, the profit on a strangle is boundless. A stock price at expiration of $200, for example, gives a profit on the strangle of $108.

The profits on the short position are the negative values of the profits for the long position. Figure 2.11 shows the profits and losses for the short strangle position as dotted lines. At any stock price from $80 to $85, the short strangle has a $7 profit. Between these two prices, the long trader cannot profit by exercising either the put or the call, so the short trader keeps the full price of both options. For stock prices below $80, the straddle buyer exercises the put, and for stock prices above $85, the straddle buyer exercises the call. Any exercise costs the short trader, who still has some

Figure 2.10   Profit and Loss at Expiration from the Options in a Strangle

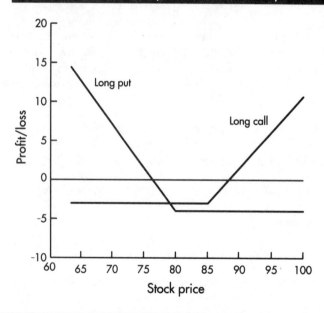

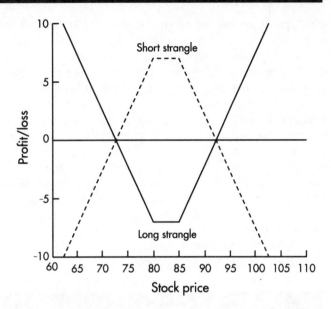

Profit and Loss at Expiration from a Strangle   **Figure 2.11**

profit if the stock price stays within the \$73–\$92 range. However, for very low stock prices, the short strangle position gives large losses, as it does for very high stock prices. Therefore, the short strangle trader is betting that stock prices will stay within a fairly wide band. In essence, the short strangle trader has a high probability of a small profit but accepts the risk of a very large loss.

Bull and Bear Spreads with Call Options

A **bull spread** in the options market is a combination of options designed to profit if the price of the underlying good rises.[5] A bull spread utilizing call options requires two calls with the same underlying stock and the same expiration date, but with different exercise prices. The buyer of a bull spread buys a call with an exercise price below the stock price and sells a call option with an exercise price above the stock price. The spread is a "bull" spread, because the trader hopes to profit from a price rise in the stock. The trade is a "spread," because it involves buying one option and selling a related option. Compared with buying the stock itself, the bull spread with call options limits the trader's risk, but the bull spread also limits the profit potential.

The cost of the bull spread is the cost of the option that is purchased, less the cost of the option that the trader sells. Letting $C_t(S_t, X_1, T)$ be the cost of the first option that is purchased at time t with exercise price X_1, and letting $C_t(S_t, X_2, T)$ be the cost of the second option with exercise price X_2, such that $X_1 < X_2$, the cost of the bull spread is:

$$C_t(S_t, X_1, T) - C_t(S_t, X_2, T)$$

At expiration, the value of the bull spread will be:

$$C_T(S_T, X_1, T) - C_T(S_T, X_2, T) = \text{MAX}\{0, S_T - X_1\} - \text{MAX}\{0, S_T - X_2\} \qquad (2.5)$$

To illustrate the bull spread, assume that the stock trades at $100. One call option has an exercise price of $95 and costs $7. The other call has an exercise price of $105 and costs $3. To buy the bull spread, the trader buys the call with the lower exercise price and sells the call with the higher exercise price. In our example, the total outlay for the bull spread is $4. Figure 2.12 graphs the profits and losses for the two call positions individually. The long position profits if the stock price moves above $102. The short position profits if the stock price does not exceed $108. As the graph shows, low stock prices result in an overall loss for the bull spread, because the cost of buying the call with the lower exercise price exceeds the proceeds from selling the call with the higher exercise price. It is also interesting to consider prices at $105 and above. For every dollar by which the stock price exceeds $105, the long call portion of the spread generates an extra dollar of profit, but the short call component starts to lose money. Thus, for stock prices above $105, the additional gains on the long call exactly offset the losses on the short call. Therefore, no matter how high the stock price goes, the bull spread can never give a greater profit than it does for a stock price of $105.

Figure 2.13 graphs the bull spread as the solid line. For any stock price at expiration of $95 or below, the bull spread loses $4. This $4 is the difference between the cash inflow for selling one call and buying the other. The bull spread breaks even for a stock price of $99. The highest possible

Figure 2.12   Profit and Loss at Expiration from the Options in a Bull Spread

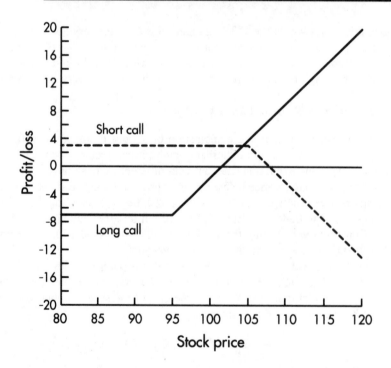

| Profit and Loss at Expiration from a Bull Spread with Calls | Figure 2.13 |

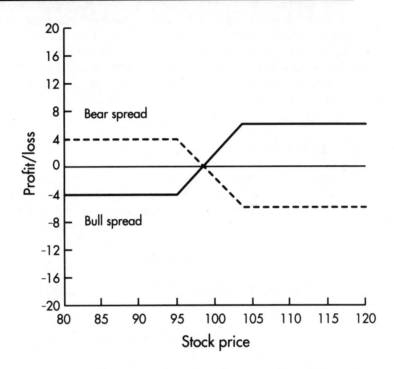

profit on the bull spread comes when the stock sells for $105. Then the bull spread gives a $6 profit. For any stock price above $105, the profit on the bull spread remains at $6. Therefore, the trader of a bull spread bets that the stock price goes up, but he hedges his bet. We can see that the bull spread protects the trader from losing any more than $4. However, the trader cannot make more than a $6 profit. We can compare the bull spread with a position in the stock itself in Figure 2.2. Comparing the bull spread and the stock, we find that the stock offers the chance for bigger profits, but it also has greater risk of a serious loss.

A **bear spread** in the options market is an option combination designed to profit from falling stock prices. To execute a bear spread with call options requires two call options with the same underlying stock and the same expiration date. The two calls, however, have different exercise prices. To execute a bear spread with calls, a trader would sell the call with the lower exercise price and buy the call with the higher exercise price. In other words, the bear spread with calls is just the short position to the bull spread with calls.

The cost of a bear spread is:

$$-C_t(S_t, X_1, T) + C_t(S_t, X_2, T)$$

At expiration, the value of the bear spread will be:

$$-C_T(S_T, X_1, T) + C_T(S_T, X_2, T) = -\text{MAX}\{0, S_T - X_1\} + \text{MAX}\{0, S_T - X_2\} \qquad (2.6)$$

Figure 2.13 shows the profit and loss profile for a bear spread with the same options we have been considering. The dotted line shows how profit and losses vary if a trader sells the call with the $95 strike price and buys the call with the $105 strike price. In a bear spread, the trader bets that the stock price will fall. However, the bear spread also limits the profit opportunity and the risk of loss compared with a short position in the stock itself. We can compare the profit and loss profiles of the bear spread in Figure 2.13 with the short position in the stock shown as the dotted line in Figure 2.2.[6]

Bull and Bear Spreads with Put Options

It is also possible to execute bull and bear spreads with put options. The bull spread consists of buying a put with a lower exercise price and selling a put with a higher exercise price. The bear spread trader sells a put with a lower exercise price and buys a put with a higher exercise price. Consistent with our notation for call options, the cost of the bull spread with puts is:

$$P_t(S_t, X_1, T) - P_t(S_t, X_2, T)$$

with exercises prices X_1 and X_2, respectively, such that $X_1 < X_2$. The value of the bull spread at expiration will be:

$$P_T(S_T, X_1, T) - P_T(S_T, X_2, T) = \text{MAX}\{0, X_1 - S_T\} - \text{MAX}\{0, X_2 - S_T\} \qquad (2.7)$$

It is also possible to initiate a bear spread with puts. The bear spread is just the opposite of a bull spread. For a put bear spread, the trader uses two options on the same underlying good that have the same time until expiration. The trader sells the put with the lower exercise price and buys the put with the higher exercise price. The bear spread with puts is simply the complementary position to the bull spread and costs:

$$-P_t(S_t, X_1, T) + P_t(S_t, X_2, T)$$

The value of the bear spread with puts at expiration is:

$$-P_T(S_T, X_1, T) + P_T(S_T, X_2, T) = -\text{MAX}\{0, X_1 - S_T\} + \text{MAX}\{0, X_2 - S_T\}$$

To illustrate bull and bear spreads with put options, consider two puts with the same expiration date and the same underlying stock. Assume that one put has an exercise price of $90 and the other has an exercise price of $110. The put with an exercise price of $90 trades at $3, while the put with an exercise price of $110 trades at $9.

The bull trader would buy the put with $X = \$90$ and sell the put with $X = \$110$, for a total cash inflow of $6. Assume the stock price at expiration is $90. The bull trader cannot exercise the put option with $X = \$90$. However, the put option with $X = \$110$ that the trader sold will be exercised, giving our trader an exercise loss of $20. Thus, the total loss for the bull trader will be $14, the initial cash inflow of $6, minus the $20 exercise loss. For any terminal stock price lower than $90, the bull trader will lose an additional dollar on the short put position. However, if the stock price falls below $90, the bull trader can exercise the long put with a striking price of $90. Thus, the gain on the long put will offset any further losses on the short put for stock prices lower than $90. Therefore, the maximum loss on the bull spread of $14 occurs with a stock price of $90 or lower.

If the stock price at expiration is $110 or higher, the short put cannot be exercised against the bull trader of our example. Also, the long put cannot be exercised, because it cannot be exercised at any price of $90 or higher. With no exercises occurring, the bull trader merely keeps the initial cash inflow that occurred when the position was assumed, and the bull trader nets a profit of $6.

For prices between $90 and $110, the short put will be exercised against the bull trader and will reduce the trader's profits or generate a loss. For example, if the stock price is $100 at expiration, the bull trader will lose $10 on the exercise of the put with $X = $110. This loss, coupled with the initial cash inflow of $6, gives a total loss on the trade of $4. Figure 2.14 shows the profits and losses from this bull trade with puts as the solid line and shows the bear spread with puts as a dotted line. As Figure 2.14 shows, the bear trader takes the opposite position from the bull trader.

In terms of our example, the bear trader would buy the put with $X = $110 and sell the put with $X = $90, for a total outlay of $6. For any terminal stock price less than $110, the bear trader can exercise the put with $X = $110 and will break even for a terminal stock price of $104. For any stock price below $90, the bear trader's short call will be exercised against her as well, giving an exercise loss on that option. This exercise loss will offset any further profits on the long put with $X = $110. As a result, the bear trader cannot make more than $14. This $14 profit occurs for any stock price of $90 or less. For example, if the terminal stock price is $85, the bear trader has an exercise profit of $25 on the long put with $X = $110 and an exercise loss of −$5 on the short put with $X = $90.

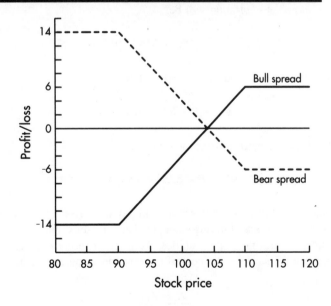

Profit and Loss at Expiration from a Bull Spread with Puts   **Figure 2.14**

This total exercise profit of $20 must be reduced by the $6 outlay required to assume the bear spread, for a net gain of $14. This gain of $14 when the stock price is $85 exactly equals the loss of $14 that the bull spread holder would incur.

The Box Spread

A **box spread** consists of a bull spread with calls plus a bear spread with puts, with the two spreads having the same pair of exercise prices. In terms of our notation, the box spread costs:

$$C_t(S_t, X_1, T) - C_t(S_t, X_2, T) + P_t(S_t, X_1, T) - P_t(S_t, X_2, T)$$

The value of the box spread at expiration is:

$$C_T(S_T, X_1, T) - C_T(S_T, X_2, T) - P_T(S_T, X_1, T) + P_T(S_T, X_2, T) =$$
$$\text{MAX}\{0, S_T - X_1\} - \text{MAX}\{0, S_T - X_2\} - \text{MAX}\{0, X_1 - S_T\} + \text{MAX}\{0, X_2 - S_T\} \qquad (2.8)$$

As an example, consider the following four transactions:

Transaction	Exercise Price
Long 1 Call	$ 95
Short 1 Call	105
Long 1 Put	105
Short 1 Put	95

The value of the box spread at expiration will be:

$$\text{MAX}\{0, S_T - \$95\} - \text{MAX}\{0, S_T - \$105\} + \text{MAX}\{0, \$105 - S_T\} - \text{MAX}\{0, \$95 - S_T\}$$

For a stock price of $102 at expiration, the payoff will be:

$$\$7 - \$0 + \$3 - \$0 = \$10$$

For a stock price of $80, the payoff at expiration will be:

$$\$0 - \$0 + \$25 - \$15 = \$10$$

In fact, for any terminal stock price, the box spread will pay the difference between the high and low exercise prices, $X_2 - X_1$, which is $10 in this example. Thus, the box spread is a riskless investment strategy. To avoid potential arbitrage opportunities, the price of the box spread must be the present value of the certain payoff. Therefore, the cost of the box spread purchased at time t must be:

$$\frac{X_2 - X_1}{(1 + r)^{(T-t)}}$$

Continuing with this example, let us assume that the options expire in one year and that the risk-free interest rate is 10 percent. Under these assumptions, the box spread must cost $9.09. Any other price would lead to arbitrage.

The Butterfly Spread with Calls

A **butterfly spread** can be executed by using three calls with the same expiration date on the same underlying stock. The long trader buys one call with a low exercise price, buys one call with a high exercise price, and sells two calls with an intermediate exercise price. Continuing to let X_i represent exercise prices such that $X_1 < X_2 < X_3$, the cost of the long butterfly spread is:

$$C_t(S_t, X_1, T) - 2C_t(S_t, X_2, T) + C_t(S_t, X_3, T)$$

The value of the butterfly spread at expiration is:

$$C_T(S_T, X_1, T) - 2C_T(S_T, X_2, T) + C_T(S_T, X_3, T) = \quad (2.9)$$
$$\text{MAX}\{0, S_T - X_1\} - 2\text{MAX}\{0, S_T - X_2\} + \text{MAX}\{0, S_T - X_3\}$$

The short trader takes exactly the opposite position, selling one call with a low exercise price, selling one call with a high exercise price, and buying two calls with an intermediate exercise price. The cost of the short position is:

$$-C_t(S_t, X_1, T) + 2C_t(S_t, X_2, T) - C_t(S_t, X_3, T)$$

The value of the short butterfly spread at expiration is:

$$-C_T(S_T, X_1, T) + 2C_T(S_T, X_2, T) - C_t(S_T, X_3, T) =$$
$$-\text{MAX}\{0, S_T - X_1\} + 2\text{MAX}\{0, S_T - X_2\} - \text{MAX}\{0, S_T - X_3\}$$

For the long trader, the spread profits most when the stock price at expiration is at the intermediate exercise price. In essence, the butterfly spread gives a payoff pattern similar to a straddle. Compared with a straddle, however, a butterfly spread offers lower risk at the expense of reduced profit potential.

As an example of a butterfly spread, assume that a stock trades at $100 and a trader buys a butterfly spread by trading options with the prices shown in the following table. As the table shows, the buyer of a butterfly spread sells two calls with a striking price near the stock price and buys one each of the calls above and below the stock price.

	Exercise Price	Option Premium
Long 1 Call	$105	$3
Short 2 Calls	100	4
Long 1 Call	95	7

Figure 2.15 graphs the profits and losses from each of these three option positions. To understand the butterfly spread, we need to combine the profits and losses, remembering that the spread involves selling two options and buying two, a total of four options with three different exercise prices.

Figure 2.15   Profit and Loss at Expiration for the Options in a Butterfly Spread

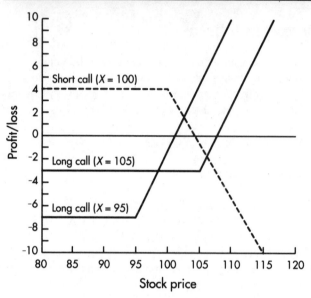

Let us consider a few critical stock prices to see how the butterfly spread profits respond. The critical stock prices always include the exercise prices for the options. First, if the stock price is $95, the call with an exercise price of $95 is worth zero and a long position in this call loses $7. The long call with the $105 exercise price also cannot be exercised, so it is worthless, giving a loss of the $3 purchase price. The short call position gives a profit of $4 per option and the spread sold two of these options, for an $8 profit. Adding these values gives a net loss on the spread of $2, if the stock price is $95. Second, if the stock price is $100, the long call with a striking price of $95 loses $2 (the $5 stock profit minus the $7 purchase price). The long call with an exercise price of $105 loses its full purchase price of $3. Together, the long calls lose $5. The short call still shows a profit of $4 per option, for a profit of $8 on the two options. This gives a net profit of $3 if the stock price is $100. Third, if the stock price is $105 at expiration, the long call with an exercise price of $95 has a profit of $3. The long call with an exercise price of $105 loses $3. Also, the short call position loses $1 per option for a loss on two positions of $2. This gives a net loss on the butterfly spread of $2. In summary we have: a $2 loss for a $95 stock price, a $3 profit for a $100 stock price, and a $2 loss for a $105 stock price.

Figure 2.16 shows the entire profit and loss graph for the butterfly spread. At a stock price of $100, we noted a profit of $3. This is the highest profit available from the spread. At stock prices of $95 and $105, the spread loses $2. For stock prices below $95 or above $105, the loss is still $2. As the graph shows, the butterfly spread has a zero profit for stock prices of $97 and $103. The buyer of the butterfly spread essentially bets that stock prices will hover near $100. Any large move away from $100 gives a loss on the butterfly spread. However, the loss can never exceed $2. Comparing

Profit and Loss at Expiration for a Butterfly Spread with Calls   **Figure 2.16**

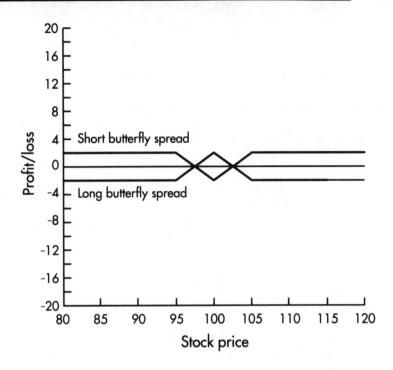

the butterfly spread with the straddle in Figure 2.9, we see that the butterfly spread resembles a short position in the straddle. Compared with the straddle, the butterfly spread reduces the risk of a very large loss. However, the reduction in risk necessarily comes at the expense of a chance for a big profit.

The Butterfly Spread with Puts

The butterfly spread can also be initiated with a combination of put options. For a long position in a butterfly spread, the trader buys a put with a low exercise price, buys a put with a high exercise price, and sells two puts with an intermediate exercise price. The short trader sells a put with a low exercise price, sells a put with a high exercise price, and buys two puts with an intermediate exercise price.

For the long position in the butterfly spread with puts, the cost is:

$$P_t(S_t, X_1, T) - 2P_t(S_t, X_2, T) + P_t(S_t, X_3, T)$$

The value at expiration is:

$$P_T(S_T, X_1, T) - 2P_T(S_T, X_2, T) + P_T(S_T, X_3, T) \qquad\qquad (2.10)$$
$$= \text{MAX}\{0, X_1 - S_T\} - 2\text{MAX}\{0, X_2 - S_T\} + \text{MAX}\{0, X_3 - S_T\}$$

For the short trader, the cost of the short position is:

$$-P_t(S_t, X_1, T) + 2P_t(S_t, X_2, T) - P_t(S_t, X_3, T)$$

The value at expiration for the short butterfly spread with puts is:

$$-P_T(S_T, X_1, T) + 2P_T(S_T, X_2, T) - P_T(S_T, X_3, T)$$
$$= -\text{MAX}\{0, X_1 - S_T\} + 2\text{MAX}\{0, X_2 - S_T\} - \text{MAX}\{0, X_3 - S_T\}$$

The long and short butterfly trades with puts give a profit pattern just like the butterfly trade with calls, as illustrated in Figure 2.16.

To explore these transactions more fully, consider the following transactions for a long butterfly spread with puts.

	Exercise Price	Option Premium
Long 1 Put	$ 95	$ 5
Short 2 Puts	100	7
Long 1 Put	105	10

The total cost of this position is $1. If the stock price at expiration is exactly $95, the put with $X = \$95$ cannot be exercised. However, both puts with $X = \$100$ will be exercised against the long trader, for an exercise loss of $10. The long trader will be able to exercise the put with $X = \$105$, for an exercise profit of $10, so the long butterfly trader will experience no net gain or loss on the exercise. The same is true for any stock price lower than $95. Lower stock prices will generate larger losses on the exercise of the puts with $X = \$100$, but these will be exactly offset by higher exercise gains on the two long puts that constitute the long butterfly spread. Thus, for any stock price of $95 or lower, there is no exercise gain or loss and the trader loses the $1 cost of the butterfly spread. At a terminal stock price of $105 or higher, no put can be exercised, so there is no exercise gain or loss, and the purchaser of the butterfly spread loses the $1 cost of the position. Figure 2.17 shows these profits and losses as a solid line.

For a stock price at expiration between $95 and $105, the long trader has an exercise gain that will offset the $1 cost of the position and may even make the entire transaction profitable. For example, if the terminal stock price is $100, the puts with $X = \$95$ and $X = \$100$ cannot be exercised. In this situation, the trader can exercise the put with $X = \$105$ for a $5 exercise profit. This exercise profit, offset by the $1 cost of the position, gives a total gain on the trade of $4, and this is the maximum profit from the trade. For terminal stock prices between $95 and $100 or between $100 and $105, the gain will be less and may even be a loss. For a terminal stock price of $96, for example, the trader will exercise the put with $X = \$105$ for a $9 exercise profit. However, the two short puts with $X = \$100$ will be exercised against her, for an exercise loss of −$8. The net exercise gain will be $1, which exactly offsets the $1 cost of the position. Thus, the trade has a zero gain/loss at a terminal stock price of $96. The same occurs if the terminal stock price is $104. For a terminal stock

Profit and Loss at Expiration for a Butterfly Spread with Puts   **Figure 2.17**

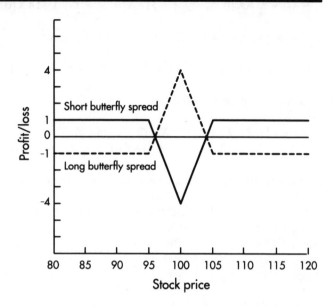

price between $96 and $104, there is some profit, with the maximum profit of $4 occurring when the stock price is $100.

As we noted at the beginning of this section, it is also possible to initiate a short butterfly position with puts. With the options of this example, the short butterfly transaction would require selling a put with $X = \$95$, selling a put with $X = \$105$, and buying two puts with $X = \$100$, for a total cash inflow of $1. This short butterfly position would have profits and losses that exactly mirror those of the long position. Figure 2.17 shows the profits and losses for this short butterfly position with puts as a dotted line.

The Condor with Call Options

A **condor** is a specialized position that involves four options on the same underlying good and the same expiration date. The four options have different exercise prices. For a long condor entered with call options, a trader buys a call with a low exercise price, sells a call with a somewhat higher exercise price, sells a call with a yet higher exercise price, and buys a call with the highest exercise price. Notice that this is like a butterfly, in that the long trader buys two calls with extreme exercise prices, and sells two calls with intermediate exercise prices. In a butterfly, the intermediate exercise price is the same for the two calls, while a condor uses two different intermediate exercise prices. Thus, the cost of a long condor is:

$$C_t(S_t, X_1, T) - C_t(S_t, X_2, T) - C_t(S_t, X_3, T) + C_t(S_t, X_4, T)$$

The value of the long condor at expiration is:

$$C_T(S_T, X_1, T) - C_T(S_T, X_2, T) - C_T(S_T, X_3, T) + C_T(S_T, X_4, T) = \qquad (2.11)$$
$$\text{MAX}\{0, S_T - X_1\} - \text{MAX}\{0, S_T - X_2\} - \text{MAX}\{0, S_T - X_3\} + \text{MAX}\{0, S_T - X_4\}$$

For the short condor position executed with calls, the cost of the position is:

$$-C_t(S_t, X_1, T) + C_t(S_t, X_2, T) + C_t(S_t, X_3, T) - C_t(S_t, X_4, T)$$

For the short condor, the value at expiration is:

$$-C_T(S_T, X_1, T) + C_T(S_T, X_2, T) + C_T(S_T, X_3, T) - C_T(S_T, X_4, T) =$$
$$-\text{MAX}\{0, S_T - X_1\} + \text{MAX}\{0, S_T - X_2\} + \text{MAX}\{0, S_T - X_3\} - \text{MAX}\{0, S_T - X_4\}$$

The following transactions illustrate a long condor position entered with call options.

	Exercise Price	*Option Premium*
Long 1 Call	$ 90	$10
Short 1 Call	95	7
Short 1 Call	100	4
Long 1 Call	105	2

The total cost of the condor is $1. If the terminal stock price is $90 or less, no call can be exercised, and the position expires worthless for a total loss of $1. If the stock price at expiration is $95, the long trader can exercise the call with $X = \$90$ for an exercise profit of $5. This gives a total profit on the position of $4. For any stock price above $95, the short call with $X = \$95$ will be exercised against the purchase of the condor; and for any stock price above $100, the short call with X = $100 will also be exercised. For example, if the terminal stock price is $102, the transactions give the following result. The long call with $X = \$90$ will have a $12 exercise profit, the short call with $X = \$95$ will generate an exercise loss of $7, and the short call with $X = \$100$ will generate an exercise loss of $2. These exercise results, coupled with the $1 initial cost of the position, give a final profit of $4.

For higher terminal stock prices, those of $105 or higher, the exercise gains and losses are exactly offsetting. For example, if the terminal stock price is $107, the exercise gains and losses are: $17 for the call with $X = \$90$, −$12 for the call with $X = \$95$, −$7 for the call with $X = \$100$, and $2 for the call with $X = \$105$, for a net exercise result of zero. This leaves a loss of $1, which was the original cost to enter the position. Figure 2.18 shows the short condor position with the dotted line. As usual, the results for the short position are a mirror image of those for the long position. In a zero-sum game, the winner's gains match the loser's losses.

The Condor with Put Options

As with the other strategies, it is also possible to initiate a condor with puts as well as with calls. Again, all options have the same underlying stock and the same expiration date. For a long condor with puts, the trader buys a put with the lowest exercise price, sells a put with a higher exercise price, sells a put with a yet higher exercise price, and buys a put with the highest exercise price. The short condor trader takes the opposite side of the long position, selling a put with the lowest exercise price,

Profit and Loss at Expiration for a Condor with Calls   **Figure 2.18**

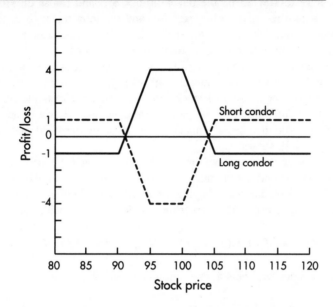

buying a put with a higher exercise price, buying a put with a yet higher exercise price, and selling a put with the highest exercise price.

The cost of a long condor with puts is:

$$P_t(S_t, X_1, T) - P_t(S_t, X_2, T) - P_t(S_t, X_3, T) + P_t(S_t, X_4, T)$$

The value of the long condor with puts at expiration is given by:

$$P_T(S_T, X_1, T) - P_T(S_T, X_2, T) - P_T(S_T, X_3, T) + P_T(S_T, X_4, T) = \qquad (2.12)$$
$$MAX\{0, X_1 - S_T\} - MAX\{0, X_2 - S_T\} - MAX\{0, X_3 - S_T\} + MAX\{0, X_4 - S_T\}$$

The following transactions illustrate a long condor initiated with puts.

	Exercise Price	*Option Premium*
Long 1 Put	$ 90	$ 2
Short 1 Put	95	5
Short 1 Put	100	9
Long 1 Put	105	13

With these prices, the long condor position costs $1. For a terminal stock price of $105 or higher, none of these puts can be exercised, so the total loss on the position is $1. For a stock price of $90, three puts will be exercised, but there will be no net gain or loss on the exercise. The long trader will exercise the put with $X = \$105$ for an exercise gain of $15, but two puts will be exercised against the trader for an exercise loss of $5 on the put with $X = \$95$ and a loss of $10 on the put with $X = \$100$. This gives a zero result from the exercise, and the long trader loses the $1 cost of the position. For any stock price less than $90, the long condor trader can exercise the put with $X = \$90$, so the exercise result is zero for any stock price of $90 or less.

As with the long condor executed with calls, the long condor with puts pays best when the terminal stock price is between the two intermediate exercise prices. In our example, this range extends from $95 to $100. For a terminal stock price of $100, for example, the long trader can exercise the put with $X = \$105$ for an exercise gain of $5. Given the $1 cost of the position, the total profit on the transaction would then be $4. This is the same for any terminal stock price in the range of $95 to $100 as Figure 2.19 shows.

The short condor trader could use puts as well, again taking the mirror position of the long trader. Specifically, the short condor with puts requires selling the put with the lowest exercise price, buying a put with a higher exercise price, buying a put with a yet higher exercise price, and selling a put with the highest exercise price. Thus, the short condor executed with puts costs:

$$-P_t(S_t, X_1, T) + P_t(S_t, X_2, T) + P_t(S_t, X_3, T) - P_t(S_t, X_4, T)$$

The value of the short condor with puts at expiration is given by:

$$- P_T(S_T, X_1, T) + P_T(S_T, X_2, T) + P_T(S_T, X_3, T) - P_T(S_T, X_4, T) =$$
$$-\text{MAX}\{0, X_1 - S_T\} + \text{MAX}\{0, X_2 - S_T\} + \text{MAX}\{0, X_3 - S_T\} - \text{MAX}\{0, X_4 - S_T\}$$

Figure 2.19   Profit and Loss at Expiration for a Condor with Puts

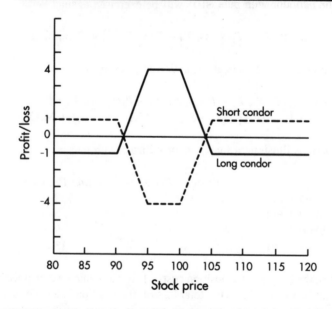

With our example prices, that would involve selling a put with $X = \$90$, buying a put with $X = \$95$, buying a put with $X = \$100$, and selling a put with $X = \$105$. Figure 2.19 shows the profits and losses for the short condor position as a dotted line.

Ratio Spreads

A **ratio spread** is a spread transaction in which two or more related options are traded in a specified proportion. For example, a trader might buy a call with a lower exercise price and sell three calls with a higher exercise price. As the ratio of one instrument to the other can be varied without limit, infinitely many different ratio spreads are possible. Consequently, we will consider just one fairly simple ratio spread as a guide.

In a ratio spread, the number of contracts bought differs from the number of contracts sold to form the spread. For example, buying two options and selling one gives a 2:1 ratio spread. The spread can be varied infinitely by changing the ratio between the options that are bought and sold. Thus, it is impossible to provide a complete catalog of ratio spreads. We illustrate the idea behind ratio spreads by considering a 2:1 ratio spread.

Earlier, we considered a bull spread using call options and illustrated this trade by considering two call options, one with an exercise price of $95 and costing $7, the other with an exercise price of $105 and costing $3. Figure 2.13 presented the profits and losses from that position. For comparison, consider a ratio spread in which a trader buys two calls with $X = \$95$ and sells one call with $X = \$105$. (In this case, the trader has utilized a 2:1 ratio.) The total cost of the position is $11. For any terminal stock price of $95 or less, neither call can be exercised, and the trader loses $11. If the stock price exceeds $95, the trader can exercise both of the purchased calls. For example, with a stock price of $105, the trader exercises both calls for an exercise profit of $20, giving a total gain on the trade of $9. For any stock price above $105, the trader will exercise the two calls purchased with $X = \$95$, but the call sold with $X = \$105$ will be exercised against her as well. This partially offsets the benefits derived from exercising the two calls with $X = \$95$. For example, a stock price of $110 gives an exercise profit on the two options with $X = \$95$ of $30. This gain is partially offset by the exercise against our trader of the option with $X = \$105$, for an exercise loss of $5. The net gain at exercise is $25, which more than compensates for the $11 cost of the position and gives a net profit of $14 on the trade.

Figure 2.20 shows the profits and losses for the bull spread with call options, repeating the information of Figure 2.13, and it shows profits and losses from the ratio spread we are considering. In comparing these two profit and loss patterns, we see that the ratio spread costs more to undertake, but that it also offers higher profits if the stock price rises sufficiently.

As we observed, the profit on the ratio spread is $9 for a terminal stock price of $105. For higher stock prices, the ratio call profits increase dramatically. By contrast, the bull spread reaches its maximum profitability of $4 at a terminal stock price of $105. By varying the ratio between the options in a spread, it is possible to create a wide variety of payoff patterns.

Summary

In this section, we have considered the wide variety of option combinations available when all of the options have a common expiration date. As the variety of combinations shows, it is possible to construct a wide range of profit and loss profiles by choosing the correct combination of options.

Figure 2.20   Profit and Loss at Expiration for a 2:1 Ratio Spread

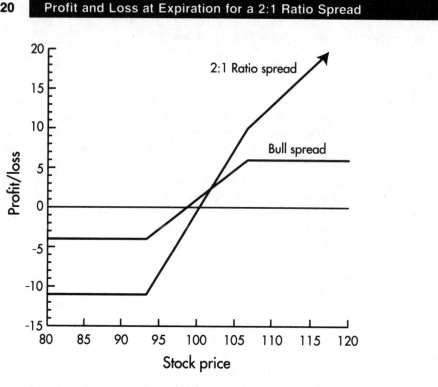

Table 2.1 summarizes the variety of positions we have considered and tabulates the cost to undertake each position, along with the value of the position at expiration. In addition, the table shows the condition that would make such a trade reasonable.

It is also possible to create an option combination with options that have different expiration dates. When an option combination has more than one expiration date represented in the options that constitute the spread, the combination is called a **calendar spread**. The absence of a uniform expiration date adds greater complication and requires that we consider calendar spreads in Chapter 5 after we introduce the pricing principles for options before expiration.

In this section, we have studied options combined with other options. However, it is also possible to combine options with other instruments to form additional profit and loss profiles. Most interesting, options can be combined with the underlying stock and with the risk-free asset. We now turn to a consideration of combinations of options with bonds and stocks.

COMBINING OPTIONS WITH BONDS AND STOCKS

Thus far, we have considered some of the most important combinations of options. We now show how to combine options with stocks and bonds to adjust payoff patterns to fit virtually any taste for risk and return combinations. These combinations show us the relationships among the different

	Option Combinations and Their Profits		Table 2.1
Position	**Cost**	**Value at Expiration**	**Trader Expects**
Long call	C_t	MAX$\{0, S_T - X\}$	Rising stock price
Short call	$-C_t$	$-$MAX$\{0, S_T - X\}$	Stock price stable or falling
Long put	P_t	MAX$\{0, X - S_T\}$	Falling stock price
Short put	$-P_t$	$-$MAX$\{0, X - S_T\}$	Stock price stable or rising
Long straddle	$C_t + P_t$	$C_T + P_T$	Stock price volatile, rising or falling
Short straddle	$-C_t - P_t$	$-C_T - P_T$	Stock price stable
Long strangle	$C_t(S_t, X_1, T)$ $+P_t(S_t, X_2, T)$	$C_T(S_T, X_1, T)$ $+P_T(S_T, X_2, T)$	Stock price very volatile, rising or falling
Short strangle	$-C_t(S_t, X_1, T)$ $-P_t(S_t, X_2, T)$	$-C_T(S_T, X_1, T)$ $-P_T(S_T, X_2, T)$	Stock price generally stable
Bull spread with calls	$C_t(S_t, X_1, T)$ $-C_t(S_t, X_2, T)$	$C_T(S_T, X_1, T)$ $-C_T(S_T, X_2, T)$	Stock price rising
Bear spread with calls	$-C_t(S_t, X_1, T)$ $+C_t(S_t, X_2, T)$	$-C_T(S_T, X_1, T)$ $+C_T(S_T, X_2, T)$	Stock price falling
Bull spread with puts	$P_t(S_t, X_1, T)$ $-P_t(S_t, X_2, T)$	$P_T(S_T, X_1, T)$ $-P_T(S_T, X_2, T)$	Stock price rising
Bear spread with puts	$-P_t(S_t, X_1, T)$ $+P_t(S_t, X_2, T)$	$-P_T(S_T, X_1, T)$ $+P_T(S_T, X_2, T)$	Stock price falling
Box spread	$C_t(S_t, X_1, T)$ $-C_t(S_t, X_2, T)$ $-P_t(S_t, X_1, T)$ $+P_t(S_t, X_2, T)$	$X_2 - X_1$	Riskless strategy
Long butterfly spread with calls	$C_t(S_t, X_1, T)$ $-2C_t(S_t, X_2, T)$ $+C_t(S_t, X_3, T)$	$C_T(S_T, X_1, T)$ $-2C_T(S_T, X_2, T)$ $+C_T(S_T, X_3, T)$	Stock price stable
Short butterfly spread with calls	$-C_t(S_t, X_1, T)$ $+2C_t(S_t, X_2, T)$ $-C_t(S_t, X_3, T)$	$-C_T(S_T, X_1, T)$ $+2C_T(S_T, X_2, T)$ $-C_T(S_T, X_3, T)$	Stock price volatile, rising or falling
Long butterfly spread with puts	$P_t(S_t, X_1, T)$ $-2P_t(S_t, X_2, T)$ $+P_t(S_t, X_3, T)$	$P_T(S_T, X_1, T)$ $-2P_T(S_T, X_2, T)$ $+ P_T(S_T, X_3, T)$	Stock price stable

Table 2.1	Option Combinations and Their Profits (continued)		
Position	**Cost**	**Value at Expiration**	**Trader Expects**
Short butterfly spread with puts	$-P_t(S_t, X_1, T)$ $+2P_t(S_t, X_2, T)$ $-P_t(S_t, X_3, T)$	$-P_T(S_T, X_1, T)$ $+2P_T(S_T, X_2, T)$ $-P_T(S_T, X_3, T)$	Stock price volatile, rising or falling
Long condor with calls	$C_t(S_t, X_1, T)$ $-C_t(S_t, X_2, T)$ $-C_t(S_t, X_3, T)$ $+C_t(S_t, X_4, T)$	$C_T(S_T, X_1, T)$ $-C_T(S_T, X_2, T)$ $-C_T(S_T, X_3, T)$ $+C_T(S_T, X_4, T)$	Stock price stable
Short condor with calls	$-C_t(S_t, X_1, T)$ $+C_t(S_t, X_2, T)$ $+C_t(S_t, X_3, T)$ $-C_t(S_t, X_4, T)$	$-C_T(S_T, X_1, T)$ $+C_T(S_T, X_2, T)$ $+C_T(S_T, X_3, T)$ $-C_T(S_T, X_4, T)$	Stock price volatile
Long condor with puts	$P_t(S_t, X_1, T)$ $-P_t(S_t, X_2, T)$ $-P_t(S_t, X_3, T)$ $+P_t(S_t, X_4, T)$	$P_T(S_T, X_1, T)$ $-P_T(S_T, X_2, T)$ $-P_T(S_T, X_3, T)$ $+P_T(S_T, X_4, T)$	Stock price stable
Short condor with puts	$-P_t(S_t, X_1, T)$ $+P_t(S_t, X_2, T)$ $+P_t(S_t, X_3, T)$ $-P_t(S_t, X_4, T)$	$-P_T(S_T, X_1, T)$ $+P_T(S_T, X_2, T)$ $+P_T(S_T, X_3, T)$ $-P_T(S_T, X_4, T)$	Stock price volatile
Ratio spreads	Too various to catalog		

Note: $X_1 < X_2 < X_3 < X_4$

classes of securities. By combining two types of securities, we can generally imitate the payoff patterns of a third. In addition, this section extends the concepts we developed earlier in this chapter. Specifically, we learn more about shaping the risk and return characteristics of portfolios by using options.

In this section, we consider five combinations of options with bonds or stocks. First, we consider the popular strategy of the **covered call** – a long position in the underlying stock and a short position in a call option. Second, we explore **portfolio insurance**. During the 1980s, portfolio insurance became one of the most discussed techniques for managing the risk of a stock portfolio. We illustrate some of the basic ideas of portfolio insurance by showing how to insure a stock portfolio. Third, we show how to use options to mimic the profit and loss patterns of the stock itself. For investors who do not want to invest the full purchase price of the stock, it is possible to create an option position that gives a profit and loss pattern much like the stock itself. Fourth, by combining options with the risk-free bond, we can synthesize the underlying stock. In this situation, the option and bond position gives the same profit and loss pattern as the stock, and it has the same value as the stock as well. Finally, we show how to combine a call, a bond, and a share of stock to create a synthetic put option.

The Covered Call: Stock plus a Short Call

In a covered call transaction, a trader is generally assumed to already own a stock and writes a call option on the underlying stock. (The strategy is "covered" because the trader owns the underlying stock, and this stock covers the obligation inherent in writing the call.) This strategy is generally undertaken to enhance income. For example, assume a trader owns a share currently priced at $100. She might write a call option on this share with an exercise price of $110 and an assumed price of $4. The option premium will be hers to keep. In exchange for accepting the $4 premium, our trader realizes that the underlying stock might be called away from her if the stock price exceeds $110. If the stock price fails to increase by $10, the option she has written will expire worthless, and she will be able to keep the income from selling the option without any further obligation. As this example indicates, the strategy turns on selling an option with a striking price far removed from the current value of the stock, because the intention is to keep the premium without surrendering the stock through exercise.

While writing covered calls can often serve the purpose of enhancing income, it must be remembered that there is no free lunch in the options market. The writer of the covered call is actually exchanging the chance of large gains on the stock position in favor of income from selling the option. For example, if the stock price were to rise to $120, the trader would not receive this benefit because the stock would be called away from her.

Figure 2.21 graphs the profits and losses at expiration for the above example. The solid line shows the profits and losses for the stock itself, while the dotted line shows the profits and losses for the covered call (the stock plus short call). For any stock price less than or equal to $110, the written call cannot be exercised against our trader, and she receives whatever profits or losses the stock earns plus the $4 option premium. Thus, she is $4 better off with the covered call than she would be with the stock alone for any stock price of $110 or less. If the stock price exceeds $110, the option will be exercised against her, and she must surrender the stock. This potential exercise places an upper limit on her profit at $14. If the stock price had risen to $120 and the trader had not written the call, her profit would have been $20 on the stock investment alone. In the covered call position, she would have made only $14, because the stock would have been called away from her. The desirability of writing a covered call to enhance income depends on the chance that the stock price will exceed the exercise price at which the trader writes the call.

Portfolio Insurance: Stock plus a Long Put

Along with program trading, portfolio insurance was a dominant investing technique developed in the 1980s and continues to be an important tool today. **Portfolio insurance** is an investment management technique designed to protect a stock portfolio from severe drops in value. Investment managers can implement portfolio insurance strategies in various ways. Some use options, while others use futures, and still others use combinations of other instruments. We analyze a simple strategy for implementing portfolio insurance with options. Portfolio insurance applies to only portfolios, not individual stocks. Therefore, for our discussion, we assume that the underlying good is a well-diversified portfolio of common stocks. We may think of the portfolio as consisting of the Standard & Poor's 100. This is convenient because a popular stock index option is based on the S&P 100. Therefore, the portfolio insurance problem we consider is protecting the value of this stock portfolio from large drops in value.[7]

Figure 2.21   Profit and Loss at Expiration for a Covered Call

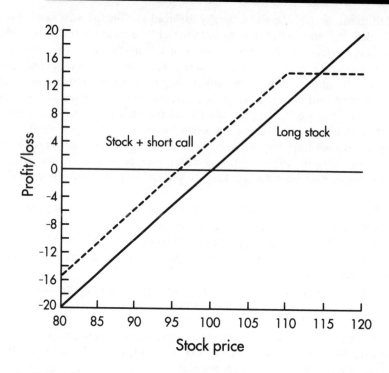

In essence, portfolio insurance with options involves holding a stock portfolio and buying a put option on the portfolio.[8] If we have a long position in the stock portfolio, the profits and losses from holding the portfolio consist of the profits and losses from the individual stocks. Therefore, the profits and losses for the portfolio resemble the typical stock's profits and losses.

Let S_t be the cost of the stock portfolio at time t, and let P_t be a put option on the portfolio. The cost of an insured portfolio is, therefore:

$$S_t + P_t$$

Because the price of a put is always positive, it is clear that an insured portfolio costs more than the uninsured stock portfolio alone. At expiration, the value of the insured portfolio is:

$$S_T + P_T = S_T + MAX\{0, X - S_T\} \tag{2.13}$$

As the profit on an uninsured portfolio is $S_T - S_t$, the insured portfolio has a superior performance when $MAX\{0, X - S_T\} - P_t - S_t > 0$.

As an example of an insured portfolio, consider an investment in the stock index at a value of 100.00. Figure 2.22 shows the profit and loss profiles for an investment in the index at 100 and for

Profit and Loss at Expiration for a Stock Index and a Put   **Figure 2.22**

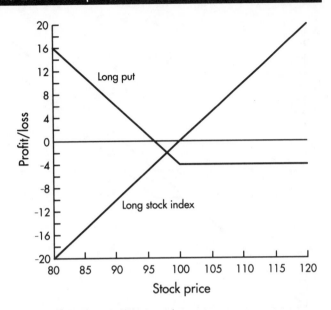

a put option on the index. The figure assumes that the put has a striking price of 100.00 and costs 4.00 (we are expressing all values in terms of the index). Figure 2.23 shows the effects of combining an investment in the index stocks with a put on the index. For comparison, Figure 2.23 also shows the profits and losses from a long position in the index itself.

The insured portfolio, the index plus a long put, offers protection against large drops in value. If the stock index suddenly falls to 90.00, the insured portfolio loses only 4.00. No matter how low the index goes, the insured portfolio can lose only 4.00 points. However, this insurance has a cost. Investment in the index itself shows a profit for any index value over 100.00. By contrast, the insured portfolio has a profit only if the index climbs above 104.00. In the insured portfolio, the index must climb high enough to offset the price of buying the insuring put option. Because the put option will expire, keeping the portfolio insured requires that the investor buy a series of put options to keep the insurance in force. In Figure 2.23, notice that the combined position of a long index and a long put gives a payoff shape that matches a long position in a call. Like a call, the insured portfolio protects against extremely unfavorable outcomes as the stock price falls. This similarity between the insured portfolio and a call position suggests that a trader might buy a call and invest the extra proceeds in a bond in order to replicate a position in an insured portfolio.

As a further comparison, we consider the likely profits from holding the stock portfolio and the insured portfolio. Let us assume that the option expires in one year. The stock portfolio is expected to appreciate about 10 percent and have a standard deviation of 15 percent. We also assume that the returns on the stock portfolio are normally distributed. Thus, a $100 investment in the stock portfolio would have an expected terminal value of $110 in one year. Under these assumptions, Figure 2.24 shows the probability distribution of the stock portfolio's terminal value. With a standard deviation

Figure 2.23 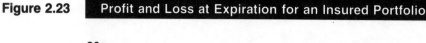 Profit and Loss at Expiration for an Insured Portfolio

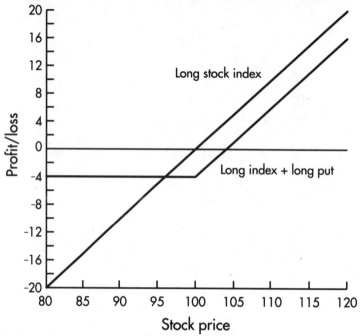

of 15 percent, there is approximately a two-thirds chance that the terminal value of the portfolio will lie between $95 and $125 dollars. This conclusion results from a feature of the normal distribution. About 67 percent of all observations from a normal distribution lie within one standard deviation of the mean.

With the insured portfolio, we have already seen that the maximum loss is $4. Therefore, the terminal value of the insured portfolio must be at least $96. However, Figures 2.23 and 2.24 imply that there is a good chance that the insured portfolio's terminal value will be $96. For the stock portfolio, any terminal value of $100 or less gives a $96 terminal value for the insured portfolio. While the insured portfolio protects against large losses, it has a lower chance of a really large payoff. For the insured portfolio to have a terminal value of $136, for example, the stock portfolio must be worth $140. This is two standard deviations above the expected return on the stock portfolio, however, and there is little chance of such a favorable outcome.

Figure 2.25 compares the distribution of returns for the stock and for the insured portfolios. The figure presents the cumulative probability distribution for each portfolio. The stock portfolio line presents the cumulative probability consistent with Figure 2.24. The kinked line in Figure 2.25 corresponds to the insured portfolio. The probability of a terminal value below $96 for the insured portfolio is zero because that is exactly what the insurance guarantees. However, there is a very good chance that the terminal value for the insured portfolio will be $96. The probability of a $96 terminal

Probability Distribution for a Stock Index's Terminal Value   **Figure 2.24**

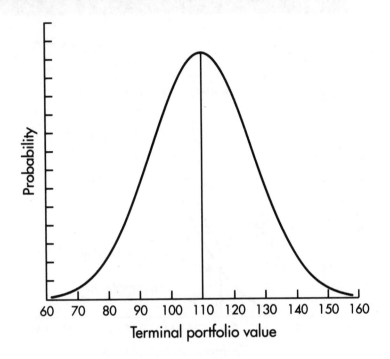

value for the insured portfolio equals the probability that the stock portfolio will be worth $100 or less. As the graph shows, this probability is 25 percent. Notice also that the probability of a $96 or lower terminal value for the stock portfolio is 18 percent. This means that there is an 82 percent chance that the stock portfolio will outperform the insured portfolio, because there is an 82 percent chance that the stock portfolio will be worth more than $96.

As we consider terminal stock portfolio values above $96, we see that the line for the insured portfolio lies above the line for the stock portfolio in Figure 2.25. Consider a $110 terminal value for the stock portfolio. Because the distribution is normal and the expected return is 10 percent, there is a 50 percent chance that the terminal value of the stock portfolio will be $110 or less. Because the line for the insured portfolio lies above the line for the stock portfolio, there is a higher probability that the insured portfolio's value will be $110 or less. The probability of a terminal value for the insured portfolio of $110 or less is 61 percent. Correlatively, there is a 50 percent chance of a terminal stock portfolio value above $110 and only a 39 percent chance of a terminal value above $110 for the insured portfolio. Thus, because the insured portfolio's cumulative probability line lies above that for the stock portfolio at higher terminal prices, the stock portfolio has a better chance of higher returns. Figure 2.25 shows that the insured portfolio sacrifices chances of a large gain to avoid the chance of a large loss. Which investment is better depends on the risk preferences of the investor. The important point to recognize is the role of options in adjusting the returns distribution for the

Figure 2.25   Comparison of Returns Distributions for an Insured and an Uninsured Stock Portfolio

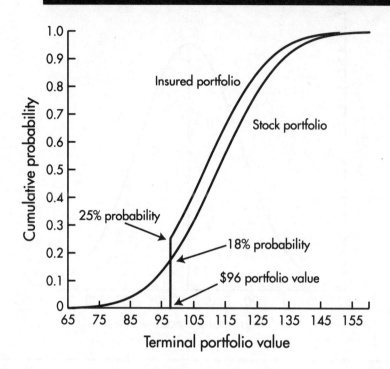

underlying investment. With options, we can adjust the distribution to fit our tastes – subject to the risk and return trade-off governing the entire market.[9]

Finally, we also observe that the insured portfolio has the same profits and losses as a call option. In fact, the profit and loss graph for the insured portfolio matches that of a call option with a striking price of 100.00 and a price of 4.00. This does not mean, however, that the insured portfolio and such a call option would have the same value. At expiration, the call will have no residual value beyond its profit and loss at that moment. By contrast, the insured portfolio will still include the underlying value of the investment in the stock index. Therefore, for a particular time horizon, two different investments can have the same profit and loss patterns without having the same value.

Mimicking and Synthetic Portfolios

We now begin to study how European options can be combined with other instruments, notably the underlying stock and the risk-free bond, to create specialized payoff patterns at expiration. As we will see, it is possible to create portfolios of European options, the underlying stock, and the risk-free bond that simulate another instrument in key respects. We define two basic types of relationships, **mimicking portfolios**, and **synthetic instruments**.[10]

A mimicking portfolio has the same profits and losses as the instrument or portfolio that it mimics, but it does not necessarily have the same value. A synthetic instrument has the same profits and losses and value as the instrument it synthetically replicates. For example, we will see that it is possible to create a portfolio of instruments that has the same value and the same profits and losses as a put. In this case, the portfolio would be known as a synthetic put.

Mimicking Stock: Long Call plus a Short Put. By combining a long position in a European call and a short position in a European put, we can create an option position that has the same profit and loss pattern at expiration as does the underlying stock. This long call/short put position costs:

$$c_t - p_t$$

At expiration, the payoff on this option combination is:

$$c_T - p_T = \text{MAX}\{0, S_T - X\} - \text{MAX}\{0, X - S_T\} \qquad (2.14)$$

Assume for the moment that the call and put are chosen so that the exercise price equals the stock price at the time the put is purchased. That is, assume $X = S_t$. Under this special condition, the payoff on the long call/short put position is:

$$\text{MAX}\{0, S_T - S_t\} - \text{MAX}\{0, S_t - S_T\}$$

If the stock price rises, $S_T > S_t$, so the call is worth $S_T - S_t$, and the put is worth nothing. Notice that $S_T - S_t$ is just the profit on the stock portfolio alone. If the stock price falls, $S_t > S_T$. In this case, the call is worth zero, and the put is worth $S_t - S_T$. As the option combination includes a short position in the put, the payoff to the portfolio is $S_T - S_t$, which is the same as the stock portfolio. Thus, the long call/short put portfolio has a value that equals the profit or loss from investing in the underlying stock. Notice again that this special condition arises when the exercise price on the options equals the stock price at the time the option combination is purchased.

To illustrate this idea, consider a stock priced at $100 and call and put options with exercise prices of $100. Assume that the call costs $7 and the put costs $3. We want to compare two investments. The first investment is buying one share of stock for $100. The second investment is buying one call for $7 and selling one put for $3.

When the options expire, the two investments have parallel profits and losses. However, the profit on the stock will always be $4 greater than the profit on the option position. For example, assume the stock price is $110 at expiration. The stock has a profit of $10, and the option investment has a profit of $6. For the option position, the put expires worthless and the call has an exercise value of $10. From this exercise value, we subtract the $4 net investment required to purchase the option position. Figure 2.26 graphs the profits and losses for both options, the stock, and the combined option position.

Investing in the stock costs $100, while the option position costs only $4. Yet the option position profits mimic those of the stock fairly closely. In a sense, the options give very high leverage by simulating the stock's profits and losses with a low investment. Many option traders view this high leverage of options as one of their prime advantages. Thus, a very small investment in the option position gives a position that mimics the profits and losses of a much more costly investment in the stock. In other words, the option position is much more elastic than the similar stock position.

Figure 2.26   Profit and Loss at Expiration for the Elements of a Mimicking Portfolio

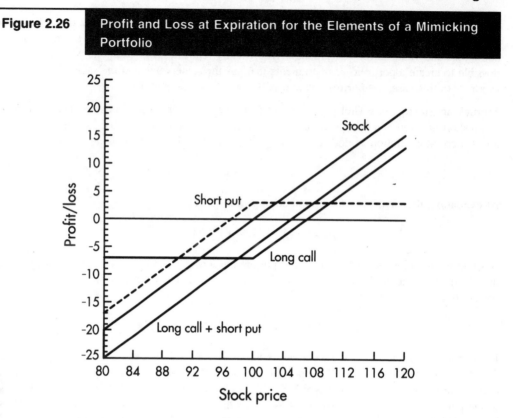

The profit on the stock is always $4 greater than the profit on the option position. However, the stock investment costs $100, while the option position costs only $4. Therefore, the stock costs $96 more than the option position to guarantee a certain $4 extra profit over the option position. While the long call plus short put option position mimics the profits and losses on the stock, it does not synthetically replicate the stock. As we will see, we can create a synthetic stock by adding investment in the risk-free bond to the option.

Synthetic Stock: Long Call, plus a Short Put, plus Bonds. As we have just seen, a long call combined with a short put can mimic the profit and loss pattern at the expiration date for the underlying stock. By adding an investment in the risk-free bond, we can create a portfolio that synthesizes the stock. In this case, the synthetic stock will have the same value as well as an identical profit and loss pattern as the stock being synthesized. Therefore, this section shows that a long call, plus a short put, plus the right investment in the risk-free bond, can synthesize a stock investment. (Again, we are focusing on European options throughout this discussion, which we denote as c_t and p_t for the values of European calls and puts at time t.) As we will demonstrate, the investment in the risk-free bond should be the present value of the exercise price on the call and the put. Therefore, this formula for a synthetic stock is:

$$S_t = c_t - p_t + Xe^{-r(T-t)} \qquad (2.15)$$

where:

r = risk-free rate of interest

At expiration, the value of this portfolio (for both American and European options) will be:

$$c_T - p_T + X = \text{MAX}\{0, S_T - X\} - \text{MAX}\{0, X - S_T\} + X$$

We know that the stock price can be above, equal to, or below the exercise price. If the stock price at expiration exceeds the exercise price, the call is worth $S_T - X$, and the put is worthless. The value of the portfolio consists of the value of the call, plus the maturing bond, or $S_T - X + X = S_T$. This is exactly the same value as the stock at the expiration date. If the stock price is below the exercise price on the expiration date of the options, then the call is worthless and the put has a value equal to $X - S_T$. Because the portfolio consists of a short position in the put, the value of the portfolio, including the maturing bond, is $S_T - X + X = S_T$. Again, the value of the long call/short put/long bond is the same as that of the underlying stock. If the terminal value of the stock equals the exercise price, X, then both the call and put are worthless and the value of the synthetic stock portfolio is just X, the value of the maturing risk-free investment. But in this situation, it remains true that the value of the synthetic stock is equal to that of the stock itself, because $S_T = X$.

We can illustrate this synthetic stock by considering the same stock selling for $100 and the same options we considered in the previous section. Comparing just the value of the stock position with the value of the option position at expiration, the stock position will always be worth $100 more than the option position. For example, assume the stock price is $120 at expiration. Then, the stock investment is worth $120. The option position will be worth $20, because the call can be exercised for $20 and the put will be worthless. To synthesize the stock, we need to buy a risk-free bond that pays $100 at expiration. We can think of this investment as buying a one-year Treasury bill with a face value of $100. Notice that the payoff on the Treasury bill equals the exercise price for the options. We now have two portfolios that will have identical values at the expiration date:

Investment	Cash Flow
Portfolio A	
Long position in the stock	$100
Portfolio B	
Long position in the call	–$7
Short position in the put	+3
A bond paying the exercise price of $100 at expiration	?

Thus far in the example, we have not said how much the bond should cost. However, we can employ our no-arbitrage principle for guidance. We know that both portfolios will have the same value in one year when the option expires. To avoid arbitrage, the two portfolios must have the same value now as well. This condition implies that the bond must cost $96 and that the interest rate must be 4.17 percent.

To see why the bond must cost $96, we consider the arbitrage opportunity that results with any other bond price. For example, assume that the bond costs $93. With this low bond price, Portfolio A is too expensive relative to Portfolio B. To exploit the arbitrage opportunity, we sell the overpriced Portfolio A and buy the underpriced Portfolio B, transacting as follows:

Transaction		Cash Flow
Sell the stock		$100
Buy the call		−7
Sell the put		+3
Buy the bond		−93
	Net Cash Flow	+$3

When the options expire in one year, we can close out all the positions without any additional investment. To close the position, we buy back the stock and honor any obligation we have from selling the put. Fortunately, we will have $100 in cash from the maturing bond we bought. For example, if the stock price at expiration is $90, our call is worthless and the put is exercised against us. Therefore, we use the proceeds from the maturing T-bill to pay the $100 exercise price for the put that is exercised against us. We now have the stock and, in return, use it to close our short position in the stock. The total result at expiration is that we can honor all obligations with zero cash flow. This is true no matter what the stock price is. Therefore, the cheap price on the bond gave us an arbitrage profit of $3 when we made the initial transaction. The transactions are an arbitrage because they require no investment and offer a riskless profit. With an initial cash inflow of $3, there is clearly no investment. Also, we make a riskless profit immediately when we transact. Any bond price below $96 will permit the arbitrage transactions we have just described.

If the bond is priced higher than $96, Portfolio B is overpriced relative to Portfolio A. We then sell Portfolio B and buy Portfolio A. Again, we have an arbitrage profit. To see how to make an arbitrage profit from a bond price that is too high, assume the bond price is $98. We then transact as follows:

Transaction		Cash Flow
Buy the stock		−$100
Sell the call		+7
Buy the put		−3
Sell the bond		+98
	Net Cash Flow	+$2

In one year, the options will expire and the bond will mature. Selling the bond means that we borrow $98 and promise to repay $100, so we will owe $100 on the bond at expiration. However, no matter what the stock price is at expiration, we can dispose of the stock and close the option positions for a cash inflow of $100. This gives exactly what we need to pay our debt on the bond. For example, assume the stock price is $93. The call we sold expires worthless, but we can exercise the put. When we exercise the put, we deliver the stock and receive the $100 exercise price. This amount repays the bond debt. Any bond price greater than $96 will permit this same kind of arbitrage transaction.

The Synthetic Put: The Put-Call Parity Relationship. We have just seen that we can buy a call, short a put, and invest in a risk-free bond to create a synthetic stock. In fact, with any three of these four instruments, we can synthesize the fourth. This section illustrates **put-call parity** – the relationship between put, call, stock, and bond prices. Specifically, put-call parity shows how to synthesize a put option by selling the stock, buying a call, and investing in a risk-free bond. Put-call parity asserts that a put is worth the same as a long call, short stock, and a risk-free investment that pays the exercise price on the common expiration date of the put and call. The put-call parity relationship is:

$$p_t = c_t - S_t + Xe^{-r(T-t)} \tag{2.16}$$

To create a put from the other instruments, we use our previous example of a stock selling at $100, a call option worth $7 with a strike price of $100, and a bond costing $96 that will pay $100 in one year. From these securities, we can synthesize the put option costing $3 with an exercise price of $100. To create a synthetic put, we transact as follows:

Investment	Cash Flow
Portfolio C	
Buy the call	−$ 7
Sell the stock	+100
Buy a bond that pays the exercise price at maturity	− 96
	−$3

In buying Portfolio C, we have the same cash outflow of $3 that buying the put requires. To show that Portfolio C is equivalent to a put with a $3 price and a $100 exercise price, we consider the value of Portfolio C when the stock price equals, exceeds, or is less than $100.

If the stock price is $100 at expiration, the call in Portfolio C is worthless, but we receive $100 from the maturing bond, with which we buy the stock. This disposes of the entire portfolio. The entire portfolio is worth zero, just as the put is worth zero. For any stock price above $100, Portfolio C, like the put itself, is worthless. We can then exercise the call and use the proceeds from the bond to pay the exercise price on the call. This gives us the stock, which we owe to cover our earlier sale of the stock. Thus, we have met all obligations arising from owning Portfolio C. To illustrate this outcome, consider a terminal stock price of $105. In this case, the put would be worthless. Therefore, Portfolio C should be worthless as well. With a stock price of $105, we would exercise the call, paying for the exercise with the proceeds of our maturing bond. We receive a stock worth $105. However, we must repay our short sale of the stock by returning this share. Therefore, there is no net cash flow at the exercise date. Finally, for a stock price less than $100, Portfolio C is worth the difference between the exercise price and the stock price. If the stock price is $95, the call option expires worthless. We receive $100 on the bond investment and use $95 of this to repurchase the stock that we owe. Thus Portfolio C is worth $5, just as the put itself would be.

Considering our profits on Portfolio C, we lose $3 for any stock price of $100 or more because Portfolio C is then worthless at expiration and it costs $3. For any stock price at expiration less than $100, Portfolio C is worth the exercise price of $100 minus the stock price. Notice that this is an exact description of the profit and losses on the put. Therefore, Portfolio C synthetically replicates the put option with an exercise price of $100 that costs $3.

Put-call parity has another important implication. Assume that $S_t = X$. In this situation, the call will be worth more than the put. To prove this principle, consider the following rearrangement of the put-call parity formula:

$$c_t - p_t = S_t - Xe^{-r(T-t)}$$

If $S_t = X$, the right-hand side of this equation must be positive, because the exercise price X is being discounted. Therefore, the quantity $c_t - p_t$ must also be positive, which implies that the call price must exceed the put price in this special circumstance.

SUMMARY

This chapter has explored the value and profits from option positions at expiration. The concept of arbitrage provided a general framework for understanding option values and profits. We began by studying the characteristic payoffs for positions in single options, noting that there are four basic possibilities of being long or short a call or a put.

We then considered how to combine options to create special positions with unique risk and return characteristics. These option combinations included straddles, strangles, bull and bear spreads, butterfly spreads, condors, and a box spread. As we observed, a trader can either buy or sell each of these option combinations and most can be created using either puts or calls. Each gives its own risk and return profile, which differs from the position in a single option.

We also considered combinations among options, stocks, and bonds. We considered the advantages and disadvantages of covered call writing, and explored how to insure a portfolio by using a put option. We also showed that a combination of options could mimic the profit and loss profile of a stock. To create a synthetic stock, we used a call, a put, and investment in a risk-free bond. The mimicking portfolio has the same profit and loss patterns, while a synthetic instrument has the identical profit and loss characteristics and the same value as the instrument being synthesized. We also showed how to create a synthetic put by trading a call, a stock, and the risk-free bond to illustrate the put-call parity relationship. In general, we conclude that put, call, bond, and stock prices are all related and that any one can be synthesized by a combination of the other three.

QUESTIONS AND PROBLEMS

1. Consider a call option with an exercise price of $80 and a cost of $5. Graph the profits and losses at expiration for various stock prices.
2. Consider a put option with an exercise price of $80 and a cost of $4. Graph the profits and losses at expiration for various stock prices.
3. For the call and put in Questions 1 and 2, graph the profits and losses at expiration for a straddle comprising these two options. If the stock price is $80 at expiration, what will be the profit or loss? At what stock price (or prices) will the straddle have a zero profit?
4. A call option has an exercise price of $70 and is at expiration. The option cost $4 and the underlying stock trades for $75. Assuming a perfect market, how would you respond if the call is an American option? State exactly how you might transact. How does your answer differ if the option is European?
5. A stock trades for $120. A put on this stock has an exercise price of $140 and is about to expire. The put trades for $22. How would you respond to this set of prices? Explain.
6. If the stock trades for $120 and the expiring put with an exercise price of $140 trades for $18, how would you trade?

7. Consider a call and a put on the same underlying stock. The call has an exercise price of $100 and costs $20. The put has an exercise price of $90 and costs $12. Graph a short position in a strangle based on these two options. What is the worst outcome from selling the strangle? At what stock price or prices does the strangle have a zero profit?

8. Assume that you buy a call with an exercise price of $100 and a cost of $9. At the same time, you sell a call with an exercise price of $110 and a cost of $5. The two calls have the same underlying stock and the same expiration. What is this position called? Graph the profits and losses at expiration from this position. At what stock price or prices will the position show a zero profit? What is the worst loss that the position can incur? For what range of stock prices does this worst outcome occur? What is the best outcome and for what range of stock prices does it occur?

9. Consider three call options with the same underlying stock and the same expiration. Assume that you take a long position in a call with an exercise price of $40 and a long position in a call with an exercise price of $30. At the same time, you sell two calls with an exercise price of $35. What position have you created? Graph the value of this position at expiration. What is the value of this position at expiration if the stock price is $90? What is the position's value for a stock price of $15? What is the lowest value the position can have at expiration? For what range of stock prices does this worst value occur?

10. Assume that you buy a portfolio of stocks with a portfolio price of $100. A put option on this portfolio has a striking price of $95 and costs $3. Graph the combined portfolio of the stock plus a long position in the put. What is the worst outcome that can occur at expiration? For what range of portfolio prices will this worst outcome occur? What is this position called?

11. Consider a stock that sells for $95. A call on this stock has an exercise price of $95 and costs $5. A put on this stock also has an exercise price of $95 and costs $4. The call and the put have the same expiration. Graph the profit and losses at expiration from holding the long call and short put. How do these profits and losses compare with the value of the stock at expiration? If the stock price is $80 at expiration, what is the portfolio of options worth? If the stock price is $105, what is the portfolio of options worth? Explain why the stock and option portfolio differ as they do.

12. Assume a stock trades for $120. A call on this stock has a striking price of $120 and costs $11. A put also has a striking price of $120 and costs $8. A risk-free bond promises to pay $120 at the expiration of the options in one year. What should the price of this bond be? Explain.

13. In the preceding question, if we combine the two options and the bond, what will the value of this portfolio be relative to the stock price at expiration? Explain. What principle does this illustrate?

14. Consider a stock that is worth $50. A put and call on this stock have exercise prices of $50 and expire in one year. The call costs $5 and the put costs $4. A risk-free bond will pay $50 in one year and costs $45. How will you respond to these prices? State your transactions exactly. What principle do these prices violate?

15. A stock sells for $80 and the risk-free rate of interest is 11 percent. A call and a put on this stock expire in one year and have exercise prices of $75. How would you trade to create a synthetic call option? If the put sells for $2, how much is the call option worth? (Assume annual compounding.)

16. Both stock and a risk-free bond paying $110 in one year cost $100. What can you say about the cost of a put and a call on this stock that both expire in one year and that both have an exercise price of $110? Explain.

17. Assume that you buy a strangle with exercise prices on the constituent options of $75 and $80. You also sell a strangle with exercise prices of $70 and $85. Describe the payoffs on the position you have created. Does this portfolio of options have a payoff pattern similar to that of any of the combinations explored in this chapter?

18. If a stock sells for $75, and a call and put together cost $9, and the two options expire in one year and have an exercise price of $70, what is the current rate of interest?

19. Assume you buy a bull spread with puts that have exercise prices of $40 and $45. You also buy a bear spread with puts that have exercise prices of $45 and $50. What will this total position be worth if the stock price at expiration is $53? Does this position have any special name? Explain.

20. Explain the difference between a box spread and a synthetic risk-free bond.

21. Within the context of the put-call parity relationship, consider the value of a call and a put option. What will the value of the put option be if the exercise price is zero? What will the value of the call option be in the same circumstance? What can you say about potential bounds on the value of the call and put option?

22. Using the put-call parity relationship, write the value of a call option as a function of the stock price, the risk-free bond, and the put option. Now consider a stock price that is dramatically in excess of the exercise price. What happens to the value of the put as the stock price becomes extremely large relative to the exercise price? What happens to the value of the call option?

NOTES

[1] Recall that we are ignoring transaction costs. In the options market, both buyers and sellers incur transaction costs. Therefore, the options market is a negative sum game if we include transaction costs in our analysis.

[2] The arbitrage arguments used in this chapter stem from a famous paper by Robert C. Merton, "Theory of Rational Option Pricing," *Bell Journal of Economics and Management Science,* 4, Spring 1973, pp. 141–83.

[3] The buyer of a straddle need not be matched with a single trader who sells a straddle. Opposite the buyer of a straddle could be two individuals, one selling a call and the other selling a put.

[4] The theoretically maximum loss for the short straddle trader occurs when the stock price goes to zero. In this case, the call cannot be exercised against the short trader, but the put will be exercised. Thus, the trader will lose $X - S = X - 0 = X$ on the exercise. This loss will be partially offset by the funds received from selling the straddle $(C_t + P_t)$, so the total loss will be: $X - C_t - P_t$.

[5] It is also possible to execute similar strategies with combinations of options and the underlying instrument.

[6] The reader should note that the use of terms such as *bear spread* and *bull spread* is not standardized. While this book uses these terms in familiar ways, other traders may use them differently.

[7] Two introductory studies of portfolio insurance are Peter A. Abken, "An Introduction to Portfolio Insurance," Federal Reserve Bank of Atlanta, *Economic Review,* 72:6, November/December 1987, pp. 2–25; and Thomas J. O'Brien, "The Mechanics of Portfolio Insurance," *Journal of Portfolio Management,* 14:3, Spring 1988, pp. 40–7. In another introductory study, "Simplifying Portfolio Insurance," *Journal of Portfolio Management,* 14:1, Fall 1987, pp. 48–51, Fischer Black shows how to insure a portfolio without using option pricing theory and how to establish an insured portfolio without a definite horizon date.

[8] It is possible to create an insured portfolio without using options. These alternative strategies employ stock index futures with continuous rebalancing of the futures position. Because of this continuous rebalancing,

these strategies are called "dynamic hedging" strategies. Hayne E. Leland discusses these dynamic strategies in "Option Pricing and Replication with Transaction Costs," *Journal of Finance,* 40, December 1985, pp. 1283–1301. With a dynamic strategy, the insurer must re-balance the portfolio very frequently, leading to a trade-off between having an exactly insured portfolio and high transaction costs. J. Clay Singleton and Robin Grieves discuss this trade-off in their paper, "Synthetic Puts and Portfolio Insurance Strategies," *Journal of Portfolio Management,* 10:3, Spring 1984, pp. 63–69. Richard Bookstaber, "Portfolio Insurance Trading Rules," *Journal of Futures Markets,* 8:1, February 1988, pp. 15–31, discusses some technological innovations in portfolio insurance strategies and foresees increasing complexity and sophistication in the implementation of insurance techniques.

[9] Several studies have explored the cost of portfolio insurance. Richard J. Rendleman, Jr., and Richard W. McEnally, "Assessing the Cost of Portfolio Insurance," *Financial Analysts Journal,* 43, May/June 1987, pp. 27–37, compare the desirability of an insured portfolio relative to a utility-maximizing strategy. They conclude that only extremely risk-averse investors will be willing to incur the costs of insuring a portfolio. Richard Bookstaber presents similar results in his paper, "The Use of Options in Performance Structuring: Modeling Returns to Meet Investment Objectives," in *Controlling Interest Rate Risk: New Techniques and Applications for Money Management,* Robert B. Platt, (ed.), New York: Wiley, 1986. According to Bookstaber, completely insuring a portfolio costs about 25 percent of the portfolio's total return. C. B. Garcia and F. J. Gould, "An Empirical Study of Portfolio Insurance," *Financial Analysts Journal,* July/August 1987, pp. 44–54, find that fully insuring a portfolio causes a loss of returns of about 100 basis points. They conclude that an insured portfolio is not likely to outperform a static portfolio of stocks and T-bills. Roger G. Clarke and Robert D. Arnott study the costs of portfolio insurance directly in their paper, "The Cost of Portfolio Insurance: Tradeoffs and Choices," *Financial Analysts Journal,* 43:6, November/December 1987, pp. 35–47. Clarke and Arnott explore the desirability of insuring only part of the portfolio, increasing the risk of the portfolio, and attempting to insure a portfolio for a longer horizon. As they conclude, transaction costs are an important factor in choosing the optimal strategy.

[10] These synthetic relationships hold for only European options. In Chapter 6, we explore the reasons for this restriction within the context of our discussion of American options.

BOUNDS ON OPTION PRICES

INTRODUCTION

This chapter continues to use no-arbitrage conditions to explore option pricing principles. In the last chapter, we considered prices options could have at expiration, consistent with no-arbitrage conditions. In this chapter, we consider option prices before expiration. Extending our analysis to options with time remaining until expiration brings new factors into consideration.

The value of an option before expiration depends on five factors: the price of the underlying stock, the exercise price of the option, the time remaining until expiration, the risk-free rate of interest, and the possible price movements on the underlying stock.[1] For stocks with dividends, the potential dividend payments during an option's life can also influence the value of the option. In this chapter, we focus on the intuition underlying the relationship between put and call prices and these factors. The next chapter builds on these intuitions to specify these relationships more formally.

We first consider how option prices respond to changes in the stock price, the time remaining until expiration, and the exercise price of the option. These factors set general boundaries for possible option prices. Later in the chapter, we discuss the influence of interest rates on option prices and we consider how the riskiness of the stock affects the price of the option.

THE BOUNDARY SPACE FOR CALL AND PUT OPTIONS

In Chapter 2, we saw that the value of a call (either European or American) at expiration must be:

$$C_T = \text{MAX}\{0, S_T - X\} \tag{3.1}$$

Similarly, the value of a put (either European or American) at expiration is:

$$P_T = \text{MAX}\{0, X - S_T\} \tag{3.2}$$

where:

> C_t = the call price at time t
> P_t = the put price at time t
> S_t = the stock price at time t
> X = the exercise price at time t
> T = the expiration date of the option

Corresponding to Equations 3.1 and 3.2, we saw that call and put options had distinctive graphs that specified their values at expiration. Figure 2.4 for a call and Figure 2.6 for a put gave the value of the options at expiration. These two figures simply graph Equations 3.1 and 3.2, respectively. Now we want to consider the range of possible values for call and put options more generally. Specifically, we want to analyze the values that options can have before expiration.[2]

Said another way, we want to explore the values of options as a function of the stock price, S, the exercise price, X, and the time remaining until expiration, $T - t$. In Chapter 2, we considered only options that were at expiration, with $t = T$. Thus, we were considering option values for various ranges of stock price and exercise prices but with zero time to expiration. Now, we want to consider option prices when the stock price, the exercise price, and the time to expiration all vary.

Before expiration, call and put values need not conform to Equations 3.1 and 3.2. Therefore, our first task is to determine the entire possible range of prices that calls and puts may have before expiration. We call this range of possibilities the **boundary space** for an option. Once we specify the largest range of possible prices, we consider no-arbitrage principles that will help us specify the price of an option more precisely.

The Boundary Space for a Call Option

To define the boundary space for a call option, we consider extreme values for the variables that affect call prices. Because we first focus on the stock price, exercise price, and the time remaining until expiration, we consider extremely high and low values for each of these variables. First, the value of a call option will depend on the stock price. We have already seen that a call option at expiration is worth more the greater the price of the stock. Second, the value of a call option depends on the exercise price of the option. Third, the value of a call can depend on the time remaining until the option expires.

The owner of a call option receives the stock upon exercise. The stock price represents the potential benefit that will come to the holder of a call, so the higher the stock price, the greater the value of a call option. We have already observed this to be true at expiration, as Equation 3.1 shows. Also, the exercise price is a cash outflow if the call owner exercises. As such, the exercise price represents a potential liability to the call owner. The lower the liability associated with a call, the better for the call owner. Therefore, the lower the exercise price, the greater the value of a call. Finally, consider the time remaining until expiration. For clarity we focus on two different American options, one of which has a longer time remaining until expiration. We see that the one with the longer time until expiration gives every benefit that the one with the shorter time until expiration does. At a given moment, if the shorter-term option permits expiration, so does the option with a longer term until expiration. In addition, the longer term option allows the privilege of waiting longer to decide whether to exercise. Generally, this privilege of waiting is quite valuable, so the option with the longer life tends to have a higher value. However, no matter what happens, the option with the longer life must have a price at least as great as the option with the shorter life. We will see that the same holds true for European options. The longer the time until expiration, the greater the value of the option, holding other factors constant.

We have seen that lower exercise prices and longer lives generally increase the value of an option. Therefore, the value of an option will be highest for an option with a zero exercise price and an infinite time until expiration. Similarly, the value will be lowest for an option with a higher exercise price and the shortest time until expiration. A call that is about to expire, with $t = T$, will be the call with the lowest price for a given stock price and a given exercise price. We already know the possible values that such an expiring option can have. This value is simply the call option's price at expiration, which is given by Equation 3.1. At the other extreme, the call with the highest possible value for a given stock price will be the call with a zero exercise price and an infinite time until expiration.

This call option with a zero exercise price and an infinite time until it expires allows us to exercise the option with zero cost and acquire the stock. In short, we can transform this option into the stock any time we wish without paying anything. Therefore, the value of this call must equal the price of the underlying stock. If we can get the stock for zero any time we wish, the price of the call cannot be more than the stock price. Also, the price of the call cannot exceed the stock price because the call can be used only to acquire the stock. Therefore, we know that a call on a given stock, with a zero exercise price, and an infinite time to expiration, must have a value equal to the stock price. In this special limiting case $C_t = S_t$.

From this analysis, we have now determined the upper and lower bounds for the price of a call option before expiration. Figure 3.1 depicts the boundaries for the price of a call option as the interior

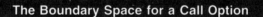

The Boundary Space for a Call Option   **Figure 3.1**

area between the upper and lower bounds. The upper bound for any call option is the stock price. The figure shows this boundary as the 45 degree line from the origin. Along this line, the call option is worth the same as the stock. The lower bound is the value of the call option at expiration. At expiration, if the stock price is at or below the exercise price, the call is worth zero. For any stock price above the exercise price, the expiring call is worth the stock price minus the exercise price. Therefore, the value of a call option must always fall somewhere on or within the bounds given by these lines. Later in this chapter, we develop principles that help us to specify much more precisely where within these bounds the actual option price must lie.

The Boundary Space for a Put Option

We now consider the range of possible put prices. We have already considered prices for puts at expiration and found the value of a put at expiration to conform to Equation 3.2. This equation gives the lower bound for the value of a put option. To find the upper bounds for a put option, we need to consider the best possible circumstances for the owner of a put option.

Upon exercise, the owner of a put surrenders the stock and receives the exercise price. The most the put holder can receive is the exercise price, and he can obtain this only by surrendering the stock. Therefore, the lower the stock price, the more valuable the put must be. This is true before expiration and at expiration, as we have already seen. The owner of an American put can exercise the option at any time. Therefore, the maximum value for an American put is the exercise price. The price of an American put equals the exercise price if the stock is worthless and is sure to remain worthless until the option expires. For a European put before expiration, the maximum possible price equals the present value of the exercise price. The European put price cannot exceed the present value of the exercise price because the owner of a European put must wait until expiration to exercise.

Figure 3.2 shows the bounds for American and European puts. The price of a put can never fall below the maximum of zero or $X - S_T$. For an American put, the price can never exceed X. For a European put, the price can never exceed the present value of the exercise price, $Xe^{-r(T-t)}$. Therefore, the interior of Figure 3.2 defines the range of possible put prices. By developing more exact no-arbitrage conditions, we can say where in this interior area the price of a put can be found.[3]

RELATIONSHIPS BETWEEN CALL OPTION PRICES

In this section, we focus on price relationships between call options. These price differences arise from differences in exercise price and time until expiration. We have already seen in an informal way that the exercise price is a potential liability associated with call ownership. The greater the value of this potential liability, the lower the value of the call option. We will illustrate this principle more formally by appealing to our familiar no-arbitrage arguments. We use similar no-arbitrage arguments to explicate other pricing relationships. Unless explicitly stated otherwise, all of these relationships hold for both American and European calls.

The Lower the Exercise Price, the More Valuable the Call

Let us consider a single underlying stock on which there are two call options. The two call options have the same expiration date, but one option has a lower exercise price than the other. In this section, we want to show why the option with the lower exercise price must be worth as much or more than

The Boundary Space for a Put Option   **Figure 3.2**

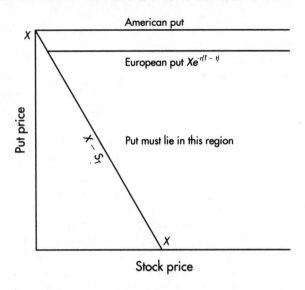

the option with the higher exercise price. For example, assume that two calls exist that violate this principle:

	Time Until Expiration	Exercise Price	Call Price
Call A	6 months	$100	$20
Call B	6 months	95	15

These two calls violate our principle because Call A has a higher exercise price and a higher call price. These prices give rise to an arbitrage opportunity, as we now show. Faced with these prices, the trader can transact as follows:

Transaction	Cash Flow
Sell Call A	+$20
Buy Call B	−15
Net Cash Flow	+$5

Once we sell Call A and buy Call B, we have a sure profit of at least $5. To see this, we consider profits and losses for various stock prices, such as $95 and below and $100 and above. If the stock price is $95, neither option can be exercised. If the stock price stays at $95 or below, both options expire worthless, and we keep our $5 from the initial transactions. If the stock price is greater than $100, say $105, Call A will be exercised against us. When that happens, we surrender the stock worth $105 and receive $100, losing $5 on the exercise against us. However, we ourselves exercise Call

B, receiving the stock worth $105 and paying the exercise price of $95. So, we can summarize our profits and losses from the exercises that occur when the stock trades at $105.

Transaction	Cash Flow
Surrender stock	−$105
Receive $100 exercise price	+100
Pay $95 exercise price	−95
Receive stock	+105
Net Cash Flow	+$5

As the calculation shows, if Call A is exercised against us, we exercise Call B and make $5 on the double exercise. Therefore, we make a total of $10, $5 from the initial transaction and $5 on the exercises.

Next, we consider what happens if the stock price lies between $95 and $100, say at $97. This outcome is also beneficial for us because the option we sold with a $100 strike price cannot be exercised against us. However, we can exercise our option. When we exercise, we pay the $95 exercise price and receive a stock worth $97. We add the $2 profit on this exercise to the $5 we made initially, for a total profit of $7. Figure 3.3 graphs the total profit on the position for all stock prices. With a stock price at or below $95, we make $5 because neither option can be exercised. With a stock price of $100 or above, we make $10: $5 from our initial transaction and $5 from the difference between the two exercise prices. If the stock price is between $95 and $100, we make $5 from our initial transaction plus the difference between the stock price and the $95 exercise price we face.

Figure 3.3   Arbitrage with Calls A and B

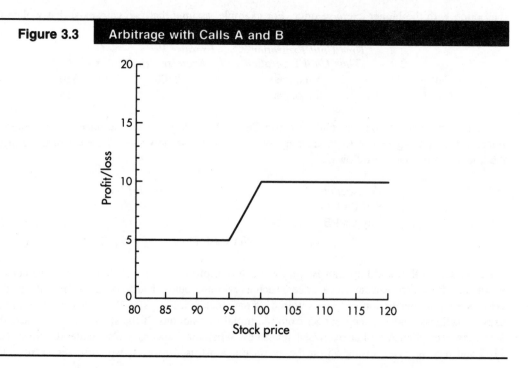

These transactions guarantee an arbitrage profit of at least $5 and perhaps as much as $10. Figure 3.3 shows that there is at least a $5 profit for any stock price. If the profit and loss graph shows profits for all possible stock prices with no investment, then there is an arbitrage opportunity. In the real world, an investment strategy that requires no initial investment may show profits for some stock price outcomes, but it must also show losses for other stock prices. Otherwise, there is an arbitrage opportunity.

In stating our principle, we said that the call with the lower exercise price must cost at least as much as the call with the higher exercise price. Why doesn't the call with the lower exercise price have to cost more than the call with the higher exercise price? In most real market situations, the call with the lower exercise price will, in fact, cost more. However, we cannot be sure that will happen as a general rule. To see why, assume the stock underlying Calls A and B trades for $5, and there is virtually no chance that the stock price could reach $90 before the two options expire. When the underlying stock is extremely far out-of-the-money, the calls might have the same, or nearly the same, price. In such a situation, both calls would have a very low price. If it is certain that the stock price can never rise to the lower exercise price, both calls would be worthless.

The Difference in Call Prices Cannot Exceed the Difference in Exercise Prices

Consider two call options that are similar in all respects except that they have exercise prices that differ by $5. We have already seen that the price of the call with the lower exercise price must equal or exceed the price of the call with the higher exercise price. Now we show that the difference in call prices cannot exceed the difference in exercise prices. We illustrate this principle by considering two call options with the same underlying stock:

	Time Until Expiration	Exercise Price	Call Price
Call C	6 months	$ 95	$10
Call D	6 months	100	4

The prices of Calls C and D do not meet our condition, and we want to show that these prices give rise to an arbitrage opportunity. To profit from this mispricing, we trade as follows:

Transaction	Cash Flow
Sell Call C	+$10
Buy Call D	−4
Net Cash Flow	+$6

Selling Call C and buying Call D gives a net cash inflow of $6. Because we sold a call, however, we also have the risk that the call will be exercised against us. We now show that no matter what stock price occurs, we still make a profit.

If the stock price is $95 or below, both options expire worthless, and we keep our initial cash inflow of $6. If the stock price exceeds $100, Call C is exercised against us, and we exercise Call D. For example, assume the stock price is $102. We exercise, pay the $100 exercise price, and receive the stock. Call C is exercised against us, so we surrender the stock and receive the $95 exercise price. Therefore, we lose $5 on the exercise. This loss partially offsets our initial cash inflow of $6. Thus, for any stock price of $100 or more, we make $1. We now consider stock prices between $95 and $100. If the stock price is $98, Call C will be exercised against us. We surrender the stock worth $98 and receive $95, for a $3 loss. The option we own cannot be exercised because the exercise price of $100 exceeds the current stock price of $98. Therefore, we lose $3 on the exercise, which partially offsets our initial cash inflow of $6. This gives a $3 net profit.

Figure 3.4 shows the profits and losses on this trade for a range of stock prices. As the figure shows, we make at least $1 and may make as much as $6. Because all outcomes show a profit with no investment, these transactions constitute an arbitrage. The chance to make this arbitrage profit stems from the fact that the call option prices differed by more than the difference between the exercise prices. In real markets, the difference between two call prices will usually be less than the difference in exercise prices. However, the difference in call prices cannot exceed the difference in exercise prices without creating an arbitrage opportunity.[4]

A Call Must Be Worth at Least the Stock Price Less the Present Value of the Exercise Price

We have already noted that a call at expiration is worth the maximum of zero or the stock price less the exercise price. Before expiration, the call must be worth at least the stock price less the present value of the exercise price. That is:

$$C_t \geq S_t - Xe^{-r(T-t)} \tag{3.3}$$

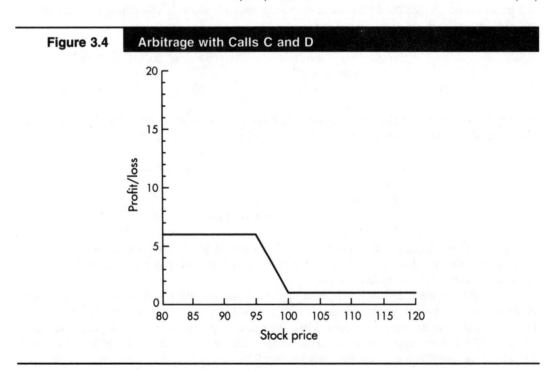

| Figure 3.4 | Arbitrage with Calls C and D |

To see why prices must observe this principle, we consider the following situation. Assume the stock trades for $103 and the current risk-free interest rate is 6 percent. A call with an exercise price of $100 expires in six months and trades for $2. These prices violate our rule, because the call option price is too low: $2 is less than the stock price less the present value of $100. These prices give rise to an arbitrage opportunity. To take advantage, we trade as follows:

Transactions	Cash Flow
Sell the stock	+$103
Buy the call option	−2
Buy a bond with remaining funds	−101
Net Cash Flow	0

With these transactions, we owe one share of stock. However, with our call option and the money we have left from selling the stock, we can honor our obligations at any time and still have a profit. For example, at the beginning of the transactions, we can exercise our option, pay the $100 exercise price, return the stock, and keep $1.

Alternatively, we can wait until our option reaches expiration in six months. Then the bond we purchased with be worth $101e^{(.06)(.5)} = $104.08. Whatever the stock is worth at expiration, we can repay with profit. For example, if the stock price is higher than the exercise price, we exercise the option and pay $100 to get the stock. This gives a profit at expiration of $4.08. If the stock price is below the exercise price, we allow our option to expire. We then buy the stock in the open market and repay our debt of one share. For example, if the stock price is $95 at expiration, our option expires, and we pay $95 for the share to repay our obligation. Our profit then is $104.08 − $95 = $9.08. Figure 3.5 graphs the profits from this transaction.

From this analysis, we can see that our option must cost at least $103 − $100e^{−(.06)(.5)} = $103 − $97.04 = $5.96. Any lower price allows an arbitrage profit. If the call is priced at $5.96, we have $97.04 to invest in bonds after selling the stock at $103 and buying the option at $5.96. At expiration, our bond investment pays $100, which is the exercise price. If the option sold at $5.96, the profit line in Figure 3.5 would shift down to show a zero profit for any stock price of $100 or more. This would eliminate the arbitrage because there would be some stock prices that would give zero profits. However, in real markets the price of this call would generally be higher than $5.96. A price of $5.96 ensures against any loss and gives profits for any stock price below $100. If there is any chance that the stock price might be below $100 at expiration, then the call of our example should be worth more than $5.96.

The More Time Until Expiration, the Greater the Call Price

If we consider two call options with the same exercise price on the same underlying good, then the price of the call with more time remaining until expiration must equal or exceed the price of the call that expires sooner. Violating this principle leads to arbitrage, as the following example shows.

Consider two options on the same underlying good.

	Time Until Expiration	Exercise Price	Call Price
Call E	3 months	$100	$6
Call F	6 months	100	5

Figure 3.5	Arbitrage of a Call Against a Stock and Bond

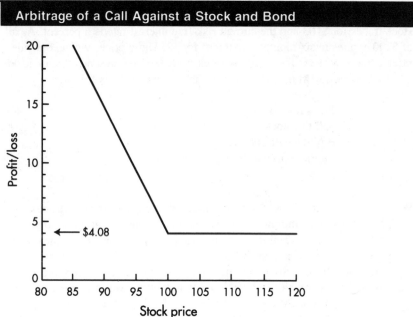

These prices violate our principle, which implies that Call F must cost at least as much as Call E. To capture the arbitrage profits, we trade as follows:

Transaction	Cash Flow
Sell Call E	+$6
Buy Call F	−5
Net Cash Flow	+$1

With a net cash inflow at the time of contracting, the transactions clearly require no investment. Therefore, they meet the first condition for an arbitrage. Next, we need to show that the strategy produces a profit for all stock price outcomes.

First, we show how to protect the arbitrage profit if the options are American options. Any time that Call E is exercised against us, we can exercise Call F to secure the stock to give to the holder of Call E. For example, assume that Call E is about to expire and is exercised against us with the stock price at $105. In that case, we simply exercise Call F and surrender the stock to the holder of Call E, as the following transactions show.

Assuming Call E and Call F Are American Options

Transaction	Cash Flow
Call E is exercised against us	
Receive $100 exercise price	+$100
Surrender stock worth $105	−105

Exercise Call F
    Receive stock worth $105   +105
    Pay $100 exercise price   −100
                        Net Cash Flow   0

As these transactions show, if the call we sold is exercised against us, we can fulfill all our obligations by exercising our call. There will be no net cash flow on the exercise, and we keep the $1 profit from our original transaction.

Notice that our concluding transactions assumed that both Call E and Call F were American options. This allowed us to exercise our Call F before expiration. Had the options been European options, we could not exercise Call F when Call E was exercised against us. However, the principle still holds for European options – the European option with more time until expiration must be worth at least as much as the option with a shorter life. We can illustrate this principle for European options with the following transactions.

Assuming Call E and Call F Are European Options

Transaction	*Cash Flow*
Call E is exercised against us	
Receive $100 exercise price	+$100
Surrender stock worth $105	−105
Sell Call F	
Receive $S - Xe^{-r(T-t)} \geq \$5$	at least +5
Net Cash Flow	at least 0

As these transactions show, we will receive at least $5 for selling Call F. Earlier, we used no-arbitrage arguments to show that an in-the-money call must be worth at least the stock price minus the present value of the exercise price. The worst situation for these transactions occurs at very low interest rates. However, the arbitrage still works for a zero interest rate. Then, Call F must still be worth at least $S - X = \$105 - \$100 = \$5$. If we get $5 from selling Call F, we still have a net zero cash flow when Call E is exercised against us. If we get more, any additional net cash flow at the time of exercise is just added to the $1 cash inflow we had at the time we initially transacted.

Do Not Exercise Call Options on No-Dividend Stocks Before Expiration

In this section, we show that a call option on a non–dividend paying stock is always worth more than its mere exercise value. Therefore, such an option should never be exercised. If the trader wants to dispose of the option, it will always be better to sell the option than to exercise it.

For a call option, the **intrinsic value** or the **exercise value** of the option equals $S_t - X$. This is the value of the option when it is exercised because the holder of the call pays X and receives S_t. We have seen that, prior to expiration, a call option must be worth at least $S_t - Xe^{-r(T-t)}$. Therefore, exercising a call before expiration discards at least the difference between X and $Xe^{-r(T-t)}$. The difference between the call price and the exercise value is the **time value** of the option. For example, consider the following values:

$$S_t = \$105$$
$$X = \$100$$
$$r = .10$$
$$T - t = 6 \text{ months}$$

The intrinsic value of this call option is $5, or $S_t - X$. However, we know that the market price of the call option must meet the following condition:

$$C_t \geq S_t - Xe^{-r(T-t)}$$
$$\geq \$105 - \$100e^{-(.1)(.5)}$$
$$\geq \$9.88$$

Therefore, exercising the call throws away at least $X - Xe^{-r(T-t)} = \$100 - \$95.12 = \$4.88$. Alternatively, it discards the difference between the lower bound on the call price and the exercise value of the call, $9.88 − $5.00 = $4.88. For a non–dividend paying stock, early exercise can never be optimal. This means that the call will not be exercised until expiration. However, this makes an American option on a non–dividend paying stock equivalent to a European option. For a stock that pays no dividends, the American option will not be exercised until expiration, and a European option cannot be exercised until expiration. Therefore, the two have the same price. Notice that this rule holds only for a call option on a stock that does not pay dividends. In some circumstances, it can make sense to exercise a call option on a dividend paying stock before the option expires. The motivation for the early exercise is to capture the dividend immediately and to earn interest on those funds. We explore these possibilities in Chapter 6.

RELATIONSHIPS BETWEEN PUT OPTION PRICES

In Chapter 2, we saw that the value of either an American put or a European put at expiration is given by:

$$P_T = \text{MAX}\{0, X - S_T\}$$

Essentially, the put holder anticipates receiving the value of the exercise price and paying the stock price at expiration. Now we want to consider put values before expiration and the relationship between pairs of puts. As we did for calls, we illustrate these pricing relationships by invoking no-arbitrage conditions. Further, the relationships hold for both American and European puts unless explicitly stated otherwise.

Before Expiration an American Put Must Be Worth at Least the Exercise Price Less the Stock Price

The holder of an American put option can exercise at any time. Upon exercising, the put holder surrenders the put and the stock and receives the exercise price. Therefore, the American put must be worth at least the difference between the exercise price and the stock price.

$$P_t \geq \text{MAX}\{0, X - S_t\}$$

where P_t is the price of an American put at time t.

We illustrate this principle by showing how to reap an arbitrage profit if the principle does not hold. Consider the following data:

$S_t = \$95$
$X = \$100$
$P_t = \$3$

With these prices, the put is too cheap. The put's price does not equal or exceed the $5 difference between the exercise price and the stock price. To take advantage of the mispricing, we transact as shown below. With these transactions, we capture an immediate cash inflow of $2. Also, we have no further obligations, so our arbitrage is complete. Notice that these transactions involve the immediate exercise of the put option. Therefore, this kind of arbitrage is possible only for an American put option. To prevent this kind of arbitrage, the price of the American put option must be at least $5. In actual markets, the price of a put will generally exceed the difference between the exercise price and the stock price.

Transaction	Cash Flow
Buy put	−$3
Buy stock	−95
Exercise option	+100
Net Cash Flow	+$2

Before Expiration a European Put Must Be Worth at Least the Present Value of the Exercise Price Minus the Stock Price

We have just seen that an American put must be worth at least the difference between the exercise price and the stock price, $X - S_t$. The same rule does not hold for a European put because we cannot exercise the European put before expiration to take advantage of the mispricing. However, a similar rule holds for a European put. Specifically, the value of a European put must equal or exceed the present value of the exercise price minus the stock price:

$$p_t \geq Xe^{-r(T-t)} - S_t$$

We can illustrate this price restriction for a European put by using our same stock and option, except we treat the put as a European put. Also, the risk-free interest rate is 6 percent, and we assume that the option expires in 3 months.

$S_t = \$95$
$X = \$100$
$p_t = \$3$
$T - t = 3$ months
$r = .06$

where p_t is the price of a European put at time t. With these values, our principle states:

$$p_t \geq Xe^{-r(T-t)} - S_t = \$100e^{-(.06)(.25)} - \$95 = \$98.51 - \$95 = \$3.51$$

The put must be worth at least \$3.51, but the actual price is only \$3, so we can reap an arbitrage profit by trading as follows:

Transaction	Cash Flow
Borrow \$98 at 6 percent for 3 months	+\$98
Buy put	-3
Buy stock	-95
Net Cash Flow	0

After making these initial transactions, we wait until the option is about to expire and we transact as follows:

Transaction	Cash Flow
Exercise option, deliver stock, and collect exercise price	+\$100.00
Repay debt = $\$98e^{(.06)(.25)}$	-99.48
Net Cash Flow	+\$.52

These transactions give an arbitrage profit of \$.52 at expiration. Notice that there was a zero net cash flow when we first transacted, so there was no investment. These initial transactions guaranteed the \$.52 profit at expiration. Therefore, we have an arbitrage.

   From these two examples, we can see that an American put must be worth at least as much as a European put. The lower bound for the price of an American put is $X - S_t$, but the lower bound for the European put is $Xe^{-r(T-t)} - S_t$. Also, we know that the American put gives all the rights of the European put, plus the chance to exercise early. Therefore, the American put must be worth at least as much as the European put.

The Longer Until Expiration, the More Valuable an American Put

Consider two American put options that are alike except that one has a longer time until expiration. The put with the longer time until expiration must be worth at least as much as the other. Informally, the put with the longer time until expiration offers every advantage of the shorter term put. In addition, the longer-term put offers the chance for greater price increases on the put after the shorter term put expires. Without this condition, arbitrage opportunities exist.

   To illustrate the arbitrage opportunity, assume the underlying stock trades for \$95 and we have two American puts with exercise prices of \$100 as follows:

	Time Until Expiration	Put Price
Put A	3 months	\$7
Put B	6 months	6

These prices permit arbitrage because the put with the longer life is cheaper. Therefore, we sell Put A and buy Put B for an arbitrage profit, as shown below.

Transaction	Cash Flow
Sell Put A	+$7
Buy Put B	−6
Net Cash Flow	+$1

After making these transactions, we must consider what happens if the Put A is exercised against us. Assume that Put A is exercised against us when the stock price is $90. In this situation, the following events occur.

Transaction	Cash Flow
On the exercise of Put A	
Receive stock worth $90	$90
Pay exercise price of $100	−100
We exercise Put B	
Deliver stock worth $90	−90
Receive exercise price of $100	+100
Net Cash Flow	0

When the holder of Put A exercises against us, we immediately exercise Put B. No matter what the stock price may be, these transactions give a zero net cash flow. Therefore, the original transaction gave us $1, which represents an arbitrage profit of at least $1. The profit could be greater if Put A expires worthless. Then we have our $1 profit to keep, plus we still hold Put B, which may have additional value. Therefore, the longer term American put must be worth at least as much as the shorter term American put. Notice that this rule holds for only American puts. Our arbitrage transactions require that we exercise Put B when the holder of Put A exercises against us. This we could do only with an American option.

For European put options, it is not always true that the longer term put has greater value. A European put pays off the exercise price only at expiration. If expiration is very distant, the payoff will be diminished in value because of the time value of money. However, the longer the life of a put option, the greater its advantage in allowing something beneficial to happen to the stock price. Thus, the longer the life of the put, the better for this reason. Whether having a longer life is beneficial to the price of a European put depends on which of these two factors dominates. We will be able to evaluate these more completely in the next chapter.

The fact that a European put with a shorter life can be more valuable than a European put with a longer life shows two important principles. First, early exercise of a put can be desirable even when the underlying stock pays no dividends. This follows from the fact that a short-term European put can be worth more than a long-term European put. Second, American and European put prices may not be identical, even when the underlying stock pays no dividends. If early exercise is desirable, the American put allows it and the European put does not. Therefore, the American put can be more valuable than a European put, even when the underlying stock pays no dividend.

The Higher the Exercise Price, the More Valuable the Put

For both American and European put options, a higher exercise price is associated with a higher price. A put option with a higher exercise price must be worth at least as much as a put with a lower exercise price. Violations of this principle lead to arbitrage.

To illustrate the arbitrage, consider a stock trading at $90 with the following two put options having the same time until expiration:

	Exercise Price	Put Price
Put C	$100	$11
Put D	95	12

These prices violate the rule, because the price of Put D is higher, even though Put C has the higher exercise price. To reap the arbitrage profit, we transact as follows:

Transaction	Cash Flow
Sell Put D	+$12
Buy Put C	−11
Net Cash Flow	+$1

If the holder of Put D exercises against us, we immediately exercise Put C. Assuming the stock price is $90 at the time of exercise, we consider the appropriate transactions when we face the exercise of Put D:

Transaction	Cash Flow
Exercise of Put D against us	
Receive stock worth $90	+$90
Pay exercise price	−95
Our exercise of Put C	
Deliver stock worth $90	−90
Receive exercise price	+100
Net Cash Flow	+$5

No matter what the stock price is at the time of exercise, we have a cash inflow of $5 if we both exercise. Further, Put D can be exercised only when it is profitable for us to exercise Put C. Notice that this principle holds for both American and European puts. Put C and Put D can be exercised either before expiration (for an American option) or at expiration only (for a European option). Figure 3.6 shows the profits for alternative stock prices. For any stock price of $100 or above, both puts expire worthless and we keep our initial $1 inflow. For a stock price between $95 and $100, we can exercise our option, but Put D cannot be exercised. For example, if the stock is at $97, we exercise and receive $100 for a $97 stock. This $3 exercise profit gives us a total profit of $4. If the stock price is below $95, both puts will be exercised. With the stock price at $90, the exercise profit on Put D is $5, as we have seen. However, our exercise profit on Put C is $10. Thus, we lose $5 on the exercise of Put D against us, but we make $10 by exercising Put C, and we still have our $1 initial inflow, for a net arbitrage profit of $6.

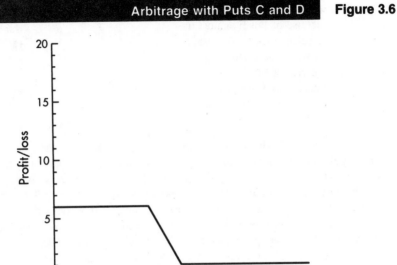

Arbitrage with Puts C and D | **Figure 3.6**

The Price Difference Between Two American Puts Cannot Exceed the Difference in Exercise Prices

The prices of two American puts cannot differ by more than the difference in exercise prices, assuming other features are the same. If prices violate this condition, there will be an arbitrage opportunity. To illustrate this arbitrage opportunity, consider the following puts on the same underlying stock:

	Exercise Price	Put Price
Put E	$100	$ 4
Put F	105	10

These prices violate our condition because the price difference between the puts is $6, while the difference in exercise prices is only $5. To exploit this mispricing, we transact as follows:

Transaction	Cash Flow
Sell Put F	+$10
Buy Put E	−4
Net Cash Flow	+$6

With this initial cash inflow of $6, we have enough to pay any loss we might sustain when the holder of Put F exercises against us. For example, assume the stock trades at $95 and the holder of Put F exercises.

Transaction	Cash Flow
The exercise of Put F against us	
Receive stock worth $95	+$95
Pay exercise price	−105
Our exercise of Put E	
Receive exercise price	+100
Deliver stock worth $95	−95
Net Cash Flow	−$5

On the exercise, we lose $5. However, we already received $6 with the initial transactions. This leaves an arbitrage profit of at least $1. As Figure 3.7 shows, we could have larger profits, depending on the stock price. If the stock price equals or exceeds $105, no exercise is possible and we keep the entire $6 of our initial transaction. For stock prices between $100 and $105, the holder of Put F can exercise against us, but we cannot exercise. For example, if the stock price is $103, we must pay $105 and receive a stock worth only $103, for a $2 exercise loss. However, with our initial cash inflow of $6, we still have a net profit of $4. For stock prices below $100, we can both exercise, as in the transactions we showed for a stock price of $95. In this case, we lose $5 on the exercise, but we still make a net profit of $1.

For Two European Puts, the Price Difference Cannot Exceed the Difference in the Present Value of the Exercise Prices

A similar principle holds for European puts, except the difference in put prices cannot exceed the difference in the present values of the exercise prices. If Puts E and F are European puts, the interest

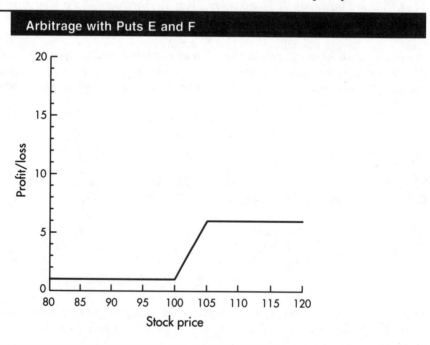

Figure 3.7   Arbitrage with Puts E and F

rate is 10 percent, and the options expire in six months, then the present values of the exercise prices are:

	Exercise Price	Present Value of Exercise Price
Put E	$100	$95.12
Put F	105	99.88

According to this principle, the price of Put F cannot exceed the price of Put E by more than $4.76 ($99.88 − $95.12). With prices of $4 and $10 for Puts E and F, there should be an arbitrage profit.

To capture the profit, we sell Put F and buy Put E. This gives a cash inflow of $6, which we invest for six months at 10 percent. The European puts cannot be exercised until expiration, at which time our investment is worth ($6e^{(.1)(.5)}$) = $6.31. The most we can lose on the exercise is $5, the difference in the exercise prices. As we saw for the American puts, this happens when the stock price is $100 or less. However, we have $6.31 at expiration, so we can easily sustain this loss. If the stock price exceeds $105, neither option can be exercised, and we keep our entire $6.31. For the European puts, the graph of the arbitrage profit is exactly like Figure 3.7, except we add $.31 to every point. If the options had been priced $4.76 apart, our investment would have yielded $5 at expiration ($4.76e^{(.1)(.5)}$). This $5 would protect us against any loss at expiration, but it would guarantee no arbitrage profit.

Summary

To this point, we have considered how call and put prices respond to stock and exercise prices and the time remaining until expiration. We have expressed all of these relationships as an outgrowth of our basic no-arbitrage condition: Prevailing option prices must exclude arbitrage profits. For call options, the story is very clear. The higher the stock price, the higher the call price. The higher the exercise price, the lower the call price. The longer the time until expiration, the higher the call price. For put options, the higher the stock price, the lower the put price. The higher the exercise price, the higher the put price. For time until expiration, the effects are slightly more complicated. For an American put, the longer the time until expiration, the more valuable the put. For a European put, a longer time until expiration can give rise to either a lower or higher put price.

We have also seen that no-arbitrage conditions restrict how call and put prices for different exercise prices can vary. For two call options or two American put options that are alike except for their exercise prices, the two option prices cannot differ by more than the difference in the exercise prices. For two European put options with different exercise prices, the option prices cannot differ by more than the present value of the difference in the exercise prices.

Throughout this discussion, we have been trying to tighten the bounds we can place on option prices. For example, Figure 3.1 gave the most generous bounds for call options. There we noted that the call price could never exceed the stock price as an upper bound. As a lower bound, the call price must always be at least zero or the stock price minus the exercise price, whichever is higher. The price relationships we considered in this section tighten these bounds by placing further restrictions on put and call prices. Figure 3.8 illustrates how we have tightened these bounds for call options. First, we showed that the call price must be at least zero or the stock price minus the present value of the exercise price. Figure 3.8 reflects this restriction by pulling in the right boundary. Now we know that the call price must lie in this slightly smaller area. Also, if we consider a call with a lower

Figure 3.8   Call Price Relationships

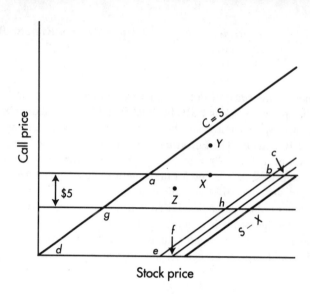

exercise price, we know that the call price must be at least as high for the call with the lower exercise price.

Further, we have considered price relationships between pairs of options that differ in some respects. For example, assume that Option X in Figure 3.8 is priced correctly. We want to consider Option Y, which is another call like X, except it has a longer time until expiration. The price of Y must equal or exceed the price of X. For example, Y in Figure 3.8 would have to lie on or above the horizontal line *abc* that runs through X. Based on our information, Y in Figure 3.8 has a permissible location.

Consider another option, Z, which is just like X except Z has an exercise price that is $5 higher than that of X. The price of Z can never fall below the stock price minus the present value of Z's exercise price. Therefore, the right boundary for the stock price minus the present value of Z's exercise price gives a floor for the price of Z. The price of Z must lie above the line *eb*. With a higher exercise price, the price of Option Z cannot exceed the price of X. Therefore, the price of Z must lie on or below the line *abc*. Combining these two restrictions, we know that the price of Z must lie in the area given by *abed*.

However, we can locate the price of Z more exactly. We know from our discussion that two calls that differ only in their exercise prices must have prices that differ no more than their exercise prices. In our example, the exercise price of Z is $5 more than the exercise price of X. In Figure 3.8, line *gh* is $5 below line *abc*. Therefore, continuing to assume that the price of X is correct, Z must have a price that lies on or above *gh*. If it did not, the price of Z would be too low relative to X. Putting these principles together, we know that the price of Z must lie within the area defined by *abhg*. Z in Figure 3.8 conforms to these rules.

We cannot specify exactly where Z must lie within area *abhg*. Option prices also depend on two additional factors: interest rates and the way in which the stock price moves. After considering these additional factors in this chapter and in Chapter 4, we will be able to pinpoint the price that an option must have.

OPTION PRICES AND THE INTEREST RATE

We now apply our no-arbitrage approach to examine the effect of interest rates on option prices. For a call option, the exercise price represents a potential liability the owner of a call option faces at expiration. Before expiration, the lower the present value of the liability associated with owning a call, the better for the call owner. Therefore, as we show in this section, call option prices increase with higher interest rates. The result may seem counterintuitive because we generally associate higher asset prices with lower interest rates. This is not so for call options, as our no-arbitrage argument shows. The owner of a put option may exercise and receive the exercise price in exchange for surrendering the stock, so the exercise price represents a potential asset for a put owner. The lower the interest rate, the higher the present value of that potential asset. Therefore, the lower the interest rate, the higher the price of a put. This section presents a no-arbitrage argument to show why the price of a put must fall as interest rates rise.

Call Prices and Interest Rates

We have already observed that the price of either an American or a European call must equal or exceed the larger of zero or the stock price minus the present value of the exercise price:

$$C_t \geq \text{MAX}\{0, S_t - Xe^{-r(T-t)}\} \tag{3.4}$$

In Equation 3.3, $Xe^{-r(T-t)}$ is the present value of the exercise price. The larger the interest rate, r, the smaller that present value, and thus a higher interest rate gives a larger value for $S_t - Xe^{-r(T-t)}$. This makes sense because the exercise price is a liability the call owner incurs upon exercise.

We can also show that the call price must rise if interest rates rise by the following no-arbitrage example. Consider a call option on a stock trading at \$100. The exercise price of the call is \$100. The option expires in six months, and the current interest rate is 10 percent. From Equation 3.3, the price of this call must equal or exceed \$4.88:

$$C_t \geq \text{MAX}\{0, \$100 - \$100e^{-(.1)(.5)}\} \geq \$4.88$$

For convenience, we assume that the option is correctly priced at \$4.88.[5]

Suddenly, interest rates jump from 10 to 12 percent, but the option price remains at \$4.88. Now the option price does not meet the condition in Equation 3.3. The option price is too low, so we want to transact to guarantee an arbitrage profit. Accordingly, we trade as follows:

Transaction	Cash Flow
Sell stock	+\$100.00
Buy call	−4.88
Buy bond maturing in 6 months and yielding 12 percent	−95.12
Net Cash Flow	0

In six months, the option is at expiration and our bond matures. The bond will pay $101.

How we deal with the call and stock depends on the stock price relative to the option price. If the stock trades for $100, the call option is worthless. In this case, we buy the stock for $100 and return it, leaving a profit of $1. If the stock price is less than $100, our profit increases. For example, with a $95 stock price, the option is worthless, and we buy the stock for $95. These transactions leave a total profit of $6. If the stock price exceeds $100, we exercise our call and pay the exercise price of $100. After exercising and returning the stock, we still have $1. Therefore, we have a profit at expiration with no investment. This arbitrage opportunity arose because the option price did not increase as the interest rate rose. With our example, the price of the call should have risen to at least $5.82 to exclude arbitrage:

$$C_t \geq \text{MAX}\{0, S_t - Xe^{-r(T-t)}\} \geq \text{MAX}\{0, \$100 - \$100e^{-(.12)(.5)}\} \geq \$5.82$$

Because the price did not respond, we were able to reap an arbitrage profit. To exclude arbitrage, the price of a call must be higher the higher the interest rate. Otherwise, a riskless profit without investment will be possible.

Put Prices and Interest Rates

Interest rates also affect put prices. When exercising, the holder of a put receives the exercise price. Therefore, for a put owner, the exercise price is a potential cash inflow. The greater the present value of that potential inflow, the higher will be the value of the put. As a consequence, the put price should be higher the lower the interest rate. If a put price fails to adjust to changing interest rates, there will be an arbitrage opportunity. This rule holds for both American and European puts.

To show how put prices depend on interest rates, consider a stock trading at $90. A European put option on this stock expires in six months and has an exercise price of $100. Interest rates are at 10 percent. We know that the European put price must meet the following condition:

$$p_t \geq \text{MAX}\{0, Xe^{-r(T-t)} - S_t\} \geq \text{MAX}\{0, \$100e^{-(.1)(.5)} - \$90\} \geq \$5.12$$

For convenience, we assume that the put is priced at $5.12.

Let us now assume that interest rates suddenly fall to 8 percent but the put price does not change. Our principle asserts that the put should be worth at least $6.08 now. With the put price staying at $5.12, we trade as follows:

Transaction	Cash Flow
Borrow $95.12 at 8 percent	+$95.12
Buy stock	−90.00
Buy put	−5.12
Net Cash Flow	0

With these transactions in place, we wait until expiration in six months to reap our arbitrage profit. At expiration, we owe $99.00 on our borrowings. From the stock and the put, we must realize enough to cover that payment. Any remaining money will be profit. If the stock price at expiration is $100, we allow our put to expire and sell the stock. We receive $100, from which we pay $99.00. This leaves a $1 profit. If the stock price at expiration is below $100, we exercise our put. For example, with a stock price of $95, we exercise our put, deliver the stock, and collect $100. This gives a $1 profit. We make exactly $1 at expiration for any stock price of $100 or less. For any stock price above $100, our put is worthless, and our profit equals the difference between the stock price and our $99 debt. From these transactions, we see that we will make at least $1 at expiration. This we achieve with zero investment. Therefore, the failure of the put option price to adjust to changing interest rates generates an arbitrage opportunity. The put price must rise as interest rates fall.

OPTION PRICES AND STOCK PRICE MOVEMENTS

Up to this point, we have studied the way in which four factors constrain call and put prices. These factors are the stock price, the exercise price, the time remaining until expiration, and the interest rate. Even with these four factors, we cannot say exactly what the option price must be before expiration. There is a fifth factor to consider – stock price movements before expiration. If we consider a stock with options on it that expire in six months, we know that the stock price can change thousands of times before the option expires. Further, for two stocks, the pattern of changes and the volatility of the stock price changes can differ dramatically. However, if we can develop a model for understanding stock price movements, we can use that model to specify what the price of an option must be.

We now make a drastic, but temporary, simplifying assumption. Between the current moment and the expiration of an option, we assume that the stock price will rise or fall by 10 percent. With this assumption about the stock's price movement, we can use our no-arbitrage approach to determine the exact value of a European call or put. Therefore, knowing the potential pattern of stock price movements gives us the final key to understanding option prices. This section illustrates how to determine option prices based on this simplifying model of stock price movements. The next chapter shows how to apply more realistic models of stock price movements to compute accurate option prices.

Let us assume that a stock trades for $100. In the next year, the price can rise or fall exactly 10 percent. Therefore, the stock price next year will be either $90 or $110. Both a put and a call option have exercise prices of $100 and expire in one year. The current interest rate is 6 percent. We want to know how much the put and call will be worth. With these data, the call price is $7.55, and the put is worth $1.89. Other prices create arbitrage opportunities. This section shows that the options must have these prices. Chapter 4 explains why these no-arbitrage relationships must hold. (As we consider a single period in this section, we employ discrete compounding.)

The Call Price

We have asserted that the call price must be $7.55, given our other data, if the call price is to exclude an arbitrage opportunity. If the option price is lower, we will enter arbitrage transactions that include buying the option. Similarly, if the option price is higher, our arbitrage transactions will include selling the call. We illustrate each case in turn. Let us begin by assuming that the call price is $7.00, which is below our no-arbitrage price of $7.55. If the call price is too low, we transact as follows:

Transaction	Cash Flow
Sell 1 share of stock	+$100.00
Buy 2 calls	−14.00
Buy bond	−86.00
Net Cash Flow	0

At expiration, the stock price will be either $110 or $90. If the stock price is $110, the calls will be worth $10 each – the stock price minus the exercise price. If the stock price is $90, the calls are worthless. In either case, the bond will pay $91.16. If the stock price is $90, we repurchase a share with our bond proceeds for $90. This leaves a profit of $1.16. If the stock price is $110, we sell our two options for $20. Adding this $20 to our bond proceeds, we have $111.16. From this amount, we buy a share for $110 to repay the borrowing of a share. This leaves a profit of $1.16. Therefore, we make $1.16 whether the stock price rises or falls. We made this certain profit with zero investment, so we have an arbitrage profit.

Now assume the call price is $8.00, exceeding $7.55. In this case, the call price is too high, so we sell the call as part of the following transactions.

Transaction	Cash Flow
Buy 1 share of stock	−$100.00
Sell 2 calls	+16.00
Sell a bond (borrow funds)	+84.00
Net Cash Flow	0

At expiration, we know we must repay $89.04. If the stock price at expiration is $90, the calls cannot be exercised against us. So we sell our stock for $90 and repay our debt of $89.04. This leaves a profit of $.96.

If the stock price goes to $110, the calls will be exercised against us. To fulfill one obligation, we deliver our share of stock and receive the exercise price of $100. We then buy back the other call that is still outstanding. It costs $10, the difference between the stock price and the exercise price. This leaves $90, from which we repay our debt of $89.04. Now we have completed all of our obligations and we still have $.96. Therefore, with a call priced at $8.00, we will have a profit of $.96 from these transactions, whether the stock price goes up or down. We captured this sure profit with zero investment, so we have an arbitrage profit.

To eliminate arbitrage, the call must trade for $7.55. If that call price prevails, both transaction strategies fail. For example, we might try to transact as follows if the call price is $7.55.

Transaction	Cash Flow
Buy 1 share of stock	−$100.00
Sell 2 calls	+15.10
Sell a bond (borrow funds)	+84.90
Net Cash Flow	0

At expiration, we owe $90.00. If the stock price is $90, our calls are worthless. However, we can sell our share for $90 and repay our debt. Our net cash flow at expiration is zero. If the stock price is $110, the calls will be exercised against us. We deliver our one share and receive $100. From this $100, we repay our debt of $90. This leaves $10, the exact difference between the stock and exercise price. Therefore, we can use our last $10 to close our option position. Our net cash flow is zero. With a call price of $7.55, our transactions cost us zero and yield zero. This is exactly the result we expect in a market that is free from arbitrage opportunities.[6]

The Put Price

Based on the same data we have just considered for the call option, the put price must be $1.89 to avoid arbitrage. We can see that this must be the case in two ways. First, we show that put-call parity requires a price of $1.89. Second, we show how any other price leads to arbitrage opportunities similar to those that occurred when the call was priced incorrectly.

From Chapter 2, we know that put-call parity expresses the value of a European put as a function of a similar call, the stock, and investment in the risk-free bond.

$$p_t = c_t - S_t + Xe^{-r(T-t)}$$

where $Xe^{-r(T-t)}$ is the present value of the exercise price. For our example, we know that the correct call price is $7.55 and that the stock trades for $100. With one year remaining until expiration, the present value of the exercise price is $94.34. According to put-call parity for our example:

$$p_t = \$7.55 - \$100.00 + \$94.34 = \$1.89$$

If the put is not worth $1.89, arbitrage opportunities arise. This makes sense because the put-call parity relationship is itself a no-arbitrage condition.[7]

We now show how to reap arbitrage profits if the put does not trade for $1.89 by considering the transactions if the put price is above or below $1.89. First, let us assume that the put price is $1.50. In this case, the put is too cheap relative to other assets. The other assets that replicate the put are too expensive, taken together. These are the call, stock, bond combination on the right-hand side of the put-call parity formula. The put-call parity relationship suggests that we should buy the relatively overpriced put and sell the relatively overpriced portfolio that replicates the put. To initiate this strategy, we transact as follows:

Transaction	Cash Flow
Buy put	−$1.50
Sell call	+7.55
Buy stock	−100.00
Borrow $93.95 and invest at 6 percent for one year	+94.35
Net Cash Flow	0

In one year, our debt is $99.59, and the put and call are at expiration. The stock price will be either $90 or $110. If the stock price is $90, we exercise our put and deliver our share of stock. This gives a cash flow of $100, from which we repay our debt of $99.59. We have no further obligations, yet $.41 remains. Thus, we make a profit with no initial investment.

If the stock price is $110, our put is worthless, and the stock will be called away from us. When the call is exercised against us, we receive $100. From this $100, we repay our debt of $99.59. Again, this leaves us with $.41. No matter whether the stock goes to $90 or to $110, we make $.41. We achieved this profit with no initial investment. Consequently, we have a certain profit with zero investment, an arbitrage profit.

Let us now assume that the put trades for $2.00. With the put being too expensive, we sell the relatively overpriced put and purchase the relatively underpriced portfolio that replicates the put. In this case, our transactions are just the reverse of those we made when the put price was too low. We transact as follows:

Transaction	Cash Flow
Sell put	+$2.00
Buy call	−7.55
Sell stock	+100.00
Lend $94.45 at 6 percent for one year	−94.45
Net Cash Flow	0

In one year, our loan matures, so we collect $100.12. If the stock price is $90, our call is worthless, and the put will be exercised against us. We must accept the $90 stock and pay the $100 exercise price. This leaves one share of stock and $.12. We use the share to cover our original sale of stock, and we have $.12 after meeting all obligations.

If the stock price goes to $110.00, the put we sold will expire worthless. We exercise our call, paying the $100 exercise price to acquire the stock. We now have $.12 and one share, so we cover our original share sale by returning the stock. Again, we have completed all transactions and $.12 remains. Therefore, no matter whether the stock goes to $90 or $110 over the one-year investment horizon, we make $.12. We did this with zero investment, so we have an arbitrage profit.

These transactions illustrate why the put must trade for $1.89 in our example. Any other price allows arbitrage. If the put price is $1.89, both of the transactions we have just considered will cost zero to execute, but they will be sure to return zero when the options expire. In a market free of arbitrage opportunities, this is just what we expect.

OPTION PRICES AND THE RISKINESS OF STOCKS

As we have seen, option prices depend on several factors, including stock prices. In this section, we explore how stock price changes affect option prices. Specifically, we consider how the riskiness of the stock affects the price of the put or call. We use a simple model of the way a stock price changes to illustrate a very important result: The riskier the underlying stock, the greater the value of an option. This principle holds for both put and call options. While it may seem odd for an option price to be higher if the underlying good is riskier, we can use no-arbitrage arguments to show why this must be true.

Essentially, a call option gives its owner most of the benefits of rising stock prices and protection from suffering the full cost of a drop in stock prices. Thus, a call option offers insurance against falling stock prices and holds out the promise of high profits from surging stock prices. The riskier the underlying stock, the greater the chance of an extreme stock price movement. If the stock price falls dramatically, the insurance feature of the call option comes into play. This limits the call holder's loss. However, if the stock price increases dramatically, the call owner participates fully in the price increase. The protection against large losses, coupled with participation in large gains, makes call options more valuable when the underlying stock is risky.

For put options, risk has a parallel effect. Put owners benefit from large stock price drops and suffer from price increases. However, a put protects the owner from the full force of a stock price rise. In effect, a put embodies insurance against large price rises. At the same time, the put allows its owner to benefit fully from a stock price drop. Because the put incorporates protection against rising prices and allows its owner to capture virtually all profits from falling prices, a put is more valuable the riskier the underlying stock.

In the preceding section, we used a very simple model of stock price movement to show how to price put and call options. In this section, we extend the same model and example to evaluate the effect of riskiness on stock prices. Earlier, we assumed a stock traded for $100 and that its price would go to either $90 or $110 in one year. We assumed that the risk-free rate of interest was 6 percent and that a call and put option both had exercise prices of $100 and expired in one year. Under these circumstances, the call was worth $7.55 and the put was worth $1.89. Any other price for the put or call led to arbitrage opportunities. To explore the effect of risk, we consider two other possible outcomes for the stock price. First, we assume that the stock is not risky. In this case, the stock price increases by the risk-free rate of 6 percent with certainty. Second, we consider stock price movements in which the stock price goes to either $80 or $120.

Option Prices for Riskless Stock

If the stock is risk free, its value grows at the risk-free rate. Otherwise, there would be an arbitrage opportunity between the stock and the risk-free bond.[8] Consequently, we consider prices of our example options assuming that the stock price in one year will be $106 with certainty. Under these circumstances, the call option will be worth $5.66, and the put will be worth zero.

The put will be worth zero one year before expiration because it is sure to be worth zero at expiration. If the stock price is sure to be $106 at expiration, the put only gives the right to force someone to accept a stock worth $106 for $100. Thus, the put is worthless because there is no chance the stock price will be below the exercise price of the put.

The call has a certain payoff at expiration because the stock price is certain. At expiration, the call is worth $MAX\{0, S_T - X\}$ = $6. With a riskless stock, the call is also riskless. Investment in the call pays a certain return of $6 in one year, so the call must be worth the present value of $6, or $5.66. Any other price for the call creates an arbitrage opportunity. For example, if the option trades at $5.80, we sell the call and invest the $5.80 at 6 percent. In one year, our investment is worth $6.15, and the exercise of the call against us costs us $6. This yields a $.15 arbitrage profit. For any other price of either the put or the call, our familiar transactions guarantee an arbitrage profit.

Earlier, we placed the following bound on the European call price before expiration:

$$c_t \geq MAX\{0, S_t - Xe^{-r(T-t)}\}$$

Now we see that this relationship holds exactly if the stock is risk free. In other words, the European call price is on the lower boundary if the stock has no risk. Therefore, holding the other factors constant, any excess value of the call above the boundary is due to the riskiness of the stock.

Comparing our two examples of stock price movements, we saw that the risk-free stock implied a call price of $5.66. If the stock price was risky, moving up or down 10 percent in the next year, the call price was $7.55. This call price difference is due to the difference in the riskiness of the stock. As we now show, higher risk implies higher option prices.

Riskier Stocks Result in Higher Option Prices

In our model of stock price movements, we assumed that stock prices change over a year in a very specific way. When we assumed that stock prices could increase or decrease 10 percent, we found certain option prices. We now consider the same circumstances but allow for more radical stock price movements of 20 percent up or down. All other factors remain the same. In summary, a stock trades today at $100. In one year, its price will be either $80 or $120. The risk-free interest rate is 6 percent. A call and put each have an exercise price of $100 and expire in one year. Under these circumstances, the call price must be $12.26, and the put price must be $6.60. Any other prices create arbitrage opportunities. Therefore, we have observed the price effects of the following three stock price movements on option prices.

Stock Price Movement	Call Price	Put Price
Stock price increases by a certain 6 percent	$ 5.66	$0.00
Stock price rises or falls by 10 percent	7.55	1.89
Stock price rises or falls by 20 percent	12.26	6.60

In these examples, we held other factors constant. Each example uses options with the same exercise price and time to expiration. Also, each example employs the same risk-free rate. As these examples illustrate, greater risk in the stock increases both put and call prices.

SUMMARY

In this chapter, we discussed the relationships that govern option prices. We began by considering general boundary spaces for calls and puts. By linking relationships between option features, such as time to expiration and exercise prices, we specified price relationships between options. For example, we saw that the price of a call with a lower exercise price must equal or exceed the price of a similar call with a higher exercise price. We discussed the five factors on which option prices depend: the exercise price, the stock price, the risk-free interest rate, the time to expiration, and the riskiness of the stock. We found that option prices have a definitive relationship to these factors, as Table 3.1 summarizes. We explore these price reactions in detail in Chapter 5.

Understanding these factors helps place bounds on call and put prices. However, to determine an exact price, we must specify how the stock price can move. To illustrate the important influence of stock price movements on option prices, we considered a very simple model of stock price movements. For example, we assumed that the stock prices can change 10 percent in the next year. With this assumption, we were able to find exact option prices. However, this assumption about the movement of stock prices is very unrealistic. A year from now, a stock may have a virtually infinite number of prices, not just two. With unrealistic assumptions about stock price movements, the option

Table 3.1	Option Price Response to Changes in Underlying Variables	
For an Increase in	**Call Price**	**Put Price**
Stock Price	Rises	Falls
Exercise Price	Falls	Rises
Time Until Expiration	Rises	Rises or Falls
Interest Rate	Rises	Falls
Stock Risk	Rises	Rises

prices we compute are likely to be unrealistic as well. In the next chapter, we work toward more realistic assumptions about stock price movements and we develop a more exact option pricing model.

QUESTIONS AND PROBLEMS

1. What is the maximum theoretical value for a call? Under what conditions does a call reach this maximum value? Explain.
2. What is the maximum theoretical value for an American put? When does it reach this maximum? Explain.
3. Answer Question 2 for a European put.
4. Explain the difference in the theoretical maximum values for an American and a European put.
5. How does the exercise price affect the price of a call? Explain.
6. Consider two calls with the same time to expiration and written on the same underlying stock. Call 1 trades for $7 and has an exercise price of $100. Call 2 has an exercise price of $95. What is the maximum price that Call 2 can have? Explain.
7. Six months remain until a call option expires. The stock price is $70 and the exercise price is $65. The option price is $5. What does this imply about the interest rate?
8. Assume the interest rate is 12 percent and four months remain until an option expires. The exercise price of the option is $70 and the stock that underlies the option is worth $80. What is the minimum value the option can have based on the no-arbitrage conditions studied in this chapter? Explain.
9. Two call options are written on the same stock that trades for $70 and both calls have an exercise price of $85. Call 1 expires in six months; Call 2 expires in three months. Assume that Call 1 trades for $6 and that Call 2 trades for $7. Do these prices allow arbitrage? Explain. If they do permit arbitrage, explain the arbitrage transactions.
10. Explain the circumstances that make early exercise of a call rational. Under what circumstances is early exercise of a call irrational?
11. Consider a European and American call with the same expiration and the same exercise price that are written on the same stock. What relationship must hold between their prices? Explain.
12. Before exercise, what is the minimum value of an American put?
13. Before exercise, what is the minimum value of a European put?
14. Explain the differences in the minimum values of American and European puts before expiration.
15. How does the price of an American put vary with time until expiration? Explain.
16. What relationship holds between time until expiration and the price of a European put?
17. Consider two puts with six months to expiration. One put has an exercise price of $110, the other has an exercise price of $100. Assume the interest rate is 12 percent. What is the maximum price difference between the two puts if they are European? If they are American? Explain the difference, if any.
18. How does the price of a call vary with interest rates? Explain.
19. Explain how a put price varies with interest rates. Does the relationship vary for European and American puts? Explain.
20. What is the relationship between the risk of the underlying stock and the call price? Explain in intuitive terms.
21. A stock is priced at $50 and the risk-free rate of interest is 10 percent. A European call and a European put on this stock both have exercise prices of $40 and expire in six months. What is

the difference between the call and put prices? (Assume continuous compounding.) From the information supplied in this question, can you say what the call and put prices must be? If not, explain what information is lacking.

22. A stock is priced at $50 and the risk-free rate of interest is 10 percent. A European call and a European put on this stock both have exercise prices of $40 and expire in six months. Assume that the call price exceeds the put price by $7. Does this represent an arbitrage opportunity? If so, explain why and state the transactions you would make to take advantage of the pricing discrepancy.

NOTES

[1] The price of an option depends on these five factors when the underlying stock pays no dividends. As we will discuss in Chapter 5, if the underlying stock pays a dividend, we must consider the dividend as a sixth factor.

[2] As in Chapter 2, the discussion of these rational bounds for option prices relies on a paper by Robert C. Merton, "Theory of Rational Option Pricing," *Bell Journal of Economics and Management Science,* 4, 1973, pp. 141–83.

[3] Scholars have tested market data to determine how well puts and calls meet these boundary conditions. Dan Galai was the first to test these relationships in his paper, "Empirical Tests of Boundary Conditions for CBOE Options," *Journal of Financial Economics,* 6, June/September 1978, pp. 182–211. Galai found some violations of the no-arbitrage conditions in the reported prices. However, these apparent arbitrage opportunities disappeared if a trader faced a 1 percent transaction cost. Mihir Bhattacharya conducted more extensive tests in his paper, "Transaction Data Tests on the Efficiency of the Chicago Board Options Exchange," *Journal of Financial Economics,* 1983, pp. 161–85. Like Galai, Bhattacharya found that a trader facing transaction costs could not exploit apparent arbitrage opportunities. However, both studies found that a very low cost trader, such as a market maker, could have a chance for some arbitrage returns.

[4] As we discuss in Chapter 5, differences between European and American call options require some slight revisions of these rules. In this section, we have said that the difference in the price of two calls cannot exceed the difference in exercise prices. Our arbitrage arguments for this principle assumed immediate exercise before expiration, thus implicitly assuming that the option is American. For a similar pair of European options, the price differential cannot exceed the present value of the difference between the two exercise prices. The arbitrage profit equals the excess difference between the exercise prices. With European options, this excess differential is not available until expiration, when traders can exercise. Therefore, for European options, the arbitrage profit will be the excess difference in the exercise prices discounted to the present.

[5] Assuming that the option is correctly priced at the lower bound implicitly assumes that the stock price has no risk. In other words, we implicitly assume that the stock price will not change before expiration. Making this assumption does not affect the validity of our example because we are focusing on the single effect of a change in interest rates.

[6] The next chapter explains why we need to buy one share of stock and sell two calls in this example. In brief, by combining a bond, a stock, and the right number of calls, we can form a riskless portfolio.

[7] The put-call parity relationship was first addressed by Hans Stoll in "The Relationship Between Put and Call Option Prices," *Journal of Finance,* 24, May 1969, pp. 801–24. Robert C. Merton extended the concept in his paper, "The Relationship Between Put and Call Option Prices: Comment," *Journal of Finance,* 28, pp. 183–4. Robert C. Klemkosky and Bruce G. Resnick tested the put-call parity relationship empirically

with market data. Their two papers are "An Ex-Ante Analysis of Put-Call Parity," *Journal of Financial Economics,* 8, 1980, pp. 363–72, and "Put-Call Parity and Market Efficiency," *Journal of Finance,* 34, 1979, pp. 1141–55. While they find that market prices do not agree perfectly with the put-call parity relationship, the differences are not sufficiently large to generate trading profits after considering all transaction costs.

[8] If the stock earned a riskless rate above the risk-free rate, we would borrow at the risk-free rate and invest in the stock. Later, we could sell the stock, repay our debt, and have a certain return from the difference in the two riskless rates. If the stock earned a riskless rate below the risk-free rate, we would sell the stock and invest the proceeds in the higher rate of the risk-free bond. Therefore, for a given horizon, there is only one risk-free rate.

INTRODUCTION

In Chapter 3 we showed how to compute call and put prices assuming that stock prices behave in a highly simplified manner. Specifically, we assumed that stock prices could rise by a certain percentage or fall by a certain percentage for a single period. After that single period, we assumed that the option expired. Under these unrealistic and highly restrictive assumptions, we found that calls and puts must each have a unique price; any other price leads to arbitrage. In this chapter, we develop similar option pricing models, but we use more realistic models of stock price movement.

To develop a more realistic option pricing model, this chapter first analyzes option pricing under the simple percentage change model of stock price movements. Now, however, we show how to find the unique prices that the no-arbitrage conditions imply. This framework is the **single-period binomial model**. Analyzing the single-period model leads to more realistic models of stock price movements, one of which is the **multi-period binomial model**. By considering several successive models of stock price changes, we come to one of the most elegant models in all of finance – the **Black-Scholes option pricing model**.

Throughout this chapter, we focus on European options. Later, in Chapter 6, we consider American option pricing and the complications arising from the potential for early exercise. At the beginning of this chapter, we focus on stocks with no dividends. Later, we consider the complications that dividends bring in evaluating the prices of European options.

OPTION! provides support for the diverse models that we study in this chapter. With **OPTION!**, we can make virtually all of the computations discussed in this chapter, including the single-period and multi-period binomial model call and put values and Black-Scholes model prices. In each case, using the software can save considerable computational labor.

THE SINGLE-PERIOD BINOMIAL MODEL

In Chapter 3, we considered a stock priced at $100 and assumed that its price would be $90 or $110 in one year. In this example, the risk-free interest rate was 6 percent. We then considered a call and put on this stock, with both options having an exercise price of $100 and expiring in one year. The call was worth $7.55, and the put was worth $1.89. As we showed in Chapter 3, any other option price creates arbitrage opportunities.

Now we want to create a synthetic European call option – a portfolio that has the same value and profits and losses as the call being synthesized. Consider a portfolio comprised of one-half share of stock plus a short position in a risk-free bond that matures in one year and has an initial purchase price of $42.45. In one year, the portfolio's value depends on whether the stock price is $110 or $90. Depending on the stock price, the half-share will be worth $55 or $45. In either event, we will owe $45.00 to repay our bond. If the stock price rises, the portfolio will be worth $10. If the stock price falls, the portfolio will be worth zero. These are exactly the payoffs for the call option. Therefore, the value of the portfolio must be the same as the value of the call option. Figure 4.1 shows values for the stock, the call, the risk-free bond, and the portfolio value at the outset and one year later. The stock price moves to $110 or $90, and the call moves accordingly to $10 or zero. The risk-free bond increases at a 6 percent rate no matter what the stock does, so borrowing $42.45 generates a debt of $45 due in one year. Likewise, our portfolio of one-half share and a $42.45 borrowing will be worth $10 or zero in one year, depending on the stock price. The diagrams in Figure 4.1 are known as binomial "trees" or "lattices."

Because our portfolio and the call option have exactly the same payoffs in all circumstances, they must have the same initial value. Otherwise, there would be an arbitrage opportunity. This means that an investment of one-half share of stock, S_t, and a bond, B_t, of $42.45 must equal the value of the call.

$$c_t = .5S_t - \$42.45 = \$50 - 42.45 = \$7.55$$

Therefore, the call must be worth $7.55, the same conclusion we reached in Chapter 3. This result shows that a combined position in the stock and the risk-free bond can replicate a call option for a one-period horizon.

Figure 4.1   **One-Period Payoffs (in dollars)**

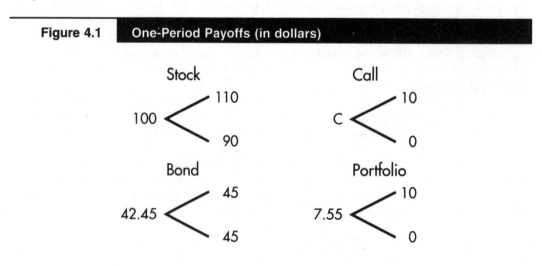

We now show how to find the replicating portfolio made of the stock and the risk-free investment. At the outset, $T - t = 1$, the value of the portfolio, $PORT_t$, depends on the stock price, the number of shares, N, and the price of the bond, B_t.

$$PORT = NS_t - B_t$$

At the end of the horizon, $T - t = 0$, the debt equals the amount borrowed, B_t, plus interest, $B_T = RB_t$. The portfolio's value also depends on the stock price. If the stock price rises, the value of the portfolio will be:

$$PORT_{U,T} = NUS_T - RB_t$$

where:

    $PORT_{U,T}$ = value of the replicating portfolio at time T if the stock price goes up
        $U = 1 +$ percentage of stock price increase
        $R = 1 + r$

Likewise, if the stock price falls, the value of the portfolio will be:

$$PORT_{D,T} = NDS_T - RB_t$$

where:

    $PORT_{D,T}$ = value of the replicating portfolio at time T if the stock price goes down
        $D = 1 -$ percentage of stock price decrease

At expiration, $T - t = 0$, the value of the call also depends on whether the stock price rises or falls. For each circumstance, we represent the call's price as c_U and c_D.

As our example shows, we can choose the number of shares to trade, N, and the amount of funds to borrow, B_t, to replicate the call. Replicating the call means that the portfolio will have the same payoff. Therefore, if the stock price rises:

$$PORT_{U,T} = NUS_T - RB_t = c_U$$

If the stock price falls:

$$PORT_{D,T} = NDS_T - RB_t = c_D$$

After these algebraic manipulations, we have two equations with two unknowns, N and B_t. Solving for the values of the unknowns that satisfy the equations, N^* and B_t^*, we find:

$$N^* = \frac{c_U - c_D}{(U - D)S_t}$$

$$B_t^* = \frac{c_U D - c_D U}{(U - D)R}$$

Therefore,

$$c_t = N*S_t - B_t*$$ (4.1)

This is the **single-period binomial call pricing model**. It holds for a call option expiring in one period when the stock price will rise by a known percentage or fall by a known percentage. The model shows that the value of a call option equals a long position in the stock, plus some borrowing at the risk-free rate. Applying our new notation to our example, we have:

$c_U = \$10$

$c_D = \$0$

$U = 1.1$

$D = .9$

$R = 1.06$

$$B_t* = \frac{c_U D - c_D U}{(U - D)R} = \frac{10(0.9) - 0(1.1)}{(1.1 - 0.9)(1.06)} = \$42.45$$

$$N* = \frac{c_U - c_D}{(U - D)S_t} = \frac{10 - 0}{(1.1 - 0.9)100} = 0.5$$

The Role of Probabilities

In discussing the single-period binomial model, we have not used the concept of probability. For example, we have not considered the likelihood that the stock price will rise or fall. While we have not explicitly used probabilistic concepts, the array of prices does imply a certain probability that the stock price will rise, if we are willing to assume that investors are risk neutral.[1] We assume a risk-neutral economy in this section to show the role of probabilities. The option prices that we compute under the assumption of risk neutrality are the same as those from strict no-arbitrage conditions without any reference to probabilities.

Assuming risk neutrality and given the risk-free interest rate and the up and down percentage movements, we can compute the probability of a stock price increase. Using our definitions of $N*$ and B_t*, the call is worth:

$$c_t = \left(\frac{c_U - c_D}{(U - D)S_t}\right)S_t - \frac{c_U D - c_D U}{(U - D)R}$$

Simplifying, we have:

$$c_t = \frac{c_U - c_D}{U - D} - \frac{c_U D - c_D U}{(U - D)R}$$

Isolating the c_U and c_D terms gives:

$$c_t = \frac{\left(\dfrac{R-D}{U-D}\right)c_U + \left(\dfrac{U-R}{U-D}\right)c_D}{R}$$

In this equation, the call value equals the present value of the future payoffs from owning the call. If the stock price goes up, the call pays C_U at expiration. If the stock goes down, the call pays C_D. The numerator of this equation gives the expected value of the call's payoffs at expiration. Therefore, the probability of a stock price increase is also the probability that the call is worth c_U. The probability of a stock price increase is $(R - D)/(U - D)$, and the probability of a stock price decrease is $(U - R)/(U - D)$.

For our continuing example, we have the following values: $c_U = \$10$, $c_D = \$0$, $U = 1.1$, $D = 0.9$, $R = 1.06$. Therefore, the probability of an increase in the stock price (π_U) is 0.8 and the probability of a decrease (π_D) is 0.2. The value of the call in our single period model is:

$$c_t = \frac{\pi_U c_U + \pi_D c_D}{R} = \frac{.8 \times 10 + .2 \times 0}{1.06} = \$7.55$$

This result shows that the value of a call equals the expected payoff from the call at expiration, discounted to the present at the risk-free rate, assuming a risk-neutral economy.

Summary

Our single-period model is a useful tool. We have seen how to replicate an option by combining a long position in stock with a short position in the risk-free asset. Also, we used the single-period model to show that the value of a call equals the present value of the call's expected payoffs at expiration. Nonetheless, our single-period model suffers from two defects. First, it holds for only a single period. We need to be able to value options that expire after many periods. Second, our assumption about stock price changes is still unrealistic. Obviously, we do not really know how stock prices can change in one period. In fact, if we define one year as a period, we know that stock prices can take almost an infinite number of values by the end of the period. We now proceed to refine our model to consider these objections.

THE MULTI-PERIOD BINOMIAL MODEL

The principles that we developed for the single-period binomial model also apply to a multi-period framework.[2] Here we illustrate the underlying principles by considering a two-period horizon. Over two periods, the stock price must follow one of four patterns. For the two periods, the stock can go: up-up, up-down, down-up, or down-down. Assuming fixed down and up percentages, the up-down and down-up sequences result in the same terminal stock price. For each terminal stock price, a call option has a specific value. Figure 4.2 shows the binomial trees for the stock and call. To clarify the notation, S_{UU} indicates the terminal stock price if the stock price goes up in both periods. C_{UU} is the resulting call price at expiration when the stock price rises in both periods. For the two-period case, the notation π_{UU} indicates the probability of an up-up sequence of price movements, and π_{DD} indicates the probability of a down-down sequence of price movements. We define other patterns accordingly.

Figure 4.2   Two-Period Payoffs

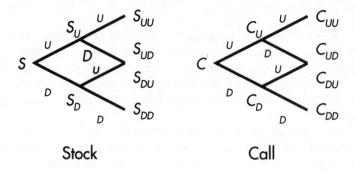

In this equation, the call value equals the expected value of the payoffs at expiration discounted at the risk-free rate.

We can express the value of a call option two periods before expiration as:

$$c_t = \frac{\pi_{UU}C_{UU} + \pi_{UD}C_{UD} + \pi_{DU}C_{DU} + \pi_{DD}C_{DD}}{R^2}$$

In this equation, the call value equals the expected value of the payoffs at expiration discounted at the risk-free rate.

We continue to use our example of a $100 stock that can rise or fall by 10 percent. The probability that the stock price will increase is .8, so this gives a .2 probability of a price drop. Also, the probability of an increase in one period is independent of the probability of an increase in any other period. We now assume that the call is two periods from expiration and that the stock trades for $100. In the first period, the stock can go up or down, giving $US_t = \$110$, $DS_t = \$90$. After the second period, there are four possible patterns with three different stock prices: $UUS_t = \$121$, $DDS_t = \$81$, and $UDS_t = DUS_t = \$99$. The probabilities of these different terminal stock prices are: $\pi_{UU} = (.8)(.8) = .64$, $\pi_{UD} = (.8)(.2) = .16$, $\pi_{DU} = (.2)(.8) = .16$, and $\pi_{DD} = (.2)(.2) = .04$. The call price at expiration equals the terminal stock price minus the exercise price of $100, or zero, whichever is larger. Therefore, we have $C_{UU} = \$21$, $C_{DD} = 0$, $C_{DU} = C_{UD} = 0$.

To determine the call price two periods before expiration, we apply our formula for a call option two periods before expiration. In doing so, we compute the expected value of the call at expiration and discount for two periods:

$$c = \frac{.64(\$21) + .16(0) + .16(0) + .04(0)}{1.06^2} = \frac{\$13.44}{1.06^2} = \$11.96$$

If the call expires in two periods and the stock trades for $100, the call will be worth $11.96. Notice that our sample call pays off at expiration only if the stock price rises twice. Any other pattern of stock price movement in our example gives a call that is worthless at expiration. With one period until expiration and the stock trading at $100, we saw that the call was worth $7.55. With the same initial stock price and two periods until expiration, the call is worth $11.96. This price difference reflects the difference in the present value of the expected payoffs from the call.

In the single-period binomial model, there are two possible stock price outcomes. With two periods until expiration, there are four possible stock price patterns. In general, there are 2^n possible stock price patterns, where n is the number of periods until expiration. Thus, the number of stock and call outcomes increases very rapidly. For example, if the option is 20 periods from expiration, there are more than 1 million stock price outcomes and the same number of call outcomes to consider.[3] It becomes apparent that we need a more general formula for the multi-period binomial pricing model. Also, for options with many periods until expiration, we need a computer. **OPTION!** can compute binomial model call and put values.

We have explored the single-period and two-period binomial model in detail and analyzed examples for each. The principles we developed remain true no matter how many periods we consider. However, the computations become more numerous and cumbersome, as we just saw. Therefore, we now make a mathematical jump to present the formula, which we discuss in intuitive terms.

The Multi-Period Binomial Call Pricing Model

In this section, we introduce the multi-period binomial call pricing model. As Equation 4.2 shows, it is undeniably complex. However, a little study will show that the equation is not really so intimidating.

$$c_t = \frac{\sum_{j=0}^{n} \left(\frac{n!}{j!(n-j)!} \right) [\pi_U{}^j \pi_D{}^{n-j}] \text{MAX}[0, U^j D^{n-j} S_t - X]}{R^n} \qquad (4.2)$$

To understand this formula, we need to break it into simpler elements. From our previous discussion, we know that the formula gives the present value of the expected payoffs from the call at expiration. The denominator R^n is the discount factor raised to n, the number of periods until expiration. The numerator gives the expected payoff on the call option. Thus, we need to focus on the numerator.

With the multiperiod model, we are analyzing an option that expires in n periods. As a feature of the binomial model, we know that the stock price either goes up or down each period. Let us say that it goes up j of the n periods. Then the stock price must fall $n - j$ periods. Our summation runs from $j = 0$ to $j = n$, which includes every possibility. When $j = 0$, we evaluate the possibility that the stock price never rises. When $j = n$, we evaluate the possibility that the stock price rises every period. The summation considers these extreme possibilities and every intermediate possibility.

For any random number of stock price increases, j, the numerator expresses three things about the call for the j stock price increases among the n periods. First, starting from the right, the numerator gives the payoff on the option if the stock price rises j times. This is our familiar expression beginning with MAX. The value of the call at expiration is either zero or the stock price minus the exercise price, whichever is greater. The expression $U^j D^{n-j} S_t$ gives the stock price at expiration if the stock price rises j periods and falls the other $n - j$ periods. Second, the numerator expresses the probability of exactly j stock price increases and $n - j$ stock price decreases. Earlier, we saw how to find the probability of up and down movements. Therefore, $\pi_U{}^j \pi_D{}^{n-j}$ gives the probability of observing j up movements and $n - j$ down movements. Third, more than one sequence of stock price movements can result in the same terminal stock price. For instance, in the two-period model we saw that UDS_t

gave the same terminal stock price as DUS_t. The numerator also computes the number of different combinations of stock price movements that result in the same terminal stock price. The expression:

$$\frac{n!}{j!(n-j)!}$$

computes the number of possible combinations of j rises from n periods. In essence, the combination weights the possibility of exactly n rises and $n - j$ falls by the number of different patterns that result in exactly j rises and $n - j$ falls. For example, only one pattern results in n rises – the stock must rise in every period. By contrast, if $j = n - j$, there will usually be many patterns that can give j rises and $n - j$ falls.

In the expression for the combination, $n!$ is call n-factorial. Its value equals n multiplied by $n - 1$ times $n - 2$ and so on down to 1:

$$n! = n(n-1)(n-2)(n-3) \ldots \quad (1)$$

To illustrate, if $n = 5$, then $5! = 5(4)(3)(2)(1) = 120$. For example, with the two-period model we could have the pattern up-down or down-up resulting in the same stock price. Thus, there are two combinations of one increase over two periods. The increase could be first or second. For any j value, the numerator in Equation 4.2 computes the number of combinations of j increases from n periods, times the probability of having exactly j increases times the payoff on the call if there are j increases. The summation ensures that the numerator reflects all possible j values.

In our two-period example, the option pays off at expiration only if the stock price rises both times. In general, many stock price patterns leave the option out-of-the-money at expiration. For valuing the option, stock price patterns that leave the option out-of-the-money are a dead end because they result in a zero option price. As a consequence, we do not need to evaluate fully stock price patterns that leave the option out-of-the-money at expiration. Instead, we need to evaluate only those values of j for which the option expires in-the-money. In our two-period example, we do not need to compute the entire formula for $j = 0$ and $j = 1$. If the stock price never goes up or goes up only once, the option expires out-of-the-money. For our two-period example, we need to consider only what happens to the option when the stock price rises twice, that is, when $j = 2$. Only then does the option finish in-the-money. Let us define m as the number of times the stock price must rise for the option to finish in-the-money. Thus, when the stock price rises exactly m times, it must fall $n - m$ times. However, this pattern still leaves the option in-the-money because the stock price rose the needed m times. Then we need consider only values of $j = m$ to $j = n$. In our two-period example, $m = 2$ because the stock price must rise in both periods for the option to finish in-the-money. Therefore, the following formula gives an alternative expression for the value of an option:

$$c_t = \frac{\sum_{j=m}^{n} \left(\frac{n!}{j!(n-j)!}\right)(\pi_U^j \pi_D^{n-j})[U^j D^{n-j} S_t - X]}{R^n} \quad (4.3)$$

Notice that the summation begins with m, the minimum number of stock price increases needed to bring the option in-the-money. Because we consider only the events that put the option in-the-money, we no longer need to worry about the call being worth the maximum of zero or the stock price less the exercise price at expiration. With at least m stock price rises, the option will be worth more than zero because it necessarily finishes in-the-money. Now we divide the formula into two parts – one associated with the stock price and the other associated with the exercise price.

$$c_t = S_t \left[\sum_{j=m}^{n} \left(\frac{n!}{j!(n-j)!} \right) (\pi_U^{\,j} \pi_D^{\,n-j}) \frac{U^j D^{n-j}}{R^n} \right] - XR^{-n} \left[\sum_{j=m}^{n} \left(\frac{n!}{j!(n-j)!} \right) \pi_U^{\,j} \pi_D^{\,n-j} \right] \qquad (4.4)$$

This version of the binomial formula starts to resemble our familiar expression for the value of the call as the stock price minus the present value of the exercise price. If the option is in-the-money and the stock price is certain to remain unchanged until expiration, the call price equals the stock price minus the present value of the exercise price. Our formula has exactly that structure except for the two complicated expressions in brackets. These two expressions reflect the riskiness of the stock. This uncertainty or riskiness about the stock gives the added value to the call above the stock price minus the present value of the exercise price.

The multi-period binomial model can reflect numerous stock price outcomes, if there are numerous periods. In our examples, we kept the period length the same and added more periods. This lengthened the total time until expiration. As an alternative, we could keep the same time to expiration and consider more periods of shorter duration. For example, we originally treated a year as a single period. For that year, we could regard each trading day as a period, giving about 250 periods per year. We could evaluate an option with the multi-period model by assuming that the stock price could change once a day.

The binomial model requires that the price move up or down a given percentage. Therefore, if we shorten the period, we need to adjust the stock price movements to correspond to the shorter period. While up or down 10 percent might be reasonable for a period of one year, it would not be reasonable for a period of one day. Similarly, a risk-free rate of 6 percent makes sense for a period of one year but not for a period of one day.

By adjusting the period length, the stock price movement, and the interest rate, we can refine the binomial model as much as we wish. For example, we could assume that the stock price could move one-hundredth of a percent every minute of the year if we wished. Under this assumption, the model would have finer partitions than exist in the market for most stock. However, with the price changing every minute and a time to expiration of one year, we would have trillions of possible stock price outcomes to consider. While having so many periods would be computationally expensive, we could apply the model if we wished. Conceptually, we could make each period so short that the stock price would change continuously. However, if the stock price truly changed continuously, there would be an infinite number of periods to consider. While we cannot compute binomial model values for an infinite number of periods, mathematical techniques do exist to compute option prices when stock prices change continuously.

BINOMIAL PUT OPTION PRICING

In discussing binomial option pricing, we have used call options as an example. To value put options, we follow the same reasoning process that we have considered in detail for call options. Rather than detail all of the reasoning leading to the formula, we begin with the formula for the price of a European put option.

$$p_t = \frac{\sum_{j=0}^{n}\left(\frac{n!}{j!(n-j)!}\right)(\pi_U^j\pi_D^{n-j})\,\mathrm{MAX}[0, X - U^jD^{n-j}S_t]}{R^n} \tag{4.5}$$

This formula matches our binomial call formula, except we substitute the expression for the value of a put at expiration, $X - U^jD^{n-j}S_t$, in place of the value of a call at expiration.

In pricing the call option, we considered only stock price patterns that left the call in-the-money at expiration. The same is true for the put. The put finishes in-the-money if the stock price does not increase often enough to make the stock price exceed the exercise price. We defined m as the number of price increases needed to bring the call into the money. If the price increases $m - 1$ or fewer times, the put finishes in-the-money. Therefore, we can also write the formula for the put as follows:

$$p_t = \frac{\sum_{j=0}^{m-1}\left(\frac{n!}{j!(n-j)!}\right)(\pi_U^j\pi_D^{n-j})[X - U^jD^{n-j}S_t]}{R^n} \tag{4.6}$$

Rearranging terms gives:

$$P_t = XR^{-n}\left(\sum_{j=0}^{m-1}\left(\frac{n!}{j!(n-j)!}\right)(\pi_U^j\pi_D^{n-j})\right) - S_t\left(\sum_{j=0}^{m-1}\left(\frac{n!}{j!(n-j)!}\right)(\pi_U^j\pi_D^{n-j})\frac{U^jD^{n-j}}{R^n}\right) \tag{4.7}$$

This formula for the put parallels our familiar expression for the put as equaling the present value of the exercise price minus the stock price. As with the call, the two bracketed expressions account for the risky movement of the stock price.

We can also value the put through put-call parity. We have the value of the call under the binomial model as given above. Put-call parity tells us that:

$$p_t = c_t - S_t + Xe^{-r(T-t)}$$

Both approaches must necessarily give the same answer.

STOCK PRICE MOVEMENTS

In actual markets, stock prices change to reflect new information. During a single day, a stock price may change many times. From the ticker, we can observe stock prices when transactions occur. When trading ceases overnight, however, we cannot observe the stock price for hours at a time. Where the price wanders during the night, no one can know. Our observations are also limited because stock prices are quoted in eighths of a dollar. The true stock price need not jump from one eighth to the next, but the observed stock price does. Sometimes the observed price remains the same from one transaction to another. But just because we observe the same price twice in succession does not mean it remained at that price between the two observations. We can never know exactly how stock prices change because we cannot observe the true stock price at every instant. Therefore, any model of stock price behavior deviates from an exact description of how stock prices move. Nonetheless, it is possible to develop a realistic model of stock price movements. In this section, we review a model that has been successful in a wide range of finance applications.

Let us consider the random information that affects the price of a stock. We assume that the information arrives continuously and that each bit of information is small in importance. Under this scenario, we consider a stock price that rises or falls a small proportion in response to each bit of information. We know that finance depends conceptually on the twin ideas of expected return and risk. Thus, we might also think of a stock as having a positive expected rate of return. In the absence of special events, we expect the stock price to grow along the path of its expected rate of return. However, the world is risky. Information about the stock is sometimes favorable and sometimes unfavorable. As this random information becomes known, it pushes the stock away from its expected growth path. When the information is better than expected, the stock price jumps above its growth path. Negative information has the opposite effect; it pushes the stock price below its expected growth path.

Finance uses a standard mathematical model that assumes that the stock grows at an expected rate μ with a standard deviation σ over some period of time Δt:

$$\Delta S = S_{t+1} - S = S_t \mu \Delta t + S_t N(0,1) \sigma \sqrt{\Delta t} \qquad (4.8)$$

where:

S_t = the stock price at the beginning of the interval
ΔS = the stock price change during time Δt
$S_t \mu \Delta t$ = expected value of the stock price change during time Δt
$N(0,1)$ = normally distributed random variable with $\mu = 0$, $\sigma = 1$
σ = standard deviation of the stock price

Equation 4.8 says that the stock price change during Δt depends on two factors: the expected growth rate in the price and the variability of the growth. First, the expected growth in the stock price over a given interval depends on the mean growth rate, μ, and the amount of time, Δt. Therefore, if the stock price starts at S_t, the expected stock price increase after an interval of Δt equals $S_t \mu \Delta t$. However, this is only the expected stock price increase after the interval. Due to risk, the actual price change can be greater or lower. Deviations from the expected stock price depend on chance and on the volatility of the stock. The equation captures risk by using the normal distribution. For convenience, the model uses the standard normal distribution, which has a zero mean and a standard deviation of 1. The standard deviation represents the variability of a particular stock. We multiply the standard deviation of the stock by a random drawing from the normal distribution to capture the riskiness of the stock. Also, the equation says that the variability increases with the square root of the interval Δt. In other words, the farther into the future we project the stock price with our model, the less certain we can be about what the stock price will be.

Dividing both sides of Equation 4.8 by the original stock price, S_t, gives the percentage change in the stock price during Δt:

$$\frac{\Delta S}{S_t} = \mu \Delta t + N(0,1) \sigma \sqrt{\Delta t}$$

From this equation, it is possible to show that the percentage change in the stock price is normally distributed:

$$\frac{\Delta S}{S_t} \sim N[\mu\Delta t, \; \sigma\sqrt{\Delta t}] \tag{4.9}$$

Figure 4.3 shows two stock price paths over the course of a year, with both stock prices starting at \$100. The straight line graphs a stock that grows at 10 percent per year with no risk. The jagged line shows a stock price path with an expected growth rate of 10 percent and a standard deviation of .2 per year. We generated the second price path by taking repeated random samples from a normal distribution to create price changes according to Equation 4.8. As the jagged line in Figure 4.3 shows, a stock might easily wander away from its growth path due to the riskiness represented by its standard deviation.

To construct Figure 4.3, we used 1,000 periods per year and a growth rate of 10 percent. To construct the straight line, we assumed that the stock price increased by .1/1000 each period. However, this gives an ending stock price of \$110.51, not the \$110 we expect if the stock price grows at 10 percent per year. This difference results from using 1,000 compounding intervals during the year.

However, we hypothesize that information arrives continuously, so that the stock price could always change. To avoid worrying about the compounding interval, we now employ continuous compounding. Therefore, we focus on logarithmic stock returns. For example, consider a beginning

Figure 4.3   Two Stock Price Paths

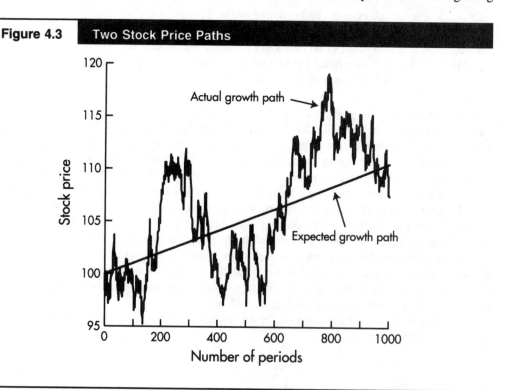

stock price of $100 and an ending price of $110 a year later. The logarithmic stock return over the year is $\ln(S_t/S_0) = \ln(\$110/\$100) = \ln(1.1) = .0953$. The logarithmic stock return is just the continuous growth rate that takes the stock price from its original value to its ending value. Thus, $\$100e^{ut} = \$100e^{.0953(1)} = \$110$. We now need a continuous growth model of stock prices consistent with our model for the percentage change stock price model of Equation 4.9. With some difficult math, it is possible to prove the following result:

$$\ln\left(\frac{S_{t+\Delta t}}{S_t}\right) \sim N[(\mu - .5\sigma^2)(\Delta t), \sigma\sqrt{\Delta t}] \tag{4.10}$$

This expression asserts that logarithmic stock returns are distributed normally with the given mean and standard deviation. For a later time, $t + \Delta t$, the expected stock price and the variance of the stock price are:

$$E(S_{t+\Delta t}) = S_t e^{\mu\Delta t}$$

$$VAR(S_{t+\Delta t}) = S_t^2 e^{2\mu\Delta t}(e^{\sigma^2\Delta t}-1)$$

Thus, the expected stock price at $t + \Delta t$ depends on the original stock price, S_t, the expected growth rate, μ, and the amount of time that elapses, Δt. Similarly, the variance of the stock price depends on the original stock price, the expected growth rate, and the elapsed time as well. The longer the time horizon, the larger the variance will be. The increasing variance reflects our greater uncertainty about stock prices far in the future.

As an example, consider a stock with an initial price of $100 and an expected growth rate of 10 percent. If the stock has a standard deviation of .2 per year, we can compute the expected stock price and variance for six months into the future. For this example, we have the following values:

$$S_t = \$100$$
$$\mu = .1$$
$$\sigma = .2$$
$$\Delta t = .5$$
$$E(S_{t+\Delta t}) = \$100e^{.1(.5)} = \$105.13$$
$$VAR(S_{t+\Delta t}) = (\$100)(\$100)(e^{2(.1)(.5)})(e^{(.2)(.2)(.5)} - 1) = \$223.26$$

The standard deviation of the price over period Δt is $14.94. Figure 4.4 shows stock price realizations that are consistent with this example. We found these prices by drawing random values from a normal distribution and using our example growth rate and standard deviation. Each dot in the figure represents a possible stock price realization. Notice that the price tends to drift higher over time, consistent with a rising expected value. This is shown by the regression line that is fitted through the points. However, there is considerable uncertainty about what the price will be at any future date. The farther we go into the future, the greater that uncertainty becomes.

Research on actual stock price behavior shows that logarithmic stock returns are approximately normally distributed. So we say that, as an approximation, stock returns follow a **log-normal distribution**. Stock returns themselves are not normally distributed. As an example, Figure 4.5 shows a distribution of stock returns with a mean of 1.2 and a standard deviation of .6. It is easy to see that

Figure 4.4   Possible Stock Prices

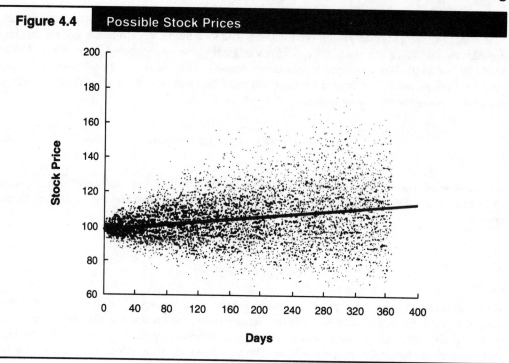

Figure 4.5   A Log-Normal Distribution

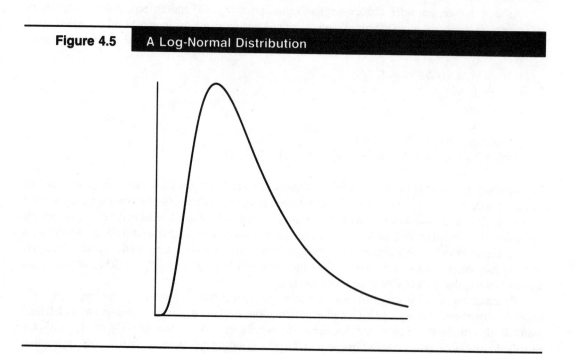

this distribution is not normal because it is skewed to the right. There is a greater chance of larger returns than one would expect with a normal distribution. Figure 4.6 shows the log-normal distribution that corresponds to the values in Figure 4.5. The values graphed in Figure 4.6 are the logarithms of the values used to construct Figure 4.5. The graph in Figure 4.6 shows a normal distribution. We will assume that stock returns are distributed as Figure 4.6 shows, except the mean and standard deviation differ from stock to stock.

While the log-normal distribution only approximates stock returns, it has two great virtues. First, it is mathematically tractable, so we can obtain solutions for the value of call options if stock returns are log-normally distributed. Second, the call option prices that we compute are very good approximations of actual market prices. In the remainder of this chapter, we treat stock returns as log-normally distributed with a specified mean and variance.

THE BINOMIAL APPROACH TO THE BLACK-SCHOLES MODEL

We have seen how to generalize the binomial model to any number of periods. Increasing the number of periods allows for many possible stock price outcomes at expiration, thereby increasing the realism of the results. However, three problems remain. First, as the number of periods increases, computational difficulties begin to arise. Second, increasing the number of periods while holding the time until expiration constant means that the period length becomes shorter. We must adjust the up and down movement factors, U and D, and the risk-free rate to fit the time horizon. Obviously, we cannot use factors with a scale appropriate to a year when the period length is, say, one day. Third, we have worked with more or less arbitrarily selected up and down factors. The price that the model gives can be only as good as its inputs. The example inputs we have been considering serve well as

The Normal Distribution　　　**Figure 4.6**

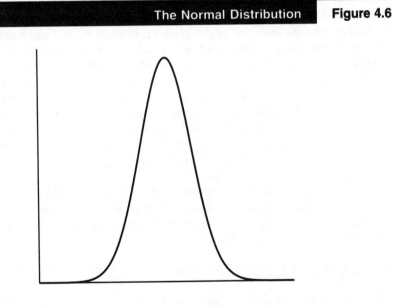

illustrations, but they are not appropriate for analyzing real options. Therefore, we need a better way to determine the up and down factors.

Modeling stock returns by a log-normal process solves these three problems simultaneously. If stock returns are log-normally distributed with the mean return given by μ and a standard deviation of σ for some unit of calendar time Δt, then we define the following binomial inputs as:

$$U = e^{\sigma\sqrt{\Delta t}}$$

$$D = \frac{1}{U}$$

(4.11)

$$\pi_u = \frac{e^{\mu\Delta t} - D}{U - D}$$

As the entire analysis takes place within a risk-neutral framework μ, the expected return on the stock must equal the risk-free rate. Therefore, the probability of an upward stock price movement becomes:

$$\pi_u = \frac{e^{r\Delta t} - D}{U - D}$$

(4.12)

Notice that the values of R, U, and D adjust automatically as the tree is adjusted to include more and more periods during the fixed calendar interval $T - t$. The absolute value of each becomes smaller, exactly as we would expect for a shorter time period. The values for U and D depend on the riskiness of the stock returns. The probability of a stock price increase depends upon the mean return on the stock. Thus, if we can estimate the standard deviation of stock returns, we have reasonable inputs to the binomial model. These can replace the arbitrary example values that we have been using.[4]

To illustrate how the binomial model gives increasingly refined estimates as the number of periods increases, consider a European call option that has one year until expiration and an exercise price of $100. Assume that the underlying stock trades for $100, with a standard deviation of 0.10. The risk-free rate of interest is 6 percent. Figure 4.7 shows how the binomial prices converge to the true option price of $7.46 as the number of periods increases. The binomial prices oscillate around the true price: for a single-period binomial model, the price is $7.76. With two periods, the binomial model gives a price of $6.96. With 20 periods, the binomial price is $7.40, and with 100 periods, the binomial price is $7.45. In general, the greater the number of periods in the lattice, the more accurate the computed binomial price. **OPTION!** can compute call and put prices for the single-period and multi-period binomial models.

As we show in the next section, using the model of stock returns discussed in this section allows us to compute the value of an option with an infinite number of periods until expiration. With the strict binomial model, we could never employ an infinite number of periods because it would take forever to add all the individual results.

THE BLACK-SCHOLES OPTION PRICING MODEL

To this point, we have developed the binomial option pricing model. We have discussed the log-normal distribution of stock returns and have presented up and down factors for the binomial model

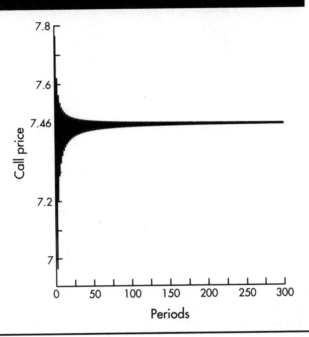

Figure 4.7

Convergence of Binomial Prices as the Number of Periods Increases

that are consistent with the log-normal distribution of stock returns. Also, we have seen how to adjust the precision of the binomial model by dividing a given unit of calendar time into more and more periods. As we deal with more periods, however, the calculations in the binomial model become cumbersome. As the number of periods in the binomial model becomes very large, the binomial model converges to the famous Black-Scholes option pricing model.

Fischer Black and Myron Scholes developed their option pricing model under the assumptions that asset prices adjust to prevent arbitrage, that stock prices change continuously, and that stock returns follow a log-normal distribution.[5] Their model also holds for European call options on stocks with no dividends. Further, they assume that the interest rate and the volatility of the stock remain constant over the life of the option. The mathematics they used to derive their result include stochastic calculus, which is beyond the scope of this text. In this section, we present their model and illustrate the basic intuition that underlies it. We show that the form of the Black-Scholes model parallels the bounds on option pricing that we have already observed. In fact, the form of the Black-Scholes model is very close to the binomial model.

The Black-Scholes Call Option Pricing Model

The following expression gives the Black-Scholes option pricing model for a call option:

$$c_t = S_t N(d_1) - X e^{-r(T-t)} N(d_2) \qquad (4.13)$$

where:

$$N(\cdot) = \text{cumulative normal distribution function}$$

$$d_1 = \frac{\ln\left(\frac{S_t}{X}\right) + (r + .5\sigma^2)(T - t)}{\sigma\sqrt{T - t}} \tag{4.14}$$

$$d_2 = d_1 - \sigma\sqrt{T - t}$$

This model has the general form we have long considered – the value of a call must equal or exceed the stock price minus the present value of the exercise price:

$$c_t \geq S_t - Xe^{-r(T-t)}$$

To adapt this formula to account for risk, as in the Black-Scholes model, we multiply the stock price and the exercise price by some factors to account for risk, giving the general form:

$$c_t = S_t \times \text{Risk Factor 1} - Xe^{-r(T-t)} \times \text{Risk Factor 2}$$

The binomial model shares this general form with the Black-Scholes model. With the binomial model, the risk adjustment factors were the large bracketed expressions of Equation 4.2. With the Black-Scholes model, the risk factors are $N(d_1)$ and $N(d_2)$. In the Black-Scholes model, these risk adjustment factors are the continuous time equivalent of the bracketed expressions in the binomial model.

Computing Black-Scholes Option Prices

In this section, we show how to compute Black-Scholes option prices. Assume that a stock trades at $100 and the risk-free interest rate is 6 percent. A call option on the stock has an exercise price of $100 and expires in one year. The standard deviation of the stock's returns is .10 per year. We compute the values of d_1 and d_2 as follows:

$$d_1 = \frac{\ln\left(\frac{100}{100}\right) + [0.06 + 0.5(0.01)]1}{0.1\sqrt{1}} = 0.65$$

$$d_2 = 0.65 - 0.1(1) = 0.55$$

Next, we find the cumulative normal values associated with d_1 and d_2. These values are the probability that a normally distributed variable with a zero mean and a standard deviation of 1.0 will have a value equal to or less than the d_1 or d_2 term we are considering. Figure 4.8 shows a graph of a normally distributed variable with a zero mean and a standard deviation of 1.0. It shows the values of d_1 and d_2 for our example. For illustration, we focus on d_1, which equals .65. In finding $N(d_1)$, we want to know which portion of the area under the curve lies to the left of .65. This is the value of $N(d_1)$. Clearly, the value we seek is larger than .5, because d_1 is above the mean of zero. We can find

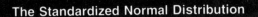

The Standardized Normal Distribution **Figure 4.8**

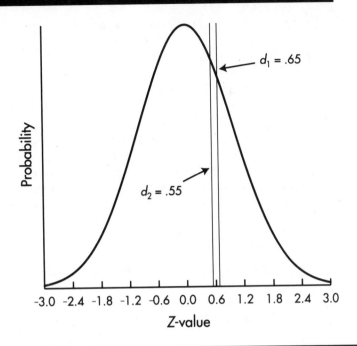

the exact value by consulting a table of the cumulative normal distribution for this variable. We present this table as Appendix A. Also, we can use **OPTION!** to find these values. For a value of .65 drawn from the border of the table, we find our probability in the interior: $N(.65) = .7422$. Similarly, $N(d_2) = N(.55) = .7088$. We now have:

$$c_t = \$100 \times .7422 - \$100 \times .9418 \times .7088 = \$7.46$$

We chose these values for our example because they parallel the values from our original binomial example. There we also assumed that the stock traded for $100 and that the risk-free rate was 6 percent. We assumed an up factor of 10 percent and a down factor of −10 percent. With a single-period binomial model and these values, we found that a call must be priced at $7.55. The two results are close. However, if we use more periods in the Binomial Model and use up and down factors that are consistent with a log-normal distribution of stock returns, the Binomial Model will converge to the Black-Scholes model price. The reader can explore this possibility by using **OPTION!**.

The Black-Scholes Put Option Pricing Model

Black and Scholes developed their option pricing model for calls only. However, we can find the Black-Scholes model for European puts by applying put-call parity:

$$p_t = c_t - S_t + Xe^{-r(T-t)}$$

Substituting the Black-Scholes call formula in the put-call parity equation gives:

$$p_t = S_t N(d_1) - Xe^{-r(T-t)}N(d_2) - S_t + Xe^{-r(T-t)}$$

Collecting like terms simplifies the equation to:

$$p_t = S_t[N(d_1) - 1] + Xe^{-r(T-t)}[1 - N(d_2)]$$

If we consider the cumulative distribution of all values from $-\infty$ to $+\infty$, the maximum value is 1.0. For any value of d_1 we consider, part of the whole must lie at or below the value and the remainder must lie above it. For example, if $N(d_1)$ is .7422, for $d_1 = .65$, then .2578 of the total area under the curve must lie at values greater than .65. Now we apply a principle of normal distributions. The normal distribution is symmetrical, so the same percentage of the area under the curve that lies above d_1 must lie below $-d_1$. Therefore, for any symmetrical distribution and any arbitrary value, w:

$$N(w) + N(-w) = 1$$

Following this pattern and substituting for $N(d_1)$ and $N(d_2)$ gives the equivalent Black-Scholes value for a put option.

$$p_t = Xe^{-r(T-t)}N(-d_2) - S_t N(-d_1) \tag{4.15}$$

This equation has the familiar form that we have been exploring since Chapter 2. We emphasize that the Black-Scholes model for puts holds only for European puts.

INPUTS FOR THE BLACK-SCHOLES MODEL

We have seen that the Black-Scholes model for the price of an option depends on five variables: the stock price, the exercise price, the time until expiration, the risk-free rate, and the standard deviation of the stock. Of these, the stock price is observable in the financial press or on a trading terminal. The exercise price and the time until expiration can be known with certainty. We want to consider how to obtain estimates of the other two parameters; the risk-free interest rate and the standard deviation of the stock.

Estimating the Risk-Free Rate of Interest

Estimates of the risk-free interest rate are widely available and are usually quite reliable.[6] There are still a few points to consider, however. First, we need to select the correct rate. Because the Black-Scholes model uses a risk-free rate, we can use the Treasury bill rate as a good estimate. Quoted interest rates for T-bills are expressed as discount rates. We need to convert these to regular interest rates and express them as continuously compounded rates. As a second consideration, we should select the maturity of the T-bill carefully. If the yield curve has a steep slope, yields for different maturities can differ significantly. With T-bills maturing each week, we choose the bill that matures closest to the option expiration.

We illustrate the computation with the following example. Consider a T-bill with 84 days until maturity. Its bid yield is 8.83 and its asking yield is 8.77. Letting BID and ASK be the bid and asked yields, the following formula gives the price of a T-bill as a percentage of its face value:

$$P_{TB} = 1 - .01\left(\frac{BID + ASK}{2}\right)\left(\frac{\text{Days Until Maturity}}{360}\right)$$

$$= 1 - .01\left(\frac{8.83 + 8.77}{2}\right)\left(\frac{84}{360}\right)$$

$$= .97947$$

In this formula, we average the bid and asked yields to estimate the unobservable true yield, which lies between the observable bid and asked yields. For our example, the price of the T-bill is 97.947 percent of its face value. To find the corresponding continuously compounded rate, we solve the following equation for r:

$$e^{r(T-t)} = \frac{1}{P_{TB}}$$

$$e^{r(.23)} = 1/.97947$$

$$.23r = \ln(1.02096) = .0207$$

$$r = .0902$$

In the equation, $T - t = .23$ because 84 days is 23 percent of a year. Thus, the appropriate interest rate in this example is 9.02 percent. Securing good estimates of the risk-free interest rate is fairly easy. However, having an exact estimate is not critical, as option prices are not very sensitive to the interest rate.

Estimating the Stock's Standard Deviation

Estimating the standard deviation of the stock's returns is more difficult and more important than estimating the risk-free rate. The Black-Scholes model takes as its input the current, instantaneous standard deviation of the stock. In other words, the immediate volatility of the stock is the riskiness of the stock that affects the option price. The Black-Scholes model also assumes that the volatility is constant over the life of the option.[7] There are two basic ways to estimate the volatility. The first method uses historical data, while the second technique employs fresh data from the options market itself. This second method uses option prices to find the option market's estimate of the stock's standard deviation. An estimate of the stock's standard deviation that is drawn from the options market is called an **implied volatility**. We consider each method in turn.[8]

Historical Data. To estimate volatility using historical data, we compute the price relatives, logarithmic price relatives, and the mean and standard deviation of the logarithmic price relatives. Letting PR_t indicate the price relative for day t so that $PR_t = P_t/P_{t-1}$, we give the formulas for the mean and variance of the logarithmic price relatives as follows:

$$\overline{PR} = \frac{1}{T}\sum_{t=1}^{T} \ln PR_t$$

$$VAR(PR) = \frac{1}{T-1}\sum_{t=1}^{T}(\ln PR_t - \overline{PR})^2$$

As an example, we apply these formulas to data in the following table, which gives 11 days of price information for a stock. With 11 price observations, we compute ten daily returns. The first column tracks the day; the second column records the stock's closing price for the day. The third column computes the price relative from the prices in column 2. The fourth column gives the log of the price relative in column 3. The last column contains the result of subtracting the mean of the logarithmic price relatives from each observation and squaring the result.

Day	P_t	PR_t	$\ln(PR_t)$	$[\ln PR_t - PR^\mu]^2$
0	100.00			
1	101.50	1.0150	0.0149	0.000154
2	98.00	0.9655	−0.0351	0.001410
3	96.75	0.9872	−0.0128	0.000234
4	100.50	1.0388	0.0380	0.001264
5	101.00	1.0050	0.0050	0.000006
6	103.25	1.0223	0.0220	0.000382
7	105.00	1.0169	0.0168	0.000205
8	102.75	0.9786	−0.0217	0.000582
9	103.00	1.0024	0.0024	0.000000
10	102.50	0.9951	−0.0049	0.000053
		Sums	.0247	0.004294

Sample μ = .0247/10 = .00247
Sample σ^2 = .004294/9 = .000477
Sample σ = .021843

The mean, variance, and standard deviation that we have calculated are all based on our sample of daily data. We use the sample standard deviation as an input to the Black-Scholes model.

Three inputs to the Black-Scholes model depend on the unit of time. These inputs are the interest rate, the time until expiration, and the standard deviation. We can use any single measure we wish, but we need to express all three variables in the same time units. For example, we can use days as our time unit and express the time until expiration as the number of days remaining. Then we must also use a daily estimation of the standard deviation and the interest rate for a single day. Generally, one year is the most convenient common unit of time. Therefore, we need to convert our daily standard deviation into a comparable yearly estimate. We have estimated our daily standard deviation of ten days. However, these are ten trading days, not calendar days. Accordingly, we recognize that we are working in trading time, not calendar time. Deleting weekend days and holidays, each year has about 250–252 trading days. We use 250 trading days per year.

We have already seen that stock prices are distributed with a standard deviation that increases as the square root of time. Accordingly, we can adjust the time dimension of our volatility estimate by multiplying it by the square root of time. For example, we convert from our daily standard deviation estimate to an equivalent yearly value by multiplying the daily estimate times the square root of 250.[9]

$$\text{Annualized } \sigma = \text{Daily } \sigma \times \sqrt{250} \qquad (4.16)$$

For our daily estimate of .021843, the estimated standard deviation in annual terms is .3454.

In our example, we have used ten days of data. In actual practice, we face a trade-off between using the most recent possible data and using more data. In statistics, we almost always get more reliable estimates by using more data. However, the Black-Scholes model takes the instantaneous standard deviation as an input. This gives great importance to using current data. If we use the last year of historical data, then we have a rich data set for estimating the old volatility. Using just ten days, as we did in our example, emphasizes current data, but it is really not very much data for getting a reliable estimate.

To emphasize the importance of using current data, consider the Crash of 1987. On Bloody Monday, October 19, 1987, the market lost about 22 percent of its value. If we used a full year of daily data to estimate a stock's historical volatility the next day, our estimate would be too low. In the light of the Crash, the instantaneous volatility had surely increased.

Implied Volatility. To overcome the limitations inherent in using historical data to estimate standard deviations, some scholars have turned to techniques of implied volatility. In this section, we show how to use market data and the Black-Scholes model to estimate a stock's volatility. There are five inputs to the Black-Scholes model, which the model relates to a sixth variable, the call price. With a total of six variables, any five imply a unique value for the sixth. The technique of implied volatility uses known values of five variables to estimate the standard deviation. The estimated standard deviation is an implied volatility because it is the value implied by the other five variables in the model.[10]

To find implied volatilities, we begin with established values for the stock price, exercise price, interest rate, time until expiration, and the call price. We use these to find the implied standard deviation. However, the standard deviation enters the Black-Scholes model through the values for d_1 and d_2, which are used to determine the values of the cumulative normal distribution. As a result, we cannot solve for the standard deviation directly. Instead, we must search for the volatility that makes the Black-Scholes equation hold. To do this, we need a computer. Otherwise, we would have to try an estimate of the standard deviation, make all of the Black-Scholes computations by hand, and adjust the standard deviation for the next try. This would be cumbersome and time-consuming. Therefore, implied volatilities are almost always found using a computer. **OPTION!** has a module for finding implied volatilities.

For most stocks with options, several options with different expirations trade at once. Some researchers have argued that all of these options should be used to find the volatility implied by each. The resulting estimates are then given weights and averaged to find a single volatility estimate. The single estimate is known as a **weighted implied standard deviation**. In principle, this is a good idea because it uses more information. Some options trade infrequently, which makes their prices less reliable for computing implied volatilities. In addition, options way out-of-the-money give somewhat spurious volatility estimates. Virtually all weighting schemes give the highest weight to options closest to-the-money. At-the-money options tend to give the least biased volatility estimates, and many option traders derive implied volatilities by focusing on at-the-money options.[11]

Consider the following example of an implied standard deviation based on a call option. We assume that $X = \$100$ and the option is at-the-money, so $S = \$100$. We also assume that the option has 90 days remaining until expiration and that the risk-free interest rate is 10 percent, so we have $T - t = 90$ days and $r = .10$. The call price is \$5.00. To find the implied standard deviation, we need to find the standard deviation that is consistent with these other values. To do this, we can compute the Black-Scholes model price for alternative standard deviations. We adjust the standard deviation to make the option price converge to its actual price of \$5.00. The sequence of standard deviations and call prices below shows this relationship. In our example, we first try $\sigma = .1$, which gives a call price of \$3.41. This price is too low. Thus, we know the correct standard deviation must be larger because the call price varies directly with the standard deviation. Next, $\sigma = .5$ results in a call price of \$11.03, which is too high. Now we know that the standard deviation must be greater than .1, but less than .5. The task is to find the standard deviation that gives a call value equal to the specified \$5.00. This happens with $\sigma = .187$. Using the implied volatility module of **OPTION!**, we find that the exact standard deviation is .186800.[12]

Standard Deviation	Corresponding Call Price	
.1	\$ 3.41	too low
.5	11.03	too high
.3	7.16	too high
.2	5.24	too high
.15	4.31	too low
.175	4.78	too low
.18	4.87	too low
.185	4.97	too low
.19	5.06	too high
.188	5.02	too high
.187	5.00	success

EUROPEAN OPTIONS AND DIVIDENDS

Most of the stocks that underlie stock options pay dividends. Yet the Black-Scholes model assumes that the underlying stock pays no dividends. While the Black-Scholes model might be elegant and provide a great deal of insight into option pricing, successful real-world application of the model depends upon resolving the dividend problem. In this section, we consider the impact of dividends on option values, and we show how slight adjustments in the Black-Scholes model allow it to apply to options on dividend-paying stocks. We continue to focus on European options.

The Effect of Dividends on Option Prices

As we have seen, the value of a call option at expiration equals the maximum of zero or the stock price minus the exercise price, and a put option at expiration is worth the maximum of zero or the exercise price minus the stock price. In our familiar notation:

$$c_T = \text{MAX}\{0, S_T - X\}$$
$$p_T = \text{MAX}\{0, X - S_T\}$$

For both the call and the put, anything that affects the stock price at expiration will affect the price of the option. Dividends that might be paid during the life of the option can affect the stock price.

We may regard a dividend as a repayment of a portion of the share's value to the shareholder. As such, we would expect the stock price to fall by the amount of the dividend payment.[13] As a metaphor, we might think of the dividend on a stock as a leakage of value from the stock. As the value of the stock drops due to the leakage of dividends, the changing stock price will affect the value of options on the stock.

A drop in the stock price due to a dividend will have an adverse effect on the price of a call and a beneficial effect on the price of a put. For a call, the stock price at expiration will be lower than it would have been had there been no dividend. Thus, the dividend will reduce the quantity $S_T - X$, thus reducing the value of the call at expiration. For the put, the dividend will reduce the stock price at expiration, and it will therefore increase the quantity $X - S_T$.

We can illustrate the effect of dividends with an example of a call and put that have a common exercise price of $100. Assume the options are moments from expiration and that the stock price is $102. Without bringing dividends into consideration, the value of the options would be:

$$c_T = MAX\{0, S_T - X\} = MAX\{0, \$102 - \$100\} = \$2$$
$$p_T = MAX\{0, X - S_T\} = MAX\{0, \$100 - \$102\} = \$0$$

Just before expiration, the stock pays a dividend of $3, causing the stock price to drop from $102 to $99. With a stock price of $99 at expiration, the call option will be worth zero, and the put will be worth $1. Failing to take into account the looming dividend payment could cause large pricing errors from a blind application of the Black-Scholes model. We now turn to adjustments in the Black-Scholes model that reflect dividends.

Adjustments for Known Dividends

For most stocks, the dividend payments likely to occur during the life of an option can be forecast with considerable precision. If we are looking ahead to a dividend forecasted to occur in three months, we expect the stock price to drop by the amount of the dividend when the stock goes ex-dividend. At the present moment, three months before the ex-dividend date, we can build that looming dividend into our analysis. To do so, we subtract the present value of the dividend from the current stock price. We then apply the Black-Scholes model as usual, except we use the adjusted stock price as an input to the model instead of the current stock price.

As an example, consider call and put options with a common exercise price of $100 and 150 days until expiration. Assume that the underlying stock trades for $102 and that you expect the stock to pay a $3 dividend in 90 days. The risk-free rate is 9 percent, and the standard deviation for the stock is 0.30. The present value of the $3 dividend is:

$$\$3e^{-r(90/365)} = \$2.93$$

According to this technique, we reduce the stock price now by the present value of the dividend, giving an adjusted stock price of $99.07. We then apply the Black-Scholes model in the usual way, except we use the adjusted stock price of $99.07 instead of the current price of $102. The following table shows the results of applying the adjusted and unadjusted models to the call and the put.

Black-Scholes Model Price	Call	Put
Adjusted for known dividends	8.91	6.21
Unadjusted	10.74	5.11

Applying the Black-Scholes model with the adjustment for known dividends gives a call value of $8.91 and a put value of $6.21. With no adjustment for dividends, the Black-Scholes prices are $10.74 for the call option and $5.11 for the put option. The difference in prices amounts to almost 20 percent. Also, as we hypothesized, subtracting the present value of the dividends from the stock price reduces the value of the call and increases the value of the put.

The same technique applies in situations when there are several dividends. The stock price should be adjusted by subtracting the present value of all dividends that are expected to occur before the expiration date of the option. Dividends expected after the option expires can be ignored because the option will already have been exercised or allowed to expire before those dividends affect the value of the stock. **OPTION!** can compute the prices of call and put options under the Black-Scholes model adjusted for known dividends.

Adjustments for Continuous Dividends – Merton's Model

Robert Merton has shown how to adjust the Black-Scholes model to account for dividends when the dividend is paid at a continuous rate. Instead of focusing on the quarterly dividends that characterize individual stocks, Merton's model applies when the dividend is paid continuously. Essentially, the adjustment for continuous dividends treats the dividend rate as a negative interest rate. We have already seen that dividends reduce the value of a call option because they reduce the value of the stock that underlies the option. In effect, we have a continuous leakage of value from the stock that equals the dividend rate. We let the Greek letter delta, δ, represent this rate of leakage.[14]

Merton's model applies particularly well to options on goods such as foreign currency. In such an option, the foreign currency is treated as paying a continuous dividend equal to the foreign interest rate. (We explore options on foreign currency in Chapter 7.) Merton's model also applies fairly well to options on individual stocks, if we treat the quarterly dividends as being earned at a continuous rate. Merton's adjustment to the Black-Scholes model for continuous dividends is:

$$c_t^M = e^{-\delta(T-t)}S_t N(d_1^M) - Xe^{-r(T-t)}N(d_2^M)$$

$$d_1^M = \frac{\ln\left(\dfrac{S_t}{X}\right) + (r - \delta + .5\sigma^2)(T - t)}{\sigma\sqrt{T - t}}$$

$$d_2^M = d_1^M - \sigma\sqrt{T - t}$$

$$(4.17)$$

where δ = the continuous dividend rate on the stock

To adjust the regular Black-Scholes model, we replace the current stock price with the stock price adjusted for the continuous dividend. That is, we replace S_t with:

$$e^{-\delta(T-t)}S_t$$

Substituting this expression into the formulas for d_1 and d_2 gives d_1^M and d_2^M as shown above. Merton's adjusted put value is:

$$p_t^M = Xe^{-r(T-t)}N(-d_2^M) - Se^{-\delta(T-t)}N(-d_1^M)$$

$$(4.18)$$

When $\delta = 0$, Merton's model reduces to the Black-Scholes model. Thus, the Merton model is a more general model than the original Black-Scholes. As an example of how to apply the continuous dividend adjustment, consider the following data:

$$S_t = \$60$$
$$X = \$60$$
$$r = .09$$
$$\sigma = .2$$
$$T - t = 180 \text{ days}$$

The stock will pay a quarterly dividend of $2 in 90 days, implying a continuous dividend rate, δ, of 13.75 percent. We compute the call price, c_t^M, as follows:

$$d_1^M = \frac{\ln\left(\frac{60}{60}\right) + [.09 - .1375 + .5(.2)(.2)]\left(\frac{180}{365}\right)}{.2\sqrt{\frac{180}{365}}}$$

$$= \frac{0 - 0.01356}{0.14045} = -0.09656$$

$$d_2^M = -0.09656 - .2\sqrt{\frac{180}{365}} = -0.23701$$

$N(d_1^M) = N(-0.09656) = 0.4615$, and $N(d_2^M) = N(-0.23701) = 0.4063$. Therefore, $N(-d_1^M) = 0.5385$, and $N(-d_2^M) = 0.5937$. The call and put values adjusted for continuous dividends are:

$$c_t^M = 60e^{-.1375(180/365)}(0.4615) - 60e^{-.09(180/365)}(0.4063) = \$2.55$$

$$p_t^M = 60e^{-0.09(180/365)}(0.5937) - 60e^{-0.1375(180/365)}(0.5385) = \$3.88$$

OPTION! allows the direct estimation of European call and put values according to Merton's model.

The Binomial Model and Dividends

The binomial model can evaluate European option prices for options on dividend paying stocks. There are three alternative dividend treatments within the context of the binomial model, and all involve adjusting the lattice to reflect the impact of dividends on the stock price. The first considers options on stocks paying a continuous dividend. This binomial approach is the analog to the Merton model. The second binomial approach applies to options on a stock that will pay a known dividend yield at a certain time. For example, a stock might pay a dividend equal to some fraction of its value on a certain date, such as a dividend of 3 percent of the stock's value 120 days from now. The third approach applies to a known dollar dividend that will occur at a certain time. For example, 90 days from now a stock might pay a $1 dividend. The binomial model can accommodate any number of dividend payments between the present and the expiration of the option.

Continuous Dividends. To apply the binomial model to options on a stock paying a continuous dividend, we need to adjust the binomial parameters to reflect the continuous leakage of value from the stock that the dividend represents. For Merton's model for European options on a stock paying a continuous dividend, we saw that the adjustment largely involved subtracting the continuous dividend rate, δ, from the risk-free rate, r. This is exactly the adjustment required for the binomial model. For options on a stock paying a continuous dividend δ, the U, D, and π_U factors are:

$$U = e^{\sigma\sqrt{\Delta t}}$$

$$D = \frac{1}{U}$$ (4.19)

$$\pi_u = \frac{e^{(r-\delta)\Delta t} - D}{U - D}$$

We illustrated Merton's model by considering a call option on a stock with a price of $60, a standard deviation of .2, and a continuous dividend rate of 13.75 percent. The call had an exercise price of $60 and expired in 180 days. The risk-free rate was 9 percent. We saw that the price of this option according to Merton's model was $2.5557. According to the binomial model, with 200 periods, the price would be $2.5516, which is almost identical. For the same data, the European put according to Merton's model was worth $3.8845. The binomial model with 200 periods gives a put price of $3.8805.

Known Dividend Yield. Consider a stock that will pay w percent of its value as a dividend in 55 days. An option on the stock expires in 120 days, and we model the price of the option using a three-period binomial model. In this situation, the dividend will occur in the second period. The binomial tree for the stock will appear as shown in Figure 4.9. At the second period in the binomial tree, the stock price will be reduced to $(1 - w)$ percent of its value. If the stock price rose in each of the first two periods, the stock price at period 2 would be $S_iUU(1 - w)$. Because of the known dividend yield

Figure 4.9	The Binomial Tree for a Stock with a Known Dividend Yield

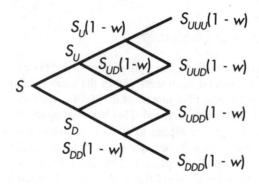

occurring at day 55, the value of the stock is reduced by the w percent dividend. Given that the stock price went up the first two periods, the value of the stock in the third period could be either $S_tUUU(1 - w)$ if the stock price goes up again, or it could be $S_tUUD(1 - w)$ if the stock price falls in the final period. To value either a call or a put in the context of the binomial model with a known dividend yield, we apply the usual technique to work from the terminal stock prices back to the current stock price and current options price. **OPTION!** can compute call and put prices under the binomial model adjusted for known dividend yields.

Extending this example, let us assume that the initial stock price is $80, that the exercise price for a call and a put is $75, that the standard deviation of the stock is 0.3, and the risk-free rate of interest is 7 percent. The percentage dividend that will be paid is 3 percent, so $w = 0.03$. With 120 days until expiration and a three-period binomial model, $\Delta t = 40/365 = 0.1096$. Therefore:

$$U = e^{.3\sqrt{.1096}} = 1.1044$$

$$D = \frac{1}{1.1044} = .9055$$

$$\pi_U = \frac{1.0077 - .9055}{1.1044 - .9055} = .5138$$

The discounting factor for a single period is $e^{-r\Delta t} = e^{-.07(40/365)} = .9924$. Figure 4.10 shows the binomial tree for the stock of our example. The top panel shows the stock price without dividends, while the bottom tree shows the effect of the 3 percent dividend on the stock price. For example, in the bottom tree, the stock price pattern generated by a rise, a rise, and a fall is:

$$S_tUUD(1 - w) = \$80(1.1044)(1.1044)(.9055)(1.0 - .03) = \$85.70$$

Figure 4.11 shows two binomial trees for the call option. The top tree in Figure 4.11 does not reflect the dividends and shows that the option's value would be $9.37. The bottom tree, which does reflect the 3 percent dividend yield, shows that the call is worth $7.94. The difference in the two prices is due entirely to taking account of the dividend.

Figure 4.12 parallels Figure 4.11, except it shows trees for the put option. The top tree shows that the put's value would be $2.67 if there were no dividend. Taking account of the dividend in the bottom tree gives a put price of $3.64. The effect of the dividend increases the put's value by 36 percent, from $2.67 to $3.64, and decreases the call's value by 15 percent, from $9.37 to $7.94.

Known Dollar Dividend. Most stocks that underlie stock options pay a fixed dollar dividend, rather than a dividend that equals some percentage of their value. This presents a complication because the tree may develop a tremendous number of branches. For example, assume that the stock price is initially $80 and that $U = 1.1$. Therefore, $D = .9091$. After one period, the stock price is either $88 or $72.73, as Figure 4.13 shows. Assume that a $2 dividend is paid just before the first period. Taking the dividend payment into account, the stock price will be either $86 or $70.73 at the first period. In the next period, the stock price will either rise or fall. If it was $86, it will then be $94.60 if the price rises again or $78.18 if the price falls. If the stock price fell in the first period to $70.73 after the dividend payment, in the second period it will either rise to $77.80 or fall to $64.30. In the normal tree, there would only be three prices to consider, because $S_tUD = S_tDU$. That is not the case with known dollar dividends. Letting DIV$ indicate a given dollar dividend, $(S_tU - \text{DIV}\$)D$ does not

Figure 4.10   Example Stock Price Lattices With and Without a Known Dividend Yield (in dollars)

Without dividends

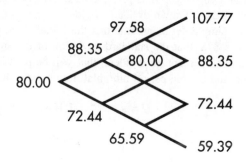

With dividends

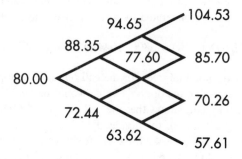

equal $(S_t D - DIV\$)U$. For many periods and multiple dividend payments, the number of nodes to evaluate can explode, making this model very difficult to apply.

We can avoid these difficulties by making a simplifying assumption. We assume that the stock price reflects the dividend, which is known with certainty, and all other factors that might affect the stock price, which are uncertain. We then adjust the uncertain component of the stock price for the impending dividends and model the uncertain component of the stock price with the binomial tree adding back the present value of all future dividends at each node. Specifically, we follow these steps:

1. Compute the present value of all dividends to be paid during the life of the option as of the present time = t.

Example Call Price Lattices With and Without a Known Dividend Yield (in dollars)   **Figure 4.11**

Without dividends

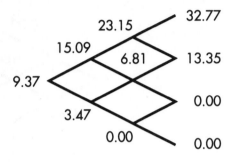

With dividends

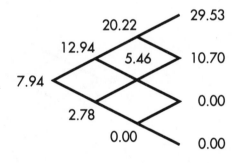

2. Subtract this present value from the current stock price to form $S'_t = S_t - PV$ of all dividends.
3. Create the binomial tree by applying the up and down factors in the usual way to the initial stock price S'_t.
4. After generating the tree, add to the stock price at each node the present value of all future dividends to be paid during the life of the option.
5. Compute the option values in the usual way by working through the binomial tree.

   To make this discussion more concrete, consider again the tree that failed to recombine in Figure 4.13. The initial stock price was $80, $U = 1.1$, $D = .9091$, and a dividend was to be paid just before the time of the first period. We now additionally assume that one period is .25 years and the interest rate is 10 percent. Therefore, the one-period discount factor is:

Figure 4.12　Example Put Price Lattices With and Without a Known Dividend Yield (in dollars)

Without dividends

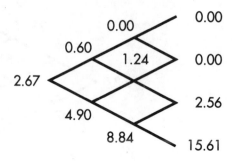

With dividends

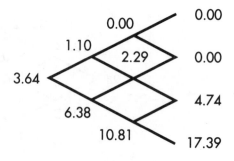

$$e^{-r(\Delta t)} = e^{-.1(.25)} = .9753$$

At the outset, the present value of the dividend is $1.95 = .9753($2). To form S'_t we subtract this present value from S_t:

$$S'_t = S_t - \text{PV of all dividends} = \$80 - \$1.95 = \$78.05$$

Figure 4.14 shows the binomial tree generated from a starting price of $78.05. Notice that the present value of the dividends ($1.95) has been added only to the first node because only the first node represents a time before the payment of the dividend. Notice also that the tree recombines at the second period, in contrast to Figure 4.13. **OPTION!** can compute call and put prices under the binomial model adjusted for known dollar dividends.

Stock Price Lattice Unadjusted for a Known Dollar Dividend   **Figure 4.13**
(in dollars)

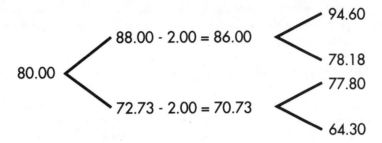

Stock Price Lattice Adjusted for a Known Dollar Dividend   **Figure 4.14**
(in dollars)

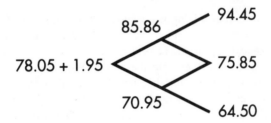

Summary

In this section, we have considered the effect of dividends on European options. In general, a dividend on a stock reduces the value of the stock by the amount of the dividend. Dividends reduce the value of call options because they reduce the stock price. Dividends increase the value of put options because the dividend reduces the price of the stock. The Black-Scholes model as originally developed pertained to only options on non–dividend paying stocks. However, the stocks that underlie most stock options do pay dividends, so the limitation of the Black-Scholes model is potentially serious.

There are several adjustments to the Black-Scholes model to account for dividends. The first one adjusts for known dividends by subtracting the present value of the dividends from the stock price and then applying the Black-Scholes model in the usual way. When the underlying stock pays a continuous dividend, Merton showed how to adjust the Black-Scholes model to account for the dividend.

We also considered adjustments to the binomial model to account for dividends. When the stock pays a known dividend yield at a given date, the binomial model can reflect the impact of this dividend on the stock price and the option quite easily. When the dividend is a given dollar amount, the binomial model requires a more elaborate adjustment, but it too can adjust the stock price and compute option values that reflect the impact of the dividend.

TESTS OF THE OPTION PRICING MODEL

If the Black-Scholes option pricing model correctly captures the factors that affect option prices, the price computed according to the model should correspond closely to the price observed in the market. Otherwise, either the model is inadequate or prices in the market are irrational. Therefore, each of the tests that we will consider in this section test a joint hypothesis – adequacy of the option pricing model and market rationality. If we find a discrepancy between the two, we can account for this divergence by claiming that the model is inadequate or by allowing that market participants are foolish. Note, however, that the Black-Scholes model was derived under the assumption that prices should not permit arbitrage. Accordingly, any major discrepancy between the model price and the market price would be serious indeed.

The Black-Scholes Study

The first empirical study of option pricing was conducted by Black and Scholes.[15] In this 1972 test, they examined over-the-counter option prices because listed options did not yet trade. Black and Scholes computed a theoretical option price based on their model. If the market price exceeded their theoretical price, they assumed that they sold the option. Similarly, if the market price was below the price they computed, they assumed that they bought the option. In both cases, they assumed that they held a stock position in conjunction with the option that gave a riskless position. (In other words, if they were long the call option, they would hold $-N(d_1)$ shares of stock as well.) This risk-free position should earn the risk-free rate if option prices in the market and their model are identical. They maintained this position until expiration, adjusting the portfolio as needed to maintain its riskless character. Their results showed significant profit opportunities. In other words, actual market prices differed significantly from the theoretical price given by the model. This difference was statistically significant but not economically important. When Black and Scholes considered transaction costs, they found that the costs of trading would erode any potential profit. Therefore, option traders could not follow their strategy and make a profit. This result helped to show the strong correspondence between market prices and option prices computed from theoretical models, such as the Black-Scholes model.

The Galai Studies

As in the Black-Scholes study, Dan Galai created hedged portfolios of options and stock and used these portfolios to study the correspondence between the Black-Scholes model price and actual market prices for options.[16] In contrast to the Black-Scholes study, Galai used listed option data from the Chicago Board Options Exchange. With options trading on an exchange, Galai had access to daily price quotations. Therefore, he was able to compute the rate of return on the hedged option-stock portfolio for each option for each day. He also adjusted the hedge ratio each day to maintain the neutral hedge – neutral in the sense that a change in the stock price would not change the overall value of the combined option-stock position. Comparing market prices with Black-Scholes model prices, Galai assumed that he sold overpriced options and bought underpriced options each day.

Galai's results showed that this strategy could earn excess returns. In other words, his initial results seemed to be inconsistent with an efficient market. However, this apparent result disappeared when Galai considered transaction costs. If transaction costs were only 1 percent, the apparent excess returns disappeared. Most traders outside the market face transaction costs of 1 percent or higher. However, market makers can transact for less than 1 percent transaction costs. This suggests that market makers could have followed Galai's strategy to earn excess returns. Yet even market makers face some additional transaction costs implied by their career choice. For instance, the market maker must buy or lease a seat on the exchange and forego alternative employment. When Galai brought these additional implicit transaction costs into the analysis, the market maker's apparent excess returns diminished or disappeared. At any rate, Galai's results showed that Black-Scholes model prices closely match actual market prices for options.

The Bhattacharya Study

Mihir Bhattacharya used an approach like the Black-Scholes and Galai studies to analyze the correspondence between actual market prices and theoretical prices.[17] Bhattacharya discusses the adherence of market prices to theoretical boundaries implied by no-arbitrage conditions. We focus on one of his three boundaries. As we discussed in Chapter 3, a call option should be worth more than its exercise value if time remains until expiration. Bhattacharya compiled a sample of 86,000 transactions and examined them to determine if immediate exercise was profitable. He found 1,100 such exercise opportunities, meaning that the stock price exceeded the exercise price plus the call price. As we argued in Chapter 3, such a price relationship should not exist. However, these exercise opportunities assumed that the exercise could be conducted without transaction costs. When Bhattacharya considered transaction costs, these apparently profitable exercise opportunities disappeared. The apparent violation of the boundary condition was observed only because transaction costs were not considered. This means that traders could not exploit the deviation from the boundary condition to make a profit.

The MacBeth-Merville Study

James MacBeth and Larry Merville used the Black-Scholes model to compute implied standard deviations for the underlying stocks.[18] They assumed that the Black-Scholes model correctly prices at-the-money options with at least 90 days until expiration. Based on these assumptions and the estimated standard deviation, they evaluated how well the Black-Scholes model prices options that are in-the-money or out-of-the-money and how well the model prices options that have fewer than 90 days until expiration. They found some systematic discrepancies between market prices and Black-Scholes model prices. First, the Black-Scholes prices tended to be less than market prices for in-the-money options and higher than market prices for out-of-the-money options. Second, this first effect is larger the farther the options are from the money. However, it is smaller the shorter the time until expiration. Therefore, we expect to find the greatest discrepancy between market prices and the Black-Scholes model price for options with a long time until expiration and options that are way in- or way out-of-the-money.

The Rubinstein Study

Mark Rubinstein compared market prices with theoretical option prices from the Black-Scholes model and other models of option prices.[19] Some other models out-performed the Black-Scholes model in some respects, yet none did so consistently. Further, Rubinstein confirmed some of the biases noted by MacBeth and Merville for the Black-Scholes model. However, none of the other models was consistently free of bias either. In general, Rubinstein was unable to conclude that there was a single model superior to the others.

Summary

Testing of the option pricing model is far from complete. Recently, attention has turned to the information inherent in option prices that might not be reflected in stock prices or that might be reflected first in option prices and later in stock prices. For example, Joseph Anthony finds that trading volume in call options leads trading volume in the underlying stock by one day.[20] While this lead-lag relationship does not necessarily imply any inefficiency in either market, it does seem to suggest that information that reaches the market affects options first.[21] In recent years the proliferation of many new kinds of options has attracted attention away from options on individual stocks. The kinds of studies on options on individual stocks that were conducted by Black and Scholes, Galai, Bhattacharya, and Rubinstein have recently been conducted for these new kinds of options. In large part, these new results corroborate the earlier results that were found for options on individual stocks. In this section, it has been possible to discuss only some of the most famous studies. There are many other worthwhile studies that have been conducted and many more still that remain to be conducted.

SUMMARY

We began this chapter by developing the binomial model. We showed that the single-period binomial model emerges directly from no-arbitrage conditions that govern all asset prices. We extended the single-period model to the multi-period binomial model. With this model, we found that we could apply our no-arbitrage principles to value options with numerous periods remaining until expiration. Throughout this development, we considered price movements that were somewhat arbitrary.

Researchers have studied the actual price movements of stocks in great detail. We found that logarithmic stock returns are distributed approximately normally and that this model of stock price movements has proven to be very useful as a working approximation of stock price behavior. Using this model of stock price behavior, a binomial model with many periods until expiration approaches the Black-Scholes model. The Black-Scholes model gives an elegant equation for pricing a call option as a function of five variables: the stock price, the exercise price, the risk-free rate, the time until expiration, and the standard deviation of the stock. Only two of these variables, the interest rate and the standard deviation, are not immediately observable. We showed how to estimate these two parameters.

OPTION! is a useful tool for analyzing the concepts we developed in this chapter. A module for the binomial model allows the user to specify one or many periods for analysis. In this module, the user specifies the up and down percentage factors. A separate module uses up and down factors that are consistent with the Black-Scholes model. With this module, we can study the convergence of the binomial price to the Black-Scholes price. Another module of **OPTION!** allows us to compute

Black-Scholes call and put values. A separate module finds the implied volatility of the stock based on the Black-Scholes model. Another module computes values of the cumulative normal distribution for input values of d_1 or d_2. Finally, **OPTION!** also includes a module to generate random price paths consistent with initial values that the user specifies.

QUESTIONS AND PROBLEMS

1. What is binomial about the binomial model? In other words, how does the model get its name?
2. If a stock price moves in a manner consistent with the binomial model, what is the chance that the stock price will be the same for two periods in a row? Explain.
3. Assume a stock price is $120 and in the next year it will either rise by 10 percent or fall by 20 percent. The risk-free interest rate is 6 percent. A call option on this stock has an exercise price of $130. What is the price of a call option that expires in one year? What is the chance that the stock price will rise?
4. Based on the data in Question 3, what would you hold to form a risk-free portfolio?
5. Based on the data in Question 3, what will the price of the call option be if the option expires in two years and the stock price can move up 10 percent or down 20 percent in each year?
6. Based on the data in Question 3, what would the price of a call with one year to expiration be if the call has an exercise price of $135? Can you answer this question without making the full calculations? Explain.
7. A stock is worth $60 dollars today. In a year, the stock price can rise or fall by 15 percent. If the interest rate is 6 percent, what is the price of a call option that expires in three years and has an exercise price of $70? What is the price of a put option that expires in three years and has an exercise price of $65? (Use **OPTION!** to solve this problem.)
8. Consider our model of stock price movements given in Equation 4.8. A stock has an initial price of $55 and an expected growth rate of .15 per year. The annualized standard deviation of the stock's return is .4. What is the expected stock price after 175 days?
9. A stock sells for $110. A call option on the stock has an exercise price of $105 and expires in 43 days. If the interest rate is .11 and the standard deviation of the stock's returns is .25, what is the price of the call according to the Black-Scholes model? What would be the price of a put with an exercise price of $140 and the same time until expiration?
10. Consider a stock that trades for $75. A put and a call on this stock both have an exercise price of $70 and they expire in 150 days. If the risk-free rate is 9 percent and the standard deviation for the stock is .35, compute the price of the options according to the Black-Scholes model.
11. For the options in Question 10, assume that the stock pays a continuous dividend of 4 percent. What are the options worth according to Merton's model?
12. Consider a Treasury bill with 173 days until maturity. The bid and asked yields on the bill are 9.43 and 9.37. What is the price of the T-bill? What is the continuously compounded rate on the bill?
13. Consider the following sequence of daily stock prices: $47, $49, $46, $45, $51. Compute the mean daily logarithmic return for this share. What is the daily standard deviation of returns? What is the annualized standard deviation?
14. A stock sells for $85. A call option with an exercise price of $80 expires in 53 days and sells for $8. The risk-free interest rate is 11 percent. What is the implied standard deviation for the stock? (Use **OPTION!** to solve this problem.)

15. For a particular application of the binomial model, assume that $U = 1.09$, $D = .91$, and that the two are equally probable. Do these assumptions lead to any particular difficulty? Explain. (Note: These are specified up and down movements and are not intended to be consistent with the Black-Scholes model.)

16. For a stock that trades at $120 and has a standard deviation of returns of .4, use the Black-Scholes model to price a call and a put that expire in 180 days and that have an exercise price of $100. The risk-free rate is 8 percent. Now assume that the stock will pay a dividend of $3 on day 75. Apply the known dividend adjustment to the Black-Scholes model and compute new call and put prices.

17. A call and a put expire in 150 days and have an exercise price of $100. The underlying stock is worth $95 and has a standard deviation of .25. The risk-free rate is 11 percent. Use a three-period binomial model and stock price movements consistent with the Black-Scholes model to compute the value of these options. Specify U, D, and π_u, as well as the values for the call and put.

18. For the situation in Problem 17, assume that the stock will pay 2 percent of its value as a dividend on day 80. Compute the value of the call and the put under this circumstance.

19. For the situation in Problem 17, assume that the stock will pay a dividend of $2 on day 80. Compute the value of the call and the put under this circumstance.

20. Consider the first tree in Figures 4.10 and 4.12. If the stock price falls in both of the first two periods, the price is $65.59. For the first tree in Figure 4.12, the put value is $8.84 in this case. Given that the exercise price on the put is $75, does this present a contradiction? Explain.

21. Consider the second tree in Figures 4.10 and 4.11. If the stock price increases in the first period, the price is $88.35. For the second tree in Figure 4.11, the call price is $12.94 in this case. Given that the exercise price on the put is $75, does this present a contradiction? Explain.

NOTES

[1] A risk-neutral investor considers only the expected payoffs from an investment. For such an investor, the risk associated with the investment is not important. Thus, a risk-neutral investor would be indifferent between an investment with a certain payoff of $50 or an investment with a 50 percent probability of paying $100 and a 50 percent probability of paying zero.

[2] The development of the binomial model stems from two seminal articles: R. Rendleman and B. Bartter, "Two-State Option Pricing," *Journal of Finance,* 34, December 1979, pp. 1093–1110, and J. Cox, S. Ross and M. Rubinstein, "Option Pricing: A Simplified Approach," *Journal of Financial Economics,* 7, September 1979, pp. 229–63. J. Cox and M. Rubinstein develop and discuss the binomial model in their book *Option Pricing,* Prentice Hall, 1973 and their paper "A Survey of Alternative Option Pricing Models," in *Option Pricing,* ed. M. Brenner, Lexington: D. C. Heath, 1983, pp. 3–33.

[3] Not every one of these stock price outcomes will be unique. Even in the two-period model we saw that $UDS = DUS$. Strictly speaking, with 20 periods, there are more than 1 million stock price paths.

[4] To this point, we have considered the binomial model in some detail and the log-normal model of stock prices. In essence, each different assumption about stock price movements leads to a different class of option pricing models. For instance, we have already observed that assuming stock prices can either rise or fall by a given amount in a period leads to the binomial model. The log-normal assumption that we have been considering assumes that the stock price path is continuous. In other words, for the stock price to go from $100 to $110, the price must pass through every value between the two. Another entire class of assumptions about stock price movements assumes that the stock price follows a jump process – the

stock price jumps from one price to another without taking on each of the intervening values. To distinguish these two models, determine whether the stock price path can be drawn without lifting pen from paper. If so, then the stock price path is continuous. The following papers analyze option pricing under alternative assumptions about stock price movements: J. Cox and S. Ross, "The Valuation of Options for Alternative Stochastic Processes," *Journal of Financial Economics,* 3, January-March 1976, pp. 145–66; R. Merton, "Option Pricing when Underlying Stock Returns Are Discontinuous," *Journal of Financial Economics,* 3, January-March 1976, pp. 125–44; F. Page and A. Saunders, "A General Derivation of the Jump Process Option Pricing Formula," *Journal of Financial and Quantitative Analysis,* 21:4, December 1986, pp. 437–46; C. Ball and W. Torous, "On Jumps in Common Stock Prices and Their Impact on Call Option Pricing," *Journal of Finance,* 40:1, March 1985, pp. 155–73; and E. Omberg, "Efficient Discrete Time Jump Process Models in Option Pricing," *Journal of Financial and Quantitative Analysis,* 23:2, June 1988, pp. 161–74.

[5] F. Black and M. Scholes, "The Pricing of Options and Corporate Liabilities," *Journal of Political Economy,* May 1973, pp. 637–59, provides the classic statement of the model. In his paper, "Fact and Fantasy in the Use of Options," *Financial Analysts Journal,* 1975, May/June, 31:4, pp. 36–41 and 61–72, Black develops many of the same ideas in a more intuitive manner. More recently, Black has told the story of how Scholes and he discovered the option pricing formula in "How We Came Up With the Option Formula," *Journal of Portfolio Management,* Winter 1989, pp. 4–8.

[6] In imperfect markets, there may not be a single interest rate but a borrowing rate and a lending rate. J. Gilster and W. Lee consider this possibility in their paper, "The Effects of Transaction Costs and Different Borrowing and Lending Rates on the Option Pricing Model: A Note," *Journal of Finance,* 39:4, September 1984, pp. 1215–21. They also consider transaction costs and show that considering both imperfections in the debt market and transaction costs results in two offsetting influences. They conclude that neither has a strong effect on the estimation of the option price and Black-Scholes option prices conform well to actual prices observed in the market. Thus, neither market imperfection is too important because the two imperfections tend to cancel each other.

[7] It is possible that the stock volatility could change over the life of the option. But shifting volatilities present difficulties in finding an option pricing model. J. Hull and A. White, "The Pricing of Options on Assets with Stochastic Volatilities," *Journal of Finance,* 42:2, June 1987, pp. 281–300, address this issue. While Hull and White acknowledge that no formula for an option price assuming changing volatility has been found, they develop techniques for approximating the value of an option with changing volatility. In doing so, they assume that changes in volatility are correlated with changes in the stock price. This problem has also been studied by L. Scott, "Option Pricing when the Variance Changes Randomly: Theory, Estimation, and an Application," *Journal of Financial and Quantitative Analysis,* 22:4, December 1987, pp. 419–38. Scott uses simulation techniques to approximate option prices but concedes that no formula for an option price under shifting volatilities has been found. Finally, James Wiggins explores this problem as well in his paper, "Option Values Under Stochastic Volatility: Theory and Empirical Estimates," *Journal of Financial Economics,* 19:2, December 1987, pp. 351–72. He also acknowledges that an actual formula for the price of an option under shifting volatilities is lacking. Wiggins applies a numerical estimation technique to develop estimates of option prices assuming that volatility follows a continuous process. Under this assumption, Wiggins is able to compute estimated option prices.

[8] There is a third potentially useful method that we do not consider in this book. M. Parkinson, "The Random Walk Problem: Extreme Value Method for Estimating the Variance of the Displacement," *Journal of Business,* 53, January 1980, pp. 61–5, showed that focusing on high and low prices for a few days could give as good an estimate as using historical data for five times as many days. His model assumes that stock prices are distributed log-normally. Compared with the use of historical data on the closing price for a given day, Parkinson's method uses both the high and low prices for the day. This method would allow a

good estimate from more recent historical data than simply focusing on the history of closing prices. M. Garman and M. Klass, "On the Estimation of Security Price Volatilities from Historical Data," *Journal of Business,* 53:1, 1980, pp. 67–78, pointed out some difficulties with Parkinson's approach. First, his method is very sensitive to any errors in the reported high and low prices. Further, if trading during the day is sporadic, Parkinson's method will generate biased estimates of volatility. In particular, with discontinuities in the trading, the reported high will almost certainly be lower than the high that would have been observed with continuous trading. Similarly, the reported low will be higher than the value that would have been achieved under continuous trading. Garman and Klass also show how to improve Parkinson's type of estimate.

[9] Similarly, assume that we estimate the standard deviation with weekly data. We would convert this raw data to annualized data by multiplying the weekly standard deviation times the square root of 52. Similarly, if we begin with monthly data, we annualize our monthly standard deviation by multiplying it times the square root of 12.

[10] In principle, we can take any five of the values as given and solve for the sixth. For example, Menachem Brenner and Dan Galai, "Implied Interest Rates," *Journal of Business,* 59, July 1986, pp. 493–507, find that interest rates implied in the options market correspond to other short-term rates of interest. These implied rates are nearer to the borrowing rate than to the lending rate. Further, in situations where early exercise is imminent, the interest rates implied in the option markets can differ widely from short-term rates on other instruments. S. Swidler takes this approach a step further in his paper, "Simultaneous Option Prices and an Implied Risk-Free Rate of Interest: A Test of the Black-Scholes Model," *Journal of Economics and Business,* 38:2, May 1986, pp. 155–64. Swidler uses two options, which allows him to estimate two parameters simultaneously – two equations in two unknowns. Swidler estimates the implied interest and the implied standard deviation. While the standard deviation can differ from stock to stock, there should be a common interest rate for all options on a given date. For most of the stocks, Swidler finds that a single interest rate can be found. Accordingly, he regards his evidence as supporting the reasonableness of the Black-Scholes model.

[11] For a discussion of these weighting techniques, see H. A. Latane and R. J. Rendleman, Jr., "Standard Deviations of Stock Price Ratios Implied in Option Prices," *Journal of Finance,* 31, 1976, pp. 369–82; D. P. Chiras and S. Manaster, "The Information Content of Option Prices and a Test of Market Efficiency," *Journal of Financial Economics,* 6, 1978, pp. 213–34; and R. E. Whaley, "Valuation of American Call Options on Dividend Paying Stocks: Empirical Tests," *Journal of Financial Economics,* 10, 1982, pp. 29–58. In his paper, "Standard Deviations Implied in Option Prices as Predictors of Future Stock Price Variability," *Journal of Banking and Finance,* 5, 1981, pp. 363–82, Stan Beckers concludes that using the option with the highest sensitivity to the standard deviation provides the best estimate of future volatility. For a review of the literature on implied volatility, see S. Mayhew, "Implied Volatility," *Financial Analysts Journal,* 51:4, July/August 1995, pp. 8–20.

[12] **OPTION!** searches for the correct standard deviation in a way similar to the sequence of standard deviations and prices shown here. However, it uses a somewhat more sophisticated procedure for choosing the next standard deviation to try.

[13] In fact, considerable research shows that the stock price falls when a stock goes ex-dividend, but the drop in the stock price does not equal the full amount of the dividend. In this text, we make the simplifying assumption that the stock price falls by the amount of the dividend. Alternatively, the reader may regard the dividend as being equal to the amount of the fall in the stock price occasioned by the dividend payment.

[14] This is not the same as capital delta, Δ, which stands for the sensitivity of the call option price to a change in the stock price.

[15] F. Black and M. Scholes, "The Valuation of Option Contracts and a Test of Market Efficiency," *Journal of Finance,* 27:2, 1972, pp. 399–417.

[16] D. Galai, "Tests of Market Efficiency of the Chicago Board Options Exchange," *Journal of Business,* 50:2, April 1977, pp. 167–97, and "Empirical Tests of Boundary Conditions for CBOE Options," *Journal of Financial Economics,* 6:2/3, June-September 1978, pp. 182–211.

[17] M. Bhattacharya, "Transaction Data Tests on the Efficiency of the Chicago Board Options Exchange," *Journal of Financial Economics,* 12:2, 1983, pp. 161–85.

[18] J. D. MacBeth and L. J. Merville, "An Empirical Examination of the Black-Scholes Call Option Pricing Model," *Journal of Finance,* 34:5, 1979, pp. 1173–86.

[19] M. Rubinstein, "Nonparametric Tests of Alternative Option Pricing Models Using All Reported Trades and Quotes on the 30 Most Active CBOE Option Classes from August 23, 1976 Through August 31, 1978," *Journal of Finance,* 40:2, 1985, pp. 455–80. The other models tested were extensions of the Black-Scholes model based on changing assumptions about how stock prices move. For instance, they included option models based on the assumption that stock prices jump from one price to another, rather than moving continuously through all intervening prices as the stock price moves from one price to another. Rubinstein tested the following models: the Black-Scholes model, the jump model, the mixed diffusion jump model, the constant elasticity of variance model, and the displaced diffusion model.

[20] J. H. Anthony, "The Interrelation of Stock and Options Market Trading-Volume Data," *Journal of Finance,* 43:4, September 1988, pp. 949–64.

[21] Option prices may react before stock prices due to the trading preferences of informed traders. We have already seen that option markets often offer lower transaction costs than the market for the underlying good. For traders with good information, the options market may be the preferred market to exploit their information. On this scenario, we would expect to see option prices and volume change before stock prices and volume. The trading of the informed traders would move option prices, and the arbitrage linkages between options and stocks would lead to an adjustment of the corresponding stock prices.

<table>
<tr><td>

CHAPTER

5

</td><td>

OPTION SENSITIVITIES AND OPTION HEDGING

</td></tr>
</table>

INTRODUCTION

Chapter 4 developed the principles of pricing for European options. There we analyzed option pricing within the framework of the binomial model and extended the discussion to encompass the Black-Scholes model, which gives a closed-form solution for the price of a European option on a non-dividend stock. We also considered the Merton model, which provides a solution for the price of a European option on a stock paying a continuous dividend.

In this chapter, we continue our exploration of these models by focusing on the response of option prices to the factors that determine the price. We noted in Chapter 4 that the price of a European option depends on the price of the underlying stock, the exercise price, the interest rate, the volatility of the underlying stock, and the time until expiration. This chapter analyzes the sensitivity of option prices to these factors and shows how a knowledge of these relationships can direct trading strategies and can improve option hedging techniques.

With **OPTION!**, we can compute all of the sensitivity measures that we consider in this chapter. Also, **OPTION!** can graph the response of the option price to the different factors.

OPTION SENSITIVITIES IN THE MERTON AND BLACK-SCHOLES MODELS

Throughout this chapter, we focus on the Merton model (given in Equations 4.17 and 4.18) and the sensitivity of option prices in this model to the underlying factors. This approach embraces the Black-Scholes model (presented in Equations 4.13–4.15), as we may regard the Merton model simply as the Black-Scholes model extended to account for stocks that pay continuous dividends. As we saw in Chapter 4, the Merton model simplifies to the Black-Scholes model if we assume that the underlying stock pays no dividends. Similarly, the sensitivities of option prices in the Merton model reduce to those for the Black-Scholes model if we assume that the underlying stock pays no dividends.

The option price sensitivities that we consider in this chapter derive from calculus. For example, the sensitivity of the option price with respect to the stock price is simply the first derivative of the option pricing formula with respect to the stock price. For readers unfamiliar with calculus, we illustrate this basic idea in two ways. The first derivative of the call price with respect to the stock price is just the change in the call price for a change in the stock price:

$$\frac{\Delta c}{\Delta S}$$

This change in the call price is measured for an extremely small change in the stock price. In fact, in terms of calculus, the change in the call price is measured for an infinitesimal change in the stock price. As a second illustration, consider a European call option on a stock priced at $100 with a standard deviation of .3. The option expires in 180 days, has a striking price of $100, and the current risk-free rate of interest is 8 percent. Table 5.1 shows the value of this call for stock prices in the neighborhood of $100. It also shows the value of $N(d_1)$ computed at each price as well. Consider a change in the stock price from $100 to $102. For this change of $2 in the stock price, the call price changes from $10.3044 to $11.5702. Therefore:

$$\frac{\Delta c}{\Delta S} = \frac{1.2658}{2.00} = .6329$$

Next consider a change in the stock price from $100.00 to $100.10. In this case, the call price would change from $10.3044 to $10.3660, giving:

$$\frac{\Delta c}{\Delta S} = \frac{0.0616}{0.10} = .6160$$

For these two cases, we now compare the relative change in call prices with $N(d_1)$. For a stock price of $100, $N(d_1) = .6151$, and our $\Delta c/\Delta S$ term has a value in that neighborhood. We also note that for

Table 5.1	Call Prices for Various Stock Prices		
	Call Price	Stock Price	$N(d_1)$
	$ 9.1111	$ 98.00	.5780
	9.4024	98.50	.5874
	9.6984	99.00	.5967
	9.9991	99.50	.6060
	10.1512	99.75	.6105
	10.3044	100.00	.6151
	10.3660	100.10	.6169
	10.4587	100.25	.6196
	10.6142	100.50	.6241
	10.9284	101.00	.6330
	11.2472	101.50	.6418
	11.5702	102.00	.6505

a $2 stock price change, $\Delta c/\Delta S$ is .6329, but for a $.10 change, $\Delta c/\Delta S = .6160$. As the change becomes smaller, the value for $\Delta c/\Delta S$ approaches the value of $N(d_1)$ for a stock price of $100, which is .6151. For an infinitesimally small change in the stock price, the change in the value of the call option will exactly equal $N(d_1)$. In fact, $N(d_1)$ is the first derivative of the call price with respect to the stock price for a non-dividend stock. The line for the call in Figure 5.1 shows how the value of our example option changes as a function of the stock price. The straight line tangent to the option price curve in the top graph of Figure 5.1 shows the instantaneous rate of change in the call price for a change in the stock price. The slope of this straight line is the first derivative of the call price with respect to the stock price. As the figure shows, the straight line indicates the slope of the call price curve at a stock price of $100, which is .6151.

All of the sensitivity measures we consider in this chapter are similarly conceived and derived. They all derive from calculus and express the sensitivity of an option price to a change in one of the underlying parameters. In the common calculus notation for our example, the first derivative of the call price with respect to the stock price is denoted as $\partial c/\partial S$. Table 5.2 presents the standard sensitivities used in option analysis for the Merton model as it applies to calls, while Table 5.3 gives the same equations for puts. (See Chapter 4 for the equations for the two models and other terms.)

As we saw in Chapter 4, the Black-Scholes model is the same as the Merton model where there are no dividends on the stock. Similarly, we can derive the sensitivities for the Black-Scholes model from those of the Merton model if we assume that the stock pays no dividends. Tables 5.4 and 5.5 parallel Tables 5.2 and 5.3 and give the sensitivities for the Black-Scholes model.

Earlier, we considered a call option on a stock priced at $100 with a standard deviation of .3 and no dividend. The call had 180 days until expiration, and we assumed a risk-free rate of 8 percent. Table 5.6 shows all of the sensitivities for calls and puts for both the Black-Scholes model (assuming no dividend) and for the Merton model (assuming a continuous dividend of 3 percent). **OPTION!** computes all of these sensitivity measures. We now consider each of the measures in turn.

DELTA

DELTA is the first derivative of an option's price with respect to a change in the price of the stock. As such, DELTA measures the sensitivity of the option's price to changing stock prices. $DELTA_c$ is always positive, while $DELTA_p$ is always negative. Thus, the value of a call increases with a stock price increase, while the value of a put decreases if the stock price increases. In Table 5.6 for the options on a non-dividend stock, $DELTA_c = .6151$ and $DELTA_p = -.3849$. These sensitivities can be interpreted as follows. If the stock price rises by $1, the price of the call will rise by approximately $.6151, while the price of the put will fall by about $.3849.

These estimations of the change in the option price are only approximate. If the change in the stock price were infinitesimal, the DELTAs would give us an exact price change for the options. Because a $1 change in the stock price is discrete, our computed prices remain estimates. If the stock price is $101, we have $c = \$10.9284$ and $p = \$6.0601$. Thus, the call price increases by $.6240 (compared with the predicted $.6151), and the put price falls by $.3759 (compared with the predicted fall of $.3849).

The lower graph of Figure 5.1 shows how the put price of our example varies with the stock price. Notice that the price of a European put can be less than its intrinsic value, as we discussed in Chapter 4. As the two panels of Figure 5.1 indicate, option prices are extremely dependent upon

Figure 5.1 Call and Put Prices as a Function of the Stock Price

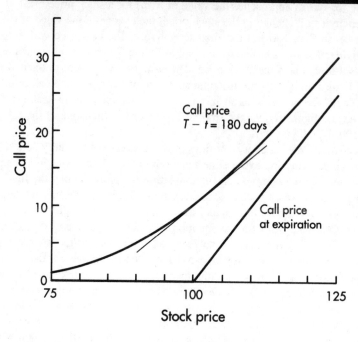

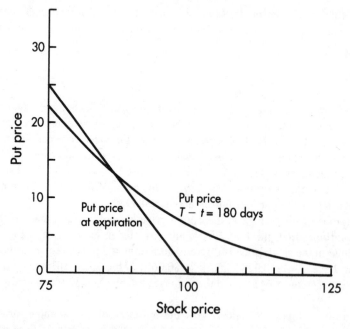

$X = \$100$; $\sigma = .3$; $r = .08$; $T - t = 180$ days

| | Call Sensitivities for the Merton Model | **Table 5.2** |

Name	Sensitivity
DELTA$_c$	$\dfrac{\partial c}{\partial S} = e^{-\delta(T-t)}N(d_1^M)$
THETA$_c$	$-\dfrac{\partial c}{\partial(T-t)} = -\dfrac{SN'(d_1^M)\sigma e^{-\delta(T-t)}}{2\sqrt{T-t}}$ $+ \delta SN(d_1^M)e^{-\delta(T-t)} - rXe^{-r(T-t)}N(d_2^M)$
VEGA$_c$	$\dfrac{\partial c}{\partial \sigma} = S\sqrt{T-t}\,N'(d_1^M)e^{-\delta(T-t)}$
RHO$_c$	$\dfrac{\partial c}{\partial r} = X(T-t)e^{-r(T-t)}N(d_2^M)$
GAMMA$_c$	$\dfrac{\partial \text{DELTA}_c}{\partial S} = \dfrac{\partial^2 c}{\partial S^2} = \dfrac{N'(d_1^M)e^{-\delta(T-t)}}{S\sigma\sqrt{T-t}}$
Note:	$N'(d_1^M) = \dfrac{1}{\sqrt{2\pi}}e^{-.5(d_1^M)^2}$

| | Put Sensitivities for the Merton Model | **Table 5.3** |

Name	Sensitivity
DELTA$_p$	$\dfrac{\partial p}{\partial S} = e^{-\delta(T-t)}[N(d_1^M) - 1]$
THETA$_p$	$-\dfrac{\partial p}{\partial(T-t)} = -\dfrac{SN'(d_1^M)\sigma e^{-\delta(T-t)}}{2\sqrt{T-t}}$ $- \delta SN(d_1^M)e^{-\delta(T-t)} + rXe^{-r(T-t)}N(-d_2^M)$
VEGA$_p$	$\dfrac{\partial p}{\partial \sigma} = S\sqrt{T-t}\,N'(d_1^M)e^{-\delta(T-t)}$
RHO$_p$	$\dfrac{\partial p}{\partial r} = -X(T-t)e^{-r(T-t)}N(-d_2^M)$
GAMMA$_p$	$\dfrac{\partial \text{DELTA}_p}{\partial S} = \dfrac{\partial^2 p}{\partial S^2} = \dfrac{N'(d_1^M)e^{-\delta(T-t)}}{S\sigma\sqrt{T-t}}$
Note:	$N'(d_1^M) = \dfrac{1}{\sqrt{2\pi}}e^{-.5(d_1^M)^2}$

Table 5.4	Call Sensitivities for the Black-Scholes Model

Name	Sensitivity
$DELTA_c$	$$\frac{\partial c}{\partial S} = N(d_1)$$
$THETA_c$	$$-\frac{\partial c}{\partial (T-t)} = -\frac{SN'(d_1)\sigma}{2\sqrt{T-t}} \\ - rXe^{-r(T-t)}N(d_2)$$
$VEGA_c$	$$\frac{\partial c}{\partial \sigma} = S\sqrt{T-t}\,N'(d_1)$$
RHO_c	$$\frac{\partial c}{\partial r} = -X(T-t)e^{-r(T-t)}N(d_2)$$
$GAMMA_c$	$$\frac{\partial DELTA_c}{\partial S} = \frac{\partial^2 c}{\partial S^2} = \frac{N'(d_1)}{S\sigma\sqrt{T-t}}$$
Note:	$$N'(d_1) = \frac{1}{\sqrt{2\pi}}e^{-.5(d_1)^2}$$

Table 5.5	Put Sensitivities for the Black-Scholes Model

Name	Sensitivity
$DELTA_p$	$$\frac{\partial p}{\partial S} = N(d_1) - 1$$
$THETA_p$	$$-\frac{\partial p}{\partial (T-t)} = -\frac{SN'(d_1)\sigma}{2\sqrt{T-t}} \\ + rXe^{-r(T-t)}N(-d_2)$$
$VEGA_p$	$$\frac{\partial p}{\partial \sigma} = S\sqrt{T-t}\,N'(d_1)$$
RHO_p	$$\frac{\partial p}{\partial r} = -X(T-t)e^{-r(T-t)}N(-d_2)$$
$GAMMA_p$	$$\frac{\partial DELTA_p}{\partial S} = \frac{\partial^2 p}{\partial S^2} = \frac{N'(d_1)}{S\sigma\sqrt{T-t}}$$
Note:	$$N'(d_1) = \frac{1}{\sqrt{2\pi}}e^{-.5(d_1)^2}$$

	Black-Scholes Model $\delta = 0.0$		Merton Model $\delta = 0.03$	
	Call	**Put**	**Call**	**Put**
Option prices	$10.3044	$ 6.4360	$ 9.4209	$ 7.0210
DELTA	.6151	−.3849	.5794	−.4060
THETA	−12.2607	−4.5701	−10.3343	−5.5997
VEGA	26.8416	26.8416	26.9300	26.9300
RHO	25.2515	−22.1559	23.9250	−23.4823
GAMMA	.0181	.0181	.0182	.0182

Option Sensitivities — Table 5.6

$S = \$100; X = \$100; r = .08; \sigma = .3; T - t = 180$ days

stock prices, and the price of the underlying stock is the key determinant of an option price. Therefore, DELTA is the most important of all of the sensitivity measures that we consider in this chapter.

DELTA-NEUTRAL POSITIONS

Consider a portfolio, P, of a short position of one European call on a non-dividend stock combined with a long position of DELTA units of the stock. The portfolio would have the value:

$$P = -c + N(d_1)S \qquad (5.1)$$

Continuing to use our sample options of Table 5.6, the cost of the portfolio, assuming a current stock price of $100, would be:

$$P = -c + N(d_1)S = -\$10.3044 + .6151(\$100.00) = \$51.2056$$

If the stock price were to suddenly change to $100.10, the portfolio's value would be:

$$P = -c + N(d_1)S = -\$10.3660 + .6151(\$100.10) = \$51.2055$$

Thus, the value of the portfolio would change by only $.0001 for a $.10 change in the stock price. If the change in the stock price were infinitesimal, the price of the portfolio would not change at all. If the change in the stock price were larger, the change in the value of the portfolio would be larger, but it would still be quite small relative to the change in the stock price. For example, if the stock price rose from $100 to $110, the portfolio's value would be:

$$P = -c + N(d_1)S = -\$17.2821 + .6151(\$110.00) = \$50.3789$$

In this case, a change of $10 in the stock price caused a change of $.8267 in the value of the portfolio. Figure 5.2 shows how the value of this portfolio changes for changes in the stock price.

Figure 5.2   Value of a Delta-Neutral Portfolio as a Function of the Stock Price (Portfolio includes –1 call and .6151 shares)

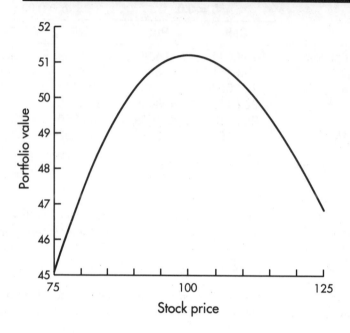

X = $100; σ = .3; r = .08; $T - t$ = 180 days

A portfolio like the one we are considering and described by Equation 5.1 is known as a **delta-neutral portfolio**. It is delta-neutral because an infinitesimal change in the price of the stock does not affect the price of the portfolio. Put another way, we could say that the DELTA of this portfolio is zero; the value of the portfolio is insensitive to the value of the stock.

As we saw in Chapter 4, the Black-Scholes model assumes that the stock price changes continuously. Imagine now that we can trade shares and options continuously as the stock price changes. We see from the equation for DELTA in Table 5.2 that DELTA changes when the stock price changes. (DELTA also changes when other factors change as well, such as the standard deviation and the time remaining until the option expires.) Assume now that we trade continuously to rebalance our portfolio as the stock price changes. In rebalancing, we seek to maintain the condition of Equation 5.1. In particular, we trade continuously to maintain our portfolio as a delta-neutral portfolio. By trading continuously, the portfolio is delta-neutral at every instant and never loses or gains value in response to changes in the stock price. By following this strategy of continuously rebalancing our portfolio, we know that it has zero price risk as a function of changing stock prices. In effect, by continuously rebalancing we have created a risk-free portfolio. Further, if the portfolio is risk-free, it must earn the risk-free rate of return.

This is the key intuition of the Black-Scholes model. Black and Scholes realized that continuous trading could maintain a delta-neutral portfolio as a risk-free portfolio earning the risk-free rate. This was an important step that enabled them to find a solution for their option pricing model.

As a practical matter, creating a delta-neutral portfolio in the manner described appears to be a difficult way of buying a risk-free security. Why not just buy a Treasury bill? Later in this chapter, we explore the valuable and practical consequences of using delta-oriented hedging technologies. However, at the present we can easily see how the idea of a delta-neutral portfolio can be useful in adjusting the riskiness of a stock trading strategy.

For the call option and the stock that we have been considering, assume that an outright investment in the stock is too risky. An investor in this position could use the idea of delta-neutrality to shape the risk characteristics of the investment to her particular needs. For example, assume that a trader holds a portfolio as follows:

$$-.5c + N(d_1)S = -.5(\$10.3044) + .6151(\$100.00) = \$56.3578$$

This portfolio is similar to the delta-neutral portfolio that we considered earlier, except instead of selling a call, the investor sells only one-half of a call. In considering the delta-neutral portfolio, we saw that selling the call in conjunction with investing in the stock gave a risk-free portfolio. Now, by selling one-half of a call, the investor diminishes but does not totally eliminate the risk. Figure 5.3 shows how the value of the delta-neutral portfolio and this new portfolio will vary as the stock price changes. This new portfolio has some risk exposure to changing stock prices, but it is much less risky than the stock itself. Later in this chapter, we consider a variety of strategies for using options to accept, avoid, or transform various investment risks.

As we noted earlier, DELTA changes as the stock price and other parameters of the option pricing model change. For our continuing example, Figure 5.4 shows how the DELTAs of the call and put vary with changing stock prices. $DELTA_c$ tends to approach 1.0 when the call option is deep-in-the-money. Similarly, when the call is deep-out-of-the-money, $DELTA_c$ approaches zero. When the stock price is near the exercise price, $DELTA_c$ is most sensitive to a change in the stock price. For $DELTA_p$, similar principles apply. $DELTA_c$ is always greater than zero, while $DELTA_p$ is always less than zero. The DELTA of a deep-in-the-money put approaches −1.0, while the DELTA of a deep-out-of-the-money put approaches zero. **OPTION!** can make graphs similar to those of Figure 5.4.

THETA

If the stock price and all other parameters of the option pricing model remain constant, the price of options will still change with the passage of time. THETA is the negative of the first derivative of the option price with respect to the time remaining until expiration. $THETA_c$ and $THETA_p$ can be greater or less than zero depending upon circumstances. However, $THETA_c$ and $THETA_p$ are generally less than zero.[1]

The tendency for option prices to change merely due to the passage of time is known as **time decay**. To see how the passage of time affects option prices, consider our continuing example of call and put options with $S = \$100$, $X = \$100$, $\sigma = .3$, $r = .08$, and $T - t = 180$ days. For these values, we noted earlier that $c = \$10.30$ and $p = \$6.44$. For these values, $THETA_c = -12.2607$ and $THETA_p = -4.5701$. These values of THETA are expressed in terms of years. Suppose that the time

Figure 5.3   Value of a Delta-Neutral Portfolio as a Function of the Stock Price (One portfolio includes 1 call and .6151 shares, and one portfolio includes −.5 calls and .6151 shares)

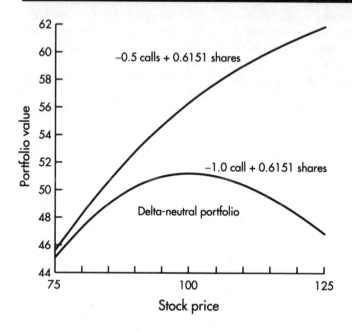

$X = \$100;\ \sigma = .3;\ r = .08;\ T - t = 180$ days

to expiration changes by .1 years (37 days) from 180 days until expiration to 143 days. Recalling that THETA is the negative of the first derivative of the option price with respect to time until expiration, we would expect the call and put prices to be $c = \$10.30 + .1(-12.2607) = \$9.07$ and $p = \$6.44 + .1(-4.5701) = \$5.98$. Recalling that all of these computed prices are approximations, the actual prices would be $c = \$9.01$ and $p = \$5.92$.

If all parameters remain constant, except that the expiration date draws nearer, both options will have to fall in value. Both the call and the put will be worthless at expiration because $S = X = \$100$. Therefore, the call and put options will lose their entire value through time decay. Figure 5.5 illustrates time decay for our sample options.

THETA$_c$ and THETA$_p$ both vary with changing stock prices and with the passage of time. For the options of our continuing example, Figure 5.6 shows how the call and put THETAs vary with the stock price. (Notice that the graph shows how a put that is deep-in-the-money can have a positive THETA.) THETA$_c$ and THETA$_p$ also both change with the passage of time. If the stock price is near the exercise price, THETA$_c$ and THETA$_p$ will become quite negative as expiration nears, as Figure 5.7 shows. However, this is not true for options that are deep-in-the-money or deep-out-of-the-money. Figure 5.7 shows how THETA$_c$ and THETA$_p$ change in very different manners depending upon

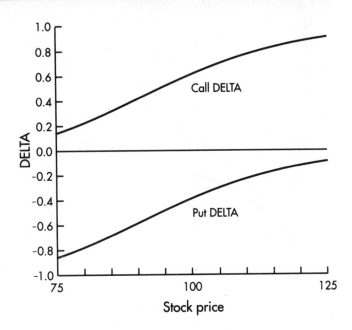

Call and Put DELTAs as a Function of the Stock Price   **Figure 5.4**

$X = \$100; \sigma = .3; r = .08; T - t = 180$ days

whether the options are in-the-money or out-of-the-money. For example, a European put that is in-the-money will have a positive THETA as expiration nears.

VEGA

VEGA is the first derivative of an option's price with respect to the volatility of the underlying stock. $VEGA_c$ and $VEGA_p$ are identical and always positive. (VEGA is sometimes known as kappa, lambda, or sigma as well. We use the term VEGA throughout.)

The VEGA is an important determinant of option prices. A sudden substantive change in the standard deviation of the underlying stock can cause a dramatic change in option values. As we noted for our example options, $c = \$10.30$ and $p = \$6.44$ when $\sigma = .3$. If volatility were to suddenly increase by .2 so that $\sigma = .5$, we would expect new prices of $c = \$10.30 + .2(26.8416) = \$15.67$ and $p = \$6.44 + .2(26.8416) = \$11.81$.

The actual call and put prices with $\sigma = .5$ would be $c = \$15.69$ and $p = \$11.82$, causing a price increase of 52 percent for the call and 84 percent for the put. During and immediately following the Crash of 1987 (when the stock market lost 20–25 percent of its value in one day), the perceived volatility for stocks increased tremendously causing an increase in option values. (Of course, calls generally lost value due to falling prices, and puts increased in value for the same reason.) Figure 5.8 shows how call and put prices vary with the standard deviation for our example options.

Figure 5.5   Call and Put Prices as a Function of the Time Until Expiration

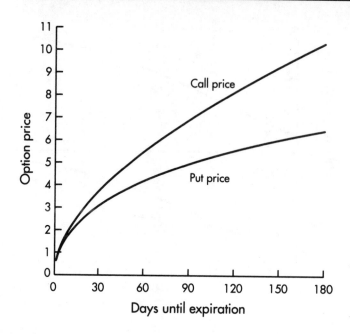

$S = \$100;\ X = \$100;\ \sigma = .3;\ r = .08$

VEGA tends to be greatest for an option near-the-money. When an option is deep-in-the-money or deep-out-of-the-money, the VEGA is low and can approach zero. Figure 5.9 shows how VEGA varies with respect to the stock price for the call and put of our continuing example. Because the two example options are at-the-money, VEGA is at its maximum. For calls or puts in-the-money or out-of-the-money, the VEGA will be lower.

RHO

RHO is the first derivative of an option's price with respect to the interest rate. RHO_c is always positive, while RHO_p is always negative. In general, option prices are not very sensitive to RHO. In Table 5.6, $RHO_c = 25.2515$ and $RHO_p = -22.1559$. If the interest rate were to increase by 1 percent, then the call price should increase by $.01(25.2515) = \$.2525$, while the price of the put should fall by $.01(-22.1559) = \$.2216$. Figure 5.10 shows how the prices of our example options would change given varying interest rates. Large changes in the interest rate have relatively little effect on the option prices.

RHO changes as a function of both the stock price and the time until expiration. RHO_c tends to be low for an option that is deep-out-of-the-money and high for a deep-in-the-money call. RHO_c tends to be sensitive to the stock price when a call is near-the-money. RHO_p is generally low for a

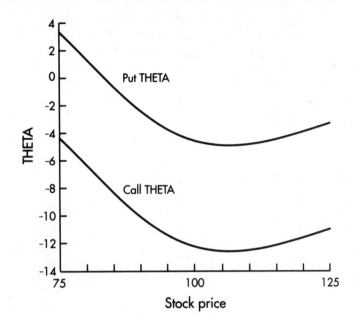

Call and Put THETAs as a Function of the Stock Price | **Figure 5.6**

$X = \$100$; $\sigma = .3$; $r = .08$; $T - t = 180$ days

deep-in-the-money put, and generally large for a deep-out-of-the-money put. When the put is near-the-money, RHO_p tends to be more sensitive to the stock price. Figure 5.11 illustrates the sensitivity of RHO_c and RHO_p to the stock price for the options in our continuing example.

RHO_c and RHO_p change as time passes, with both tending toward zero as expiration approaches. The interest rate affects the price of an option in conjunction with the time remaining until expiration mainly through the time value of money. If little time remains until expiration, the interest rate is relatively unimportant, and the price of an option becomes less sensitive to the interest rate. For our example options, Figure 5.12 shows how RHO_c and RHO_p tend to zero as expiration approaches.

GAMMA

Unlike the other sensitivity measures we have considered thus far, GAMMA does not measure the sensitivity of the price of an option to one of the parameters. Instead, GAMMA measures how DELTA changes with changes in the stock price. The GAMMA of a put and a call are always identical, and GAMMA can be either positive or negative. (In terms of calculus, GAMMA is the second derivative of the option price with respect to the stock price.) GAMMA is the only second-order effect that we consider, but it is an important one.

From our example computations in Table 5.6, we see that $GAMMA_c = GAMMA_p = .0181$. The table also shows $DELTA_c = .6151$, and $DELTA_p = -.3849$. If the stock price were to increase by \$1

Figure 5.7   Call and Put THETAs as a Function of the Time Until Expiration

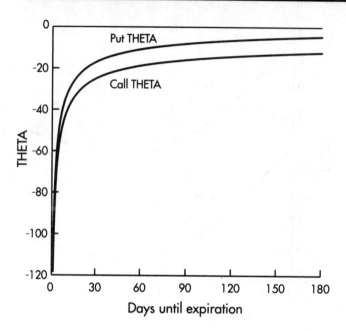

$X = \$100$; $\sigma = .3$; $r = .08$

from $100 to $101, we would expect the two DELTAs to change. The new expected DELTA$_c$ = .6151 + 1(.0181) = .6332, and the new expected DELTA$_p$ = −.3849 + 1(.0181) = −.3668. With a stock price of $101, the actual values are: DELTA$_c$ = .6330, and DELTA$_p$ = −.3670.

GAMMA tends to be large when an option is near-the-money. A large GAMMA for a given stock price simply means that the DELTA is highly sensitive to changes in the stock price around its current level. For our sample options, Figure 5.4 shows that DELTA$_c$ and DELTA$_p$ are sensitive to the stock price when the price is near the exercise price of $100. When an option is deep-in-the-money, the DELTA is near 1.0 and is not very sensitive to changing stock prices. Because of DELTA's low sensitivity to stock prices, the GAMMA for a call or a put that is deep-in-the-money must be low. A similar principle applies for a call or a put that is deep-out-of-the-money. In such a situation, the DELTA of either a call or a put will be quite low and will be insensitive to changing stock prices. Due to this low sensitivity, the GAMMA will be small for either a call or a put that is deep-out-of-the-money.

Figure 5.4 shows how DELTA$_c$ and DELTA$_p$ vary with the stock price for our sample options. GAMMA essentially measures the slope of the graphs in Figure 5.4. Because the slopes of the graphs in Figure 5.4 are near zero for calls or puts that are deep-in-the-money or deep-out-of-the-money, GAMMA must be low as well. When the call or put are near-the-money, the rate of change in the

Call and Put Prices as a Function of the Standard Deviation   **Figure 5.8**

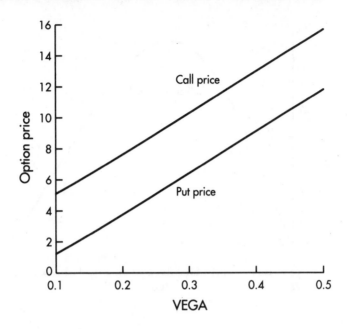

$S = \$100$; $X = \$100$; $r = .08$; $T - t = 180$ days

DELTA as a function of the stock price is high – that is, the slope of the graph in Figure 5.4 is high. Therefore, for near-the-money options, GAMMA must be large.

Figure 5.13 shows how GAMMA varies with the stock price for our sample options. The figure applies to both the put and the call because the GAMMAs are the same for a put and call with the same underlying instrument, time to expiration, and strike price. As the figure shows, GAMMA is large when the option is near-the-money and small when the option is deep-in-the-money or when it is deep-out-of-the-money.

GAMMA also varies with the time remaining until expiration. For an option that is near-the-money, GAMMA increases as expiration approaches. This large GAMMA reflects the heightened sensitivity of the DELTA to the stock price when the option is near-the-money and expiration is near. For an option that is deep-out-of-the-money or deep-in-the-money, GAMMA will fall dramatically as expiration becomes very close. For in-the-money or out-of-the-money options, with expiration distant, the GAMMA will tend to rise as time passes. However, it is difficult to make solid generalizations about how GAMMA will change without actually calculating the effects of the passage of time. Both our example options are at-the-money, so the GAMMAs of the call and put will rise as expiration nears. Figure 5.14 shows how GAMMA varies with time remaining until expiration for options at-the-money, in-the-money, and out-of-the-money.

Figure 5.9	Call and Put VEGA as a Function of the Stock Price

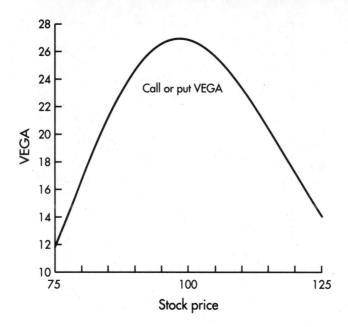

$X = \$100$; $r = .08$; $T - t = 180$ days

Positive and Negative GAMMA Portfolios

Earlier in this chapter, we created an example of a delta-neutral portfolio. For our sample call option, we saw that we could create a delta-neutral portfolio consisting of a long position of .6151 shares of the underlying stock and a short position of one call. Figure 5.2 shows how the value of this portfolio changes as the stock price changes. As the price of the stock moves away from $100, the value of the portfolio decreases.

The underlying stock has a DELTA of 1.0, which never changes. The change in the value of the stock is always 1:1 for changes in the value of the stock. Because the DELTA of the stock never changes, its GAMMA must be zero; the DELTA of the stock is completely insensitive to changes in the stock price. For our example call, the GAMMA is .0181. Because we have sold one call with a GAMMA of .0181 and .6151 shares with a GAMMA of zero, the GAMMA of this portfolio must be −.0181. Because the portfolio has a negative GAMMA, the DELTA of the portfolio must decrease if the stock price changes.

For small changes in the stock price, we know that the price of the portfolio of −1 call and .6151 shares will not change because the portfolio was constructed to be delta-neutral. For large changes in the stock price, however, the value of this portfolio will fall. The following data show

Call and Put Prices as a Function of the Interest Rate   **Figure 5.10**

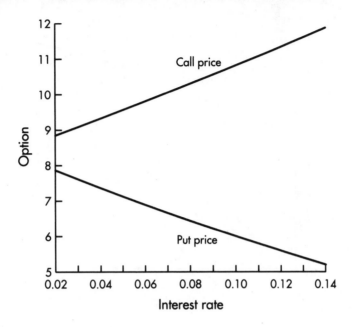

$S = \$100;\ X = \$100;\ \sigma = .3;\ T - t = 180$ days

the value of the elements of the portfolio and the total portfolio for stock prices of $90, $100, and $110.

Stock Price	Call Price	.6151 Shares	Portfolio Value (−1 Call + .6151 Shares)
$ 90	$ 5.12	$55.36	$50.24
100	10.30	61.51	51.21
110	17.28	67.66	50.38

The negative GAMMA of this portfolio ensures that large changes in the stock price will make the portfolio lose value. This is true whether the stock price rises or falls.

By contrast, consider a delta-neutral portfolio with a positive GAMMA. We can construct such a portfolio by combining our example put with the underlying stock to form a new portfolio. From Table 5.6, $p = \$6.4360$, $\text{DELTA}_p = -.3849$, and $\text{GAMMA}_p = .0181$. A portfolio of one put and .3849 shares of stock will be delta-neutral, will be worth $44.926, and will have a GAMMA of .0181. The following table shows how the value of this positive GAMMA portfolio will vary with large changes in the stock price.

Figure 5.11   Call and Put RHOs as a Function of the Stock Price

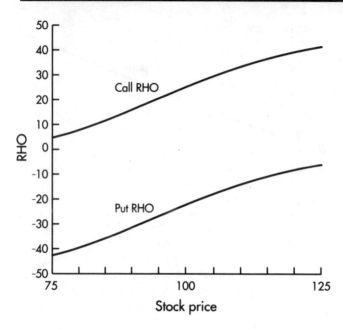

$X = \$100$; $\sigma = .3$; $r = .08$; $T - t = 180$ days

			Portfolio Value
Stock Price	*Put Price*	*.3849 Shares*	*(1 Put + .3849 Shares)*
$ 90	$11.25	$34.64	$45.89
100	6.44	38.49	44.93
110	3.41	42.34	45.75

These examples of a negative GAMMA portfolio and a positive GAMMA portfolio show the desirability of positive GAMMAs. If a trader holds a position with a positive GAMMA, large changes in the stock price will cause the portfolio value to increase. We have explored this within the context of a delta-neutral portfolio, but the principle holds for all portfolios.

CREATING NEUTRAL PORTFOLIOS

We have seen that a trader can create a delta-neutral portfolio from a stock and a call or from a stock and a put. In some situations, a trader might like to create a position that is neutral with respect to some other parameter, such as the THETA or VEGA of a portfolio. We now focus on stock plus option portfolios and show how to ensure various types of neutrality for these portfolios.

We saw that a stock plus call or a stock plus put portfolio could be created as a delta-neutral portfolio. In general, a stock plus a single option portfolio can be made neutral with respect to just

Call and Put RHOs as a Function of the Time Until Expiration   **Figure 5.12**

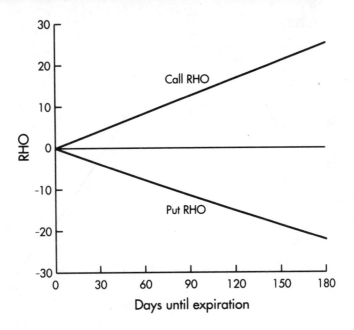

$S = \$100; \ X = \$100; \ \sigma = .3; \ r = .08$

one parameter. For example, when we created the delta-neutral portfolios analyzed earlier, we found that the resulting portfolios were not gamma-neutral. A portfolio comprising a stock and a single option can never be delta-neutral and gamma-neutral unless the GAMMA of the option happens to be zero. However, we can control both the DELTA and the GAMMA of a stock plus option portfolio by creating a portfolio of a stock and two different options.

To illustrate this idea, we introduce another call option on the same underlying stock that we have been considering. This call option has the same time to expiration, but its exercise price is $X = \$110$. For this call, we have $c = \$6.06$, $\text{DELTA}_c = .4365$, and $\text{GAMMA}_c = .0187$. To create a portfolio that is delta-neutral and gamma-neutral using our stock and these two calls, we create a portfolio that meets the two following conditions:

$$N_s\text{DELTA}_s + N_1\text{DELTA}_1 + N_2\text{DELTA}_2 = 0$$
$$N_s\text{GAMMA}_s + N_1\text{GAMMA}_1 + N_2\text{GAMMA}_2 = 0$$

where N_s, N_1, and N_2 are the number of shares, the number of the first call (with $X = \$100$), and the number of the second call (with $X = \$110$) to be held in the portfolio. We choose to create the portfolio with one share of stock, so $N_s = 1$. This leaves two equations with two unknowns, N_1 and N_2. We must choose these values to meet the two neutrality conditions.

Figure 5.13   GAMMA as a Function of the Stock Price

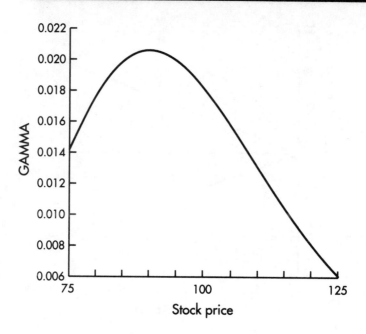

$X = \$100; \sigma = .3; r = .08; T - t = 180$ days

For our example stock and options, we have:

$$1(1) + N_1(.6151) + N_2(.4365) = 0$$
$$1(0) + N_1(.0181) + N_2(.0187) = 0$$

If $N_1 = -5.1917$ and $N_2 = 5.0251$, the conditions will be met. Therefore, we create a delta-neutral and gamma-neutral portfolio by buying one share, selling 5.1917 calls with $X = \$100$, and buying 5.0251 calls with $X = \$110$. The resulting portfolio will be both delta-neutral and gamma-neutral.

This portfolio may be delta-neutral and gamma-neutral, but its value will still be sensitive to other parameters, such as the standard deviation of the underlying stock or the time until expiration. If we wanted to make the portfolio neutral with respect to DELTA, GAMMA, and VEGA, for example, we would need to add a third option to the portfolio. In general, we need to use one option for each sensitivity parameter that we want to control.

OPTION SENSITIVITIES AND OPTION TRADING STRATEGIES

Thus far in this chapter, we have seen that a trader can use a knowledge of option sensitivities to control risk. By the same token, this knowledge can be used to guide speculative trading strategies

GAMMA as a Function of the Time Until Expiration   **Figure 5.14**

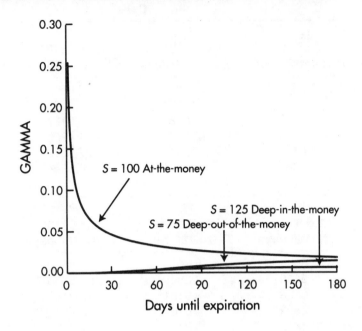

$X = \$100$; $\sigma = .3$; $r = .08$; $T - t = 180$ days

as well. By knowing the sensitivities of the various positions, a trader can create strategies to exploit certain expectations efficiently. Further, a trader should be aware of the various sensitivities of a position so she does not suffer unpleasant surprises.

In Chapter 2, we considered a wide variety of strategies, such as straddles, strangles, butterfly spreads, and condors, and we evaluated the profitability of these trades at expiration. Now, armed with the Black-Scholes model and the Merton model, we can understand how the value of these positions will behave prior to expiration. Further, given a knowledge of the sensitivities, we can analyze how a given trading strategy is likely to behave when the stock price changes, when volatility changes, or when the option approaches expiration. To explore the characteristics of option strategies, we consider the sample options shown in Table 5.7, which we use to illustrate some of the typical strategies.

The Straddle

Consider a long straddle consisting of call $C2$ and put $P2$ from Table 5.7. The cost of this position is $16.74. If the stock price at expiration is $100, which is the common exercise price for the two options, the position will expire worthless. At expiration, the value of the straddle will equal the intrinsic value of the call if the stock price exceeds $100, or it will equal the intrinsic value of the put if the stock price is below $100.

| Table 5.7 | Sample Options |

Calls

	C1 X = $90 T − t = 180 days	C2 X = $100; T − t = 180 days	C3 X = $110; T − t = 180 days	C4 X = $100; T − t = 90 days
Price	16.33	10.30	6.06	6.91
DELTA	.7860	.6151	.4365	.5820
GAMMA	.0138	.0181	.0187	.0262
THETA	−11.2054	−12.2607	−11.4208	−15.8989
VEGA	20.4619	26.8416	27.6602	19.3905
RHO	30.7085	25.2515	18.5394	12.6464

Puts

	P1 X = $90 T − t = 180 days	P2 X = $100; T − t = 180 days	P3 X = $110; T − t = 180 days	P4 X = $100; T − t = 90 days
Price	2.85	6.44	11.80	4.95
DELTA	−.2140	−.3849	−.5635	−.4180
GAMMA	.0138	.0181	.0187	.0262
THETA	−4.2839	−4.5701	−2.9612	−8.0552
VEGA	20.4619	26.8416	27.6602	19.3905
RHO	−11.9582	−22.1559	−33.6087	−11.5295

$S = \$100$; $r = .08$; $\sigma = .3$; $\delta = 0$

At the present, 180 days before expiration, the straddle has a DELTA of .2302, so the value of the straddle will vary directly with the stock price but at a much reduced rate. The GAMMA of the straddle is .0362, so large shifts in the stock price will be beneficial. The VEGA of the straddle is 53.6832, indicating that any increase in volatility will increase the value of the position. The THETA of the straddle is -16.8308, emphasizing that the passage of time will reduce the value of the position. In fact, if the stock price remains at $100 for the 180 days that remain until expiration, the value of the straddle will decay from $16.74 to zero over this period. A single day is .00273973 years. Therefore, with a THETA of −16.8308, we would expect a loss in the value of the straddle from day 180 to day 179 of −$.046, assuming the stock price remains steady at $100. While the straddle might lose only about $.05 of its value per day due to time decay, it will decay to just $11.86 in 90 days. Figure 5.15 shows how the profit and loss from this straddle varies for 180, 90, and zero days to expiration as a function of the stock price.

Time decay works to the benefit of the seller of this straddle, reducing the potential liability each day. By the same token, the seller is exposed to volatility risk. If the volatility of the underlying stock increases, both option values will rise and the short straddle position will lose. Finally, the positive GAMMA on the straddle is unfortunate from the point of view of the seller.

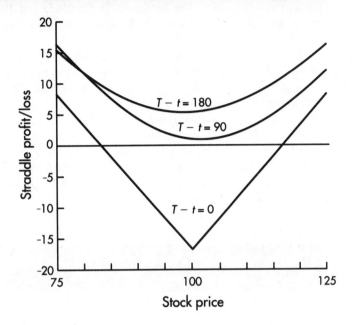

The Profit/Loss of a Straddle as a Function of the Stock Price
with Various Times Remaining Until Expiration

Figure 5.15

$X = \$100$; $\sigma = .3$; $r = .08$

The Strangle

As we saw in Chapter 2, a strangle is similar to a straddle because it involves the purchase of a put and a call. Unlike a straddle, however, the striking prices of the put and call are not identical. To purchase a strangle, the trader buys a call with a lower exercise price and purchases a put with a higher exercise price. Here we consider two different strangle purchases using the example options detailed in Table 5.7.

The first strangle covers the exercise price range from $90 to $110. To purchase the strangle, the trader buys $C1$ with an exercise price of $90 and buys $P3$ with an exercise price of $110. For $C1$, we have $c = \$16.33$, DELTA = .7860, GAMMA = .0138, THETA = −11.2054, VEGA = 20.4619, and RHO = 30.7085. For $P3$, $p = 11.80$, DELTA = −.5635, GAMMA = .0187, THETA = −2.9612, VEGA = 27.6602, and RHO = −33.6087. Because both options are $10 into-the-money, they are fairly expensive, and the total cost of this strangle is $28.13. $C1$ has a large DELTA because it is well into-the-money. For $C1$ RHO is positive, but RHO is negative for $P3$. As a result the strangle is not very sensitive to interest rates.

As a second strangle, we focus on an exercise price range from $100 to $110. This strangle requires the purchase of $C2$ and $P3$. For $C2$, $c = 10.30$, DELTA = .6151, GAMMA = .0181, THETA =

−12.2607, VEGA = 26.8416, and RHO = 25.2515. $P3$ is the same put we considered in the preceding paragraph. This second strangle costs $22.10. The DELTA of the call (.6151) and put (−.5635) almost offset each other, so this strangle is almost delta-neutral. However, the strangle has a positive GAMMA and a high positive sensitivity to volatility. The RHOs of $C2$ (25.2515) and $P3$ (−33.6087) have different signs and largely offset each other. Therefore, the strangle has a low sensitivity to interest rates.

Figure 5.16 shows the profit and loss profiles for both strangles as a function of the current stock price. At the current stock price of $100, the profit or loss on the two positions is equal. For any stock price below $100, the first strangle has a greater profit (or a smaller loss). If the stock price moves above $100, the second strangle has a greater profit.

Notice that the two strangles have quite different risk profiles. As we noted earlier, the first strangle (with X_1 = $90 and X_2 = $110) is almost delta-neutral. The second strangle (with X_1 = $100 and X_2 = $110) is more sensitive to changes in the stock price around S = $100. The VEGA for the first strangle is 48.1221, while the VEGA for the second strangle is 54.5018. As both strangles employ the same put ($P3$), this difference in VEGA is due to the difference in VEGA between $C1$ and $C2$, and demonstrates the greater sensitivity to risk of the first strangle.

Figure 5.16   The Profit/Loss of Two Strangles as a Function of the Stock Price

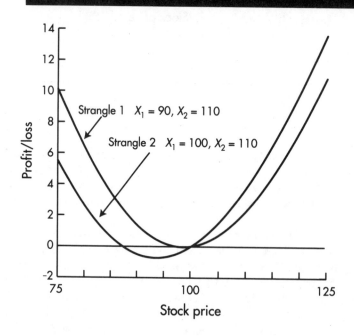

σ = .3; r = .08; $T - t$ = 180 days

The Butterfly Spread with Calls

In a butterfly spread, a purchaser employs calls with three different exercise prices with the same underlying good and the same expiration. To illustrate the investment characteristics of this position, we use calls $C1-C3$ from Table 5.7. To purchase a butterfly spread, the trader would buy $C1$ (with $X = \$90$), buy $C3$ (with $X = \$110$), and sell two $C2$ (with $X = \$100$). Thus the position is long $C1$, long $C3$, and short two $C2$. This position costs $1.79:

$$16.33 - 2(10.30) + 6.06 = \$1.79$$

At a price of $1.79, we might expect future payoffs to be unlikely and small, and we should be aware of potential risks. From Chapter 2, we know that a butterfly spread with calls has the greatest payoff at expiration if the stock price equals the exercise price of the calls that were sold. For our example, that price would be $100. If the stock price at expiration were $100, $C1$ (with $X = \$90$) would be worth $10, and all other options in the spread would expire worthless.

The DELTA of this butterfly spread is:

$$.7860 - 2(.6151) + .4365 = -.0077$$

Thus, the DELTA of the spread is almost zero, but just slightly negative. Any change in the stock price will cause a slight fall in the value of the position. Further, the GAMMA is near zero, but also slightly negative:

$$.0138 - 2(.0181) + .0187 = -.0037$$

There is also little to hope for a change in volatility because the VEGA for the spread is negative:

$$20.4619 - 2(26.8416) + 27.6602 = -5.5611$$

Therefore, the position is not very sensitive to volatility, but an increase in volatility would cause some loss in value.

The butterfly spread has a RHO of -1.2551:

$$30.7085 - 2(25.2515) + 18.5394 = -1.2551$$

The value of the butterfly spread will vary inversely with interest rates, but the position is not very sensitive to interest rates.

The THETA for the butterfly spread is:

$$-11.2054 - 2(-12.2607) - 11.4208 = 1.8952$$

The positive THETA indicates that time decay will increase the value of the position.

These relationships are clear from Figure 5.17. As we noted, DELTA for the spread is slightly negative. In Figure 5.17, this leads to a shallow curve for the figure, with a downward slope for stock prices greater or less than $100. The negative GAMMA is shown in the figure as the increasing

Figure 5.17   The Profit/Loss of a Butterfly Spread as a Function of the Stock Price

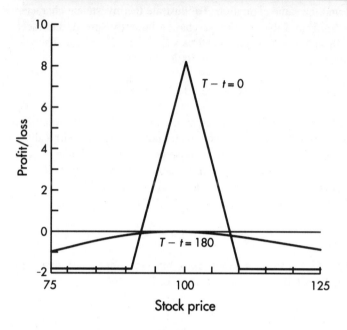

$\sigma = .3$; $r = .08$; $T - t = 180$ days; $X_1 = \$90$; $X_2 = \$100$; $X_3 = \$110$

downward curvature of the line. Figure 5.17 also shows the profit and loss on the butterfly spread as a function of the stock price at expiration. If the stock price remains at \$100, time decay will cause the value of the butterfly spread to rise to \$10 at expiration. Thus, time decay increases the value of this position, consistent with the positive THETA noted earlier.

The Bull Spread with Calls

To create a bull spread with calls, a trader purchases a call with a lower exercise price and sells a call with a higher exercise price. The two calls have the same underlying good and same term to expiration. We illustrate the bull spread with calls by considering options $C1$ and $C2$ from Table 5.7. These calls have exercise prices of \$90 and \$100, respectively. Option $C1$ costs \$16.33, and Option $C2$ costs \$10.30. Therefore, the spread will cost \$6.03.

The sensitivities for the spread are: DELTA = .7860 − .6151 = .1709; GAMMA = .0138 − .0181 = −.0043; THETA = −11.2054 + 12.2607 = 1.0553; VEGA = 20.4619 − 26.8416 = −6.3797; and RHO = 30.7085 − 25.2515 = 5.4570. Therefore, we see that a stock price increase will cause an increase in the value of the spread, which will be partially offset for large stock price changes by the negative GAMMA. Time decay will cause an increase in the value of the spread, as shown by the positive THETA. The spread has a negative VEGA, indicating that an increase in the stock's volatility will cause a decrease in the value of the spread. Finally, the RHO is positive, so an increase in interest rates will cause the spread to increase in value.

Figure 5.18 shows the profit and loss profile for the spread as a function of the price of the underlying stock. The graph shows that the value of the spread is positively related to the stock price. Further, Figure 5.18 illustrates that time decay will cause an increase in profits on the position. If no other parameters change, the profit and loss profile for the spread will collapse to its value at expiration as shown in the graph.

The VEGA of the option with the higher exercise price ($C2$ with $X = \$100$) is larger than that of $C1$ (with $X = \$90$). Because the position is long $C1$ and short $C2$, the spread's VEGA is negative. Therefore, an increase in volatility will cause the price of the spread to fall. Figure 5.19 shows the profitability of the spread as a function of the standard deviation.

A Ratio Spread with Calls

As discussed in Chapter 2, there are infinite possible ratio spreads because a new position can be created merely by changing the ratio between the options that comprise the spread. Therefore, we illustrate the general technique of ratio spreads with a fairly simple ratio spread using just two options.

The Profit/Loss of a Bull Spread with Calls as a Function of the Stock Price	**Figure 5.18**

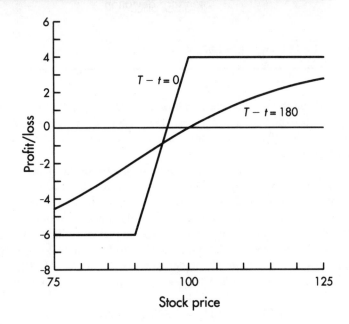

$\sigma = .3$; $r = .08$; $T - t = 180$ days; $X_1 = \$90$; $X_2 = \$100$

Figure 5.19 The Profit/Loss of a Bull Spread with Calls as a Function of the Standard Deviation

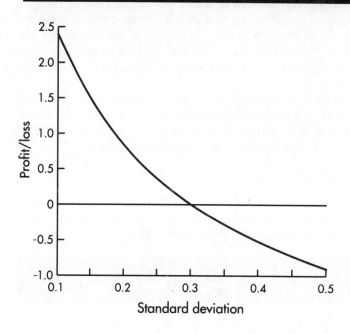

S = $100; *r* = .08; *T* – *t* = 180 days; X_1 = $90; X_2 = $100

Earlier, we considered the straddle composed of call *C*2 and put *P*2 from Table 5.7. We noted that the straddle costs $16.74 and has a DELTA = .6151 − .3849 = .2302. The straddle had a VEGA = 26.8416 + 26.8416 = 53.6832. Thus, the straddle is essentially a volatility strategy with a relatively low DELTA and a high VEGA.

Consider now a trader's desire to create a position with most of the characteristics of a straddle, but to make it more purely a volatility strategy. In other words, the trader anticipates a volatility increase for the underlying stock but does not wish to take a position on whether stock prices might rise or fall. Therefore, this trader would like to create a delta-neutral position with a high VEGA. The trader can create such a position by using a ratio spread that is similar to the straddle. However, instead of buying one *C*2 and one *P*2, the trader decides to buy one *C*2 and enough puts (*P*2) to create a delta-neutral position. Therefore, the trader buys one *C*2 and 1.5981 *P*2, which costs $10.30 + 1.5981(6.44) = $20.59. This position is delta-neutral because the DELTA of the spread is:

$$DELTA = .6151 + 1.5981(-.3849) = 0.0$$

The other sensitivities for the ratio spread are: GAMMA = .0181 + 1.5981(.0181) = .0470; THETA = −12.2607 + 1.5981(−4.5701) = −19.5642; VEGA = 26.8416 + 1.5981(26.8416) = 69.7372; and RHO =

25.2515 + (1.5981)(−22.1559) = −10.1558. Therefore, this ratio spread has zero DELTA and a high VEGA. The value of the spread will suffer from time decay and will fall if interest rates rise.

Figure 5.20 shows the profitability of the straddle and the ratio spread as a function of the stock price. The ratio spread is much less sensitive to changing stock prices. This is consistent with its creation as a delta-neutral position. Both the straddle and the spread are essentially a bet on increasing volatility. However, the ratio spread is a purer bet on volatility because it is insensitive to stock price changes. Figure 5.21 shows how the profitability of the straddle and the ratio spread change with changing volatility. Clearly, the ratio spread is more sensitive to changing volatility, as is shown by its greater slope in Figure 5.21.

One of the advantages of ratio spreads is the ability to avoid risk exposure to one parameter and to accept risk exposure to another. For example, one could use a ratio spread of the form we have considered to create a position that is vega-neutral but with a large DELTA, indicating a high sensitivity to changes in the stock price. This vega-neutral position could be created by buying $C2$ and selling $P2$ in a ratio of 1:1. The resulting spread would have a DELTA = 1.0. Thus, with a ratio spread of two options, one can maintain neutrality with respect to one parameter and accept sensitivity with respect to a second parameter.

| The Profit/Loss of a Straddle and a Ratio Spread as a Function of the Stock Price | Figure 5.20 |

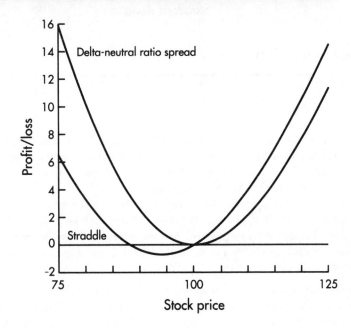

$\sigma = .3$; $r = .08$; $T - t = 180$ days; $X = \$100$

Figure 5.21	The Profit/Loss of a Straddle and a Ratio Spread as a Function of the Standard Deviation

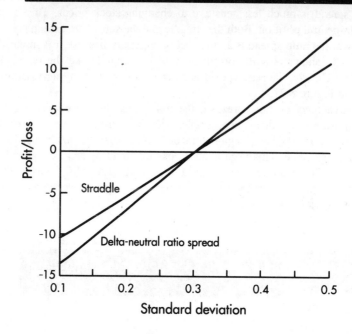

$S = \$100;\ r = .08;\ T - t = 180$ days; $X = \$100$

The Calendar Spread

All of the option strategies we have considered thus far have employed options with the same expiration date. A **calendar spread** or a **time spread** is an option combination that employs options with different expiration dates but a common underlying stock. These spreads all have a horizon that terminates by the time the near-expiration option expires.

By using calendar spreads, a trader can adopt speculative strategies designed to exploit beliefs about future stock prices. Bullish and bearish calendar spreads are both possible. The trader can also exploit differential sensitivities to create positions that are neutral with respect to some option parameter, while selecting exposure to others. For example, a trader might create a delta-neutral calendar spread that will profit with time decay.

A Calendar Spread with Calls. As a first example of a calendar spread, consider calls $C2$ and $C4$ in Table 5.7. These calls are identical, except that call $C2$ expires in 180 days and $C4$ expires in 90 days. Assume that a trader creates a calendar spread by buying $C2$ and selling $C4$. The cost of this position is: $\$10.30 - \$6.91 = \$3.39$. The sensitivities for the spread are: DELTA = .6151 − .5820 = .0331; GAMMA = .0181 − .0262 = −.0081; THETA = −12.2607 − (−15.8989) = 3.6382; VEGA = 26.8416 − 19.3905 = 7.4511; and RHO = 25.2515 − 12.6464 = 12.6051. In purchasing this position, the trader has obtained a position that will gain value for an increase in the stock price, volatility, and interest rate. Further, the position will increase in value with time decay.

Figure 5.22 shows the profitability of the calendar spread at the time it is initiated (with 180 days until C2 expires and 90 days until C4 expires). It also shows the value of the spread in 90 days (when C4 expires and C2 has 90 days remaining until expiration). We first consider the value profile of the spread at the time it is initiated. At $S = \$100$, the spread is worth $3.39, the price the trader paid. As we have seen, it is essentially delta-neutral and gamma-neutral, with a relatively low sensitivity to the standard deviation and the interest rate. The spread does have a positive THETA, however, indicating that time decay will increase the value of the position.

This positive time decay is also shown in Figure 5.22, because the figure shows the profitability of the position in 90 days, when C4 expires. If the stock price is at $100, C4 will expire worthless, but C2 will be worth $6.91. Therefore, the price of the spread will rise from $3.39 to $6.91 over 90 days if the stock price does not change. This increase in profits is strictly due to time decay. Therefore, this type of calendar spread with calls is essentially an attempt to take advantage of time decay.

A Calendar Spread with Puts. Consider the spread in which a trader buys a put with a distant expiration and sells a put with a nearby expiration. We illustrate this spread by considering puts P2

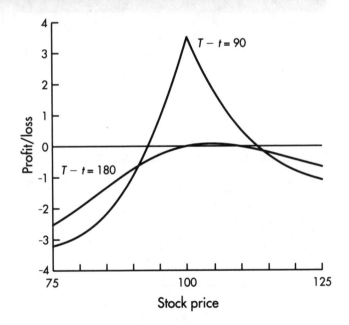

The Value of a Calendar Spread with Calls as a Function of the Stock Price   **Figure 5.22**

$r = .08$; $T_1 - t = 180$ days; $T_2 - t = 90$ days; $X_1 = X_2 = \$100$

and $P4$ from Table 5.7. The trader buys $P2$ for $6.44 and sells put $P4$ for $4.95, for a total cost of $1.49.

The sensitivities for the spread are: DELTA $= -.3849 - (-.4180) = .0331$; GAMMA $= .0181 - .0262 = -.0081$; THETA $= -4.5701 - (-8.0552) = 3.4851$; VEGA $= 26.8416 - 19.3905 = 7.4511$; and RHO $= -22.1559 - (-11.5295) = -10.6264$. The most important features of this spread are its low DELTA and its significantly positive THETA. The position is not very sensitive to changes in stock prices, but it should appreciate with time decay. Figure 5.23 shows the profitability of this spread as a function of the stock price at the time it is initiated (when $P2$ has 180 days until expiration and $P4$ has 90 days until expiration). The figure also shows the profitability of the spread at the expiration date of the nearby put. Notice that this graph is almost (but not quite) identical to Figure 5.22. Implementing a calendar spread with puts or calls gives virtually the same profit and loss profile. If the stock price remains constant at $S = \$100$, the value of the spread will rise from $1.49 to $4.95 over the 90 days until $P4$ expires. Thus, this calendar spread with puts is essentially an attempt to exploit time decay.

SUMMARY

This chapter has explored the sensitivity of option prices to the key parameters that determine the price of an option – the stock price, the standard deviation of the stock's returns, the interest rate,

---

Figure 5.23   The Value of a Calendar Spread with Puts as a Function of the Stock Price

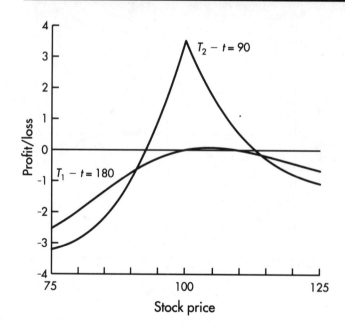

$r = .08$; $T_1 - t = 180$ days; $T_2 - t = 90$ days; $X_1 = X_2 = \$100$

and the time remaining until expiration. We explored these measures within the context of the Merton model and showed that the Merton model embraces the Black-Scholes model. Given a knowledge of these sensitivities, a trader can use options more effectively, both for hedging and for speculating.

We have seen that DELTA measures the sensitivity of the price of an option to the price of the underlying stock. GAMMA measures the tendency for DELTA to change as the stock price changes, providing a measure of a second order for the key sensitivity DELTA. VEGA gauges the sensitivity of an option's price to the volatility of the underlying stock, while RHO measures the sensitivity of the option price to the interest rate. Finally, THETA measures the sensitivity of the option price to the time to expiration of the option.

By combining options with the underlying stock or by combining options into portfolios, the trader can create positions with exactly the desired risk exposures. For example, we saw that a trader could use a stock and a call to create a portfolio that is delta-neutral. A delta-neutral portfolio does not change in value as the stock price changes infinitesimally. We also saw how to use two options in conjunction with a stock to make a portfolio both delta-neutral and gamma-neutral.

In many instances, a trader will seek exposure to one or more of the option parameters as a speculative technique. For example, we saw how traders can use straddles to accept exposure to volatility while minimizing exposure to changes in the stock price. Such a strategy is essentially a bet on increasing volatility. We also observed that strangles created with different pairs of exercise prices could have substantially different DELTAs, even when all other factors are equal. A speculator interested in making money is well advised to master these relationships. A hedger needs to know how a given position responds to changing parameters to understand a hedge completely and to create more effective hedges. Given a knowledge of these sensitivities, a speculator or a hedger can understand the full spectrum of risk entailed by a position.

QUESTIONS AND PROBLEMS

1. Consider Call A, with: $X = \$70$; $r = .06$; $T - t = 90$ days; $\sigma = .4$; and $S = \$60$. Compute the price, DELTA, GAMMA, THETA, VEGA, and RHO for this call.
2. Consider Put A, with: $X = \$70$; $r = .06$; $T - t = 90$ days; $\sigma = .4$; and $S = \$60$. Compute the price, DELTA, GAMMA, THETA, VEGA, and RHO for this put.
3. Consider a straddle comprised of Call A and Put A. Compute the price, DELTA, GAMMA, THETA, VEGA, and RHO for this straddle.
4. Consider Call A. Assuming the current stock price is $60, create a delta-neutral portfolio consisting of a short position of one call and the necessary number of shares. What is the value of this portfolio for a sudden change in the stock price to $55 or $65?
5. Consider Call A and Put A from above. Assume that you create a portfolio that is short one call and long one put. What is the DELTA of this portfolio? Can you find the DELTA without computing? Explain. Assume that a share of stock is added to the short call/long put portfolio. What is the DELTA of the entire position?
6. What is the GAMMA of a share of stock if the stock price is $55 and a call on the stock with $X = \$50$ has a price $c = \$7$, while a put with $X = \$50$ has a price $p = \$4$? Explain.
7. Consider Call B written on the same stock as Call A with: $X = \$50$; $r = .06$; $T - t = 90$ days; $\sigma = .4$; and $S = \$60$. Form a bull spread with calls from these two instruments. What is the price of the spread? What is its DELTA? What will the price of the spread be at expiration if the terminal stock price is $60? From this information, can you tell whether THETA is positive or negative for the spread? Explain.

8. Consider again the sample options, $C2$ and $P2$, of the chapter discussion as given in Table 5.7. Assume now that the stock pays a continuous dividend of 3 percent per annum. See if you can tell how the sensitivities will differ for the call and a put without computing. Now compute the DELTA, GAMMA, VEGA, THETA, and RHO of the two options if the stock has a dividend.

9. Consider three calls Call C, Call D, and Call E, all written on the same underlying stock. $S = \$80$; $r = .07$; $\sigma = .2$. For Call C, $X = \$70$ and $T - t = 90$ days. For Call D, $X = \$75$ and $T - t = 90$ days. For Call E, $X = \$80$, and $T - t = 120$ days. Compute the price, DELTA, and GAMMA for each of these calls. Using Calls C and D, create a delta-neutral portfolio assuming that the position is long one Call C. Now use calls C, D, and E to form a portfolio that is delta-neutral and gamma-neutral, again assuming that the portfolio is long one Call C.

NOTE

[1] THETA$_p$ could be positive for a put that is deep-in-the-money. For example, if $S = \$50$, $X = \$100$, $r = .08$, $\sigma = .3$, and $T - t = 180$ days, $p = \$46.1354$, and THETA$_p = 7.6377$. Notice that the put is worth less than $X - S$ because the put is European and the owner cannot exercise. However, if none of the parameters change over the life of the option, the put price must rise to $50 at the expiration date.

AMERICAN OPTION PRICING

INTRODUCTION

Chapter 4 considered the principles of pricing for European options – those that can be exercised at only the expiration of the option. There we considered the binomial model and saw how it could be extended logically to the Black-Scholes model. Strictly speaking, the Black-Scholes model holds for only European options on non–dividend paying stocks. However, we saw that it is possible to extend the Black-Scholes model to account for dividends by several adjustment procedures, such as the known dividend adjustment and Merton's model, which accounts for continuous dividends. In addition, we saw that the binomial model can price options on stocks that pay dividends, either in the form of a proportional dividend or an actual dollar dividend. Therefore, the tools for pricing European options are quite robust. However, all of the models considered in Chapter 4 pertain strictly to European options.

This chapter focuses on American options – those that can be exercised at any time during the option's life. Most publicly traded options are American options, so it is important to develop techniques for pricing these instruments. However, the early exercise feature of American options brings with it substantial complexity. As we will see, there are no general closed-form pricing models for American options that would parallel the Black-Scholes model for European options.

This chapter begins by analyzing the differences between American and European options. It then considers some attempts to estimate the value of American options. Also, we consider a special case in which there is an exact option pricing formula. Later in the chapter, we return to the binomial model and show how it can be used to price American options with a high degree of accuracy. **OPTION!** can compute prices for all of the option models considered in this chapter.

AMERICAN VERSUS EUROPEAN OPTIONS

Consider two calls or two puts that have the same underlying good, the same exercise price, and the same time to expiration, but one option is American and the other is European. In this context,

American options are just like European options, except the American option allows the privilege of early exercise. Because of this parallel between the two kinds of options, we analyze American options by contrasting them with the simpler European options that we have already considered, under the assumption that the options are parallel – have the same underlying good, the same exercise price, and the same time until expiration. The difference in price between parallel American and European options must stem from the early exercise feature of the American option. Thus, if we know the price of a European option, we can price the parallel American option by determining the impact of the early exercise privilege. The value of the right to exercise before expiration is the **early exercise premium**. Much of our analysis of American options will concentrate on valuing the early exercise premium.

Because an American option affords every benefit of a parallel European option, plus the potentially valuable benefit of early exercise, we know that, for parallel options:

$$C_t \geq c_t \text{ and } P_t \geq p_t$$

where American options are denoted by upper case ''C'' or ''P,'' and European options are indicated by lower case ''c'' or ''p.'' While the American option must be worth at least as much as the parallel European option, it may not actually be worth more – the early exercise premium may have no value in some circumstances. In some situations, however, the early exercise premium may be extremely valuable, and the American option can be worth much more than the parallel European option.

American versus European Puts

In Chapter 3, we considered various boundary conditions that limited the arbitrage-free range of option prices. Due to its early exercise feature, an American put can always be converted into its exercise value $X - S_t$. Therefore:

$$P_t \geq X - S_t$$

For a European put, we saw in Chapter 3 that:

$$p_t \geq Xe^{-r(T-t)} - S_t$$

The difference in prices of parallel American and European options depends largely on the extent to which the option is in-the-money, the interest rate, and the amount of time remaining until expiration. The early exercise of an American put discards the value of waiting to see how stock prices evolve. On the other hand, by exercising immediately, the owner of an American put captures the exercise value, $X - S_t$, and can invest those proceeds from the time of exercise until the expiration date of the option. The greater this amount of time, and the higher the interest rate, the greater the incentive for early exercise.

To illustrate this idea consider a European put option with an exercise price of $100 and 180 days until expiration. The underlying stock has a standard deviation of .1 and the risk-free rate is 10 percent. If the stock price is $100, the European put is worth $.9749, well above its immediate exercise value of zero. However, if the stock price is $85, the European put is worth $10.33, well below $X - S_t = \$15$. With a stock price of $85, we know that the parallel American put would be worth at least $15. Figure 6.1 graphs the value of this European put and the quantity $X - S_t$ for various stock prices. As the graph shows, for stock prices near $85, the value of the European put approaches its lower bound of $Xe^{-r(T-t)} - S_t$ and changes almost 1:1 for changes in the stock price. Figure 6.1 suggests why American puts can be worth considerably more than their parallel European puts. With lower interest rates or a shorter time to expiration, the difference between $X - S_t$ would be lower relative to the value of the European put. For example, for this option with a stock price of $85 and only 20 days until expiration, the European put would be worth $14.45, much closer to the exercise value of $15.

Notice that this substantial difference in the value of American and European puts arises without any consideration of dividends because the stock considered in our previous example had no dividends. As Figure 6.1 shows, the difference between $X - S_t$ and the value of a European put is larger when the put is deep-in-the-money. For a put, large dividends reduce the value of the underlying stock substantially and tend to push a put deeper in-the-money. Thus, dividends can also increase the difference in value between European and American puts.

For an American put on a dividend paying stock, the optimal time to exercise is generally immediately after a dividend payment. Certainly, exercising just before a dividend payment would not make sense; it would be much better to wait for the dividend payment to reduce the stock price and push the put further in-the-money.

In this discussion of early exercise of American puts, the critical point to realize is that a substantial difference between European and American puts can arise even when there are no dividends. Further, it can be quite rational to exercise an American put before expiration on a non–dividend paying stock.

The Boundary Space for European and American Puts **Figure 6.1**

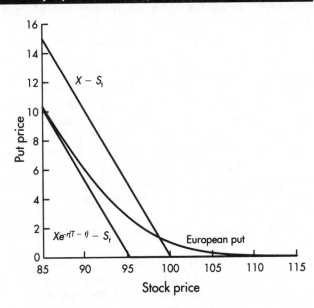

American versus European Calls

In understanding the differences between American and European calls, we begin with the simpler situation in which the underlying stock pays no dividends. For calls on a non–dividend paying stock, early exercise is never rational, and the price of an American and European call will be the same.

In Chapter 3, we explored boundary conditions for European call options and showed that before expiration the call must be worth at least as much as the stock price minus the present value of the exercise price. That is:

$$c_t \geq S_t - Xe^{-r(T-t)}$$

The immediate exercise value of a call is only $S_t - X$. As long as there is some time remaining until expiration and the interest rate is not zero, the European call will be worth more than the immediate exercise value.

Relative to its parallel European call, an American call gives benefits from the right to exercise early. However, the boundary condition on the call shows that early exercise is never desirable if the underlying stock pays no dividend. Therefore, the right to exercise early that is inherent in the American call can have no value; and for calls on a non–dividend paying stock, the price of an American call is the same as the price of a parallel European call.

We now consider the importance of dividends on call values. If the underlying stock pays a dividend, it can be rational to exercise early, and an American call can be worth more than its parallel European call. We emphasize this point by considering a radical situation. Assume that a stock trades for $80 and the firm has announced that it will pay a liquidating dividend of $80 one minute before the options on this stock expire. Assume that American and European calls on this share have an exercise price of $60 and the present time is two minutes before expiration. (The time is just before expiration in this example so that we can ignore the time value of money.) What would be the value of the American and European calls?

For the owner of the American call, the strategy is clear. The owner should exercise the option immediately, paying the exercise price of $60 and receiving the liquidating dividend of $80. This gives a cash flow of +$20, so the value of the American call must be $20. The European call cannot be exercised until expiration. But, under the terms of this example, the stock will be worth zero at the expiration of the option due to the payment of the liquidating dividend one minute before expiration. Therefore, the European call must be worth zero. Another way to see that the European call is worth zero is from the adjustment for known dividends, discussed in Chapter 4. There we saw that one could adjust the stock price by subtracting from the stock price the present value of all dividends to be paid during the life of the option. The Black-Scholes model could then be applied as usual if we substituted this dividend-adjusted stock price for the current stock price as an input to the model. In our present example, we would subtract the $80 dividend from the $80 stock price, giving an adjusted stock price of zero. Because the call is at expiration, it will be worth the maximum of zero or the adjusted stock price minus the exercise price. Therefore, the European call will be worth zero in this extreme circumstance.

In less extreme circumstances – when the dividend is smaller relative to the value of the stock and when there is more time remaining until expiration – it can still be rational to exercise before expiration. The decision to exercise early depends mainly on the amount of the dividend, the interest rate, and the time remaining until expiration. Our extreme example shows a general principle about early exercise. If there is to be early exercise of a call, it should occur immediately before a dividend payment. Later in this chapter, we will explore more fully the conditions that lead to the early exercise of calls. We now turn to models for pricing American options.

PSEUDO-AMERICAN CALL OPTION PRICING

The **pseudo-American call option pricing model** was created by Fischer Black.[1] It does not provide an exact pricing technique for American calls but does provide an estimated call price that draws on the intuitions of the Black-Scholes model. Later we explore more exact methods for pricing American calls, but the pseudo-American model is important because it clearly shows the factors that lead to early exercise and highlights the differences between European and American calls. Essentially, the valuation technique requires four steps.

1. From the current stock price, subtract the present value of all dividends that will be paid before the option expires. So far, this is the same procedure we followed for the known dividend adjustment for European calls.
2. For each dividend date, reduce the exercise price by the present value of all dividends yet to be paid, including the dividend that is about to go ex-dividend.
3. Taking each dividend date and the actual expiration date of the option as potential expiration dates, compute the value of a European call using the adjusted stock and exercise prices.
4. Select the highest of these European call values as the estimate of the value of the American call.

Each step has a clear rationale. In the first step, we adjust the stock price to reflect its approximate value after it pays the dividends. In the second step, we effectively add back the value of dividends to be received from the stock if we exercise. This is accomplished by reducing the liability of the exercise price by the present value of the dividends we will capture if we exercise. In the third step, we evaluate different exercise decisions. If we exercise, we will do so just before a dividend payment to capture the dividend from the stock. Thus, in the third step, we consider the payoffs from each potential exercise date. Finally, in the fourth step, we compare the different payoffs associated with each exercise strategy that we computed in the third step. Assuming that we plan to follow the best exercise strategy, we approximate the current American call price as the highest of these computed European call prices.

As an example, consider the following data.

$$S_t = \$60$$
$$X = \$60$$
$$T - t = 180 \text{ days}$$
$$r = .09$$
$$\sigma = .2$$
$$D_1 = \$2, \text{ to be paid in 60 days}$$
$$D_2 = \$2, \text{ to be paid in 150 days}$$

What is the pseudo-American call worth? The present value of the dividends is:

$$D_1 e^{-rt} + D_2 e^{-rt} = \$2e^{-(.09)(60/365)} + \$2e^{-(.09)(150/365)} = \$3.90$$

We subtract this present value from the stock price, so we use \$56.10 as our stock price in all subsequent calculations. We will use this adjusted stock price to compute call values, assuming the option expires at three different times: the actual expiration date, the date of the last dividend, and the date of the first dividend. Three inputs remain constant for each computation: $S = \$56.10$, $r = .09$, and $\sigma = .2$. The time until expiration will vary, and we must adjust the exercise price for different dividend amounts.

We begin with the actual expiration date. Applying the Black-Scholes model with $T - t = 180$ days and $X = \$60$ gives a call value of \$2.57. (This is the same as the known dividend adjustment for European calls discussed in Chapter 4.) Next, we deal with each dividend date, starting with the final dividend. The dividend is just about to be paid, so we adjust the exercise price by subtracting \$2. Thus, for $X = \$58$ and $T - t = 150$ days, the call value is \$2.97. Next, we consider the date of the first dividend. The present value of the dividends at that time consists of the dividend that is just about to be paid, \$2, plus the present value of the second dividend that will be paid in 90 days, $\$2e^{-(.09)(90/365)} = \$1.96$. Together, these dividends have a present value of \$3.96, so we adjust the exercise price to \$56.04. Therefore, for $X = \$56.04$ and $T - t = 60$ days, the call price is \$2.28.

Now we have three estimated call prices corresponding to two dividend dates and the actual expiration date of the option. The estimates are \$2.28 for the first dividend date, \$2.97 for the second date, and \$2.57 for the actual expiration date. Therefore, we take the largest value, \$2.97, as the estimate of the pseudo-American call value. The average error for this pseudo-American model is about 1.5 percent.[2]

The strategy behind the pseudo-American option technique is to realize that an American call on a dividend paying stock can be analyzed as consisting of a series of options. Given that early exercise is optimal only just prior to a dividend payment, we may think of the American call as consisting of a portfolio of European options that expire just before each dividend and at the actual exercise date. In the pseudo-American technique, we evaluate each of those European options and treat the American option as being worth the maximum of all of the European options.

EXACT AMERICAN CALL OPTION PRICING

In general, there is no closed-form solution to the value of an American call option on a dividend paying stock. However, an exact pricing formula is possible in one special case. It is possible to compute the exact price for an option on a stock that pays a single dividend during the life of the option.[3] The model is also known as the **compound option model**.

As discussed in the previous section on the pseudo-American model, an American call option really consists of a series of options that expire just before the various dividend dates and at the actual expiration of the option. We now focus on the situation when there is just one dividend between the present and the expiration date of the option, time T. We assume that the dividend occurs at time t_1. The time line in Figure 6.2 shows the decision points that we must consider. As t_1 approaches, the owner of the call must decide whether to exercise. If she exercises, she does so the instant before t_1 and receives the stock with dividends and pays the exercise price. If she does not exercise, the stock pays the dividend and she continues to hold a call on the stock, now without the dividend. The instant after the dividend payment occurs, the call is effectively a European call because there are no more dividend payments and early exercise on a European call is never rational. Letting S_1 be the stock price just after the dividend, D_1, is paid, and letting C_1 be the call price just after the dividend is paid, her choice is:

Decision Points for Options on a Dividend Paying Stock   **Figure 6.2**

Exercise: Receive stock with dividend and pay the exercise price.
$S_1 + D_1 - X$

Don't Exercise: Own call on the stock with the stock's value reduced by the dividend amount.
C_1

Considering the American call before the dividend date, we can see that it is really a compound option or an option on an option. It is an option on an option because she has the option to refrain from exercising and to own a European option.

The exercise decision as t_1 approaches depends principally on the stock price. If the stock reaches some critical level, the owner should exercise. If it is below that level, the call owner will be better off not exercising and owning the resulting (effectively European) call. The critical stock price, S^*, is the stock price at which the owner is indifferent about the exercise decision; and the owner will be indifferent if the exercise decision leaves her wealth unchanged. The critical stock price is the stock price that makes the two outcomes equal:

$$S^* + D_1 - X = C_1 \tag{6.1}$$

For example, assume that the dividend date t_1 is at hand and that 90 days remain until the option expires. The exercise price is \$100, the standard deviation of the stock is .2, the risk-free rate is 10 percent, and the dividend that is to be paid is \$5. If the stock price immediately after the dividend is paid is \$100.67, the call option is worth \$5.67. For these data, $S^* = \$100.67$, because:

$$\$100.67 + \$5.00 - \$100.00 = \$5.67$$

If the stock price is higher than \$100.67 the instant before t_1, the call owner should exercise. If the stock price is less than \$100.67, she should not exercise.

We now turn to the valuation of the American call before the dividend date. In this case, the value of the call is:

$$C_t = (S - D_1 e^{-r(t_1-t)})N(b_1) - (X - D_1)e^{-r(t_1-t)}N(b_2) \tag{6.2}$$
$$+ (S - D_1 e^{-r(t_1-t)})N_2\left(a_1; -b_1; -\sqrt{\frac{t_1-t}{T-t}}\right) - Xe^{-r(T-t)}N_2\left(a_2; -b_2; -\sqrt{\frac{t_1-t}{T-t}}\right)$$

where:

$$a_1 = \frac{\ln\left(\dfrac{S - D_1 e^{-r(t_1 - t)}}{X}\right) + (r + .5\sigma^2)(T - t)}{\sigma\sqrt{T - t}}$$

$$a_2 = a_1 - \sigma\sqrt{T - t}$$

$$b_1 = \frac{\ln\left(\dfrac{S - D_1 e^{-r(t_1 - t)}}{S^*}\right) + (r + .5\sigma^2)(t_1 - t)}{\sigma\sqrt{t_1 - t}}$$

$$b_2 = b_1 - \sigma\sqrt{t_1 - t}$$

The function $N_2(a; b; \rho)$ is the standardized cumulative bivariate normal distribution. For two variables, x and y, that are distributed according to the standardized bivariate normal function and have a correlation of ρ, $N_2(a; b; \rho)$ is the probability that $x \le a$ and that $y \le b$. N_2 is like the standard normal function used in the Black-Scholes model, except it takes into account two variables that are correlated. Considered singly, variables x and y are distributed normally with a mean of zero and a standard deviation of 1.0. Assume for the moment that $a = 0$, $b = 0$, and the correlation between x and y is zero, so $\rho = 0$. In that case, N_2 would give the probability of both x and y being less than or equal to zero. Considered alone, the chance that $x \le 0$ is 50 percent, and the same is true of y considered by itself. Because we assume that the correlation between the two is zero, the joint probability of both x and y being less that 0 is just the product of the two individual probabilities, or 25 percent. **OPTION!** can compute these bivariate probabilities.

We now examine the formula, which bears close similarities to the Black-Scholes model. At time t, the value of the call must equal the present value of the expected payoffs on the option. We have already seen that these are somewhat complex. First, at the dividend date, if the stock price exceeds the critical stock price, the call owner will exercise. In that case the payoff is the stock with dividend minus the exercise price, and this payoff occurs at t_1. If the stock price is less than the critical price at t_1, she will not exercise. The payoffs from the option then become either zero, if the exercise price equals or exceeds the stock price at expiration, or the stock price less the exercise price, if the stock price exceeds the exercise price at expiration. In the exact American call pricing formula the cumulative normal (N) and bivariate cumulative normal (N_2) express various probabilities of certain stock price outcomes. These probabilities give different weights to possible outcomes from the option investment. For example, the term:

$$N_2\left(a_2; -b_2; -\sqrt{\frac{t_1 - t}{T - t}}\right) \tag{6.3}$$

measures the probability that $S^* + D_1 \le S_t$ and that $S_T \ge X$. This probability would be associated with the payoff that arises when the owner does not exercise the option at the dividend date, but the option is in-the-money at expiration. Thus, without exploring all of the mathematics, we see that the call price is a function of the payoffs that arise in the various possible circumstances, such as not exercising and having the call finish in the money, coupled with the probability of those circumstances arising.

We now show how to compute the exact value of an American call on a stock with one dividend according to this model. Continuing with our example, we have an American call with an exercise price of \$100 on a stock with a standard deviation of .2. The risk-free rate is 10 percent. The stock will pay a \$5 dividend when the option has 90 days remaining until expiration. We will find the price of the call when it has 180 days remaining until expiration and the stock price is \$110.

The first step is to compute the value of the stock less the present value of the dividend:

$$S - D_1 e^{-r(t_1-t)} = \$110 - \$5 e^{-.1(90/365)} = \$105.12$$

Other terms are:

$$a_1 = \frac{\ln\left(\dfrac{110.00 - 4.88}{100.00}\right) + [.1 + .5(.2)(.2)](180/365)}{.2\sqrt{180/365}}$$

$$= \frac{.0499 + .0592}{.1404} = .7771$$

$$a_2 = .7771 - .2\sqrt{180/365} = .6367$$

$$b_1 = \frac{\ln\left(\dfrac{110.00 - 4.88}{100.67}\right) + [.1 + .5(.2)(.2)](90/365)}{.2\sqrt{90/365}}$$

$$= \frac{.0433 + .0296}{.0993} = .7341$$

$$b_2 = .7341 - .2\sqrt{90/365} = .6348$$

$$\sqrt{\frac{t_1 - t}{T - t}} = \sqrt{\frac{90}{180}} = .7071$$

Given these values, we now compute the cumulative normal and cumulative bivariate normal terms.

$$N(b_1) = N(.7341) = .768556$$
$$N(b_2) = N(.6348) = .737221$$

$$N_2\left(a_1;\ -b_1;\ -\sqrt{\frac{t_1 - t}{T - t}}\right) = N_2(.7771;\ -.7341;\ -.7071) = .099098$$

$$N_2\left(a_2;\ -b_2;\ -\sqrt{\frac{t_1 - t}{T - t}}\right) = N_2(.6367;\ -.6348;\ -.7071) = .101320$$

We now compute the value of the American call as:

$$C_t = (105.12)(.768556) + (105.12)(.099098)$$
$$- 100e^{-.1(180/365)}(.101320) - (100.00 - 5.00)e^{-.1(90/365)}(.737221)$$
$$= 80.79 + 10.42 - 9.64 - 68.33$$
$$= \$13.24$$

Thus, with 180 days until expiration, this American call should be worth $13.24. This compares with a pseudo-American value in the same circumstances of $12.91. **OPTION!** can compute the value of a call under the exact American call option pricing model.

Strictly speaking, this model holds for only an American call on a stock paying a single dividend before the option's expiration date. However, when there is more than one dividend, exercise is normally rational for only the final dividend. Therefore, we can use the exact pricing model if we subtract the present value of all dividends other than the final one from the stock price and then use the adjusted stock price in all computations. (Notice that this parallels the logic of the known dividend adjustment to the Black-Scholes model.)

As we have just noted, it is for only this special case of a call with one dividend that we can compute an exact American option price. For all other circumstances, we must use a variety of approximation techniques, which we will now consider.

ANALYTICAL APPROXIMATIONS OF AMERICAN OPTION PRICES

In Chapter 4, we considered the Merton model, which extended the Black-Scholes model to European options on stocks that pay a continuous dividend at a constant rate. The analytical approximations that we now consider apply to American options on an underlying instrument that pays a continuous dividend at a constant rate. The Merton model provides a closed-form solution to the problem of European options on stocks with continuous dividends. For American options, no closed-form solutions are available. The analytical approximations for American options considered in this section are extremely accurate and computationally inexpensive. **OPTION!** can compute both call and put values according to the analytical approximation presented in this section.

To understand the incentive for early exercise of an option on a stock with a continuous dividend, consider again the Merton model developed in Chapter 4.

$$c_t^M = Se^{-\delta(T-t)}N(d_1^M) - Xe^{-r(T-t)}N(d_2^M)$$

The difference in value between this European option and a parallel American option arises from the potential benefits of early exercise. Thus, we focus on an option that is deep in-the-money. In such a situation, d_1^M will be large, as will d_2^M. Consequently, $N(d_1^M)$ and $N(d_2^M)$ will approach 1.0. In the limit then, for an option that is extremely deep-in-the-money, Merton's model approaches:

$$c_t = S_t e^{-\delta(T-t)} - Xe^{-r(T-t)}$$

By contrast, an American option would have to be worth at least its immediately available exercisable proceeds:

$$C_t \geq S_t - X$$

If a trader owns the American option, she has a choice between these two quantities. Which is preferable depends upon how deep-in-the-money the option is, the dividend rate on the stock, δ, the interest rate, r, and the time remaining until the option expires, $T - t$. If the stock price reaches a critical level, S^*, such that:

$$S_t^* - X = c(S^*, X, T - t) + \text{Early exercise premium} \qquad (6.4)$$

the owner of an American option is indifferent about exercising. If the stock price exceeds S^*, she will exercise immediately to capture the exercise proceeds $S_t - X$. If the stock price is below S^*, she will not exercise. Figure 6.3 presents a graph of these relationships. Notice that the European call in Figure 6.3 can be worth less than $S_t - X$ because of the dividend. (As we noted above, a deep-in-the-money European call will tend to its lower bound of $S_t e^{-\delta(T-t)} - X e^{-r(T-t)}$.) At the critical stock price, S^*, the European call is worth exactly $S^* - X$. For any stock price greater than S^*, the European call will be worth less than the exercisable proceeds for the American call. This explains why the owner of the American call is indifferent about exercise at a stock price of S^*; at that stock price the American and European calls are worth the same, $S^* - X$. For higher stock prices, the value of the European call falls below that of the American, and the value of the American call becomes equal to its exercisable proceeds. Thus, the owner of the American call should exercise to capture the quantity $S_t - X$. Those funds can then be invested from the exercise date to the expiration date to earn a return that will be lost if the option is not exercised.

A similar argument applies to American put options. As the stock price falls well below the exercise price, there comes a point at which:

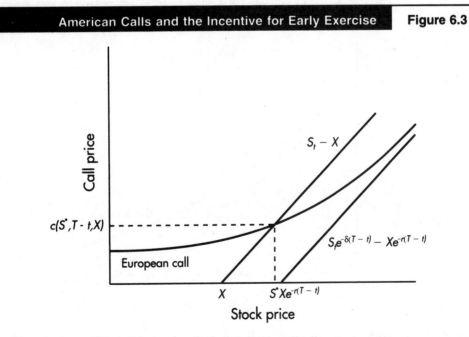

American Calls and the Incentive for Early Exercise   **Figure 6.3**

$$X - S** = p(S**, X, T - t) + \text{Early exercise premium} \tag{6.5}$$

$S**$ is the critical stock price for an American put. If the stock price falls below $S**$, the American put should be exercised to capture the exercised proceeds of $X - S_t$. Figure 6.4 presents a graph of this relationship for the European and American put. As the graph shows, for any stock price less than $S**$, the American put should be exercised immediately.

While a complete discussion of the mathematics is beyond the scope of this text, we present the formulas for an analytic approximation of the American call and put options and discuss the computation of call and put values under the terms of the model.

The analytic approximation for an American call is:

$$C_t = c_t + A_2 \left(\frac{S_t}{S*} \right)^{q_2} \qquad \text{if } S_t < S* \tag{6.6}$$
$$= S_t - X \qquad\qquad \text{if } S_t \geq S*$$

where:

$$A_2 = \frac{S*[1 - e^{-\delta(T-t)}N(d_1)]}{q_2}$$

and $S*$ is the solution to:

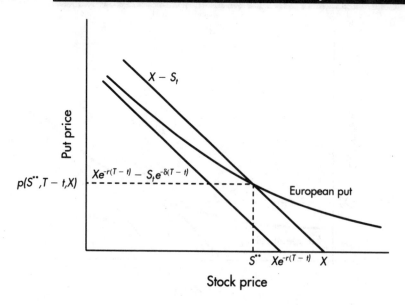

Figure 6.4   American Puts and the Incentive for Early Exercise

$$S^* - X = c_t(S^*, X, T - t) + \{1 - e^{-\delta(T-t)}N(d_1)\}(S^*/q_2) \qquad (6.7)$$

$N(d_1)$ and $p(S^*, X, T - t)$ are evaluated at S^*. To find S^* requires an iterative search for the value that makes the equation balance. Other terms are:

$$q_2 = \frac{1 - n + \sqrt{(n - 1)^2 + 4k}}{2}, \qquad n = \frac{2(r - \delta)}{\sigma^2}, \qquad k = \frac{2r}{\sigma^2(1 - e^{-r(T-t)})}$$

For an American put, the analytic approximation is:

$$P_t = p_t + A_1\left(\frac{S_t}{S^{**}}\right)^{q_1} \qquad \text{if } S_t > S^{**} \qquad (6.8)$$

$$= X - S_t \qquad \text{if } S_t \leq S^{**}$$

where:

$$A_1 = \frac{S^{**}[1 - e^{-\delta(T-t)}N(-d_1)]}{q_1}$$

$$q_1 = \frac{1 - n - \sqrt{(n - 1)^2 + 4k}}{2}$$

S^{**} is found by an iterative search to make the following equation hold:

$$X - S^{**} = p_t(S^{**}, X, T - t) - [1 - e^{-\delta(T-t)}N(-d_1)](S^{**}/q_1) \qquad (6.9)$$

$N(-d_1)$ and $p_t(S^{**}, X, T - t)$ are evaluated at the critical stock price S^{**}.

To illustrate the application of this model, consider an American call option on an underlying stock that is currently priced at $60, has a standard deviation of .2, and pays a continuous dividend of 13.75 percent. The call has a striking price of $60 and 180 days until expiration. The risk-free rate is 9 percent. In Chapter 4, we illustrated the Merton model with a European call having the same terms and found that the price of the European call was $2.5557.

The first step in computing the value of this American call is to find the value of the intermediate terms n, k, and q_2. They are:

$$n = \frac{2(.09 - .1375)}{(.2)(.2)} = -2.375$$

$$k = \frac{2(.09)}{(.2)(.2)\left[1 - e^{-.09\left(\frac{180}{365}\right)}\right]} = 103.6555$$

$$q_2 = \frac{1 - (-2.375) + \sqrt{(-2.375 - 1)^2 + 4(103.6555)}}{2} = 12.007537$$

We next search for the critical stock price, S^*, and find that $S^* = 70.2336$. (This search must be done by trial and error until the correct one is discovered.) If the actual stock price equaled the critical price, the European call would be worth \$9.0152. Then, d_1 and $N(d_1)$, computed at that critical stock price of \$70.2336, would be 1.024716 and .847251, respectively. Based on these values, we calculate A_2 as:

$$A_2 = \frac{70.2336\left[1 - e^{-.1375\left(\frac{180}{365}\right)}.847251\right]}{12.007537} = 1.218344$$

We can now compute the American call price. Because the current stock price of \$60 lies below the critical price of \$70.2336, the value of the American call is:

$$C_t = 2.5557 + 1.218344\left(\frac{60}{70.2336}\right)^{12.007537} = 2.5557 + .183878 = 2.7395$$

Thus, the early exercise premium is \$.18. Because this computation involves an iterative search for S^*, it is quite tedious to perform without a computer. **OPTION!** solves for the critical stock price and the price of American calls and puts directly using this analytic approximation.

THE BINOMIAL MODEL AND AMERICAN OPTION PRICES

Thus far in this chapter, we have considered various option pricing models for finding the value of American options on dividend paying stocks. As we have seen, there is no general exact solution for this problem. In fact, only for the case of an American call on a stock paying a single dividend during the option's life is it possible to compute an exact price. In all other circumstances, we must rely on estimation techniques. The analytic approximation method we have studied in this chapter applies to only continuous dividends. With stocks typically paying discrete dividends, the need for other estimation techniques is particularly important.

The binomial model applies to both American calls and puts on stocks with all kinds of dividend payments. These include the case of no dividends, continuous dividends, known dividend yields, and known dollar dividends. There is a common strategy for the binomial model that applies to all types of dividend patterns, and we begin our discussion by analyzing the underlying strategy for the binomial model for American options. We then consider each of the different dividend strategies in turn.

No Dividends

In Chapter 3, we explored the boundary conditions on the pricing of European options on stocks paying no dividends. For non-dividend stocks we saw that it can never be optimal to exercise a call before expiration. This means that the American call and the European call on a non-dividend stock must have the same value. Therefore, for the case of a call on a non-dividend stock we can price the American call as if it were a European call. It can often be advantageous to exercise puts on non-dividend stocks, so the value of European and American puts can differ substantially. We illustrate this point for an American put and explicate the basic strategy for applying the binomial model to American options.

The Basic Strategy

In Chapter 4, we explored the binomial model for European options on stocks with and without dividends. For European options on non-dividend stocks, we derived the possible stock prices at expiration and determined the value of the option (call or put) at expiration from our no-arbitrage condition. We then computed the value of an option one period before expiration as the expected value of the option at expiration discounted for one period. We continued this strategy, working through the binomial lattice, until we found the value of the option at the current time.

For options on stocks with dividends, we applied the binomial model by creating a lattice for the stock that reflected the timing and amount of dividend payments that the stock would make. These adjustments affected the distribution of possible stock values at the expiration date. We then computed the option values in the usual way by working from the exercise date back to the present.

To apply the binomial model for American options, we follow the same basic valuation strategy as for European options. There is, however, one important difference. For the option lattice for an American option, the option value is set equal to the maximum of:

1. The expected option value in one period discounted for one period at the risk-free rate.
2. The immediate exercise value of the option, $S_t - X$ for a call, or $X - S_t$ for a put.

Except for this treatment of each node in the lattice for an American option, the binomial model for an American option is applied in exactly the same way as it is for a European option.

We illustrate this technique by considering an American put on a stock that pays no dividend. We assume the following data:

$S_t = \$80$
$X = \$75$
$r = .07$
$\sigma = .3$
$T = 120$ days

Assuming a three-period binomial model, a single period is 40 days or .1096 years. This gives a discount factor of .9924 per period, and the following parameter values:

$U = 1.1044$
$D = .9055$
$\pi_u = .5138$

Figure 6.5 shows the stock price tree consistent with these data. (The careful reader may recall the same example from Figure 4.10.) The upper tree of Figure 6.6 repeats the upper tree from Figure 4.12, which is the binomial tree for a European put option on this stock. As the tree shows, the value of the European put is $2.67 at node c. The lower tree in Figure 6.6 is the binomial tree for an American put. Aside from the upper tree's being for a European put and the lower tree's pertaining to an American put, all other circumstances are the same. An examination of the two trees shows that they are identical except for the prices at nodes a, b, and c.

| **Figure 6.5** | Three-Period Stock Price Lattice (in dollars) |

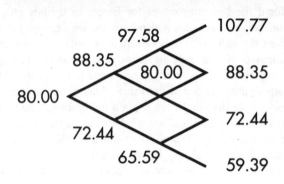

Before turning to the differences at nodes a, b, and c, we first consider why the other nodes are identical. First, consider the nodes at expiration. At expiration, European and American options are identical. Both can be exercised and both have the same payoffs from the exercise decision. Therefore, European and American options at expiration must have the same value. Second, consider a node one period before expiration, such as the middle node of the tree at which the stock price is $80 and both the European and American put prices are $1.24. If the stock price one period prior to expiration is $80, the American put cannot be exercised because the put is out-of-the-money. Therefore, it offers no advantage over the parallel European put. Consequently, the value must be the same.

These reflections lead us to see a condition for an American and a European option to have identical prices at a given node: If the option cannot be exercised at the given node, and if all nodes that can be reached subsequent to the node under consideration have identical prices for American and European options, then the price of the American and European options must be identical at the node in question. We can illustrate this point from the same tree by considering the node two periods before expiration in which the stock price is $88.35 and the value of the put (either European or American) is $.60. The American put cannot be exercised at that node because it is out-of-the-money with a stock price of $88.35. Further, all subsequent nodes have identical prices for the American and European puts. Therefore, the price of the European and American puts must be the same at that node.

We now turn to consider those nodes at which prices differ for the European and American put. At node a, the stock price is $65.59, the European put price is $8.84, and the American put price is $9.41. The European put price is just the expected value of the put's expiration values contingent upon the stock's rising or falling. The value at node a for the American put is:

$$P = MAX(X - S, p) = MAX(\$75 - \$65.59, \$8.84) = \$9.41$$

If the stock price reaches node a, the holder of an American put should exercise and capture the exercise value of $9.41. This is higher than the present value of the expected payoff at expiration, which is the price of the European put – $8.84. As this example shows, the American put derives its higher value from its right to exercise early when conditions warrant.

Three-Period Price Lattices for a European and an American Put (in dollars)

Figure 6.6

European put

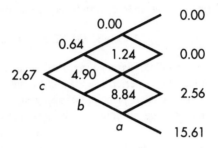

American put

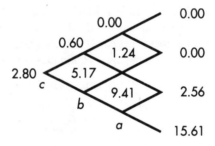

At node b, the stock price is $72.44, and the European put is worth $4.90. The owner of the American put could exercise immediately for an exercise value of $75.00 − $72.44 = $2.56, but this would be foolish. One period later, the put will be worth $1.24 if the stock price rises or $9.41 if the stock price falls. Given that the probability of a stock price rise is .5138, the present value of the put's expected value in one period is:

$$[.5138(\$1.24) + .4862(\$9.41)]e^{-.07\left(\frac{40}{365}\right)} = \$5.21(.9924) = \$5.17$$

The value of the put at node b is therefore:

$$MAX\{\$2.56, \$5.17\} = \$5.17$$

Therefore, at node b, the put should not be exercised; and it is worth $5.17 − the present value of the expected put value in one period.

At node c, the present time at which we want to value the option, the same rule applies. The American put cannot be exercised rationally because it is out-of-the-money with $75 − $80 = −$5. The present value of the expected value of the put in one period is:

$$[.5138(\$.60) + .4862(\$5.17)]e^{-.07\left(\frac{40}{365}\right)} = \$2.80$$

The value of the American put at node c, which represents the present time, is:

$$\text{MAX}\{-\$5.00, \$2.80\} = \$2.80$$

Because the exercise value (−$5.00) is negative, the value of the American put equals the present value of the expected value in one period ($2.80), and it should not be exercised.

This example illustrates the basic principle of applying the binomial model to American options. As we work back through the tree, discounting the next period's expected option values, we must ask at every node whether the immediate exercise value or the computed present value is greater. The value at the node is the maximum of those two quantities. Further, we may note that the stock tree is unaffected by whether the option we are analyzing is an American or a European option. We now consider how to apply the binomial model to American options on dividend paying stocks.

Continuous Dividends

In Chapter 4, we explored Merton's model, which adjusts the Black-Scholes model to price European options on stocks that pay a continuous dividend. We also showed how to use the binomial model to price European options on stocks that pay continuous dividends. There we saw that the parameters for the binomial model for a stock paying a continuous dividend were:

$$U = e^{\sigma\sqrt{\Delta t}}$$

$$D = \frac{1}{U} \tag{6.10}$$

$$\pi_U = \frac{e^{(r-\delta)\Delta t} - D}{U - D}$$

As we have discussed in this chapter, the stock price tree is identical whether we are pricing European or American options. Therefore, these parameters apply to generating the binomial tree of stock prices for American options on stocks paying a continuous dividend. As an examination of these parameters shows, the stock price tree will be identical in both cases. However, the probability of a stock price increase varies inversely with the level of the continuous dividend rate, δ.

To illustrate the binomial model for pricing options on stocks with continuous dividends, consider the following data:

$S_t = \$60$
$X = \$60$
$T = 180$ days
$\sigma = .2$
$r = .09$

Based on these data, consider a European and an American call option on this stock in the context of a two-period binomial model.

$$U = e^{\sigma\sqrt{\Delta t}} = e^{.2\sqrt{\frac{90}{365}}} = 1.104412$$

$$D = \frac{1}{U} = .905460$$

$$\pi_U = \frac{e^{(r-\delta)\Delta t} - D}{U - D} = \frac{e^{(.09-.1375)\left(\frac{90}{365}\right)} - .905460}{1.104412 - .905460} = .416663$$

The single-period discount factor is $e^{-.09(90/365)} = .978053$. Figure 6.7 gives the two-period stock price tree for these data, while Figure 6.8 shows the trees for a European and an American call. At expiration, the call will be in-the-money only if the stock price rises twice to a terminal price of \$73.18. In this case, both the European and American calls are worth \$13.18. One period before expiration, the present value of the expected terminal call value is:

$$\$13.18(.416663)(.978053) = \$5.37$$

This is the value of the European call at the node with a stock price of \$66.26. For the American call, the same expected value prevails, but the owner of the American call could exercise. The exercise value of the American call is \$66.26 − \$60.00 = \$6.26. Therefore, the value of the American call is:

$$C = \text{MAX}\{S - X, c\} = \text{MAX}\{\$6.26, \$5.37\} = \$6.26$$

Therefore, if the stock price reaches \$66.26 in one period, the holder of the American call should exercise. In terms of the binomial tree for the American call, the value at this node becomes \$6.26. At the present time, the present values of the expected call values one period hence are \$2.19 for the European call and \$2.55 for the American call. Thus, the current price of the European call is \$2.19. At the present, the stock price and exercise price are both \$60, so the American option cannot be

Two-Period Stock Price Lattice (in dollars)   **Figure 6.7**

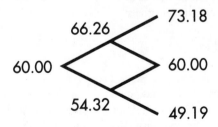

| Figure 6.8 | Two-Period Price Lattices for a European and an American Call (in dollars) |

European call

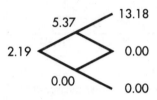

American call

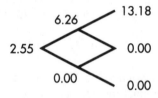

exercised rationally. This means that the current American call price is $2.55, based on a two-period tree. With 200 periods, the European call value is $2.55 and the American call price is $2.73. Table 6.1 shows how the two call prices converge to their true value as the number of periods in the binomial tree ranges from 1 to 200. For comparison, the Merton model price for the European option is $2.5557, and the American analytic approximation is $2.7395. Thus, the binomial method provides estimates that are extremely close to other model prices.

Known Dividend Yields

In Chapter 4, we considered options on a stock that pays a known dividend yield at a certain date. For example, a stock might pay a dividend equal to 1 percent of its value in 90 days. The dividend payment obviously affects the stock price tree for the binomial model, and the loss of value from the stock will affect the value of calls and puts. This is true for both European and American options. While the existence of the dividend will affect the value of European calls and puts, they do not call for European option owners to make any special decisions, as they cannot exercise even if they wished. For the holder of an American call or put, there is an exercise decision because the American

The Convergence of European and American Call Prices		Table 6.1
Number of Periods	**European Call**	**American Call**
1	3.3129	3.3129
2	2.1894	2.5530
3	2.8139	2.9399
4	2.3625	2.6380
5	2.7099	2.8517
10	2.4763	2.6909
25	2.5861	2.7554
50	2.5396	2.7216
100	2.5476	2.7256
200	2.5516	2.7275

option owner can exercise immediately before the dividend payment (in the case of a call), exercise immediately after the dividend payment (in the case of a put), or not exercise. While the dividend will affect the stock price tree, we note again that the stock price tree will be identical whether we are considering a European or an American option.

To apply the binomial model for an American call or put, we begin with the terminal stock price and the value of the option at expiration and work from expiration back to the present in the normal way. However, at each node, we must take account of the potential for early exercise. As we have seen, we take early exercise into account by finding the value of a European option at each node and compare this value with the exercise value of the American option. If the exercise value exceeds the European value, the option price at the node should be the exercise value. Otherwise, the price at the node should be the European option price.

To see how to apply the binomial model to compute American option prices on a stock with a known dividend yield, consider the following data. A stock is currently priced at $80 and it will pay a dividend equal to 3 percent of its value in 55 days. The standard deviation of the stock is .3, and the risk-free rate is 7 percent. A call option on this stock has 120 days until expiration and an exercise price of $75. Based on these data, and with a three-period binomial model, $\Delta t = 40/365 = 0.1096$. Therefore:

$$U = e^{.3\sqrt{.1096}} = 1.1044$$

$$D = \frac{1}{1.1044} = .9055$$

$$\pi_U = \frac{1.0077 - .9055}{1.1044 - .9055} = .5138$$

The discounting factor for a single period is $e^{-r\Delta t} = e^{-.07(40/365)} = .9924$. Figure 6.9 shows the stock price tree for this example. (This same example was considered in Chapter 4 for European calls.) In terms of Figure 6.9, the dividend occurs between time 1 (day 40) and time 2 (day 80). The call owner might exercise at time 1 before the dividend is paid, but if she waits until time 2, the dividend will already be paid, and the dividend's value will be lost from the stock.

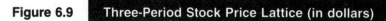

Figure 6.9 | **Three-Period Stock Price Lattice (in dollars)**

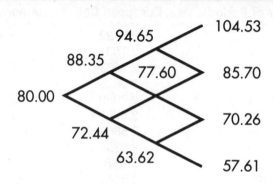

Figure 6.10 shows option price trees for European and American calls consistent with the stock price tree of Figure 6.9. At expiration and the period prior to expiration, the European and American call option trees are identical. This is because the exercise value for the American option never exceeds the value of the European call. In the first period, if the stock price rises from $80 to $88.35, the owner of an American call should exercise. We can see the desirability of exercise in this case as follows. At the node with a stock price of $88.35, the present value of the expected value of the call in the next period is $12.94, the value of the European call. With a stock price of $88.35 and an exercise price of $75.00, the American call can (and should) be exercised for an exercise value of $13.35. Thus, in the tree for the American call, the value at this node is the exercise value of $13.35. This difference in the two trees affects the current value of the European and American calls, which are $7.94 and $8.15, respectively. With 200 periods, the European and American calls are worth $7.61 and $8.04, respectively. The binomial model applies to options on stocks with any number of dividend yields during the life of the option.

For these options, none of the other models we have considered apply. From the valuation date, the dividend amount is uncertain, as it will be 3 percent of whatever stock price prevails in 55 days. Therefore, the exact American option pricing model does not apply. Further, the analytic approximation method for American options does not apply because the dividend is not continuous. For European options, we cannot apply the known dividend adjustment because the dollar amount of the dividend is unknown. Similarly, we cannot apply the Merton model because the dividend is not continuous. Of all the methods we have studied, only the binomial model can deal with the known dividend yield for an American option. **OPTION!** can compute prices for American call and put options on stocks with as many as three known dividend yields by using the binomial model.

Known Dollar Dividends

For options on stocks with known dollar dividends, the binomial model can be applied in a manner almost identical to that appropriate for known dividend yields. The first step is to generate the tree describing the potential stock price movements. As we saw in Chapter 4 when we considered the pricing of European options on stocks with known dollar dividends, there can be a problem with the

Three-Period Price Lattices for a European and an American Call (in dollars) Figure 6.10

European call

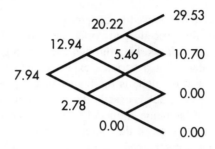

American call

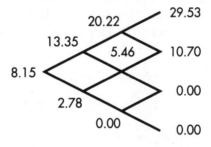

tree failing to recombine after the dividend has been paid. In this situation, the number of nodes can increase dramatically, particularly when there are many periods and several dividends. (For details on why the tree fails to recombine, see Chapter 4.)

We can solve this problem as we did in Chapter 4 by making a simplifying assumption. We assume that the stock price reflects the dividend, which is known with certainty, and all other factors that might affect the stock price, which are uncertain. We then adjust the uncertain component of the stock price for the impending dividends and model the uncertain component of the stock price with the binomial tree adding back the present value of all future dividends at each node. Specifically, we follow these steps:

1. Compute the present value of all dividends to be paid during the life of the option as of the present time = t.
2. Subtract this present value from the current stock price to form $S'_t = S_t - $ PV of all dividends.

3. Create the binomial tree by applying the up and down factors in the usual way to the initial stock price S'_t.
4. After generating the tree, add to the stock price at each node the present value of all future dividends to be paid during the life of the option.
5. Compute the option values in the usual way by working through the binomial tree.

These were exactly the steps we used in Chapter 4.

The application of this procedure to American options is exactly the same as with European options, with one exception. In working through the tree to generate the option price tree, we must compare the present value of next period's expected option value with the exercise value of the option. The option price at the node is the higher of the present value or the exercise value. The computation of the value at a node is exactly the same as in other cases we have already considered, such as the application of the binomial model to options on stocks with known dividend yields.

We illustrate the application of the binomial model to options on stocks with a known dollar dividend by considering a comprehensive example. A stock now trades for $50, has a standard deviation of .4, and will pay a dividend of $2 in 90 days. An American call and put on this stock expire in 120 days, and both have an exercise price of $50. The risk-free rate of interest is 9 percent, and we will model the price of the options with a five-period binomial model.

According to the five steps outlined earlier, we subtract the present value of the dividends to be paid during the life of the option from the current stock price. The present value of the dividend is $1.96, so the adjusted stock price, S', is $48.04. A single period is 24 days, and the discount factor for one period is .9941. The parameters for the binomial model with five periods are:

$$\Delta t = \frac{24}{365} = .065753 \text{ years}$$

$$U = e^{\sigma\sqrt{\Delta t}} = e^{.4\sqrt{.065753}} = 1.108015$$

$$D = \frac{1}{U} = .902515$$

$$\pi_U = \frac{e^{r\Delta t} - D}{U - D} = \frac{e^{.09(.065753)} - .902515}{1.108015 - .902515} = .503262$$

The top panel of Figure 6.11 shows the stock price lattice generated with a starting price of $48.04 and the up and down factors shown above. This upper lattice does not reflect the dividend. Having generated this lattice, we account for dividends by adding the present value of all future dividends to be paid during the life of the option to each node. The bottom lattice of Figure 6.11 shows the adjusted stock prices. As the dividend will be paid in 90 days, the dividend falls between the third and fourth periods. This means that for periods four and five, there are no dividends to consider, and the two lattices have identical stock prices in periods four and five. For all periods before the dividend, the stock price at each node is adjusted by adding the present value of the dividend. For example, the node for the second period represents a time that is 48 days from now. At that time, the dividend will be 42 days away, and the present value of the dividend at that point is $1.98. Therefore, if we compare the stock prices in the two lattices for period 2, the prices in the bottom lattice will exceed their counterparts in the upper lattice by $1.98. All other stock prices in

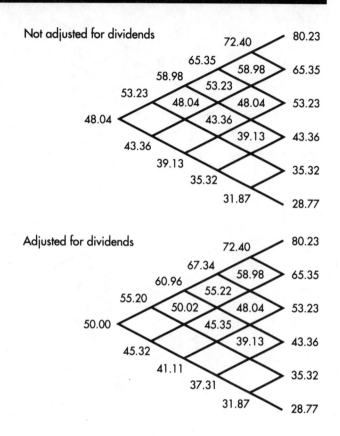

Figure 6.11

Five-Period Stock Price Lattices Unadjusted and Adjusted for a Known Dollar Dividend (in dollars)

periods 1–3 are adjusted similarly. The bottom stock price lattice in Figure 6.11 is the lattice that we will use to compute the option prices.

In Figure 6.12, the upper lattice pertains to the American call, while the lower lattice prices the American put. Some prices are preceded by an asterisk, indicating that the price represents the exercise value of the option at that node. For example, the call lattice has a price of $17.34 in period 4. The present value of the two option values in period 4 is $15.93. However, the stock price at that node is $67.34, implying an exercise value of $17.34. Because the exercise value exceeds $15.93, the call value at that node is $17.34. Working back through the lattice to the present shows an American call value of $4.48 and an American put value of $4.90. With the five-period lattice, the European call and put are worth $4.31 and $4.81, respectively. For the same data, except using a lattice with 200 periods, the American call is worth $4.59, and the American put is $4.78. With a 200-period lattice, the European call and put are $4.17 and $4.66, respectively. We also note that this example can be

| Figure 6.12 | Five-Period Price Lattices for an American Call and Put on a Stock with a Known Dollar Dividend (in dollars) |

American call

30.23
22.70
*17.34   15.35
11.36   9.27
7.22   5.44
3.12   1.62   3.23
4.48   0.81
1.76   0.00   0.00
0.41
0.00   0.00
0.00
0.00

American put

0.00
0.00
0.00   0.00
0.80   0.00   0.00
2.51   1.62
4.27   3.28
4.90   7.01   0.00
7.38   10.87   6.64
10.61
14.39   14.68
18.13   21.23

solved using the exact American call option pricing model, which gives a call price of $4.59, the same as the binomial model with 200 periods.

SUMMARY

This chapter explored the pricing of American options. We began by reviewing the differences between American and European options. For non-dividend stocks, the American and European calls have the same value, as early exercise is never desirable. For puts, however, we showed that there are incentives to early exercise even when there are no dividends. Therefore, the price of an American put can exceed that of a European put even in the absence of dividends. When the underlying stock pays dividends, circumstances can arise in which it would be desirable to exercise a call and a put before expiration, and the prices of American and European options diverge.

The discussion then turned to models for pricing American options, beginning with Black's pseudo-American option pricing model. We then considered the exact pricing model for an American call with a single dividend before the option's expiration. We noted that this is the only situation in which an exact pricing formula exists for American options. In all other pricing situations, we must use approximation techniques.

When the underlying stock pays a continuous dividend, an approximation for American options applies. This analytical approximation is analogous to the Merton model for European options and accurately estimates the prices of American calls and puts when the underlying instrument pays a continuous dividend.

Most stocks pay discrete dividends, so the analytical approximation does not apply. Accordingly, we turned to the binomial model and showed how it can apply to American options when the underlying good pays dividends in a variety of different ways. We considered the binomial model for American options when the underlying good pays a continuous dividend, when it pays a known dividend yield, and when it pays a known dollar dividend. In the last two cases, the binomial model can accommodate any number of dividends.

Many of the calculations of this chapter are quite tedious and time-consuming. (Imagine, for instance, the tedium of computing the binomial model price for a lattice of 100 periods.) **OPTION!** computes option prices for all of the models considered in this chapter.

QUESTIONS AND PROBLEMS

1. Explain why American and European calls on a non-dividend stock always have the same value.
2. Explain why American and European puts on a non-dividend stock can have different values.
3. Explain the circumstances that might make the early exercise of an American put on a non-dividend stock desirable.
4. What factors might make an owner exercise an American call?
5. Do dividends on the underlying stock make the early exercise of an American put more or less likely? Explain.
6. Do dividends on the underlying stock make the early exercise of an American call more or less likely? Explain.
7. Explain the strategy behind the pseudo-American call pricing strategy.
8. Consider a stock with a price of $140 and a standard deviation of .4. The stock will pay a dividend of $2 in 40 days and a second dividend of $2 in 130 days. The current risk-free rate of interest is 10 percent. An American call on this stock has an exercise price of $150 and expires in 100 days. What is the price of the call according to the pseudo-American approach?
9. Could the exact American call pricing model be used to price the option in Question 8? Explain.
10. Explain why the exact American call pricing model treats the call as an "option on an option."
11. Explain the idea of a bivariate cumulative standardized normal distribution. What would be the cumulative probability of observing two variables both with a value of zero, assuming that the correlation between them was zero? Explain.
12. In the exact American call pricing model, explain why the model can compute the call price with only one dividend.
13. What is the critical stock price in the exact American call pricing model?
14. Explain how the analytical approximation for American option values is analogous to the Merton model.

15. Explain the role of the critical stock price in the analytic approximation for an American call.

16. Why should an American call owner exercise if the stock price exceeds the critical price?

17. Consider the binomial model for an American call and put on a stock that pays no dividends. The current stock price is $120, and the exercise price for both the put and the call is $110. The standard deviation of the stock returns is .4, and the risk-free rate is 10 percent. The options expire in 120 days. Model the price of these options using a four-period tree. Draw the stock tree and the corresponding trees for the call and the put. Explain when, if ever, each option should be exercised. What is the value of a European call in this situation? Can you find the value of the European call without making a separate computation? Explain.

18. Consider the binomial model for an American call and put on a stock whose price is $120. The exercise price for both the put and the call is $110. The standard deviation of the stock returns is .4, and the risk-free rate is 10 percent. The options expire in 120 days. The stock will pay a dividend equal to 3 percent of its value in 50 days. Model and compute the price of these options using a four-period tree. Draw the stock tree and the corresponding trees for the call and the put. Explain when, if ever, each option should be exercised.

19. Consider the binomial model for an American call and put on a stock whose price is $120. The exercise price for both the put and the call is $110. The standard deviation of the stock returns is .4, and the risk-free rate is 10 percent. The options expire in 120 days. The stock will pay a $3 dividend in 50 days. Model and compute the price of these options using a four-period tree. Draw the stock tree and the corresponding trees for the call and the put. Explain when, if ever, each option should be exercised.

20. Consider the analytic approximation for American options. A stock sells for $130, has a standard deviation of .3, and pays a continuous dividend of 3 percent. An American call and put on this stock both have an exercise price of $130, and both expire in 180 days. The risk-free rate is 12 percent. Find the value of the call and put according to this model. Demonstrate that you have found the correct critical stock price for both options.

21. An American call and put both have an exercise price of $100. An acquaintance asserts that the critical stock price for both options is $90 under the analytic approximation technique. Comment on this claim and explain your reasoning.

NOTES

[1] Fischer Black first proposed this idea in his paper "Fact and Fantasy in the Use of Options," *Financial Analysts Journal,* July/August 1975, pp. 36–72.

[2] R. E. Whaley, "Valuation of American Call Options on Dividend Paying Stocks: Empirical Tests," *Journal of Financial Economics,* 10, March 1982, pp. 29–58.

[3] This model was developed in a series of papers. R. Roll, "An Analytical Formula for Unprotected American Call Options on Stocks with Known Dividends," *Journal of Financial Economics,* 5, 1977, pp. 251–58; R. Geske, "A Note on an Analytic Valuation Formula for Unprotected American Call Options on Stocks with Known Dividends," *Journal of Financial Economics,* 7, 1979, pp. 375–80; R. Whaley, "On the Valuation of American Call Options on Stocks with Known Dividends," *Journal of Financial Economics,* 9, 1981, pp. 207–11; R. Geske, "Comments on Whaley's Note," *Journal of Financial Economics,* 9, 1981, pp. 213–15.

CHAPTER 7

OPTIONS ON STOCK INDEXES, FOREIGN CURRENCY, AND FUTURES

INTRODUCTION

This chapter considers three different kinds of options: options on stock indexes, options on foreign currency, and options on futures. We consider these options together because the principles that determine their prices are almost identical. In essence, the three types of options considered in this chapter are united by the fact that the good underlying each option can be treated as paying a continuous dividend. The pricing of these options is further unified by the conceptual connections among the different options. For example, we will consider options on stock index futures as well as options on stock indexes themselves, and we will analyze options on foreign currency futures as well as options on foreign currencies alone.

While there may be common principles for the pricing of these three types of options, the market for each option is quite large and has its own features. These were explored in Chapter 1. Consequently, this chapter begins by analyzing the pricing principles for these options. As noted above, the underlying instruments may all be treated as paying a continuous dividend – particularly when we think of a dividend as a leakage of value from the instrument paying the dividend. For a stock index, the continuous dividend really is a dividend – the aggregate dividends on the stocks represented in the index. For a foreign currency, we may treat the foreign interest rate as a continuous dividend. For futures, the cost of financing and storing the underlying good (a bond, 5,000 bushels of wheat, or the proverbial pork bellies) is a leakage of value from the commodity.

Because the underlying good pays a continuous dividend, we know that the Merton model, which was discussed in Chapter 4, pertains directly to pricing these three types of European options. Also, the binomial model directly applies as well. For American options, discussed in Chapter 6, two approaches are clearly applicable. First, the analytic approximation technique works extremely well in pricing the types of options discussed in this chapter. Second, we can also apply the binomial model under the assumption of continuous dividends.

EUROPEAN OPTION PRICING

In Chapter 4, we considered the Merton model, which extends the Black-Scholes model, to provide an exact pricing model for European options on stocks that pay dividends at a continuous rate. We also discussed the binomial model and saw that it can apply to European option pricing on stocks that pay a continuous dividend. In this section, we extend both of these models to the pricing of European options on stock indexes, foreign currency, and futures.

The Merton Model

The Merton model extends the Black-Scholes model by treating continuous dividends as a negative interest rate. In Chapter 4, we saw how dividends reduce the value of a call option because they reduce the value of the stock that underlies the option. In effect, a continuous dividend implies a continuous leakage of value from the stock that equals the dividend rate. We let the Greek letter delta, δ, represent this rate of leakage.[1] Merton's adjustment to the Black-Scholes model for continuous dividends is:

$$c_t^M = e^{-\delta(T-t)}S_t N(d_1^M) - Xe^{-r(T-t)}N(d_2^M)$$

$$d_1^M = \frac{\ln\left(\frac{S_t}{X}\right) + (r - \delta + .5\sigma^2)(T - t)}{\sigma\sqrt{T - t}}$$

$$d_2^M = d_1^M - \sigma\sqrt{T - t}$$

(7.1)

where δ = the continuous dividend rate on the stock

To adjust the regular Black-Scholes model, we replace the current stock price with the stock price adjusted for the continuous dividend. That is, we replace S_t with:

$$e^{-\delta(T-t)}S_t$$

(7.2)

Substituting this expression into the formulas for d_1 and d_2 gives d_1^M and d_2^M as shown above. Merton's adjusted put value is:

$$p_t^M = Xe^{-r(T-t)}N(-d_2^M) - Se^{-\delta(T-t)}N(-d_1^M)$$

(7.3)

When $\delta = 0$, Merton's model reduces immediately to the Black-Scholes model.

We can determine the price of options on stock indexes, foreign currency, and futures if we can determine the correct term to substitute for expression 7.2 in the Black-Scholes model.

The Binomial Model

In Chapter 4, we saw that the price at time t of a European call, c_t, and a European put, p_t, could be expressed as follows under the terms of the binomial model.

$$c_t = \frac{\sum\limits_{j=m}^{n} \left(\dfrac{n!}{j!(n-j)!}\right)(\pi_U{}^j\pi_D{}^{n-j})[U^jD^{n-j}S_t - X]}{R^n}$$ (7.4)

$$p_t = \frac{\sum\limits_{j=0}^{n} \left(\dfrac{n!}{j!(n-j)!}\right)(\pi_U{}^j\pi_D{}^{n-j})\text{MAX}[0,\, X - U^jD^{n-j}S_t]}{R^n}$$ (7.5)

where:

$U = 1 +$ percentage increase in a period if the stock price rises
$D = 1 -$ percentage decrease in a period if the stock price falls
$R = 1 +$ risk-free rate per period
$\pi_U =$ probability of a price increase in any period
$\pi_D =$ probability of a price decrease in any period

These pricing models apply for any time span divided into n periods, where m is the minimum number of price increases to bring the call in-the-money at expiration.

To apply the binomial model to options on goods paying a continuous dividend, we need to adjust the binomial parameters to reflect the continuous leakage of value from the stock that the dividend represents and to accurately reflect the price movements on the stock. For Merton's model for European options on a stock paying a continuous dividend, we saw that the adjustment largely involved subtracting the continuous dividend rate, δ, from the risk-free rate, r. This is exactly the adjustment required for the binomial model. For options on a good paying a continuous dividend δ, the U, D, and π_U factors are:

$$U = e^{\sigma\sqrt{\Delta t}}$$

$$D = \frac{1}{U}$$ (7.6)

$$\pi_U = \frac{e^{(r-\delta)\Delta t} - D}{U - D}$$

We can apply this binomial model to options on stock indexes, foreign currency, or futures by determining the appropriate δ and the correct price of the instrument to take the place of S_t in the binomial model.

Options on Stock Indexes

The Merton model and the binomial model apply directly to pricing options on stock indexes. Because a stock index merely summarizes the performance of some set of stocks, we may think of the stock index as representing a portfolio of stocks, some of which pay dividends. Because we are pricing an option on this portfolio of stocks, we are concerned with only the dividends on the entire portfolio – we need to consider the dividend on individual stocks insofar as they determine the overall dividend for the portfolio. Almost all individual stocks pay periodic discrete dividends (usually following a quarterly payment pattern). However, for stock indexes, including many stocks, the assumption of a continuous dividend payment is fairly realistic. In general, the greater the number of stocks represented in a stock index, the more realistic the assumption of continuous dividends.[2]

To illustrate the application of the Merton model to pricing options on stock indexes, consider a stock index that has a current value of 350.00. The standard deviation of returns for the index is .2, the risk-free rate is 8 percent, and the continuous dividend rate on the index is 4 percent. European call and put options on this stock index expire in 150 days and have a striking price of 340.00. Therefore, the dividend rate of 4 percent takes the role of δ in the Merton model and the index value of 350.00 takes the role of S_t. For these data, we find the value of the call and put in index units as follows:

$$d_1^M = \frac{\ln\left(\dfrac{350}{340}\right) + [.08 - .04 + .5(.2)(.2)]\left(\dfrac{150}{365}\right)}{.2\sqrt{\dfrac{150}{365}}}$$

$$= \frac{.028988 + .024658}{0.128212} = .418413$$

$$d_2^M = .418413 - .2\sqrt{\frac{150}{365}} = .290201$$

$N(d_1^M) = N(.418413) = .662177$; $N(d_2^M) = N(.290201) = .614169$; $N(-d_1^M) = N(-.418413) = .337823$, and $N(-d_2^M) = N(-.290201) = .385831$. Therefore, the call and put are worth:

$$c_t^M = e^{-.04(150/365)}350.00(.662177) - 340.00\ e^{-.08(150/365)}(.614169) = \$25.92$$

$$p_t^M = 340.00e^{-.08(150/365)}(.385831) - 350.00\ e^{-.04(150/365)}(.337823) = \$10.63$$

For a five-period binomial model price on the same options, the call is worth $26.37, while the put is worth $11.08. With 200 periods, the call price is $25.94, and the put price is $10.65. (The calculations for the binomial model are not shown here, but similar calculations for other options appear later in this chapter.)

Options on Foreign Currency

We now explore the application of the Merton model to pricing options on a foreign currency. We will look at the issues from the point of view of a U.S. option trader. In terms of the Merton model, the dollar value of the foreign currency takes the role of the stock price, S_t, and the foreign interest rate takes the role of the continuous dividend rate, δ. The standard deviation in the Merton model is that of the underlying asset, so the correct standard deviation to use in the model is the standard deviation of the foreign currency.

As an example, consider a European call and a European put option on the British pound. The pound is currently worth $1.40 and has a standard deviation of .5, reflecting difficulties in the European Monetary System (EMS). The current British risk-free rate is 12 percent, while the U.S. rate is 8 percent. The call and put both have a striking price of $1.50 per pound and both expire in 200 days.

According to the Merton model, the call is worth $.1452, while the put value is $.2700. Both of these prices are the dollar price for an option on a single British pound. We illustrate the computation of the price of the currency options using a five-period binomial model. The binomial parameters are:

$$U = e^{\sigma\sqrt{\Delta t}} = e^{.5\sqrt{.1096}} = 1.1800$$

$$D = \frac{1}{U} = .847452$$

$$\pi_U = \frac{e^{(r-\delta)\Delta t} - D}{U - D} = .445579$$

The one-period discount factor is $e^{-.08(40/365)} = .9913$. Figure 7.1 shows the five-period binomial lattice for the foreign currency price, while Figure 7.2 shows the lattices for the call and the put. The price of the call is $.1519, and the put is worth $.2766. For a 200-period lattice, the call is worth $.1454 and the put is worth $.2702. These 200-period binomial estimates are extremely close to the values from the Merton model.

Options on Futures

In simplest terms, a futures contract is an agreement entered at one date calling for the delivery of some good at a future date. The price is established at the time the contract is entered, and the

A Five-Period Binomial Lattice for the British Pound (in dollars)   **Figure 7.1**

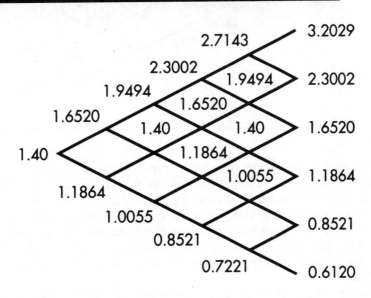

Figure 7.2 The Five-Period Lattices for Foreign Currency Call and Put Prices (in dollars)

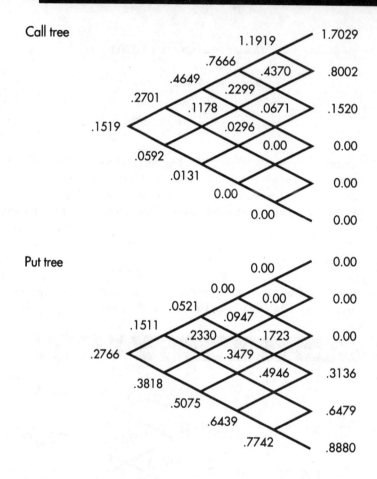

Call tree

Put tree

exchange of goods for the contract price occurs at the expiration of the futures contract. For example, a trader might buy a futures contract for 100 Troy ounces of gold for delivery in one year at a price of $400 per ounce. The current cash market price of gold might be $361.94 at the time of contracting. The trader has the obligation to pay $400 per ounce for the gold and take delivery of the metal in one year. The seller of the futures has complementary obligations. The purchaser of the futures contract profits if the price of the good at delivery exceeds the futures contract price. By contrast, the seller of the futures hopes that the futures contract price will exceed the price of the underlying good at expiration.[3]

Consider a good such as gold that has a large stock relative to consumption, that is easily storable, and does not have a seasonal production pattern (like wheat) or a seasonal consumption pattern (like gasoline). Further, assume that it is possible to sell gold short and obtain the use of the proceeds from the short sale.[4] When these conditions hold, the futures price at time t, F_t, for delivery of the good at time T is given by:

$$F_t = \text{SPOT}_t e^{r(T-t)} \tag{7.7}$$

If this relationship between the spot, or cash, price and the futures price did not prevail, there would be immediate arbitrage opportunities.

For example, assume a continuously compounded risk-free rate of 10 percent. If the spot price is $361.94 and the futures calls for delivery in one year, then the futures price must be $400 to avoid arbitrage. To see this, first assume that the futures price is too high – say $410. In this situation a trader would borrow $361.94 for 10 percent for one year, would use the borrowed funds to buy the gold for $361.94 per ounce, would sell the futures contract at a price of $410, and would store the gold for one year until the expiration of the futures. (We ignore market imperfections and storage costs for simplicity.) In one year, the trader could deliver the gold against the futures and collect $410, the futures contract price. From this $410, the trader would repay the debt, which would be $400, leaving a profit of $10. Notice that the trader had a zero cash flow at the outset of these transactions and that the profit was certain once those initial transactions were made. Thus, the $10 is an arbitrage profit.

Now assume that the futures price is too low relative to the spot price. If the futures is $380, for example, the trader would transact as follows: Sell the gold short and receive $361.94, invest $361.94 for one year at 10 percent, and buy the futures contract for $380. In one year, the trader's loan will be worth $400. From this $400, the trader will pay $380 to receive one ounce of gold in completion of the futures contract. The trader will then complete the short sale by returning the ounce of gold to the party from whom it was borrowed to consummate the short sale. The trader now has $20, which represents a riskless profit with no investment. The trader had a zero net cash flow at the outset, and once the transactions were in place, the profit was assured.

The only price relationship that rules out arbitrage is one that conforms to Equation 7.7. The futures price must equal the cash price compounded at the risk-free rate of interest from the contract date to the expiration of the futures. The relationship expressed in Equation 7.7 is called the **cost-of-carry model**. In general, all precious metals (gold, silver, platinum, and palladium) and all financial instruments (equities and debt) conform almost perfectly to this relationship. To the degree that a commodity fails to conform to the cost-of-carry model, the pricing techniques discussed in this chapter do not pertain to pricing futures options on that commodity.

In terms of the Merton model, the rate at which the spot price grows, r, takes the place of δ, and the futures price takes the place of the stock price in Equation 7.1. In other words, for futures on commodities that conform to the cost-of-carry model, $\delta = r$.[5] When we make this substitution in Equation 7.1, the formula becomes considerably simpler due to the equivalence of δ and r. For European futures options, the price of the futures call, c_t^F, and put, p_t^F, are:

$$c_t^F = e^{-r(T-t)}[F_t N(d_1^F) - X N(d_2^F)]$$

$$p_t^F = e^{-r(T-t)}[X N(-d_2^F) - F_t N(-d_1^F)] \tag{7.8}$$

$$d_1^F = \frac{\ln\left(\dfrac{F_t}{X}\right) + (.5\sigma^2)(T-t)}{\sigma\sqrt{T-t}}$$

$$d_2^F = d_1^F - \sigma\sqrt{T-t}$$

Equation 7.8 employs the standard deviation of the futures price.[6]

The binomial model also applies to options on futures, and the parameters of Equations 7.4 and 7.5 can be applied directly. Notice that the probability of a futures price increase becomes:

$$\pi_U = \frac{e^0 - D}{U - D} = \frac{1 - D}{U - D}$$

As an example, consider European options on a stock index futures that expire in one year. The current cash market price of the index is 480.00, and the risk-free rate is 7 percent. Therefore, according to the cost-of-carry model, the futures price must be:

$$F_t = 480.00e^{.07(365/365)} = 514.80$$

European call and put options on this futures contract have an exercise price of 500.00, and the standard deviation of the futures price is .2. The price of the call and put according to the Merton/Black model must be:

$$d_1^F = \frac{\ln\left(\frac{514.80}{500.00}\right) + .5(.2)(.2)}{.2} = .245852$$

$$d_2^F = .245852 - .2 = .045852$$

$N(d_1^F) = .597102$, and $N(d_2^F) = .518286$. Therefore, the call and put prices are:

$$c_t^F = e^{-.07}[514.80(.597102) - 500.00(.518286)] = \$44.98$$

$$p_t^F = e^{-.07}[500.00(.481714) - 514.80(.402898)] = \$31.18$$

For a binomial model with five periods, the call and put prices are $46.49 and $32.69, respectively. With 200 periods the binomial model gives prices of $44.95 and $31.15 for the call and put, respectively.

Options on Futures versus Options on Physicals

For some goods, such as foreign currencies, options trade on the futures contract and on the good itself. For example, in Chapter 1 we saw that the Philadelphia Stock Exchange trades options on foreign currencies, while the Chicago Mercantile Exchange trades options on foreign currency futures. The differences between options on futures and options on the underlying good itself depends critically on whether the option is a European or an American option.

At the expiration of a futures contract, the futures price must equal the spot price. This is necessary to avoid arbitrage. For example, in the gold market if the spot price is $400 per ounce and the futures contract is at expiration, the futures contract price must also be $400. If it were not, there is a simple and immediate arbitrage opportunity. If the futures price at expiration exceeds the spot price, a trader would buy the physical good and deliver it in the futures market to capture the higher futures price. By contrast, if the futures price is below the spot price, the arbitrageur would buy a futures contract, take delivery of gold, and sell the gold for the higher spot price. To avoid both of these potential arbitrage plays, the spot price and the futures price must be equal at the expiration of the futures contract.

The no-arbitrage condition has important implications for pricing European futures options. Because a European option can be exercised only at expiration, a European futures option can be exercised only when the futures price and the spot price are identical. This restriction on exercise means that the payoffs on European futures options and options on physicals are identical. Therefore, the price of a European futures option and a European option on the physical must always be identical.

For American options, the analysis is more complex because the trader can exercise an American option at any time. The relationship between prices of American options on futures and physicals depends on the relationship between the futures price and the spot price prevailing at a given time prior to expiration. For precious metals and financials, the futures price before expiration almost always exceeds the spot price. In the markets for some commodities, the spot price often exceeds the futures price. This happens in markets for industrial metals such as copper, in markets for agricultural goods, and in the energy market. While a complete explanation for why these price relationships arise lies beyond the scope of this book, we offer a very brief explanation. In essence, the futures price will lie above the spot price if supplies of the underlying good are large relative to consumption, if the underlying good is easily storable and transportable, if the market for the underlying good is well developed, if supply of and demand for the underlying good are free of seasonal fluctuations, and if it is easy and cheap to effect short sales for the underlying good. These conditions prevail for precious metals and financials. By contrast, industrial metals, agricultural commodities, and energy products are strongly affected by supply and demand seasonalities, by poorly developed cash markets, and by costly transportation and storage. These factors allow the spot price to exceed the futures price on occasion.[7]

Without regard to the economic factors that cause the futures price or the spot price to be higher, the relationship between the futures and spot price determines the relationship between prices for American futures options and American options on the physical. When the futures price exceeds the spot price, the price of an American futures call must exceed the price of an American call on the physical, and the price of an American futures put must be less than the price of an American put on the physical. When the spot price exceeds the futures price, the price of an American futures call must be below the price of an American call on the physical and the price of an American futures put must exceed the price of an American put on the physical.

OPTION SENSITIVITIES

In Chapter 5, we considered the sensitivity of option prices to changes in the underlying parameters. Our exploration focused on the Merton model, and we analyzed the DELTA, GAMMA, THETA, VEGA, and RHO of European calls and puts. In this section, we extend that analysis to options on stock indexes, foreign currencies, and futures. The principles are virtually identical, but we must make slight substitutions in the definitions of the sensitivities to account for differences in the underlying instruments. Tables 7.1 and 7.2 present the call and put sensitivities for the Merton model. These are the same tables discussed in Chapter 5. These same sensitivities apply to options on stock indexes, options on foreign currencies, and options on futures with the following substitutions:

Table 7.1	Call Sensitivities for the Merton Model
Name	**Sensitivity**
DELTA$_c$	$\dfrac{\partial c}{\partial S} = e^{-\delta(T-t)}N(d_1^M)$
THETA$_c$	$-\dfrac{\partial c}{\partial(T-t)} = -\dfrac{SN'(d_1^M)\sigma e^{-\delta(T-t)}}{2\sqrt{T-t}}$ $+ \delta SN(d_1^M)e^{-\delta(T-t)} - rXe^{-r(T-t)}N(d_2^M)$
VEGA$_c$	$\dfrac{\partial c}{\partial \sigma} = S\sqrt{T-t}\,N'(d_1^M)e^{-\delta(T-t)}$
RHO$_c$	$\dfrac{\partial c}{\partial r} = X(T-t)e^{-r(T-t)}N(d_2^M)$
GAMMA$_c$	$\dfrac{\partial DELTA_c}{\partial S} = \dfrac{\partial^2 c}{\partial S^2} = \dfrac{N'(d_1^M)e^{-\delta(T-t)}}{S\sigma\sqrt{T-t}}$
Note:	$N'(d_1^M) = \dfrac{1}{\sqrt{2\pi}}e^{-.5(d_1^M)^2}$

Table 7.2	Put Sensitivities for the Merton Model
Name	**Sensitivity**
DELTA$_p$	$\dfrac{\partial p}{\partial S} = e^{-\delta(T-t)}[N(d_1^M) - 1]$
THETA$_p$	$-\dfrac{\partial p}{\partial(T-t)} = -\dfrac{SN'(d_1^M)\sigma e^{-\delta(T-t)}}{2\sqrt{T-t}}$ $- \delta SN(-d_1^M)e^{-\delta(T-t)} + rXe^{-r(T-t)}N(-d_2^M)$
VEGA$_p$	$\dfrac{\partial p}{\partial \sigma} = S\sqrt{T-t}\,N'(d_1^M)e^{-\delta(T-t)}$
RHO$_p$	$\dfrac{\partial p}{\partial r} = -X(T-t)e^{-r(T-t)}N(-d_2^M)$
GAMMA$_p$	$\dfrac{\partial DELTA_p}{\partial S} = \dfrac{\partial^2 p}{\partial S^2} = \dfrac{N'(d_1^M)e^{-\delta(T-t)}}{S\sigma\sqrt{T-t}}$
Note:	$N'(d_1^M) = \dfrac{1}{\sqrt{2\pi}}e^{-.5(d_1^M)^2}$

Sensitivities of Options on Stock Indexes. Interpret S_t as the price of the stock index and δ as the continuous dividend yield on the stock index. Adjust the computation of d_1 and d_2 by making these same substitutions.

Sensitivities of Options on Foreign Currency. Interpret S_t as the price of the foreign currency and δ as the continuous interest rate on the foreign risk-free instrument. Adjust the computation of d_1 and d_2 by making these same substitutions.

Sensitivities of Options on Futures. Interpret S_t as the price of the futures contract and δ as being equal to the risk-free rate, so that $r - \delta = 0$. Adjust the computation of d_1 and d_2 by making these same substitutions.

Because these sensitivities are so similar, we illustrate all with an example of a European option on the British pound. The current value of a British pound is $1.56. The U.S. risk-free rate of interest is 8 percent, while the risk-free rate on the British pound is 11 percent. The standard deviation of the British pound is .25, and the option expires in 90 days. The exercise price of the options we consider is $1.50. In terms of the Merton model, our inputs would be $S = \$1.56$, $X = \$1.50$, $\sigma = .25$, $T - t = 90$ days, $\delta = .11$, and $r = .08$. With these values a European call is worth $.1002, and a European put is worth $.0526. Table 7.3 shows the sensitivity values for this option.

PRICING AMERICAN OPTIONS

Chapter 6 explored the pricing of American stock options. There we saw that exact solutions for pricing American style options are generally not available. Further, we noted that the key feature that made American call option pricing distinct from European call option pricing was the payment of dividends by the underlying good. In this section, we explore the pricing of American options on stock indexes, foreign currency, and futures.

As we have discussed earlier in this chapter, we may regard futures, foreign currencies, and stock indexes as goods that pay continuous dividends. This makes them particularly well suited to analysis by the Barone-Adesi and Whaley analytic approximation. Therefore, we begin our analysis of American options on stock indexes, foreign currency, and futures by applying the analytic approximation to these instruments.

Foreign Currency Option Sensitivities	Table 7.3	
	Merton Model	
	Call	**Put**
Option Prices	$.1002	$.0526
DELTA	.6082	–.3650
THETA	–.1085	–.1578
VEGA	.2859	.2859
RHO	.2093	–.1534
GAMMA	1.9058	1.9058

$S = \$1.56$; $X = \$1.50$; $\sigma = .25$; $T - t = 90$ days; $r = .08$; $\delta = .11$

The binomial model also applies to these instruments, and we consider it in detail later in this chapter. The binomial model has special applicability to options on stock indexes because stock indexes actually have dividend payment patterns that are discrete. As we will see later in this chapter, there are certain periods of the year when stocks tend to pay dividends. This seasonality in dividend payments from stocks implies that stock indexes will also exhibit a seasonal dividend pattern. The binomial model is particularly well suited to handling this type of dividend pattern.

Analytical Approximations

As we discussed in Chapter 6, we may analyze the value of an American option as being comprised of the value of a corresponding European option, plus an early exercise premium. The value of an American option must always be at least the amount of its immediately available exercisable proceeds. For a call:

$$C_t \geq S_t - X$$

If a trader owns the American option, she has a choice between the exercisable proceeds or the value of the European call. Which is preferable depends upon how deep-in-the-money the option is, the dividend rate on the stock, δ, the interest rate, r, and the time remaining until the option expires, $T - t$. If the stock price reaches a critical level, S^*, such that:

$$S_t^* - X = c(S^*, X, T - t) + \text{Early exercise premium} \tag{7.9}$$

the owner of an American call option is indifferent about exercising. If the stock price exceeds S^*, she will exercise immediately to capture the exercise proceeds $S_t - X$. If the stock price is below S^*, she will not exercise. At the critical stock price, S^*, the European call is worth exactly $S^* - X$. For any stock price greater than S^*, the European call will be worth less than the exercisable proceeds for the American call. This explains why the owner of the American call is indifferent about exercise at a stock price of S^*; at that stock price the American and European calls are worth the same, $S^* - X$. For higher stock prices, the value of the European call falls below that of the American, and the value of the American call becomes equal to its exercisable proceeds. Thus, the owner of the American call should exercise to capture the quantity $S - X$. Those funds can then be invested from the exercise date to the expiration date to earn a return that will be lost if the option is not exercised.

A similar argument applies to American put options. As the stock price falls well below the exercise price, there comes a point at which:

$$X - S^{**} = p(S^{**}, X, T - t) + \text{Early exercise premium} \tag{7.10}$$

S^{**} is the critical stock price for an American put. If the stock price falls below S^{**}, the American put should be exercised to capture the exercised proceeds of $X - S_t$. From Chapter 6, the analytic approximation for an American call on a stock is:

$$C_t = c_t + A_2 \left(\frac{S_t}{S^*}\right)^{q_2} \qquad \text{if } S_t < S^* \tag{7.11}$$

$$= S_t - X \qquad \text{if } S_t \geq S^*$$

where:

$$A_2 = \frac{S^*[1 - e^{-\delta(T-t)}N(d_1)]}{q_2}$$

and S^* is the solution to:

$$S^* - X = c_t(S^*, X, T - t) + \{1 - e^{-\delta(T-t)}N(d_1)\}(S^*/q_2) \qquad (7.12)$$

$N(d_1)$ and $p(S^*, X, T - t)$ are evaluated at S^*. To find S^* requires an iterative search for the value that makes the equation balance. Other terms are:

$$q_2 = \frac{1 - n + \sqrt{(n-1)^2 + 4k}}{2}, \qquad n = \frac{2(r-\delta)}{\sigma^2}, \qquad k = \frac{2r}{\sigma^2(1 - e^{-r(T-t)})}$$

For an American put, the analytic approximation is:

$$P_t = p_t + A_1 \left(\frac{S_t}{S^{**}}\right)^{q_1} \qquad \text{if } S_t > S^{**} \qquad (7.13)$$

$$= X - S_t \qquad \text{if } S_t \leq S^{**}$$

where:

$$A_1 = \frac{S^{**}[1 - e^{-\delta(T-t)}N(-d_1)]}{q_1}$$

$$q_1 = \frac{1 - n - \sqrt{(n-1)^2 + 4k}}{2}$$

S^{**} is found by an iterative search to make the following equation hold:

$$X - S^{**} = p_t(S^{**}, X, T - t) - [1 - e^{-\delta(T-t)}N(-d_1)](S^{**}/q_1) \qquad (7.14)$$

$N(-d_1)$ and $p_t(S^{**}, X, T - t)$ are evaluated at the critical stock price S^{**}. We now consider how this model can apply to options on stock indexes, foreign currency, and futures.

The Analytic Approximation for Options on Stock Indexes. To apply the Barone-Adesi and Whaley model to options on stock indexes, we merely need to reinterpret certain parameters in the model. Specifically, we interpret S in the model to indicate the price of the stock index in question and δ as the aggregate dividend rate on all of the stocks represented in the index. S^* and S^{**} are the critical levels of the stock index that would trigger exercise.

As an example, assume that a stock index has a current value of $400, that the risk-free rate of interest is 7 percent, that the continuous dividend rate on the stocks comprising the index is 3.5 percent, that the standard deviation of the stock index is .18, that the time to expiration is 140 days, and that the exercise price is $380. For these values, the Barone-Adesi and Whaley model gives a call price $C = 32.14$ and a put price $P = 7.41$, where these option values are expressed in index units. For the call, the critical price is $S^* = 822.31$, while for the put the critical price is $S^{**} = 328.50$. Because the current index value is below S^* and above S^{**}, there is no incentive to exercise. **OPTION!** solves for the critical stock index value and the price of American calls and puts on stock indexes using this analytic approximation. It also can graph the value of American options as a function of the underlying parameter values.

The Analytic Approximation for Options on Foreign Currencies. As with options on stock indexes, we can apply the Barone-Adesi and Whaley model to American options on foreign currencies by reinterpreting Equations 7.11 and 7.13. To apply these equations to options on foreign currency, we interpret S as the current value of the foreign currency and the dividend rate, δ, as the risk-free rate of interest on the foreign currency.

Earlier in this chapter, we considered an example of a British pound in the context of the Merton model. In that example, the pound was worth $1.40 and had a standard deviation of .5. The British risk-free rate is 12 percent, while the U.S. rate is 8 percent. The exercise price for both a call and a put is $1.50, and the two options expire in 200 days. Using the Merton model, we found that the European option values would be $c = \$.1452$ and $p = \$.2700$. For these same parameter values, American options would be worth: $C = \$.1498$ and $P = \$.2718$. The critical prices are $S^* = \$2.52$ and $S^{**} = \$.69$. Thus, it would be unwise to exercise either the call or the put. These values were found by letting the spot value of the pound ($1.40) take on the role of S in the analytic approximation formula, while the British interest rate (12 percent) played the role of the dividend, δ. **OPTION!** can compute and graph American foreign currency option values under the Barone-Adesi and Whaley model.

The Analytic Approximation for Options on Futures. The Barone-Adesi and Whaley model applies with equal facility to options on futures. In Equations 7.11 to 7.13, we interpret S as the futures price, and we assume that the rate of return on the underlying asset equals the risk-free rate. That is, we assume that $r = \delta$. This assumption is valid if the futures contract is a financial asset or a precious metal.

To apply this model to futures, consider an American call and put on platinum. The cost-of-carry model holds very well for this precious metal, justifying our assumption that $r = \delta$. Assume that the current spot price of platinum is $500 per ounce, that the risk-free rate of interest is 11 percent, that an American futures call and put expire in 75 days, and that the two options have an exercise price of $500. If platinum conforms to the cost-of-carry, the futures price must be:

$$F = Se^{r(T-t)} = \$500e^{.11(75/365)} = \$511.43$$

The volatility of the futures price is .25. In applying Equations 7.11 to 7.13 above, we replace S with the futures price of $511.43 and replace δ with the risk-free rate of 11 percent. For these data, the American option prices are $C = \$28.5323$ and $P = \$17.2875$, with critical futures prices $S^* = \$622.98$ and $S^{**} = \$401.2984$. For the corresponding European options, the prices are: $c = \$28.37$ and $p = \$17.1955$. The early exercise premium on the call is about $.16 and for the put the premium is about $.09.

Earlier we noted that the value of an American call on a futures would be higher than the value of an American call on the physical good if the futures price exceeded the spot price. We also said that the American put on the futures would be worth less than the corresponding American put on the physical if the futures price exceeded the cash price. This example confirms that point because the prices of options on physical platinum (given the spot price of $500 and assuming the same standard deviation of .25 pertains to the futures price and to the spot price) are: $C = \$22.09$ and $P = \$22.09$. Thus, the call price on the physical good is lower and the put price on the physical good is higher than the corresponding option on the futures.[8]

Summary. In this section, we have seen that the Barone-Adesi and Whaley analytical approximation applies to options not only on stocks but on stock indexes, on foreign currency, and on futures. To apply the model to these disparate instruments, we merely need to reinterpret some of the parameters in the model.

It is worth emphasizing that the Barone-Adesi and Whaley model assumes that the underlying good in each case pays at a continuous rate, whether it be dividends on a stock index, the foreign interest rate for foreign currency options, or the cost-of-carry rate on the good underlying a futures contract. This assumption is virtually without flaw for options on foreign currency and on futures, and it is quite reasonable for options on stock indexes. However, we must note that the dividend flow from stock indexes is not really continuous. To deal with discontinuous dividend flows, we now consider the binomial model and its applications to options on stock indexes, foreign currency, and futures.

The Binomial Model

In Chapter 6, we considered the application of the binomial model to pricing American options when the underlying good paid no dividend, a continuous dividend, a known dividend yield, or a known dollar dividend. Because this chapter considers options on stock indexes, foreign currency, and futures, we are most interested in applying the binomial model to a dividend payment stream that is continuous or that pays known dividends. As Chapter 6 has already shown how to apply the binomial model to the non-dividend case and to the case of known dividend yields, we focus on the dividend patterns of greatest interest, continuous dividends and known dollar dividends.

Review of the Basic Strategy for the Binomial Model. As in Chapters 4 and 6, we follow a common strategy for computing option prices under the binomial model. For options on stocks with dividends, we applied the binomial model by creating a lattice for the stock that reflected the timing and amount of dividend payments that the stock would make. These adjustments affected the distribution of possible stock values at the expiration date. We then computed the option values in the usual way by working from the exercise date back to the present.

To apply the binomial model for American options, we follow the same basic valuation strategy, with one important difference. For the option lattice for an American option, the option value is set equal to the maximum of:

1. The expected option value in one period discounted for one period at the risk-free rate.
2. The immediate exercise value of the option, $S_t - X$ for a call, or $X - S_t$ for a put.

Except for this treatment of each node in the lattice for an American option, the binomial model for an American option is applied in exactly the same way as it is for a European option. As we work back through the tree, discounting the next period's expected option values, we must ask at every node whether the immediate exercise value or the computed present value is greater. The value at the node is the maximum of those two quantities. Further, we may note that the stock tree is unaffected by whether the option we are analyzing is an American or a European option.

Review of the Binomial Model and Continuous Dividends. In Chapter 4, we explored Merton's model, which adjusts the Black-Scholes model to price European options on stocks that pay a continuous dividend. We also showed how to use the binomial model to price European options on stocks that pay continuous dividends. There we saw that the parameters for the binomial model for a stock paying a continuous dividend were:

$$U = e^{\sigma\sqrt{\Delta t}}$$

$$D = \frac{1}{U}$$

$$\pi_U = \frac{e^{(r-\delta)\Delta t} - D}{U - D}$$

(7.15)

As we have discussed in this chapter, the stock price tree is identical whether we are pricing European or American options. Therefore, these parameters apply to generating the binomial tree of stock prices for American options on stocks paying a continuous dividend. As an examination of these parameters shows, the stock price tree will be identical in both cases. However, the probability of a stock price increase varies inversely with the level of the continuous dividend rate, δ.

Review of the Binomial Model and Known Dollar Dividends. To apply the binomial model to options on goods with known dollar dividends, the first step is to generate the tree describing the potential stock price movements. As we saw in Chapter 4 when we considered the pricing of European options on stock with known dollar dividends, there can be a problem with the tree failing to recombine after the dividend has been paid. In this situation, the number of nodes can increase dramatically, particularly when there are many periods and several dividends. (For details on why the tree fails to recombine, see Chapter 4.)

We can solve this problem as we did in Chapter 4 by making a simplifying assumption. We assume that the stock price reflects the dividend, which is known with certainty, and all other factors that might affect the stock price, which are uncertain. We then adjust the uncertain component of the stock price for the impending dividends and model the uncertain component of the stock price with the binomial tree adding back the present value of all future dividends at each node. Specifically, we follow these steps:

1. Compute the present value of all dividends to be paid during the life of the option as of the present time = t.
2. Subtract this present value from the current stock price to form $S_t' = S_t - $ PV of all dividends.
3. Create the binomial tree by applying the up and down factors in the usual way to the initial stock price S_t'.
4. After generating the tree, add to the stock price at each node the present value of all future dividends to be paid during the life of the option.
5. Compute the option values in the usual way by working through the binomial tree.

These were exactly the steps we used in Chapter 6 to resolve this difficulty.

The application of this procedure to American options is exactly the same as with European options, with a single exception. In working through the tree to generate the option price tree, we must compare the present value of next period's expected option value with the exercise value of the option. The option price at the node is the higher of the present value or the exercise value. The computation of the value at a node is exactly the same as in other cases we have already considered.

The Binomial Model for Options on Stock Indexes. As we have just discussed, the binomial model can apply to options on stock indexes for both a continuous dividend on the stock index and for specific dividends at certain times. Stock indexes in fact tend to pay dividends in a discrete manner, with higher dividend payments coming at certain times of the year. Figure 7.3 shows the typical dividend pattern on the S&P 500 index and is a function of the tendency of firms to pay dividends at the end of each calendar quarter.

In this section, we explore how to apply the binomial model to options on stock indexes with discrete dividend patterns of the type shown in Figure 7.3. Later in this chapter, we show how to apply the binomial model to continuous payments on futures options and foreign currency.

To make the discussion more concrete, let us consider a stock index with a current value of $1,200. An American call and put option on the index expire in 125 days and have a common exercise price of $1,250. The volatility of the index is .2. The current risk-free interest rate is 8 percent. During the life of these options, the index will pay two dividends. The first dividend occurs on day 15 and

The Seasonal Pattern of Dividends on the S&P 500 Stock Index   **Figure 7.3**

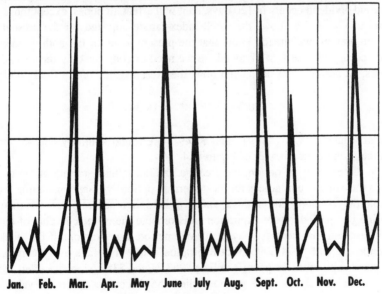

Jan.   Feb.   Mar.   Apr.   May   June   July   Aug.   Sept.   Oct.   Nov.   Dec.

Source: Reprinted by permission of Chicago Mercantile Exchange.

will be 15 index units, while the second falls on day 120 and will be 20 index units. The present value of the two dividends at the present date is:

$$PV = 15.00e^{-.08(15/365)} + 20.00e^{-.08(120/365)} = 34.4316$$

The next step is to subtract this value from the current index to form $S_t' = 1200.00 - 34.4316 = 1165.5684$.

We now compute the up and down factors and apply them to S_t' to form the stock index tree. We will form a tree with five periods, so each period consists of 25 days.

$$\Delta t = \frac{25}{365} = .0685 \text{ years}$$

$$U = e^{\sigma\sqrt{\Delta t}} = e^{.2\sqrt{.0685}} = 1.0537$$

$$D = \frac{1}{U} = .9490$$

$$\pi_U = \frac{e^{r\Delta t} - D}{U - D} = \frac{e^{.08(.0685)} - .9490}{1.0537 - .9490} = .5396$$

The upper panel in Figure 7.4 shows the stock index lattice for this example. However, we must still adjust this lattice by adding to each node the present value of all dividends to be received from that point to the expiration date of the option. The nodes occur at 0, 25, 50, 75, 100, and 125 days from the present. The first dividend occurs in 15 days, so it will affect only the node representing the present. The second dividend occurs in 120 days, so it will affect all nodes, except those at expiration. The lower panel of Figure 7.4 shows the stock index lattice adjusted for the present value of the dividends. For the present, we already know that the present value of the both dividends is $34.43. All later periods occur after the first dividend, so we need to consider only the second dividend for subsequent nodes. At period 1, 25 days from now, the present value of the final dividend is:

$$20.00e^{-.08(120-25)/365} = 19.59$$

The other present values ($19.70, $19.80, and $19.91) are found similarly and are included in the stock index lattice in the bottom panel of Figure 7.4.

To compute the price of an option, we create a parallel lattice, starting at the expiration date. Figure 7.5 shows the call and put lattices for the American options we are considering. For the option, the value at expiration is simply the intrinsic value of the option at that point. We then consider the nodes representing one period before expiration and compute the expected value of the payoffs one period later and discount that expected payoff for one period. For example, if the stock index value falls in four periods, it will be at $996.29 at expiration, while if it falls every period, it will be at $897.33. For a put at expiration, the payoffs will be $253.71 and $352.67, respectively, as the adjusted lattice for the stock index shows. One period earlier, the discounted expected value of these two payoffs is:

$$\{.5396(253.71) + .4604(352.67)\} \times .9945 = 297.63$$

| The Five-Period Stock Index Price Lattice (in dollars) | Figure 7.4 |

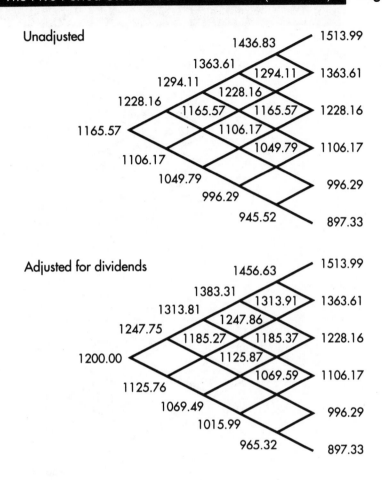

Unadjusted

					1436.83		1513.99
			1363.61			1294.11	1363.61
		1294.11		1228.16			1228.16
	1228.16		1165.57		1165.57		
1165.57				1106.17		1049.79	1106.17
	1106.17						996.29
		1049.79					
			996.29		945.52		897.33

Adjusted for dividends

					1456.63		1513.99
			1383.31			1313.91	1363.61
		1313.81		1247.86			1228.16
	1247.75		1185.27		1185.37		
1200.00				1125.87		1069.59	1106.17
	1125.76						996.29
		1069.49					
			1015.99		965.32		897.33

In terms of the adjusted lattice for the stock index, this corresponds to a stock index price at time four of $965.32.

Because we are working with American options, the holder of the put has the right to exercise at any time. At the fourth period, if the stock index price is $965.32, the immediate exercise value is $1,250 − 965.32 = 284.68. The holder of the put faces the following choice at the node we are considering. She may exercise the option for an immediate cash inflow of 284.68 index units or continue to hold the put, with its expected present value of 297.63 index units. A rational trader would hold at this point. The node in the put lattice that we are considering must have the maximum of the immediate exercise value ($284.68) or the discounted expected value of the payoffs in one period ($297.63). Thus, the node in the put lattice in Figure 7.5 has the value $297.63. Asterisks in the option lattices indicate an entry resulting from an exercise. For example, if the stock price falls

Figure 7.5 The Five-Period Lattice for an American Call and Put on the Stock Index (in dollars)

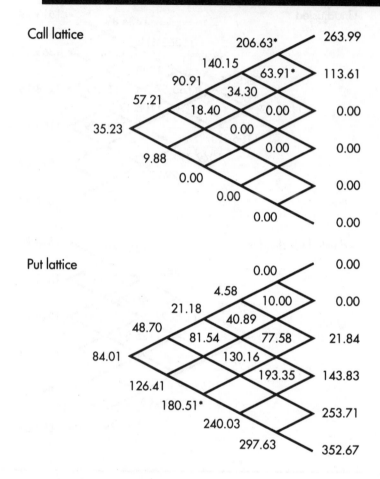

Call lattice

263.99
206.63*
140.15
113.61
90.91   63.91*
57.21   34.30
18.40   0.00
35.23   0.00   0.00
9.88   0.00   0.00
0.00   0.00
0.00   0.00
0.00   0.00

Put lattice

0.00   0.00
4.58   0.00
21.18   10.00
48.70   40.89
81.54   0.00
84.01   130.16   21.84
77.58
126.41   193.35   143.83
180.51*   253.71
240.03
297.63   352.67

*Indicates an entry resulting from an exercise.

in both of the first two periods, the put holder should exercise. Figure 7.5 shows that the value of an American call on the stock index would be 35.23 index units, while the American put is worth 84.01 index units. As the figure also shows, early exercise of either option is unlikely.

The Binomial Model for Options on Foreign Currency. We now illustrate how the binomial model applies to options on foreign currency by considering the binomial model with continuous dividends. This continuous dividends approach applies to stock index options and options on futures as well.

We illustrate the application of the binomial model to American options on foreign currency with the same example considered earlier in this chapter, except we now allow the option to be an

American option. Earlier, we analyzed a European call and put option on the British pound. Say the pound is worth $1.40 and has a standard deviation of .5. The British risk-free rate is 12 percent, while the U.S. rate is 8 percent. The call and put both have a striking price of $1.50 per pound and both expire in 200 days.

With a five-period binomial model, we found that the parameters were $U = 1.1800$; $D = .847452$; and $\pi_U = .445579$. The one-period discount factor is $e^{-.08(40/365)} = .9913$. All of these values are the same whether the option under consideration is European or American. Consequently, the lattice for the foreign currency remains the same as well. As we saw for the European options, the five-period lattice gave a call price of $.1519 and a put price of $.2766. For a 200-period lattice the call was $.1454 and the put was $.2702. For comparison, the Merton model gave a call price of $.1452 and a put price of $.2700.

To compute the price of American options on the foreign currency, we apply our familiar technology of constructing and evaluating lattices for the call and the put. For each node, we compute the expected value of the payoffs one period later and discount them for one period. Because we are now analyzing American options, we must check each node to determine whether the intrinsic value or our discounted expected value is greater. The node in question takes on the maximum of these two values.

Figure 7.6 gives the call and put lattices for these American options. An asterisk indicates a node at which early exercise is optimal. Because early exercise is optimal in some instances for both the call and the put, the price of these American options must be greater than the European counterpart. The price of the American call is $.1565, and the American put is $.2773. This gives an early exercise premium of $.0046 on the call and $.0007 for the put.

The Binomial Model for Options on Futures. We now apply the binomial model to options on futures. Generally, the goods underlying futures contracts may be thought of as paying a rate of return that equals the cost-of-carry. Earlier, we saw that this rate must equal the risk-free rate of interest to avoid arbitrage – at least if markets were sufficiently perfect. Equation 7.6 gave the parameters for the binomial model as it applies to options on goods paying a continuous return. For futures, we assume that $r = \delta$. The parameters for the binomial model are the same for a European or an American option.

As an example, we consider again the option on the stock index futures contract that we analyzed above. A stock index stands at $480 and the risk-free rate of interest is 7 percent. A call and a put on the stock index futures contract expire in one year. Therefore, the futures prices must be $514.80, as we saw above. If the standard deviation of the futures contract is .2 and the exercise price on both the call and put is $500, we saw that the five-period binomial prices for the European call and put were $46.49 and $32.69, respectively.

For these options, the binomial parameters are:

$$U = e^{\sigma\sqrt{\Delta t}} = e^{.2\sqrt{.2}} = 1.0936$$

$$D = \frac{1}{U} = .9144$$

$$\pi_U = \frac{e^{(r-\delta)\Delta t} - D}{U - D} = .4777$$

Figure 7.6 The Five-Period Lattice for an American Call and Put on the British Pound (in dollars)

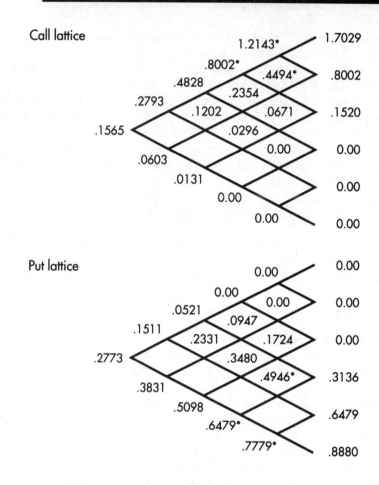

Call lattice

Put lattice

*Indicates a node at which early exercise is optional.

The discount factor per period is .9861. Figure 7.7 shows a five-period binomial lattice for the futures price. At the end of one year, the futures price will range between $329.11 and $805.25. Figure 7.8 shows the American call and put lattices for options on this futures contract. The asterisks indicate nodes at which the exercise value was substituted for the computed present value of the next period's expected payoffs. As we saw earlier in this chapter, the five-period binomial price for European options was $46.49 and $32.69 for the call and put, respectively. As Figure 7.8 shows, the American option prices from a five-period binomial analysis are $47.28 and $33.28 for the call and put, respectively.

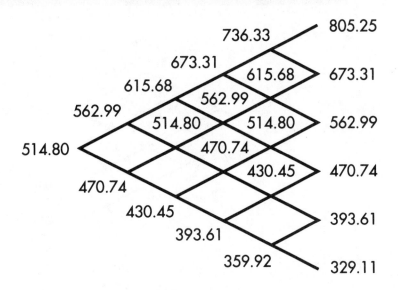

The Five-Period Lattice for the Futures Price (in dollars) | **Figure 7.7**

SUMMARY

This chapter has applied familiar ideas to new instruments – options on stock indexes, options on foreign currency, and options on futures contracts. We considered both European and American options. For European options on stock indexes, foreign currency, and futures, we saw that they can be priced by the Merton model or by the binomial model. For American options, we analyzed the analytic approximation of Barone-Adesi and Whaley and considered the binomial model.

In essence, the Merton model applies directly, given a slight reinterpretation of the parameters of the model. The reinterpretation requires that we substitute the stock index value, the foreign currency value, or the futures price for the stock price in the Merton model. We also substitute the dividend rate on the stock index, the foreign interest rate on the foreign currency, or the cost-of-carry on the futures, which we presume to equal the risk-free rate. With these substitutions, we can apply the Merton model to price the options considered in this chapter. The binomial model applies in a straightforward way to European stock index options, options on foreign currency, and options on futures.

For American options, we saw that both the Barone-Adesi and Whaley model and the binomial model are well suited to analyzing the options considered in this chapter. It is reasonable to regard foreign currencies and futures as paying a continuous yield and it is a reasonable assumption for stock indexes as well. Thus, the analytic approximation works quite well for the types of options considered in this chapter.

Figure 7.8 The Five-Period Lattice for the American Call and Put Futures Options (in dollars)

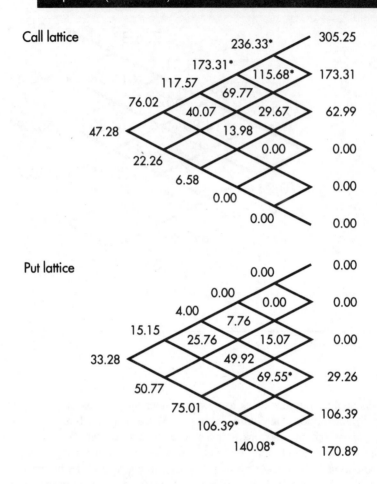

Call lattice

Put lattice

*Indicate nodes where the exercise value was substituted for the computed present value of next period's expected payoffs.

The binomial model applies to all of the American options discussed in this chapter as well. It is particularly well suited to pricing options on stock indexes. While it may be reasonable to assume that stock indexes pay a continuous dividend, we saw that there are significant discontinuities in the dividend stream for many real-world stock indexes. The binomial model is ideal for pricing options on goods that pay discrete dividends.

QUESTIONS AND PROBLEMS

1. Explain why interest payments on a foreign currency can be treated as analogous to a dividend on a common stock.
2. Why do we assume that the cost-of-carry for a futures is the same as the risk-free rate?
3. Explain verbally how to adjust a price lattice for an underlying good that makes discrete payments.
4. If a European and an American call on the same underlying good have different prices when all of the terms of the two options are identical, what does this difference reveal about the two options? What does it mean if the two options have identical prices?
5. Consider an option on a futures contract within the context of the binomial model. Assume that the futures price is $100, the risk-free interest rate is 10 percent, the standard deviation of the futures is .4, and the futures expires in one year. Assuming that a call and a put on the futures also expire in one year, compute the binomial parameters U, D, and π_U. Now compute the expected futures price in one period. What does this reveal about the expected movement in futures prices?
6. For a call and a put option on a foreign currency, compute the Merton model price, the binomial model price for a European option with three periods, the Barone-Adesi and Whaley model price, and the binomial model price with three periods for American options. Data are as follows: The foreign currency value is $2.50; the exercise price on all options is $2; the time until expiration is 90 days; the risk-free rate of interest is 7 percent; the foreign interest rate is 4 percent; the standard deviation of the foreign currency is .2.
7. Consider a call and a put on a stock index. The index price is $500, and the two options expire in 120 days. The standard deviation of the index is .2, and the risk-free rate of interest is 7 percent. The two options have a common exercise price of $500. The stock index will pay a dividend of 20.00 index units in 40 days. Find the European and American option prices according to the binomial model, assuming two periods. Be sure to draw the lattices for the stock index and the options that are being priced.
8. Consider two European calls and two European put options on a foreign currency. The exercise prices are $.90 and $1, giving a total of four options. All options expire in one year. The current risk-free rate is 8 percent, the foreign interest rate is 5 percent, and the standard deviation of the foreign currency is .3. The foreign currency is priced at $.80. Find all four option prices according to the Merton model. Compare the ratios of the option prices with the ratio of the exercise prices. What does this show?

NOTES

[1] This is not the same as capital delta, Δ, which stands for the sensitivity of the call option price to a change in the stock price.

[2] Even large indexes, such as the S&P 500, exhibit a distinct seasonal pattern in their index payments. Therefore, continuous dividends for a stock index represents something of an assumption.

[3] Our discussion of futures abstracts derives from considerable institutional detail. For instance, there is a fairly complex margining system that essentially requires traders to pay any paper losses in cash each day between the futures contracting date and the delivery date. Further, it is fairly easy to complete futures contract obligations without actually making delivery.

[4] When these conditions are not met, the pricing relationships discussed in this section do not hold. Slight deviations from these idealized conditions lead to slight pricing discrepancies, while some commodities do not obey the pricing rule at all. For details see Robert W. Kolb, *Understanding Futures Markets*, 5th ed., Cambridge, MA: Blackwell Publishing Company, 1997, Chapters 1–3.

[5] Notice that this equivalence of δ and r implies that the expected change in the futures price is zero. As the futures requires no investment and we are employing risk-neutrality arguments, the expected payoff from all investments is the risk-free rate. The risk-free rate applied to zero investment gives a zero expected profit.

[6] The application of this model to options on futures was first presented in Fischer Black, "The Pricing of Commodity Contracts," *Journal of Financial Economics*, 3, March 1976, pp. 167–79.

[7] For a detailed explanation of these pricing relationships see Chapter 3 of *Understanding Futures Markets*.

[8] Notice that the call and put on the physical have the same price of $22.09. This will always be the case if the price of the spot good equals the exercise price.

THE OPTIONS APPROACH TO CORPORATE SECURITIES

INTRODUCTION

In this chapter, we apply the concepts developed in this book to the analysis of corporate securities such as stocks and bonds. Virtually all securities have option features, and the options approach to corporate securities can help us understand these securities more fully.

Since the Black-Scholes model first appeared in the early 1970s, research on options has expanded rapidly. Option theory has given insight into several areas of finance, one of the most fruitful being corporate finance. In this chapter, we explore the insights that option theory brings to understanding corporate securities. By thinking of corporate securities as embracing options, we can build a deeper understanding of the value of securities such as stocks and bonds.[1]

The chapter begins by considering a firm with a simple capital structure of equity and a single pure discount bond. We show that the equity of the firm can be regarded as a call option on the entire firm with an exercise price equal to the obligation to the bondholders. Similarly, we can analyze the bond as involving an option as well. For this simple case, we show that the corporate bond can be regarded as consisting of a risk-free bond plus a short position in a put option. Of course, most firms have a more complex financial structure, but considering this simple case introduces the option dimension of most corporate securities.

In realistic situations, the options embedded in corporate securities are more complex. In many firms, some debt is subordinated to more senior debt, meaning that the firm pays on the junior debt after the senior debt claims have been satisfied. We show that the options approach to junior and senior debt analyzes these bonds as involving different exercise prices. When a firm has equity and coupon bonds, the analysis of the equity shows that the stock owners have a series of options. As another example, convertible debt includes a specific option – the option to convert the debt instrument into shares of the firm. The option to convert debt to equity is an option purchased by and held by the bond owner. Most corporate bonds are callable, so the issuer of the bond is entitled to retire the bond under specified circumstances. This call feature gives the issuer of the bond options with specified exercise prices. Understanding the option features of these different debt instruments gives a clearer understanding of their pricing. As we will see, these option features of corporate bonds have value and affect the value of the bonds in which they are embedded.

A **warrant** is a security that gives the owner the option to convert the warrant into a new share of the issuing firm by paying a stated exercise price. This definition shows that a warrant is very similar to an option. However, there is an important difference. An option has an existing share as its underlying good. By contrast, the exercise of a warrant requires that the firm issue a new share of stock. As we will see, this difference leads to a slight difference in the valuation of options and warrants.

EQUITY AND A PURE DISCOUNT BOND

We begin our analysis of corporate securities by focusing on a firm with an extremely simple capital structure. This firm has common stock and a single bond for its financing. The bond is a pure discount bond that matures in one year. In this section, we want to understand these securities from the options point of view.

Common Stock as a Call Option

For this firm financed by common stock and a single pure discount bond, we assume the bond issue is a pure discount bond, with face value FV. Let the current time be $t = 0$ and the maturity date of the bond be $t = m$. Between the present and $t = m$, the firm operates, generating cash flows. We further assume that the firm is operated by agents of the shareholders for the benefit of the shareholders. Also, during this period, new information about the prospects of the firm becomes available. At any time, the value of the firm equals the present value of the firm's future cash flows. The firm value also equals the total value of its outstanding securities. At $t = 0$, the firm's value, V_0, is:

$$V_0 = S_0 + B_0 \tag{8.1}$$

where:

S_0 = entire value of all stocks outstanding at time zero
B_0 = entire value of all bonds outstanding at time zero

The value of the bonds equals the present value of the face value, discounted at the appropriate risky discount rate r' for m periods.

$$B_0 = FVe^{-r'm} \tag{8.2}$$

When the bond matures, the firm can either pay the indebtedness, FV, or default. If the firm defaults, the bondholders take over the firm to salvage whatever they can. If the firm has a value greater than its indebtedness, FV, the firm will pay the bondholders, and the firm will then belong entirely to the stockholders. Thus, the stockholders' payoff at $t = m$, S_m, is either zero (if they default) or the value of the firm minus the debt to the bondholders ($V_m - FV$). In other words, the stock is just like a European call, with a payoff that equals:

$$S_m = \text{MAX}(0, V_m - FV) \tag{8.3}$$

Therefore, the stock is a call option on the firm with an exercise price equal to the debt obligation, FV. Figure 8.1 shows the position of the stockholders. If the firm value at expiration is less than or equal to FV, then the stockholders do not have enough to pay the bondholders. Accordingly, they default and receive nothing. If the firm value exceeds FV, the stockholders pay the bondholders and keep any excess value.

From our analysis of stock options, we know the call value must equal or exceed the stock price minus the present value of the exercise price. Applying that principle to our treatment of stock itself as an option, we have:

$$S_0 \geq V_0 - \text{FV}e^{-r't} \tag{8.4}$$

This formula emphasizes another principle of option pricing. We know that call prices increase for higher risk in the underlying good. In analyzing common stock as an option on the value of the firm, we see that increasing the risk of the firm will make the stock more valuable. This is true even if the increasing risk does not increase the expected value of the firm at the expiration of the bond. The reason for this increase in value is the same that we saw for stock options. The stockholders have an incentive to increase risk. If the higher risk pays off, the stockholders keep all the benefits. If the risk does not pay off, the limited liability feature of stock protects the stockholders from losing more than their investment. Therefore, increasing risk gives a better chance for a very positive outcome for the stockholders, while the option protects against very negative outcomes. However, increasing the risk of the firm without increasing its expected value cannot increase the value of the firm as a whole. The increase in the value of the stock must come at the expense of the bondholders. Increasing

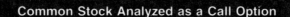

Common Stock Analyzed as a Call Option **Figure 8.1**

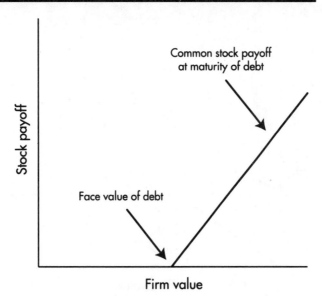

the risk of the firm without increasing the firm's expected value transfers wealth from bondholders to stockholders. Bondholders are aware of this incentive for the stockholders. As a result, bond covenants often prevent the borrower from increasing the risk of the firm.

The Option Analysis of Corporate Debt

Let us now examine the same simple firm from the perspective of the debt holder. The stockholders have promised to pay FV to the debt holders at $t = m$. However, the stockholders will pay only if the firm's value exceeds FV at the maturity of the debt. Otherwise, they will let the bondholders have the firm. Therefore, the payoff for the bondholders at $t = m$, B_m, will be the lesser of the firm's value or FV. Figure 8.2 graphs the payoffs that the bondholders receive. As the figure shows, the bondholders receive the entire value of the firm if the firm value at the maturity of the debt is less than the debt obligation, FV. However, the bondholders never receive more than the promised payment of FV. Thus, the payoff to the bondholders, B_m, is the lesser of the firm's value, V_m, or FV.

$$B_m = \text{MIN}(V_m, \text{FV}) \tag{8.5}$$

We have already seen the payoff to the stockholders at $t = m$ and know that the value of the bonds and stocks must equal the value of the firm. Therefore:

$$B_m = V_m - \text{MAX}(0, V_m - \text{FV}) \tag{8.6}$$

Figure 8.2   The Option Analysis of Corporate Debt

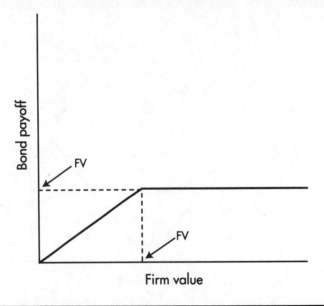

This equation shows that the bondholders have effectively purchased the entire firm and written a European call option to the stockholders. The call option is on the entire firm. The face value of the debt, FV, is the exercise price. This conclusion exactly complements our analysis of the stock as a call option on the value of the firm.

A closer analysis of Figure 8.2 shows that it has the same payoff shape that we studied in Chapter 2. In essence, the bondholders' payoff consists of two embedded positions. The general shape matches that of a short position in a put. However, the entire position can never be worth less than zero. The bondholders effectively hold a short position in a put with an exercise price of FV, in addition to a long position in a risk-free bond paying FV. To see why this is so, assume that the firm's value at maturity exactly matches the obligation to the bondholders, $V_m = FV$. From Figure 8.2, we see that the bondholders receive FV for this terminal firm value. With $V_m = FV$, the put option the bondholders issued expires worthless.

Now consider any lower value for the firm at maturity. If the firm value is lower than FV, the stockholders exercise their put option, forcing the firm upon the bondholders. Now the bondholders receive their risk-free payment of FV but lose an amount equal to the shortfall in the firm's value below FV. In our notation, the bondholders receive FV. They also lose either zero, if the firm's value exceeds FV, or they lose $FV - V_m$, if the debt obligation exceeds the value of the firm:

$$B_m = FV - MAX(0, FV - V_m) \qquad (8.7)$$

As this equation shows, the bondholders receive a payoff equal to a long position in a riskless bond and a short position in a put with an exercise price of FV.

Thus, we have seen that we can analyze the position of the bondholders in two ways:

1. The bond consists of ownership of the entire firm with a short position in a call on the entire firm given to the shareholders. The exercise price of the call possessed by the shareholders is FV.
2. The bond consists of a risk-free bond paying FV combined with a short position in a put option sold to the shareholders, which allows the shareholders to put the entire firm to the bondholders for an exercise price of FV.

From our exploration of put-call parity in Chapter 2, we know that the following relationship must hold:

$$S_t - c_t = Xe^{-r(T-t)} - p_t \qquad (8.8)$$

We can apply put-call parity to our present situation by recalling that the value of the entire firm, V_0, plays the role of the stock and that the exercise price equals the promised payment to the bondholders, FV.

$$V_0 - S_0 = B_0 \quad \text{or} \quad V_0 - c_t = FVe^{-r(T-t)} - p_t \qquad (8.9)$$

In Equation 8.9, notice that the promised payment on the bond, FV, is discounted at the risk-free rate of interest, r, not the risky rate of interest, r'. This difference reflects the analysis of the risky bond as consisting of a risk-free bond with a promised payment of FV plus a short position in the put option on the entire firm. The difference in price between the risk-free and risky bond equals the short position in the put.

SENIOR AND SUBORDINATED DEBT

Many firms have two or more debt issues in their capital structure. Thus, we now consider a firm with three securities: stock, senior debt, and subordinated debt. Subordinated debt is a bond issue that receives payment only after the firm fully meets senior debt obligations. Let the two debt issues be pure discount bonds that both mature at $t = m$. The face values on the two obligations are FV_s for the senior debt and FV_j for the junior or subordinated debt. We want to analyze the subordinated debt in option terms.

The holders of the subordinated debt receive payment only after the firm fully meets the claims of the senior debtholders. Therefore, for any firm value V_m that is less than FV_s, the junior debtholders receive zero. If the firm value exceeds FV_s, the subordinated debtholders receive at least some payment. The subordinated debtholders receive full payment if the firm's value equals or exceeds the entire amount due on both debt issues, $V_m \geq FV_s + FV_j$. Figure 8.3 shows the payoffs for the senior and junior debt. The payoffs on the junior debt match a portfolio of a long call with a striking price of FV_s and a short call with a striking price of FV_j, as Figure 8.4 shows. The stockholders in this firm own a call on the value of the firm with a striking price equal to $FV_s + FV_j$. For the call option represented by the stock to come into the money, the value of the firm must exceed the total payoff of the two debt issues. Therefore, the payoff on the call in this situation is:

$$S_m = \text{MAX}[0, V_m - (FV_s + FV_j)]$$

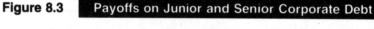

Figure 8.3   Payoffs on Junior and Senior Corporate Debt

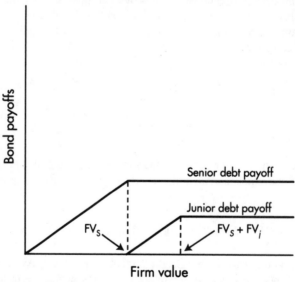

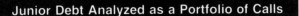

Junior Debt Analyzed as a Portfolio of Calls   Figure 8.4

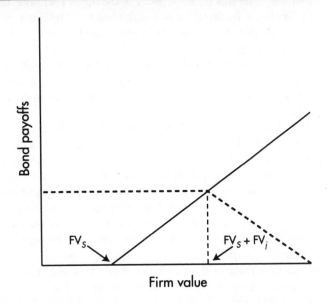

As always, the value of the firm must equal the value of all outstanding securities. However, the different classes of securities offer different ways to create various options and provide different divisions of the corporate pie when the bonds mature.

CALLABLE BONDS

The typical corporate bond is a callable bond. A **callable bond** is a bond that can be redeemed at the will of the issuer by the payment of a specified amount. Usually, the bond is not callable until a specified number of years after its issuance. Thereafter, the issuer may call the bond at any time. As an example, a firm might issue a bond today that is callable in five years (and thereafter), with a required payment equal to 110 percent of the face value of the bond. Typical call provisions allow this required payment to decline in subsequent years. In some cases, the bond is callable only on certain dates.

The issuer of the bond has an incentive to call the bond if the coupon rate exceeds the current market rate of interest. For example, if the callable bond were issued at 11 percent and current rates for similar debt are 6 percent, the issuer might wish to call the 11 percent bond and issue new debt at the prevailing market rate of 6 percent.

When it issues a callable bond, the firm itself retains a valuable option to require the bondholder to surrender the bond in return for the payment of a certain amount. Therefore, the call feature of a corporate bond means that the issuing firm has a call option on the outstanding bond. The exercise price of this call option is the call price that the firm must pay to call the bond.

For the bondholder, a callable bond is less desirable than a bond with no call feature. The bondholder knows that the issuer will exercise the call feature only when it benefits the issuing firm.

In our example, the bondholder receiving an 11 percent coupon payment in a 6 percent interest rate environment certainly would prefer that the issuer not call the bond. Therefore, in accepting a callable bond, the bondholder is implicitly buying a (non-callable) bond and selling a call option on the bond to the issuer. As we have seen, this call option held by the issuer has greater value when market rates of interest lie below the coupon rate on the bond.

The value of the non-callable bond varies inversely and smoothly with interest rates over the entire range of rates. By contrast, the value of a callable bond parallels the value of the non-callable bond for higher interest rates. For low interest rates, however, the value of the callable bond remains constant at a lower level.

To understand the difference in the values of callable and non-callable bonds, consider the following example of two similar bonds. One is non-callable, the other is callable on a single date in five years at a call price of $1,100.[2] We assume that both bonds have an initial maturity of 30 years, have an 8 percent coupon, and a $1,000 face value. We further assume that the non-callable bond has an 8 percent yield at issuance, so it is priced at its face value of $1,000. The callable bond is identical in its promised coupon payments and maturity and differs from the non-callable bond only in its call feature. As we have seen, this means that the buyer of the callable bond grants the issuer a call option which has some value. Therefore, we know that the price of the callable bond at issuance must be less than the otherwise identical non-callable bond.

Figure 8.5 illustrates the values of the two bonds five years after issuance, when both bonds have 25 years remaining until maturity. If market rates of interest are 8 percent, the non-callable bond will still be worth $1,000. The callable bond will be priced below $1,000 because of the call feature. If interest rates are higher, at 10 percent for example, the price of the non-callable bond will

Figure 8.5   Callable versus Non-Callable Bonds

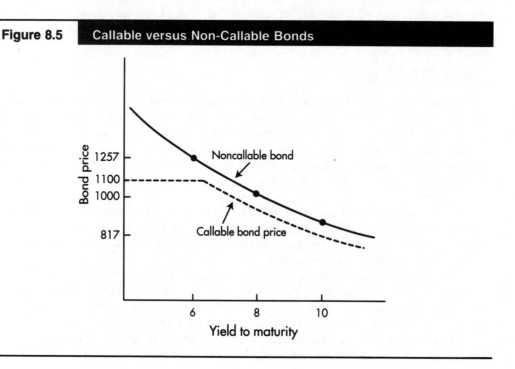

be $817, and the price of the callable bond will still be somewhat lower. If interest rates are substantially lower than 8 percent, say 6 percent for example, the price of the non-callable bond will be $1,257. At this point we can see that there will be a substantial divergence between the price of the callable and non-callable bond. The call price for the bond of $1,100 is effectively the upper bound on the price of the callable bond, even in a low interest rate environment. Investors will not be willing to pay more than $1,100 for the callable bond because they know it can be called away from them at that price.

The issuing firm holds a call option on the bond and a short position in the underlying bond. If interest rates fall, the value of bonds will rise in general. However, the callable bond is a single security, meaning that the bond and the call option on the bond are inextricably bound together. To capture the value of the call option, the issuer must exercise the call feature of the bond. This union of the call and the underlying bond in a single security helps to explain why the value of the callable bond cannot rise significantly above its call price. The resulting pricing is depicted in Figure 8.5. Summarizing, for prices at or below the call price on the callable bond, the two bonds will behave similarly. However, the callable bond will always be worth somewhat less than an otherwise similar bond due to the presence of the call feature. For higher prices on the non-callable bond, the price of the callable bond will be capped at or near the call price of the bond.

Figure 8.5 does not show the exact price of the callable bond because it does not attempt to exactly price the call that is embedded in the callable bond. However, we know that the price of the embedded call will depend on the time until expiration, the prevailing interest rate, the price of the otherwise similar bond, the call price, and the volatility of the price of the otherwise similar bond.

CONVERTIBLE BONDS

Many corporate bonds are convertible into shares of the issuing firm. The holder of the bond has the option to convert the bond into shares under the terms specified in the bond indenture. For example, a firm might issue a $1,000 face value convertible bond with a 20-year maturity and a coupon rate of 9 percent. The bond could be converted into eight shares of stock by surrendering the bond.[3] We assume that a share of the issuing firm was worth $100 at the time of issuance. We can analyze this type of convertible bond as consisting of two elements: a regular bond with no conversion feature, plus a call option on eight shares of stock with the exercise price of the option being the value of the bond. The number of shares received for the bond upon conversion is the **conversion ratio**. Because the purchase of a convertible bond receives a call option on the shares of the issuing firm, the convertible bond sells for more than an otherwise similar non-convertible bond. This means that the issuing firm can issue a convertible bond at a lower interest rate than an otherwise similar non-convertible bond. However, the firm gives a call option to secure this lower interest rate.

At any time during its life, the bond must be worth at least its conversion value. In our example, we assume that the conversion ratio was eight shares, so the bond must be worth at least eight times the current share price. If this condition were not met, there would be an immediate arbitrage opportunity because a trader could buy the bond, exercise the conversion feature to secure the shares, and sell the shares for more than the price of the bond. Of course, the bond can sell for more than its conversion value because the bond always has all of the features of a straight bond.

At the maturity of the bond, the bond will pay its face value, will be converted, or the firm will default. The firm will default if the face value exceeds the value of the firm. In the case of default, the owners of the convertible bond will take over the entire firm. Assuming the firm does not default, the convertible bond will be worth the maximum of the face value or the conversion ratio times the stock price.

In many instances, the bond indenture prohibits the issuing firm from paying a dividend during the life of the convertible bond. In this case, the bond will not be converted prior to its maturity date. This is clear by analogy to a call. Exercising a call or converting a convertible bond on a non-dividend stock terminates the option in favor of its intrinsic value. As we saw for a call, the owner is better off selling the call and buying the stock in the open market. Similarly, the holder of a convertible bond on a non-dividend stock will not exercise because doing so discards the excess value of the call option over and above its intrinsic value.

Some convertible bonds are also callable. For convertible callable bonds, both the issuer and the bondholder hold an option associated with the bond. As we have seen, the issuer has a call option on the underlying bond, and the owner of a convertible bond has a call option on the firm's shares. Consider a convertible bond that could be profitably converted and assume that the underlying shares pay no dividend. As we have just seen, the bondholder will not willingly convert prior to the maturity of the bond because converting the bond discards the time value that is inherent in the option. However, the issuer would like the holder of the convertible to convert as soon as possible for the same reason. Therefore, the issuer of a convertible callable bond can force conversion by calling the bond. As soon as the convertible callable bond can be converted, the issuer should call the bond to force conversion. If it behooves the bondholder to delay conversion, it must benefit the issuer to force conversion. After all, the bond is an asset to the bondholder, but a liability to the issuer. Therefore, forcing conversion eliminates the time premium associated with the conversion option.

WARRANTS

A typical warrant allows the owner to surrender the warrant and pay a stated price for a share of common stock of the firm that issues the warrant. Usually, warrants are created with three to seven years to expiration. As such, a warrant is very much like a call option on the stock of the issuing firm. However, a call option has as its underlying instrument an existing share. By contrast, the exercise of a warrant requires the issuing firm to create a new share and deliver it to the exerciser of the warrant. Therefore, the exercise of a warrant involves a dilution of ownership because a new share is created. Warrants are often attached to bonds as a "sweetener" to make the bonds more salable. Often these warrants are detachable and can even trade in a separate market. However warrants are issued, they are valuable instruments with all of the features of a call option, except for the fact that they command a newly created share upon exercise rather than an existing share.

At the expiration date of the warrant, exercise would make sense only if the resulting share value from exercise exceeds the exercise price. Let V_B = the share price before exercise, X = the exercise price of the warrant, n = the number of shares outstanding before exercise, and q = the number of warrants. The value of the firm after exercise will be $nV_B + qX$ because the total exercise price on the warrants is qX, and the firm's value increases by the influx of cash from the exercise of the warrants. There will be $n(1 + q/n)$ shares outstanding after exercise. Therefore, the value of a share after exercise will be:

$$\frac{nV_B + qX}{n + q} \tag{8.10}$$

As an example, consider a firm with 100 outstanding shares priced at $48 per share and assume that the shares pay no dividend. The firm has warrants for 10 shares outstanding with an exercise price on the warrants of $50. If the warrants are exercised, the firm will be worth $5,300, the present value of the firm plus the $500 exercise price of the warrants. The firm will then have 110 shares outstanding after it issues the 10 shares to meet the exercise of the warrants. Consequently, each share after exercise would be worth $48.18. With an exercise price of $50 and a post-exercise share price of $48.18, exercise is not feasible. Thus, exercise will only be feasible if the stock price equals or exceeds the exercise price.

As with a call option, a warrant should not be exercised until expiration. The reasoning is the same; early exercise discards the time premium associated with the option. Instead of exercising the call or warrant, the owner should sell the call or warrant and purchase the underlying good.

The value of a European warrant equals the value of a parallel European call after adjustment for the dilution of ownership caused by the exercise of the warrant. If q warrants are exercised and n shares are outstanding before exercise, there will be $n(1 + q/n)$ shares outstanding after exercise. The European warrant gives title to one of those shares. Therefore, the value of a European warrant at time t, W_t, must be:

$$W_t = \frac{c_t}{1 + \dfrac{q}{n}}$$

In other words, the value of a European warrant equals the value of a European call option divided by one plus the proportion of shares created in response to the exercise of the warrant.

SUMMARY

In this chapter, we have explored how various corporate securities can be analyzed in terms of the option concepts developed throughout this book. We began by considering an extremely simple firm drawing its capital from only common stock and a single pure discount bond. For such a firm, we saw that the common stock can be treated as a call option on the entire firm. In this case, the call option has an exercise price equal to the payment promised to the bondholders, and the expiration date for the option is the maturity of the bond.

The bond itself can be analyzed in option terms as well. We used put-call parity to show that the bond can be analyzed in two equivalent ways. First, the bond represents ownership of the entire firm coupled with a short position in a call on the entire firm given to the shareholders. The exercise price of the call possessed by the shareholders is the payment promised to the bondholders. As a second and equivalent analysis, the bond consists of a risk-free bond paying the face value of the bond combined with a short position in a put option sold to the shareholders, which allows the shareholders to put the entire firm to the bondholders for an exercise price of the face value of the bond.

We next considered a firm with stock, senior debt, and subordinated debt in its capital structure. The stock owners have essentially the same position as in the simplest case. They own a call on the entire firm, and the exercise price of the call is the total set of payments promised to both the senior and subordinated debtholders. The subordinated debtholder essentially holds a long call on the firm with an exercise price equal to the payment promised to the senior bondholders coupled with a short call on the entire firm with an exercise price equal to the payment promised to the junior debtholders. If the shareholders decide not to exercise their call, it will be because the value of the firm is less than the exercise price that the stockholders face – the payments promised to the junior and senior debtholders. The junior debtholders can then claim the firm by exercising their call on the senior debtholders; they merely must pay the senior debtholders as promised. However, the junior debtholders have also issued a call because the stockholders may call the firm away from them by making the promised payment.

Both callable and convertible bonds have options imbedded in them. As we saw, a callable bond consists of a straight bond, but the issuer of the bond retains a call option on the bond. Thus, the issuer is long this call and the bondholder has sold the call to the issuer. This call gives the issuer of the bond the right to purchase the bond and avoid any further payments by paying the call price. In a bond convertible into common stock, the owner of the bond has a call option on the shares of the firm. The bondholder in this case can convert a bond into shares by surrendering the bond and paying the stipulated price to acquire the shares permitted by the bond covenant. In both the case of the callable bond and the convertible bond, the imbedded options have value, and this value can be a considerable proportion of the total value of the bond.

Finally, we considered the pricing of warrants. We noted that a warrant is similar to a call option. However, a call option gives the holder the right to buy an existing share, while a warrant gives the holder the right to buy a newly issued share from the firm. Therefore, the exercise of the warrant involves a dilution of ownership in the firm, and a warrant is, therefore, slightly less valuable than an otherwise similar call option.

QUESTIONS AND PROBLEMS

1. Explain why common stock is itself like a call option. In the option analysis of common stock, what plays the role of the exercise price and what plays the role of the underlying stock?
2. Consider a firm that issues a pure discount bond that matures in one year and has a face value of $1,000,000. Analyze the payoffs that the bondholders will receive in option pricing terms, assuming the only other security in the firm is common stock.
3. Consider a firm with common stock and a pure discount bond as its financing. The total value of the firm is $1,000,000. There are 10,000 shares of common stock priced at $70 per share. The bond matures in ten years and has a total face value of $500,000. What is the interest rate on the bond, assuming annual compounding? Would the interest rate become higher or lower if the volatility of the firm's cash flows increases?
4. A firm has a capital structure consisting of common stock and a single bond. The managers of the firm are considering a major capital investment that will be financed from internally generated funds. The project can be initiated in two ways, one with a high fixed cost component and the other with a low fixed cost component. Although both technologies have the same expected value, the high fixed cost approach has the potential for greater payoffs. (If the product is successful, the high fixed cost approach gives much lower total costs for large production levels.) What does option theory suggest about the choice the managers should make? Explain.
5. In a firm with common stock, senior debt, and subordinated debt, assume that both debt instruments mature at the same time. What is the necessary condition on the value of the firm at maturity for each security holder to receive at least some payment? With two classes of debt, does option theory counsel managers to increase the riskiness of the firm's operations? Would there be any

difference on this point between a firm with a single debt issue and two debt issues? Which bondholders would tend to be more risk averse as far as choosing a risk level for the firm's operations? Explain.

6. Consider a firm financed solely by common stock and a single callable bond issue. Assume that the bond is a pure discount bond. Is there any circumstance in which the firm should call the bond before the maturity date? Would such an exercise of the firm's call option discard the time premium? Explain.

7. Consider a firm financed by only common stock and a convertible bond issue. When should the bondholders exercise? Explain. If the common shares pay a dividend, would it make sense for the bondholders to exercise before the bond matures? Explain by relating your answer to our discussion of the exercise of American calls on dividend-paying stocks.

8. Warrants are often used to compensate top executives in firms. Often these warrants cannot be exercised until a distant expiration date. This form of compensation is used to align the manager's incentives with the maximization of the shareholders' wealth. Explain how the manager's receiving warrants might thwart the efforts to change his or her incentives.

NOTES

[1] Of course the original Black-Scholes paper, "The Pricing of Options and Corporate Liabilities," *Journal of Political Economy*, 81, 1973, pp. 637–59, already focused on the option characteristics of stocks and bonds.

[2] Generally, bonds are not callable until their first call date and are then callable at any time thereafter.

[3] Other features are possible. For example, some bonds can be converted to preferred stock. Some convertible bonds can be converted only by surrendering the bond and making a cash payment. Some convertible bonds can be converted only on certain dates. Further, some convertible securities are preferred stock that can be converted into common stock.

EXOTIC OPTIONS

INTRODUCTION

In recent years, financial engineers have created a variety of complex options that are collectively known as **exotic options**. The payoffs on these options are considerably more diverse than the payoffs on the straightforward options we have considered. For example, the payoff on a **lookback call option** depends on the minimum stock price experienced during some past period. Other exotic options have different and more complicated payoff structures. This chapter explores the pricing and uses of these exotic options.

We contrast these exotic options with the plain vanilla options explored earlier in this book. For a **plain vanilla option**, the value of an option at any particular moment depends on only the current price of the underlying good, the exercise price, the risk-free rate of interest, the volatility of the underlying good, the time until expiration, and the dividend rate on the underlying good. Further, there is a fixed underlying good, a fixed and stated exercise price, a known time to expiration, and no special conditions on any of the option parameters.

With respect to the price of the underlying good, it is important to emphasize that the price of a plain vanilla option depends on only the current price of the underlying good, so the price of the option is independent of the price path followed by the underlying good. As we will see in this chapter, many exotic options exhibit **path dependence** – the price of the option today depends on the previous or future price path followed by the underlying good. For example, the price of a lookback call option depends on the minimum price reached by the underlying good over some past period. Further, the price of an average price option depends on the future average price of the underlying good. Thus, to price a path-dependent option, it is not enough to know the current price of the underlying good. Instead, we must have information about the previous path that the price of the underlying good traversed.[1]

This chapter considers nine classes of exotic options: forward-start options, compound options, chooser options, barrier options, binary options, lookback options, average price options, exchange options, and rainbow options. Because of the complexity of these options, we focus on European options, emphasizing cases in which closed-form solutions are available. Thus, all of the exotic options are analyzed as extended instances of the Merton continuous dividend model. In their working paper, "Exotic Options," Mark Rubinstein and Eric Reiner have presented a unified and comprehensive treatment of these exotic options, which this chapter relies on heavily. We also refer to other studies and original contributions for each of the types of exotic options.

This chapter explores each type of exotic option in a separate section that discusses the payoff structure of the option, presents the valuation formula for the option, and shows a calculation example. The **OPTION!** software that accompanies this book can compute the value of all of the exotic options discussed in this chapter.

ASSUMPTIONS OF THE ANALYSIS AND THE PRICING ENVIRONMENT

In this chapter, we focus exclusively on European exotic options for which closed-form solutions exist. For most American exotic options, and for some European exotic options, there is no exact pricing formula. For these options, simulation or approximation methods must be used to estimate the price. This process adds considerable complexity. By focusing on European exotic options with closed-form solutions, we can gain a rich understanding of exotic options, while avoiding much mathematical complexity.

In our analysis, we make the usual assumptions underlying the Black-Scholes model and the Merton model. Particularly, we assume that the price of the asset underlying the exotic option follows a lognormal random walk, that there are no arbitrage opportunities, and that the price of the underlying asset is expected to appreciate at the risk-free rate of interest, less any payouts from the asset such as dividends. These assumptions allow us to evaluate options in a risk-neutral framework. As we explored in Chapter 4, these assumptions lead to the Black-Scholes model and the Merton model. Because we will refer to it often in this chapter, we repeat the Merton model here for convenience:

$$c_t^M = e^{-\delta(T-t)}S_t N(d_1^M) - Xe^{-r(T-t)}N(d_2^M)$$

$$p_t^M = Xe^{-r(T-t)}N(-d_2^M) - e^{-\delta(T-t)}S_t N(-d_1^M) \qquad (9.1)$$

$$d_1^M = \frac{\ln\left(\dfrac{S_t}{X}\right) + (r - \delta + .5\sigma^2)(T - t)}{\sigma\sqrt{T - t}}$$

$$d_2^M = d_1^M - \sigma\sqrt{T - t}$$

FORWARD-START OPTIONS

In a **forward-start option**, the price of the option is paid at the present, but the life of the option starts at a future date. Further, the exercise price is typically specified to be the current price at the beginning of the option's life – that is, the option contract specifies that the option will be at-the-money when the option's life begins. Forward-start call options are often used in executive compensation packages. An executive might receive a forward-start call option on the firm's shares with an exercise price to equal the firm's share price at the time the option life starts.

For a forward-start option, there are three dates to consider: the valuation date, t; the date that the option life begins, which is called the **grant date**, tg; and the date when the option eventually expires, T. Thus it must be the case that:

$$t \leq tg \leq T$$

Accordingly, the time until the option life begins will be $tg - t$; and when the option's life begins, the time until expiration will be $T - tg$.

The value of a forward-start option is simply the value of an option with the current stock price, an exercise price equal to the current stock price, and a time to expiration of $T - tg$, with this value being discounted by the dividend rate on the underlying good over the period until the option is granted, $tg - t$:

$$\text{Forward-Start Call} = e^{-\delta(tg-t)}C_{tg}{}^{M} \qquad (9.2)$$
$$\text{Forward-Start Put} = e^{-\delta(tg-t)}P_{tg}{}^{M}$$

where $C_{tg}{}^{M}$ and $P_{tg}{}^{M}$ are the values of the call and put options, respectively, according to the Merton model, with a time to expiration of $T - tg$. The idea here is that the price of the underlying good and the exercise price on the forward-start option will change proportionally. (For a forward-start option specified to be at-the-money on the grant date, the stock and exercise price at that time will be equal.) Therefore, a forward-start option today is essentially a deferred granting of an option with a stock and exercise price equal to today's stock price and a time to expiration that equals the period from the grant date to the final expiration date.[2]

To illustrate the value of these forward-start options more fully, consider the following data:

$$S = \$100$$
$$X = \$100$$
$$T - t = 1 \text{ year}$$
$$\sigma = 0.2$$
$$r = 0.1$$
$$\delta = 0.05$$
$$tg = 0.5 \text{ years}$$

Using these data we will price a call option. Notice that the time to expiration as of the grant date is $T - tg = 0.5$ years, so this is the time to expiration that will be used in the Merton model. We first compute d_1^M and d_2^M:

$$d_1^M = \frac{\ln\left(\dfrac{100}{100}\right) + [0.1 - 0.05 + 0.5(0.2)(0.2)](0.5)}{0.2\sqrt{0.5}} = 0.247487$$

$$d_2^M = 0.247487 - 0.141421 = 0.106066$$

With these values for d_1^M and d_2^M, $N(d_1^M) = 0.597734$ and $N(d_2^M) = 0.542235$. So the value of the underlying call option is:

$$c_{tg}{}^{M} = e^{-\delta(T-tg)}S_t N(d_1^M) - Xe^{-r(T-tg)}N(d_2^M)$$
$$= e^{-0.05(0.5)}100(0.597734) - 100e^{-0.1(0.5)}(0.542235)$$
$$= 6.7186$$

The value of the forward-start call is:

$$\text{Forward-start call} = e^{-\delta(tg-t)}C_{tg}^M = e^{-0.05(0.5)}6.7186 = 6.5527$$

With the same input values, the forward-start put is worth \$4.2042.

COMPOUND OPTIONS

A **compound option** is an option on an option; in other words when one option is exercised, the underlying good is another option. In this section, we consider the pricing of the four types of possible compound European options: a call on a call, a call on a put, a put on a call, and a put on a put. For example, consider the owner of a call on a call. The owner of the compound call has until the expiration date of the compound option (the call on a call) to decide whether to exercise the compound option. If so, she will receive the underlying call option with its own exercise price and time until expiration. If that underlying option is exercised, she will receive the underlying good.

For the underlying option, we will let X be the exercise price and T be the expiration date. For the compound option, let x be the exercise price and te be the time at which the compound option expires. Because these are European options, the owner of the compound option cannot exercise until the expiration date of the compound option, te. If she exercises the compound option, she will immediately receive the underlying call. Therefore, when the compound option is at expiration, the choice is simple: pay x and receive the underlying option or do nothing and allow the option to expire worthless. Thus, when the compound option reaches expiration, the trader will exercise the compound call if the price of the underlying call is worth more than the exercise price of the compound option, x. At the expiration date of the compound option, the underlying call (or underlying put) can be priced according to the Merton model with inputs S_{te} for the price of the underlying good, X for the exercise price, $T - te$ for the time remaining until expiration, σ for the volatility of the underlying good, r for the risk free rate, and δ for the dividend rate on the underlying good.

Before the expiration date of the compound option, that is from t until te, the value of the compound option depends on the value of the underlying good in a compound manner. First, the value of the underlying option is largely a function of the value of the underlying good. Second, the value of the compound option also depends on the price of its underlying good, which is the option underlying the compound option.

The valuation of these compound options is highly analogous to the valuation of an American option with a dividend payment between the valuation date and the expiration date that we studied in Chapter 6. There we saw that the value depends on the critical stock price, S^*, that made the owner of the underlying call indifferent between exercising and allowing the option to expire worthless. In the case of an option on an underlying call, the critical stock price will be the stock price that leaves the owner of the underlying call indifferent between exercising or not. Therefore, for a compound option on an underlying call, the critical price is the stock price at which the value of the underlying call equals the cost of acquiring it, which is x. Thus, the critical stock price for an underlying call (a call on a call or a put on a call) is the value of S^* that makes the following equation hold:

$$S^* e^{-\delta(T-te)}N(z) - Xe^{-r(T-te)}N(z - \sigma\sqrt{T - te}) - x = 0 \tag{9.3}$$

where:

$$z = \frac{\ln\left(\dfrac{S^*}{X}\right) + (r - \delta + 0.5\sigma^2)(T - te)}{\sigma\sqrt{T - te}}$$

For a compound option on an underlying put (a call on a put or a put on a put), the critical stock price satisfies the following relationship:

$$-S^* e^{-\delta(T-te)}N(-z) + Xe^{-r(T-te)}N(-z + \sigma\sqrt{T - te}) - x = 0 \tag{9.4}$$

Before we can write the valuation formula for a call on a call, we must define three additional variables:

$$w_1 = \frac{\ln\left(\dfrac{S}{S^*}\right) + (r - \delta + 0.5\sigma^2)(te - t)}{\sigma\sqrt{te - t}}$$

$$w_2 = \frac{\ln\left(\dfrac{S}{X}\right) + (r - \delta + 0.5\sigma^2)(T - t)}{\sigma\sqrt{T - t}}$$

$$\rho = \sqrt{\frac{te - t}{T - t}}$$

With these definitions, the value of a call on a call, CC_t, is:

$$CC_t = Se^{-\delta(T-t)}N_2(w_1; w_2; \rho) - Xe^{-r(T-t)}N_2(w_1 - \sigma\sqrt{te - t}; w_2 - \sigma\sqrt{T - t}; \rho) \tag{9.5}$$
$$- xe^{-r(te-t)}N(w_1 - \sigma\sqrt{te - t})$$

In Equation 9.5, the three terms correspond to the key factors that determine the value of the compound option, S, k, and K. The function N_2 is the bivariate normal cumulative probability already discussed in Chapter 6.[3]

To apply this formula, consider the following data:

$S = \$100$
$\sigma = 0.2$
$r = 0.1$
$\delta = 0.05$
$X = 100$ (the exercise price on the underlying option)
$x = 8$ (the exercise price on the compound option)
$T - t = 1$ year (the expiration date of the underlying option)
$te = .25$ years (the expiration date of the compound option)

With these data, we must first find the critical value that would make the option owner indifferent between exercising the compound option and allowing it to expire. The critical price depends on the value of z, which in turn depends on S^*. This means that the values of S^* and z must be solved simultaneously. This can be done by an iterative search over potential values of S^*. This is best done by computer. For these data, the critical value is \$99.235871. This can be verified by computing z and the resulting value of zero in the equation for finding S^*.

Having found S^*, the values of w_1 and w_2 are given by:

$$w_1 = \frac{\ln\left(\frac{100}{99.235871}\right) + [0.1 - 0.05 + .5(0.2)(0.2)](0.25)}{0.2\sqrt{0.25}}$$

$$= \frac{0.0076706 + 0.0175}{0.1}$$

$$= 0.251706$$

$$w_2 = \frac{\ln\left(\frac{100}{100}\right) + [0.1 - 0.05 + 0.5(0.2)(0.2)](1.0)}{0.2(1.0)} = \frac{0 + 0.07}{0.2} = 0.35$$

The correlation coefficient is:

$$\rho = \sqrt{\frac{0.25}{1.0}} = 0.5$$

With these values of w_1, w_2, and ρ, we can compute all of the values for the unit and bivariate cumulative normal probabilities:

$$N_2(w_1; w_2; \rho) = N_2(0.251706; 0.35; 0.5) = 0.458898$$
$$N_2(w_1 - \sigma\sqrt{te - t}; w_2 - \sqrt{T - t}; \rho) = N_2(0.151706; 0.15; 0.5) = 0.395366$$
$$N(w_1 - \sigma\sqrt{te - t}) = N(0.251706 - 0.1) = 0.560291$$

These probabilities can be found and verified by using **OPTION!** We can now use these intermediate results to compute the value of our compound option:

$$CC_t = 100e^{-0.05(1.0)}(0.458898) - 100e^{-0.1(1.0)}(0.395366) - 8e^{-0.1(0.25)}(0.560291)$$
$$= 3.5059$$

Using the appropriate definition for the critical stock price given in Equation 9.3 for compound calls or Equation 9.4 for compound puts, the following formulas give the value of a call-on-a-put (CP_t), a put-on-a-call (PC_t), and a put-on-a-put (PP_t):

$$CP_t = -Se^{-\delta(T-t)}N_2(-w_1; -w_2; \rho) + Xe^{-r(T-t)}N_2(-w_1 + \sigma\sqrt{te - t}; -w_2 + \sigma\sqrt{T - t}; \rho) \qquad (9.6)$$
$$- xe^{-r(te-t)}N(-w_1 + \sigma\sqrt{te - t})$$

$$PC_t = -Se^{-\delta(T-t)}N_2(-w_1;\ w_2;\ -\rho) + Xe^{-r(T-t)}N_2(-w_1 + \sigma\sqrt{te-t};\ w_2 - \sigma\sqrt{T-t};\ -\rho) \qquad (9.7)$$

$$+\ xe^{-r(te-t)}N(-w_1 + \sigma\sqrt{te-t})$$

$$PP_t = Se^{-\delta(T-t)}N_2(w_1;\ -w_2;\ -\rho) - Xe^{-r(T-t)}N_2(w_1 - \sigma\sqrt{te-t};\ -w_2 + \sigma\sqrt{T-t};\ -\rho) \qquad (9.8)$$

$$+\ xe^{-r(te-t)}N(w_1 - \sigma\sqrt{te-t})$$

With the same input values used for the call-on-a-call, the resulting compound option values are: $CP_t = 0.6490$; $PC_t = 1.3675$; and $PP_t = 3.1498$.

Figure 9.1 shows how compound option values vary as a function of the underlying stock price. Panels A–D correspond to call-on-a-call, call-on-a-put, put-on-a-call, and put-on-a-put compound options respectively. For each graph, we use the same parameters as our example calculation. As Figure 9.1A shows, the value of a call-on-a-call is an increasing function of the stock price, while Figure 9.1B shows that the value of a call-on-a-put is a decreasing function of the stock price. Both of these compound calls vary in price as would the price of the underlying options. However, as Figures 9.1C–D show, the value of a put-on-a-call is a decreasing function of the stock price, while the price of a put-on-a-put increases with an increasing stock price.

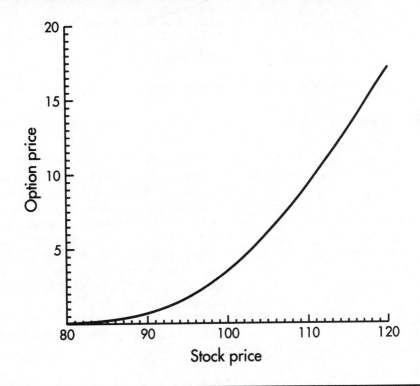

Call-on-a-Call Price as a Function of the Stock Price   **Figure 9.1A**

Figure 9.1B   Call-on-a-Put Price as a Function of the Stock Price

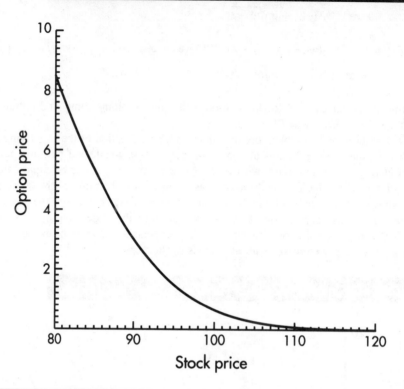

CHOOSER OPTIONS

The owner of a **chooser option** has the right to determine whether the chooser option will become a call or a put option by a specified choice date. After the choice date, the option becomes a plain vanilla call or put, depending on the owner's choice. Chooser options are also known as **as-you-like-it options**. Bankers Trust offers several types of chooser options in the over-the-counter market.[4] Chooser options are useful for hedging a future event. For example, while Congress considered the North American Free Trade Agreement (NAFTA) in 1993, there was considerable uncertainty about the bill's passage. Passage was expected to be beneficial to the value of the Mexican peso; rejection of the bill was expected to send the peso tumbling. Traders could hedge this uncertainty with a chooser option on the Mexican peso. If NAFTA passed, one could choose to let the option be a call; if the bill failed, the owner could choose to let the option be a put.[5]

In considering chooser options, there are three dates to consider: the valuation date, t; the choice date, when the owner must choose for the option to be a call or put, tc; and the expiration of the option, T. The dates must have the following relative values:

$$t \leq tc \leq T$$

Put-on-a-Call Price as a Function of the Stock Price | Figure 9.1C

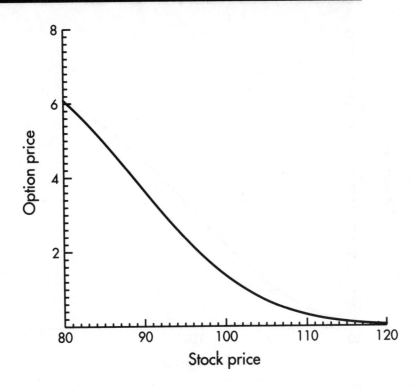

The problem is to evaluate the option at time t, before the choice date. After the choice date, the value of the option will simply be the value of the plain vanilla call or put given by the Merton model. We will focus on simple chooser options, in which the potential put and call have a common exercise price and expiration date. Complex choosers allow the potential call and put to have different exercise prices, different expiration dates, or both different exercise prices and expiration dates.

For a simple chooser, there are two extreme values for the choice date, tc, to consider. If the choice must be made immediately, $t = tc$, then the owner of the chooser will choose that the option be a call or a put, whichever has a greater value:

$$\text{If } t = tc, \text{ then Chooser}_t = \text{MAX} \begin{Bmatrix} C(S, X, T - t, \sigma, r, \delta) \\ P(S, X, T - t, \sigma, r, \delta) \end{Bmatrix}$$

If the choice date is at the expiration of the option, $tc = T$, then the chooser is really a straddle. Viewed from the valuation date, t, the value of the straddle is the value of the call and the put:

$$\text{If } t = T, \text{ then Chooser}_t = C(S, X, T - t, \sigma, r, \delta) + P(S, X, T - t, \sigma, r, \delta)$$

Figure 9.1D   Put-on-a-Put Price as a Function of the Stock Price

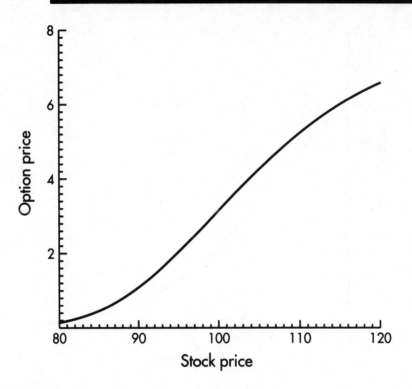

Thus, these extreme values for the choice date determine the upper and lower bounds for the value of a simple chooser. If the choice date is now, $t = tc$, then the chooser value is at the lower bound and equals the maximum of the call or put value. If the choice can be deferred until the expiration date, $tc = T$, then the value of the chooser is the same as a straddle and equals the combined value of the plain vanilla call plus the plain vanilla put.

   In the normal event, when the choice date, tc, is after t but before T, one will not want to choose whether the option is a call or put until the choice date. Therefore, the payoff on a chooser comes on the choice date and it will be:

$$\text{Chooser}_{tc} = \text{MAX} \begin{Bmatrix} C(S_{tc}, X, T - tc, \sigma, r, \delta) \\ P(S_{tc}, X, T - tc, \sigma, r, \delta) \end{Bmatrix}$$

Applying put-call parity, the value of the Chooser at tc is:

$$\text{Chooser}_{tc} = \text{MAX} \begin{Bmatrix} C(S_{tc}, X, T - tc, \sigma, r, \delta) \\ C(S_{tc}, X, T - tc, \sigma, r, \delta) + Xe^{-r(T-tc)} - S_{tc}e^{-\delta(T-tc)} \end{Bmatrix}$$

This is equivalent to:

$$\text{Chooser}_{tc} = C(S_{tc}, X, T - tc, \sigma, r, \delta) + \text{MAX}\{0, Xe^{-r(T-tc)} - S_{tc}e^{-\delta(T-tc)}\}$$

Viewed from the present valuation date, t, this payoff at tc means that the value of the chooser will be the same as the following portfolio:

$$C(S, X, T - t, \sigma, r, \delta) + P(Se^{-\delta(T-tc)}, Xe^{-r(T-tc)}, tc - t, \sigma, \delta)$$

Therefore, the value of a simple chooser at time t is:

$$\text{Chooser}_t = Se^{-\delta(T-t)}N(w_1) - Xe^{-r(T-t)}N(w_1 - \sigma\sqrt{T - t}) + Xe^{-r(T-t)}N(-w_2 + \sigma\sqrt{tc - t}) - Se^{-\delta(T-t)}N(-w_2)$$

$$(9.9)$$

where the values of w_1 and w_2 are:

$$w_1 = \frac{\ln\left(\dfrac{S}{X}\right) + (r - \delta + 0.5\sigma^2)(T - t)}{\sigma\sqrt{T - t}}$$

$$w_2 = \frac{\ln\left(\dfrac{S}{X}\right) + (r - \delta)(T - t) + 0.5\sigma^2(tc - t)}{\sigma\sqrt{tc - t}}$$

In Equation 9.9, the value of the chooser has two parts. The first portion, with the form $S - X$, corresponds to the value of the potential call, while the second portion, with the form $X - S$, corresponds to the value of the potential put.

As a calculation example, consider the following data:

$S = \$100$
$X = \$100$
$T - t = 1$ year
$\sigma = 0.25$
$r = 0.10$
$\delta = 0.05$
$tc = 0.5$ years

With these values, we first compute w_1 and w_2, finding that $w_1 = 0.3250$ and $w_2 = 0.371231$. The cumulative normal values required are:

$$N(w_1) = N(0.3250) = 0.627409$$

$$N(-w_2) = N(-0.371231) = 0.355233$$

$$N(w_1 - \sigma\sqrt{T - t}) = N(0.3250 - 0.25) = 0.529893$$

$$N(-w_2 + \sigma\sqrt{tc - t}) = N(-0.371231 + 0.17678) = 0.422910$$

Applying these values to Equation 9.9, we find:

$$\text{Chooser}_t = 100(0.951229)(0.627409) - 100(0.904837)(0.529893)$$
$$+ 100(0.904837)(0.422910) - 100(0.951229)(0.355233)$$
$$= 16.2100$$

We can verify that the value of this chooser lies between the lower and upper bounds by computing the value of the corresponding plain vanilla call and put. With the same parameter values the call is worth \$11.7343 and the put is worth \$7.0951. We noted that the lower bound for the price of the chooser would be the maximum value of either the plain vanilla call or the put. The upper bound for the price of the chooser is the combined value of the call and put, which is equivalent to the straddle:

$$\text{MAX\{plain vanilla call or put\}} \leq \text{Chooser} \leq \text{plain vanilla call} + \text{plain vanilla put}$$
$$\text{MAX\{11.7343, 7.0951\}} \leq \text{Chooser} \leq 11.7343 + 7.0951$$
$$11.7343 \leq \text{Chooser} = 16.21 \leq 18.8294$$

Figure 9.2 shows how the value of a chooser option varies with the stock price, by using the same parameter values as our example chooser and allowing the stock price to vary. The parabolic shape of the graph reflects the characteristic graph of a straddle, such as that shown in Figure 5.20. Figure 9.3 shows more specifically how the value of our example chooser will vary with the time until the choice must be made. If the choice must be made immediately, Figure 9.3 shows that the value of the chooser will be \$11.73, which equals the value of the plain vanilla call. If the choice can be deferred until expiration, Figure 9.3 shows that the value of the chooser is the same as the value of the straddle, which is \$18.83.

BARRIER OPTIONS

Barrier options can be ''in'' options or ''out'' options. An ''in'' barrier option has no value until the price of the underlying good touches a certain barrier price. When that happens, the option becomes a plain vanilla option. Accordingly, an ''out'' option is initially like a plain vanilla option, except if the price of the underlying good penetrates the stated barrier, the option immediately expires worthless. Barrier options can be either calls or puts, permitting eight types of barrier options:

Down-and-In Call	Down-and-Out Call
Up-and-In Call	Up-and-Out Call
Down-and-In Put	Down-and-Out Put
Up-and-In Put	Up-and-Out Put

Barrier options may also pay a rebate, which is a booby prize. For an ''out'' barrier option, the rebate is paid immediately when the barrier is hit and the option passes out of existence. For an ''in'' barrier option, the rebate is paid if the option expires without ever hitting the barrier price. Barrier options are also known as **knock-in** and **knock-out** options. Barrier options exhibit path dependence. The value of a barrier option at the present depends on the previous sequence of stock prices, particularly on whether the stock price has already hit the barrier for an ''in'' option. The present price of a

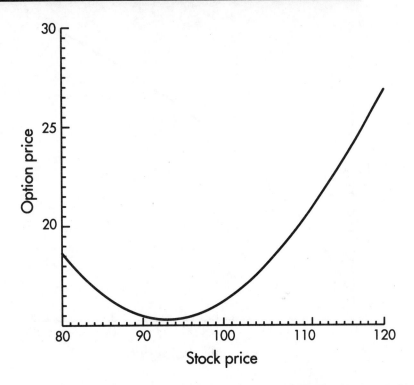

Figure 9.2

The Price of a Simple Chooser Option as a Function of the Stock Price

barrier option can also depend on the future price path of the underlying stock – Will the price hit the barrier between now and expiration?

Barrier options may be viewed as conditional plain vanilla options. ''In'' barrier options become plain vanilla options if the barrier is hit. ''Out'' barrier options are plain vanilla options, with the condition that they may pass out of existence if the barrier is hit. These conditions make barrier options inferior to unconditional plain vanilla options, so barrier options will be cheaper than otherwise identical plain vanilla options. This cheapness gives barrier options a special usefulness in hedging applications. For example, a portfolio manager may expect the value of her portfolio to increase but wish to protect against the possibility of a large drop in value. Accordingly, she might buy a put option with an exercise price slightly below the present price of the portfolio. As we have seen in Chapter 2, this is essentially a portfolio insurance strategy. By buying a down-and-in put instead of a plain vanilla put, the portfolio manager can get the same protection, but at a cheaper price.

Figure 9.4 shows how payoffs arise for a down-and-in option. As mentioned earlier, the stock price must be above the barrier for such an option to be interesting; if the stock price is below the barrier, the barrier option has already become a plain vanilla option. Thus, the initial stock price will exceed the barrier, but the exercise price may be either higher or lower than the barrier. The top

Figure 9.3   Price of a Chooser Option as a Function of the Days Until the Choice Date

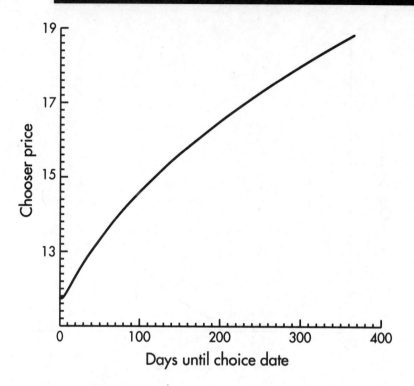

panel of Figure 9.4 shows a situation in which the barrier, BARR, exceeds the exercise price, X. Three stock price paths are shown in this panel. First, the stock price may penetrate the barrier and terminate above the exercise price but below the barrier. Second, the stock price may penetrate the barrier, and the terminal price might exceed the barrier. (We distinguish these two cases because the probabilities associated with these two price paths are different, even though they have the same payoff.) Third, the stock price may never penetrate the barrier, and the payoff is the rebate amount, REBATE. The bottom panel shows a similar situation, except in this case the exercise price exceeds the barrier. In price path 4, the stock price penetrates the barrier but terminates above the exercise price. In price path 5, the barrier is never hit so the payoff is REBATE. As Figure 9.4 pertains only to down-and-in options, we must also consider down-and-out options, particularly the fact that the rebate is paid immediately upon the barrier being pierced. This gives a sixth payoff possibility.

As an example, we focus on the payoffs from a down-and-in call. For this option, there are three possible payoff outcomes: if the barrier is never touched, the payoff is REBATE; if the barrier is touched, and $S_T > X$, the payoff is $S_T - X$; and if the barrier is touched, and $S_T \leq X$, the payoff is 0. There are alternative ways that these various payoffs may be earned because the exercise price can

Alternative Stock Price Paths for Down-and-In Barrier Options   **Figure 9.4**

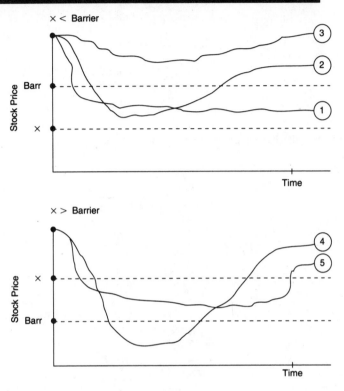

be either above or below the barrier price. To price a down-and-in call, we must consider these five price paths and their associated payoffs, for a stock price at expiration of S_T:

1. BARRIER $\geq S_T \geq X$; payoff is $S_T - X$
2. $S_T \geq$ BARRIER $\geq X$, and the barrier was touched; payoff is $S_T - X$
3. $S_T \geq$ BARRIER $\geq X$, and the barrier was never touched; payoff is REBATE
4. $S_T \geq X \geq$ BARRIER, and the barrier was touched; payoff is $S_T - X$
5. $S_T \geq X \geq$ BARRIER, and the barrier was never touched; payoff is REBATE

The value of a down-and-in call is the present expected value of these payoffs. In addition for an "out" option, there is a sixth price path and payoff to consider, which is presented later. For each type of option, we need expressions for these possible payoffs and price paths.

  We define some intermediate values prior to considering the six payoff/probability expressions that cover both "in" and "out" barrier options:

$$\lambda = \frac{r - \delta + 0.5\sigma^2}{\sigma^2}$$

$$\mu = r - \delta - 0.5\sigma^2$$

$$a = \frac{\mu}{\sigma^2} \qquad b = \frac{\sqrt{\mu^2 + 2r\sigma^2}}{\sigma^2}$$

Letting BARR indicate the barrier price, we define:

$$w_1 = \frac{\ln\left(\dfrac{S}{X}\right)}{\sigma\sqrt{T - t}} + \lambda\sigma\sqrt{T - t}$$

$$w_2 = \frac{\ln\left(\dfrac{S}{\text{BARR}}\right)}{\sigma\sqrt{T - t}} + \lambda\sigma\sqrt{T - t}$$

$$w_3 = \frac{\ln\left(\dfrac{\text{BARR}^2}{SX}\right)}{\sigma\sqrt{T - t}} + \lambda\sigma\sqrt{T - t}$$

$$w_4 = \frac{\ln\left(\dfrac{\text{BARR}}{S}\right)}{\sigma\sqrt{T - t}} + \lambda\sigma\sqrt{T - t}$$

$$w_5 = \frac{\ln\left(\dfrac{\text{BARR}}{S}\right)}{\sigma\sqrt{T - t}} + b\sigma\sqrt{T - t}$$

Tables 9.1 through 9.4 present expressions for the present values of payoffs resulting from particular price paths with their associated probabilities. Table 9.5 shows the value of each possible barrier option in terms of the expressions in Tables 9.1 through 9.4.

As an example, consider a down-and-in call with the exercise price lying above the barrier ($X > \text{BARR}$). According to Table 9.5, the value of this call will be DC4 + DC5. This analysis corresponds to the bottom panel of Figure 9.4. The value of this down-and-in call is the present value of the two payoffs, $S_T - X$ or REBATE, multiplied by their associated probabilities.[6]

Pursuing this same example, we will compute the value of a down-and-in call (with $X > \text{BARR}$) using the following data:

	Valuation Expressions for Down Calls	Table 9.1

DC1
$$Se^{-\delta(T-t)}N(w_1) - Xe^{-r(T-t)}N(w_1 - \sigma\sqrt{T-t})$$

DC2
$$Se^{-\delta(T-t)}N(w_2) - Xe^{-r(T-t)}N(w_2 - \sigma\sqrt{T-t})$$

DC3
$$Se^{-\delta(T-t)}\left(\frac{BARR}{S}\right)^{2\lambda}N(w_4) - Xe^{-r(T-t)}\left(\frac{BARR}{S}\right)^{2\lambda-2}N(w_4 - \sigma\sqrt{T-t})$$

DC4
$$Se^{-\delta(T-t)}\left(\frac{BARR}{S}\right)^{2\lambda}N(w_3) - Xe^{-r(T-t)}\left(\frac{BARR}{S}\right)^{2\lambda-2}N(w_3 - \sigma\sqrt{T-t})$$

DC5
$$REBATE\,e^{-r(T-t)}\left\{ N(w_2 - \sigma\sqrt{T-t}) - \left(\frac{BARR}{S}\right)^{2\lambda-2}N(w_4 - \sigma\sqrt{T-t}) \right\}$$

DC6
$$REBATE\left\{ \left(\frac{BARR}{S}\right)^{a+b}N(w_5) + \left(\frac{BARR}{S}\right)^{a-b}N(w_5 - 2b\sigma\sqrt{T-t}) \right\}$$

	Valuation Expressions for Down Puts	Table 9.2

DP1
$$Xe^{-r(T-t)}N(-w_1 + \sigma\sqrt{T-t}) - Se^{-\delta(T-t)}N(-w_1)$$

DP2
$$Xe^{-r(T-t)}N(-w_2 + \sigma\sqrt{T-t}) - Se^{-\delta(T-t)}N(-w_2)$$

DP3
$$Xe^{-r(T-t)}\left(\frac{BARR}{S}\right)^{2\lambda-2}N(w_4 - \sigma\sqrt{T-t}) - Se^{-\delta(T-t)}\left(\frac{BARR}{S}\right)^{2\lambda}N(w_4)$$

DP4
$$Xe^{-r(T-t)}\left(\frac{BARR}{S}\right)^{2\lambda-2}N(w_3 - \sigma\sqrt{T-t}) - Se^{-\delta(T-t)}\left(\frac{BARR}{S}\right)^{2\lambda}N(w_3)$$

DP5
$$REBATE\,e^{-r(T-t)}\left\{ N(w_2 - \sigma\sqrt{T-t}) - \left(\frac{BARR}{S}\right)^{2\lambda-2}N(w_4 - \sigma\sqrt{T-t}) \right\}$$

DP6
$$REBATE\left\{ \left(\frac{BARR}{S}\right)^{a+b}N(w_5) + \left(\frac{BARR}{S}\right)^{a-b}N(w_5 - 2b\sigma\sqrt{T-t}) \right\}$$

$$S = \$100$$
$$X = \$100$$
$$T - t = 1 \text{ year}$$
$$\sigma = 0.2$$
$$r = 0.1$$
$$\delta = 0.05$$
$$BARR = 97$$
$$REBATE = 2$$

Table 9.3	Valuation Expressions for Up Calls

UC1
$$Se^{-\delta(T-t)}N(w_1) - Xe^{-r(T-t)}N(w_1 - \sigma\sqrt{T-t})$$

UC2
$$Se^{-\delta(T-t)}N(w_2) - Xe^{-r(T-t)}N(w_2 - \sigma\sqrt{T-t})$$

UC3
$$Se^{-\delta(T-t)}\left(\frac{BARR}{S}\right)^{2\lambda}N(-w_4) - Xe^{-r(T-t)}\left(\frac{BARR}{S}\right)^{2\lambda-2}N(-w_4 + \sigma\sqrt{T-t})$$

UC4
$$Se^{-\delta(T-t)}\left(\frac{BARR}{S}\right)^{2\lambda}N(-w_3) - Xe^{-r(T-t)}\left(\frac{BARR}{S}\right)^{2\lambda-2}N(-w_3 + \sigma\sqrt{T-t})$$

UC5
$$REBATEe^{-r(T-t)}\left\{ N(-w_2 + \sigma\sqrt{T-t}) - \left(\frac{BARR}{S}\right)^{2\lambda-2}N(-w_4 + \sigma\sqrt{T-t})\right\}$$

UC6
$$REBATE\left\{ \left(\frac{BARR}{S}\right)^{a+b} N(-w_5) + \left(\frac{BARR}{S}\right)^{a-b} N(-w_5 + 2b\sigma\sqrt{T-t})\right\}$$

Table 9.4	Valuation Expressions for Up Puts

UP1
$$Xe^{-r(T-t)}N(-w_1 + \sigma\sqrt{T-t}) - Se^{-\delta(T-t)}N(-w_1)$$

UP2
$$Xe^{-r(T-t)}N(-w_2 + \sigma\sqrt{T-t}) - Se^{-\delta(T-t)}N(-w_2)$$

UP3
$$Xe^{-r(T-t)}\left(\frac{BARR}{S}\right)^{2\lambda-2}N(-w_4 + \sigma\sqrt{T-t}) - Se^{-\delta(T-t)}\left(\frac{BARR}{S}\right)^{2\lambda}N(-w_4)$$

UP4
$$Xe^{-r(T-t)}\left(\frac{BARR}{S}\right)^{2\lambda-2}N(-w_3 + \sigma\sqrt{T-t}) - Se^{-\delta(T-t)}\left(\frac{BARR}{S}\right)^{2\lambda}N(-w_3)$$

UP5
$$REBATEe^{-r(T-t)}\left\{ N(-w_2 + \sigma\sqrt{T-t}) - \left(\frac{BARR}{S}\right)^{2\lambda-2}N(-w_4 + \sigma\sqrt{T-t})\right\}$$

UP6
$$REBATE\left\{ \left(\frac{BARR}{S}\right)^{a+b} N(-w_5) + \left(\frac{BARR}{S}\right)^{a-b} N(-w_5 + 2b\sigma\sqrt{T-t})\right\}$$

where BARR is the barrier price and REBATE is the rebate amount. The value of this down-and-in call will be DC4 + DC5, so we will need the intermediate values of λ, w_2, w_3, and w_4. These values are: $\lambda = 1.75$; $w_2 = 0.502296$; $w_3 = 0.045408$; and $w_4 = 0.197704$. The needed cumulative normal values are:

	Valuation of Barrier Options	Table 9.5
	$X >$ **BARR**	$X <$ **BARR**
Down-and-In Call (DIC)	DC4 + DC5	DC1 – DC2 + DC3 + DC5
Up-and-In Call (UIC)	UC1 + UC5	UC2 – UC4 + UC3 + UC5
Down-and-In Put (DIP)	DP2 + DP3 – DP4 + DP5	DP1 + DP5
Up-and-In Put (UIP)	UP1 – UP2 + UP3 + UP5	UP4 + UP5
Down-and-Out Call (DOC)	DC1 – DC4 + DC6	DC2 – DC3 + DC6
Up-and-Out Call (UOC)	UC6	UC1 – UC2 – UC3 + UC4 + UC6
Down-and-Out Put (DOP)	DP1 – DP2 – DP3 + DP4 + DP6	DP6
Up-and-Out Put (UOP)	UP2 – UP3 + UP6	UP1 – UP4 + UP6

$$N(w_3) = 0.518109$$

$$N(w_2 - \sigma\sqrt{T - t}) = 0.618787$$

$$N(w_3 - \sigma\sqrt{T - t}) = 0.438571$$

$$N(w_4 - \sigma\sqrt{T - t}) = 0.499084$$

With these intermediate values, we can compute the values of DC4 and DC5 from Table 9.1:

$$DC4 = 100(0.951229)\left(\frac{97}{100}\right)^{3.5}(0.518109) - 100(0.904837)\left(\frac{97}{100}\right)^{1.5}(0.438571)$$

$$= 44.300383 - 37.911247$$

$$= 6.389136$$

$$DC5 = 2(0.904837)\left\{0.618787 - \left(\frac{97}{100}\right)^{1.5}(0.499084)\right\} = 0.256960$$

The value of the down-and-in call with an exercise price above the barrier, $DIC_{X>BARR}$ is the sum of the two portions: DC4 for the present value of the $S_T - X$ payoff plus DC5 for the present value of the rebate payoff, where each payoff is weighted by the probability that it will be received:

$$DIC = DC4 + DC5 = 6.3891 + 0.2570 = 6.6461$$

Figure 9.5 shows how our sample down-and-in call price varies as a function of the barrier price. If the barrier price is $50, the option is worth little because the stock price stands at $100, and the chance of its falling to $50 within the next year is small. By contrast, if the barrier is near $100, the chance of hitting the barrier is much greater, so the barrier option price is closer to that of a plain vanilla call. With these same parameter values, a plain vanilla call would be worth $9.94.

For our particular barrier option, with BARR = $97 and REBATE = $2, the computed price was $6.6461. Only $0.26 of this price was attributable to the barrier, which was DC5. For the same barrier

Figure 9.5   Down-and-In Call Price as a Function of the Barrier Price

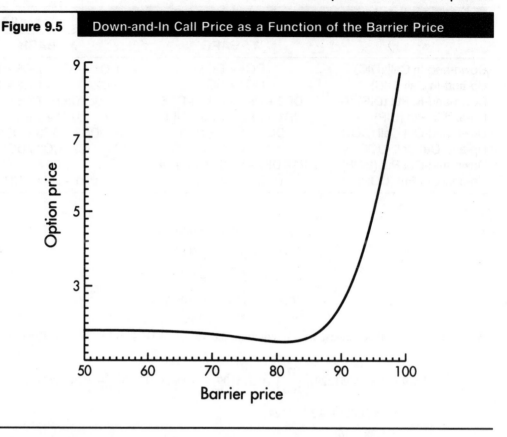

option with BARR = $97 and REBATE = 0, the price of the option is $6.3891. By focusing on this same option but assuming that REBATE = 0, we can see how the price of the barrier option approaches the price of a plain vanilla call as the barrier is set closer to the current stock price of $100. Assuming that REBATE = 0, our option would be worth $6.39 with BARR = $97, $7.46 with BARR = $98, $8.64 with BARR = $99, and $9.94 (the same as the plain vanilla call) with BARR = $99.9999.

BINARY OPTIONS

Binary options have discontinuous payoffs, either paying nothing or a considerable amount depending on the satisfaction of some condition. For example, a **cash-or-nothing call** is a type of binary option that pays a fixed cash amount if the stock price terminates above the exercise price or pays nothing if the terminal stock price is below the exercise price. Other types of binary options that we will consider are **asset-or-nothing options**, **gap options**, and **supershares**. These binary options are also known as **digital options**, a name that reflects the all-or-nothing character of their payoffs.[7]

Cash-or-Nothing Options

A cash-or-nothing call pays a fixed cash amount, Z, if the terminal stock price, S_T, exceeds the exercise price, X; otherwise the call pays nothing. Similarly, a cash-or-nothing put pays a fixed cash amount,

Z, if the terminal stock price is below the exercise price. These options require no payment of an exercise price. Instead, the exercise price merely determines whether the option owner receives a payoff. Viewed from the perspective of the valuation date, t, the value of a cash-or-nothing call will be the present value of the fixed cash payoff multiplied by the probability that the terminal stock price will exceed the exercise price.

From the Merton model, the probability of the option finishing in the money is d_2^M. The present value of the fixed cash payoff, Z, is $Ze^{-r(T-t)}$. Therefore, the value of a cash-or-nothing call is:

$$CONC_t = Ze^{-r(T-t)}N(d_2^M) \tag{9.10}$$

By analogous reasoning, the value of a cash-or-nothing put is:

$$CONP_t = Ze^{-r(T-t)}N(-d_2^M) \tag{9.11}$$

Consider now a cash-or-nothing call and put with the following parameter values:

$S = \$100$
$X = \$105$
$T - t = 0.5$ years
$\sigma = 0.2$
$r = 0.1$
$\delta = 0.05$
$Z = 100$

where Z is the fixed cash amount that the option owner receives if the option finishes in-the-money. For these values:

$$d_2^M = \frac{\ln\left(\frac{S_t}{X}\right) + (r - \delta + .5\sigma^2)(T - t)}{\sigma\sqrt{T - t}} - \sigma\sqrt{T - t}$$

$$= \frac{\ln\left(\frac{100}{105}\right) + [0.1 - 0.05 + 0.5(0.2)(0.2)](0.5)}{0.2\sqrt{0.5}} - 0.2\sqrt{0.5}$$

$$= -0.238933$$

and $N(d_2^M) = N(-0.238933) = 0.405579$. For the put $N(-d_2^M) = N(0.238933) = 0.594421$. The values of the two options are:

$$CONC_t = Ze^{-r(T-t)}N(d_2^M) = 100e^{-0.1(0.5)}(0.405579) = 38.5799$$

$$CONP_t = Ze^{-r(T-t)}N(-d_2^M) = 100e^{-0.1(0.5)}(0.594421) = 56.5431$$

Notice that a portfolio consisting of a cash-or-nothing call and put (with the same payoff and term to expiration) has a certain payoff. Specifically, the portfolio will pay the common amount Z. Therefore:

$$CONC_t + CONP_t = Ze^{-r(T-t)}, \text{ for a common expiration and a common } Z$$

Figure 9.6 shows how the values of these options vary as a function of the stock price. The value of the two options together equals the present value of Z no matter what the stock price might be.

Asset-or-Nothing Options

Asset-or-nothing options are similar to cash-or-nothing options, with one major difference. Instead of a fixed cash amount, the payoff on an asset-or-nothing option is the underlying asset. If the terminal asset price exceeds the exercise price, the owner of a call receives the asset, but if the terminal asset price is below the exercise price, the call expires worthless. For a put, if the terminal asset price is less than the exercise price, the put owner receives the asset, but if the terminal asset price exceeds

| **Figure 9.6** | The Value of Cash-or-Nothing Options as a Function of the Stock Price |

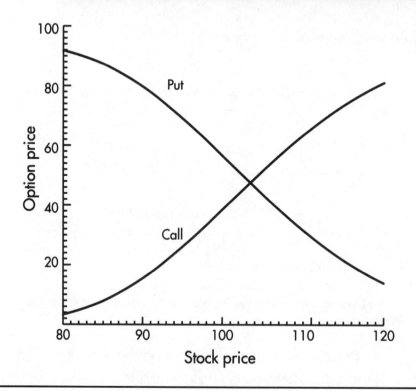

the exercise price, the put expires worthless. As with cash-or-nothing options, the exercise price is never paid. Instead, the value of the asset relative to the exercise price determines whether the option pays off or is worthless.

For an asset-or-nothing call (AONC), the value is simply the present value of the asset, depreciated for dividends between the present and expiration, multiplied by the probability that the terminal asset price will exceed the exercise price. Similarly, the asset-or-nothing put (AONP) is worth the present value of the asset, discounted for the dividends between the present and expiration, multiplied by the probability that the terminal asset price will be below the exercise price. Thus, the values of the options are:

$$\text{AONC}_t = e^{-\delta(T-t)}S_t N(d_1^M) \tag{9.12}$$

$$\text{AONP}_t = e^{-\delta(T-t)}S_t N(-d_1^M)$$

A portfolio of an asset-or-nothing call and put, with the same term to expiration and underlying asset, is worth the present value of the asset discounted for the dividends to be paid over the life of the option:

$$\text{AONC}_t + \text{AONP}_t = e^{-\delta(T-t)}S_t N(d_1^M) + e^{-\delta(T-t)}S_t N(-d_1^M)$$

$$= e^{-\delta(T-t)}S_t [N(d_1^M) + N(-d_1^M)]$$

$$= e^{-\delta(T-t)}S_t$$

As an example, consider asset-or-nothing options with the following parameters:

$$S = \$100$$
$$X = \$90$$
$$T - t = 0.5 \text{ years}$$
$$\sigma = 0.2$$
$$r = 0.1$$
$$\delta = 0.05$$

With these values: $d_1^M = 0.992499$; $N(d_1^M) = N(0.992499) = 0.839523$; and $N(-d_1^M) = N(-0.992499) = 0.160477$. The option values with these parameters are:

$$\text{AONC}_t = e^{-\delta(T-t)}S_t N(d_1^M) = e^{-.1(0.5)}100(0.839523) = 81.8795$$

$$\text{AONP}_t = e^{-\delta(T-t)}S_t N(-d_1^M) = e^{-.1(0.5)}100(0.160477) = 15.6515$$

Figure 9.7 graphs the value of our two sample options as a function of the stock price. Notice that the shape of the value curves in this figure are quite similar to those for the cash-or-nothing options in Figure 9.6. When the stock price is high, say around $120, the asset-or-nothing put is worth very little, reflecting the slight chance that the terminal stock price will be below the exercise price of $90. With a high stock price, the call is worth very nearly the same as the stock. For example, with a stock price of $100, the call is worth $81.88, as we have seen, and the present value of the asset is $97.53, so the call is worth 83.95 percent of the asset. For a stock price of $120, with a

Figure 9.7   The Value of Asset-or-Nothing Options as a Function of the
Stock Price

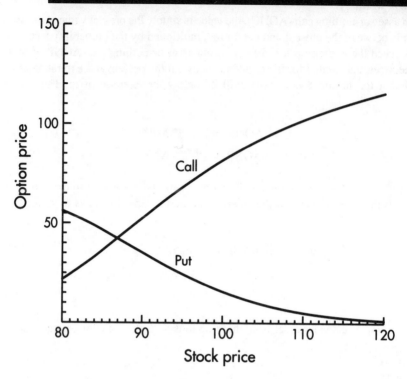

present value of $117.04, the call is worth $115.72, or 98.87 percent of the present value of the asset. Finally, if the stock is at $150, the call is worth $146.29, which equals the present value of the stock.

Gap Options

Gap options are similar to plain vanilla options, except the payoff is determined as a function of the exercise price. The payoff on a gap option depends on the usual factors in a plain vanilla option but is also affected by the gap amount, which may be negative or positive. Letting the value of the gap be indicated by g, the value of a gap call (GAPC$_t$) and a gap put (GAPP$_t$) are:

$$\text{GAPC}_t = e^{-\delta(T-t)}S_t N(d_1^M) - (X + g)e^{-r(T-t)}N(d_2^M) \tag{9.13}$$
$$\text{GAPP}_t = (X + g)e^{-r(T-t)}N(-d_2^M) - e^{-\delta(T-t)}S_t N(-d_1^M)$$

These formulas are very similar to those for plain vanilla options according to the Merton model, with the values for d_1^M and d_2^M being identical to those from the Merton model. In the valuation formulas, the gap amount is added to the exercise price so the quantity $X + g$ replaces X in the valuation formulas (but not in the formulas for d_1^M and d_2^M).

As an example of gap options, consider the following parameters:

$$
\begin{aligned}
S &= \$100 \\
X &= \$90 \\
T - t &= 0.5 \text{ years} \\
\sigma &= 0.3 \\
r &= 0.1 \\
\delta &= 0.05
\end{aligned}
$$

With these values, we will compute the value of a gap call with a positive gap $g = 5$ and a gap put with a negative gap, $g = -5$. Both options have common values for d_1^M and d_2^M:

$$
d_1^M = \frac{\ln\left(\dfrac{100}{90}\right) + [0.1 - 0.05 + 0.5(0.3)(0.3)](0.5)}{0.3\sqrt{0.5}} = 0.720591
$$

$$
d_2^M = d_1^M - \sigma\sqrt{T - t} = 0.720591 - 0.3\sqrt{0.5} = 0.508459
$$

Corresponding cumulative values are $N(d_1^M) = 0.764420$, $N(d_2^M) = 0.694434$, $N(-d_1^M) = 0.235580$, and $N(-d_2^M) = 0.305566$. With $g = +5$ for the gap call and $g = -5$ for the gap put, the option values are:

$$
\begin{aligned}
\text{GAPC}_t &= 100e^{-0.05(0.5)}0.764420 - (90 + 5)e^{-0.1(0.5)}0.694434 \\
&= 11.8008 \\
\text{GAPP}_t &= (90 - 5)e^{-0.1(0.5)}0.305566 - 100e^{-0.05(0.5)}0.235580 \\
&= 1.7300
\end{aligned}
$$

Figure 9.8 focuses on the gap call of this example. As Equation 9.13 makes clear, a positive gap for a call effectively increases the exercise price, which is a liability from the point of view of the call's owner. Therefore, a positive gap for a call decreases the value of the call relative to an otherwise identical plain vanilla call. In Figure 9.8, the lower line graphs the value of the gap call of our computational example. The upper line graphs the value of the otherwise similar call with a zero gap, $g = 0$. When $g = 0$, the gap option becomes a plain vanilla option.

Supershares

A supershare is a financial instrument whose value depends on an underlying portfolio of other financial assets. A supershare represents a contingent claim on a fraction of the underlying portfolio. The contingency is that the value of the underlying portfolio must lie between a lower and an upper bound on a certain future date. If the value of the underlying portfolio lies between the bounds, the supershare is worth a proportion of the portfolio. If the value of the portfolio lies outside the bounds, the supershare expires worthless.[8]

Figure 9.8   Gap Call Prices as a Function of the Stock Price

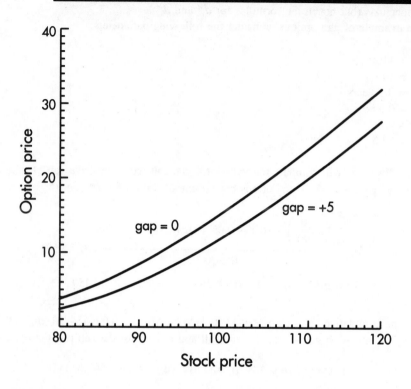

The basic idea behind supershares is the creation of a financial intermediary that holds a portfolio of securities and issues two kinds of claims against that portfolio. The first kind of claim is a supershare, which has an uncertain payoff depending on the performance of the portfolio. The second kind of claim is a purchasing power bond that pays a given rate of real interest. In our analysis, we are concerned with the claim that has an uncertain payoff – the supershare.

Letting X_L indicate the lower bound and X_H represent the upper bound, the payoffs for the supershare on the expiration date, T, are as follows:

$$S_T/X_L \text{ if } X_L \leq S_T \leq X_H; \text{ 0 otherwise}$$

A supershare is essentially like a portfolio of two asset-or-nothing calls, in which the owner of a supershare purchases an asset-or-nothing call with an exercise price of X_L and sells an asset-or-nothing call with an exercise price of X_H. This is quite similar to the bull spread considered in Chapter 2. As such the price of a supershare is:

$$SS = \frac{Se^{-\delta(T-t)}}{X_L}[N(w_L) - N(w_H)] \tag{9.14}$$

where:

$$w_L = \frac{\ln\left(\frac{S}{X_L}\right) + (r - \delta + 0.5\sigma^2)(T - t)}{\sigma\sqrt{T - t}}$$

and:

$$w_H = \frac{\ln\left(\frac{S}{X_H}\right) + (r - \delta + 0.5\sigma^2)(T - t)}{\sigma\sqrt{T - t}}$$

As a calculation example, consider the following data:

$$S = \$100$$
$$X_L = \$100$$
$$X_H = \$105$$
$$T - t = 0.5 \text{ years}$$
$$\sigma = 0.2$$
$$r = 0.1$$
$$\delta = 0.05$$

With these input values, $w_L = 0.247487$, $w_H = -0.097511$, $N(w_L) = 0.597735$, and $N(w_H) = 0.461160$. The value of this supershare is:

$$SS = \frac{100e^{-0.05(0.5)}}{100}[0.599735 - 0.461160] = 0.1352$$

Figure 9.9 shows how the price of this supershare varies with the stock price. The higher, more sharply curved line in the figure is the graph of our example supershare. Notice that the price of the supershare is $.1352 when the stock price is $100. The value of the supershare reaches its highest value for stock prices in the neighborhood of $100–$105. This neighborhood is exactly the range of the lower and upper bounds that determine the payoff. Notice also that the shape of this line is quite similar to that of a short position in a strangle as in Figure 5.16.

The flatter curve in Figure 9.9 is for the same supershare, except it assumes that the underlying stock has a standard deviation of 0.4. With a higher standard deviation, there is less chance that the terminal stock price will fall in the range of $100–$105, so the supershare written on a higher risk stock has a lower value.

LOOKBACK OPTIONS

For a plain vanilla option, the payoff depends on only the terminal stock price, not the price at any other time. For a **lookback option**, the exercise price and the option's payoff are functions of the

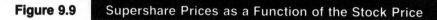

Figure 9.9   Supershare Prices as a Function of the Stock Price

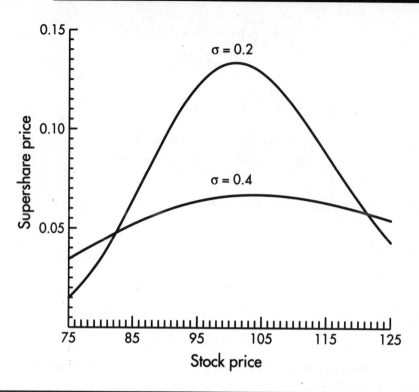

price of the underlying good up to the expiration of the option. For lookback calls, the exercise price is the minimum stock price experienced over the life of the option. For lookback puts, the exercise price is the maximum stock price over the same period. It is said of lookback options that they allow the option owner to "buy at the low and sell at the high." Of course, this opportunity will be priced in a rational market.

Consider the decision to purchase a lookback at time t with expiration at time T. The payoffs on the lookback call (LBC) and put (LBP) would be:

$$\text{LBC: MAX}\{0,\ S_T - \text{MIN}[S_t,\ S_{t+1},\ \ldots,\ S_T]\}$$
$$\text{LBP: MAX}\{0,\ \text{MAX}[S_t,\ S_{t+1},\ \ldots,\ S_T] - S_T\}$$

In effect, a lookback call allows the purchaser to acquire the asset at its minimum price over the life of the option, while the lookback put allows the owner to sell the asset at its maximum price over the relevant interval. Of course, the option to make these transactions has considerable value. Notice that lookbacks should always be exercised. For a call, the terminal stock price will always exceed some price experienced on the asset during its life. For a put, the terminal stock price will always be less than some stock price during the interval. Lookback options are clearly path-dependent options because the value ultimately depends on the minimum or maximum stock price reached over the life of the option, not merely on the terminal price when the option expires.[9]

Assuming that the stock price is observed continuously, the value of a lookback call is:

$$
\begin{aligned}
\text{LBC} = {}& Se^{-\delta(T-t)} - \text{MINPRI}e^{-r(T-t)}N\left(\frac{b + \mu(T - t)}{\sigma\sqrt{T - t}}\right) \\
& + \text{MINPRI}e^{-r(T-t)}\lambda e^{b(1-1/\lambda)}N\left(\frac{-b + \mu(T - t)}{\sigma\sqrt{T - t}}\right) \\
& - Se^{-\delta(T-t)}(1 + \lambda)N\left(\frac{-b - \mu(T - t) - \sigma^2(T - t)}{\sigma\sqrt{T - t}}\right)
\end{aligned}
\tag{9.15}
$$

where MINPRI is the minimum price of the underlying asset experienced during the life of the option and:

$$
b = \ln\left(\frac{S}{\text{MINPRI}}\right); \qquad \mu = r - \delta - 0.5\sigma^2; \qquad \lambda = \frac{0.5\sigma^2}{r - \delta}
$$

$$
\begin{aligned}
\text{LBP} = {}& -Se^{-\delta(T-t)} + \text{MAXPRI}e^{-r(T-t)}N\left(\frac{-b - \mu(T - t)}{\sigma\sqrt{T - t}}\right) \\
& - \text{MAXPRI}e^{-r(T-t)}\lambda e^{b(1-1/\lambda)}N\left(\frac{b - \mu(T - t)}{\sigma\sqrt{T - t}}\right) \\
& + Se^{-\delta(T-t)}(1 + \lambda)N\left(\frac{b + \mu(T - t) + \sigma^2(T - t)}{\sigma\sqrt{T - t}}\right)
\end{aligned}
\tag{9.16}
$$

where MAXPRI is the maximum price experienced during the life of the option. The variables λ and μ are the same as defined for the lookback call, but the definition of b for the lookback put is:

$$
b = \ln\left(\frac{S}{\text{MAXPRI}}\right)
$$

As an example of lookback call pricing, consider the following values:

$$
\begin{aligned}
S &= \$100 \\
\text{MINPRI} &= \$90 \\
T - t &= 0.5 \text{ years} \\
\sigma &= 0.3 \\
r &= 0.1 \\
\delta &= 0.05
\end{aligned}
$$

Using these data, we will compute the value of the lookback call. The intermediate values we need are:

$$b = \ln\left(\frac{100}{90}\right) = 0.105361$$

$$\lambda = \frac{0.5(0.3)(0.3)}{0.10 - 0.05} = 0.9$$

$$\mu = [0.1 - 0.05 - 0.5(0.3)(0.3)] = 0.005$$

The value for the lookback call, taking into account all of the discounting and showing the value of the arguments for the cumulative normal function, is:

$$LBC = 97.5310 - 85.6106N(0.508462)$$
$$+ 85.6106 \, (0.9)e^{0.105361(-0.1111)}N(-0.484891)$$
$$- 97.5310(1.9)N(-0.720594)$$

Thus, the value of the lookback call is:

$$LBC = 97.5310 - 59.4510 + 23.9027 - 43.6551 = 18.3275$$

Because lookbacks offer cheap exercise prices for call and high payoffs for puts, lookbacks are worth considerably more than their plain vanilla counterparts. For a plain vanilla call with the same parameters, including the exercise price of $90, the price would be $15.10. The lookback call has a price that is $3.23 higher. The difference could be even more severe. For example, consider the same input values used for the lookback call, but assume that the minimum price to date is $100. The price of this lookback would be $16.4920. The corresponding plain vanilla call would be $9.3970.

Figure 9.10 graphs our sample option using the same parameters. The upper line of Figure 9.10 shows the value of the lookback call. The lower line shows the value of an otherwise similar plain vanilla call option with an exercise price $X = \$90$. Notice that the volatility of these options is $\sigma = 0.3$. For higher volatility stocks, the value of both the lookback call and the plain vanilla call will be higher. Figure 9.11 shows the value of a lookback call and a corresponding plain vanilla call with the same parameter values as our sample option, except the volatility of the options is $\sigma = 0.9$. Comparing Figures 9.10 and 9.11 shows that the higher the volatility of the underlying stock, the greater will be the difference between the lookback and plain vanilla calls. The large percentage difference in the price of the lookback and plain vanilla calls emphasizes the costliness of lookbacks.

The high premiums on lookback options has hindered their popularity in actual markets. This limitation has led to the creation of **partial lookback options**. These partial lookbacks restrict the minimum or maximum used in computing the payoff in some way.[10]

AVERAGE PRICE OPTIONS

An **Asian option** is an option whose payoff depends on the average of the price of the underlying good or the average of the exercise price. (These options are called "Asian options" because Bankers Trust was the first to offer such products and offered them initially in their Tokyo office.[11]) In an **average price option**, the average price of the underlying good essentially takes the place of the terminal price of the underlying good in determining the payoff.

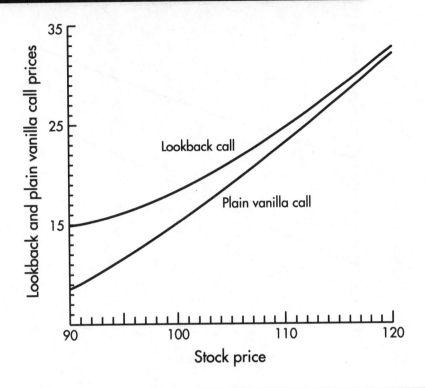

Asian options are extremely useful in combating price manipulations. For example, consider a corporate executive's given options on the firm's shares as part of her compensation. If the option payoff were determined by the price of the firm's shares on a particular day, the executive could enrich herself by manipulating the price of her shares for that single day. However, if the payoff of the option depended on the average closing price of the shares over a six-month period, it would be more difficult for her to profit from a manipulation. Asian options were first used in this kind of application. As a further example, commodity-linked bonds have two forms of payoffs, the payoffs from a straight bond and an option on the average price of the linked commodity. By making the payoff depend on the average price of the commodity, such as oil, the chance of a manipulation is lessened.[12]

The average price may be computed as either a geometric average or as an arithmetic average. Unfortunately, there is no closed-form solution for the price of an arithmetic-average price option, even though most actual average price options are based on an average price. These options must be valued by simulation techniques. It is possible, however, to compute the value of a geometric-average price option, and this section focuses exclusively on a geometric-average price call option.

Figure 9.11   The Value of a Lookback Call and a Plain Vanilla Call as a Function of the Stock Price

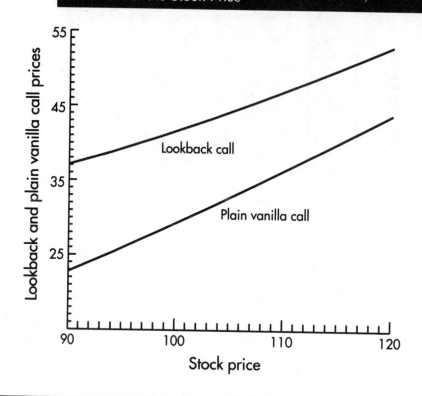

Of fundamental concern is the frequency with which the price is observed over the averaging period. If the price is observed at the close of each day, then the geometric average price will be computed by multiplying the available n daily price observations together and then taking the nth root of the product. An average price option may exist with some of the averaging period already under way. Alternatively, the time for averaging may lie in the future. Therefore, there are three time variables to consider:

t_0 = the time until the averaging period begins
t_1 = the time since the averaging period began
t_2 = the time remaining for averaging

It is typical for the averaging period to last until the option expires, we assume the typical case in this analysis. Therefore, $t_2 = T - t$, when the option expires at time T and is valued at time t. Thus, there are three possibilities to consider:

1. The averaging period has already begun prior to the present time t
   In this case, $t_0 = 0$ and $t_1 > 0$.

2. The averaging period begins immediately at time t

   In this case, $t_0 = t_1 = 0$.
3. The averaging period will begin sometime later, after time t but before time T

   In this case, $t_0 > 0$ and $t_1 = 0$.

If the averaging period has already started, there is an average price A available to compute. If the averaging period starts in the future, the average price, AVGPRI, is one.

We begin the presentation of the pricing formula by defining several intermediate variables:

$$W = A^{\left(\frac{t_1}{t_1+t_2+h}\right)} S^{\left(\frac{t_2+h}{t_1+t_2+h}\right)}$$

$$M = \left(t_0 + t_2\frac{t_2 + h}{2(t_1 + t_2 + h)}\right)[r - \delta - 0.5\sigma^2]$$

$$\Sigma^2 = t_0 + \left(\frac{t_2(t_2 + h)(2t_2 + h)}{6(t_1 + t_2 + h)^2}\right)\sigma^2$$

$$w_1 = \frac{\ln\left(\dfrac{W}{X}\right) + M}{\Sigma} + \Sigma$$

where h is the frequency of price observations used to compute the average price. For example, if the price is observed daily, $h = 1/365$ years. The price of the geometric-average price call, AVGPRI, is:

$$\text{AVGPRI} = We^{-r(T-t)}e^{(M+0.5\Sigma^2)}N(w_1) - Xe^{-r(T-t)}N(w_1 - \Sigma) \qquad (9.17)$$

As a calculation example, consider a geometric average price option for which averaging has been under way for one-half year, and the option expires in a half year. For this option, the price is observed daily to compute the average price. The data are:

$S = \$100$
$X = \$90$
$\sigma = 0.2$
$r = 0.1$
$\delta = 0.05$
$t_0 = 0.0$
$t_1 = 0.5$ years
$t_2 = 0.5$ years
$h = $ each day or $1/365$ years
$A = \$95$

For these data, we have: $W = 97.474774$; $M = 0.00376$; $\Sigma^2 = 0.001671$; and $w_1 = 2.084497$. The value of the option is:

$$\text{AVGPRI} = (97.474774)e^{-0.1(0.5)}e^{[0.00376+0.5(0.001671)]}(0.981443) - 90e^{-0.1(0.5)}(0.979504)$$

$$= 91.419406 - 83.855912$$

$$= 7.5634$$

Figure 9.12 shows the relationship between the value of our example average price call and the average price of the underlying good.

EXCHANGE OPTIONS

We now consider an option to exchange one asset for another. Upon exercising, the owned asset is exchanged for the acquired asset. The valuation of an exchange option depends upon the usual parameters for the individual assets – price, risk, and dividend rate. In addition, the time until expiration and the correlation of returns between the assets that affect the valuation. We will treat the owned asset as asset 1 and the asset to be acquired as asset 2. Thus, an exchange option may be regarded as a call on asset 2 with the exercise price being the future value of asset 1.

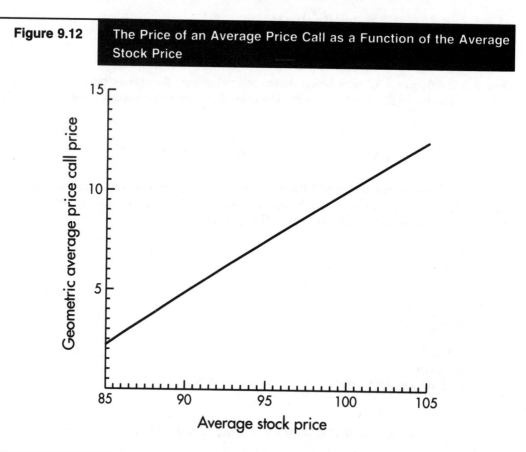

Figure 9.12   The Price of an Average Price Call as a Function of the Average Stock Price

Although exchange options were first priced in 1978, these options have existed for quite some time in the form of incentive fee arrangements, margin accounts, exchange offers and standby commitments.[13] Consider an example from the merger market. A target firm is offered the opportunity to exchange shares from the target firm for shares in the acquiring firm. The shareholders in the target firm now hold an exchange option to exchange their shares for those of the acquirer. The value of this option can range from zero to the quite valuable. To know how valuable this kind of option is, we need a pricing formula.

The value of a European exchange option (EXOPT) is:

$$EXOPT = S_2 e^{-\delta_2(T-t)} N(w_1) - S_1 e^{-\delta_1(T-t)} N(w_2) \qquad (9.18)$$

where:

$$\Sigma^2 = \sigma_1^2 + \sigma_2^2 - 2\rho\sigma_1\sigma_2$$

$$w_1 = \frac{\ln\left(\dfrac{S_2}{S_1}\right) + (\delta_1 - \delta_2 + 0.5\Sigma^2)(T - t)}{\Sigma\sqrt{T - t}}$$

$$w_2 = \frac{\ln\left(\dfrac{S_2}{S_1}\right) + (\delta_1 - \delta_2 - 0.5\Sigma^2)(T - t)}{\Sigma\sqrt{T - t}}$$

This formula is quite similar to the Merton model, except the volatility of the portfolio of the two assets, Σ, takes the place of the volatility of the underlying stock, σ, and the price of the asset to be sacrificed, S_1, takes the place of the exercise price, X. As a computational example, consider the following data:

$S_1 = \$100$
$S_2 = \$100$
$\sigma_1 = 0.3$
$\sigma_2 = 0.2$
$\delta_1 = 0.05$
$\delta_2 = 0.05$
$T - t = 0.5$ years
$\rho = 0.5$

According to our convention, asset 1 is the owned asset that may be exchanged for asset 2. With these values we have: $\Sigma^2 = 0.07$; $w_1 = 0.093541$; $w_2 = -0.093541$; $N(w_1) = 0.537262$; and $N(w_2) = 0.462737$. The value of the option to exchange asset 1 for asset 2 is:

$$EXOPT = 100e^{-0.05(0.5)}0.537263 - 100e^{-0.05(0.5)}0.462737$$
$$= 52.399840 - 45.131198$$
$$= 7.2687$$

For our sample exchange option, Figure 9.13 shows how the price of the option varies with the volatilities of the individual assets. The bottom line shows how the value of the option varies with the volatility of asset 1; the upper line pertains to the volatility of asset 2. Each line shows the sensitivity of the option's value to changes in the volatility of one asset, holding the volatility of the other asset constant. For our example option, $\sigma_1 = 0.3$ and $\sigma_2 = 0.2$. The bottom line shows that the option is worth $6.04 at that level of volatility. As σ_1 varies (and σ_2 remains constant) the value of the exchange option varies directly. The upper line shows the same relationship for asset 2. For the same sample exchange option, Figure 9.14 shows that the value of the option varies inversely with the correlation between the two assets.

RAINBOW OPTIONS

This section considers a class of exotic options known as **rainbow options**. We will limit our discussion to "two-color" rainbow options – options on two risky assets. This section distinguishes and analyzes five types of two-color rainbow options: the best of two risky assets and a fixed cash amount, the better of two risky assets, the worse of two risky assets, the maximum of two risky

Figure 9.13   The Value of an Exchange Option as a Function of Individual Asset Volatilities

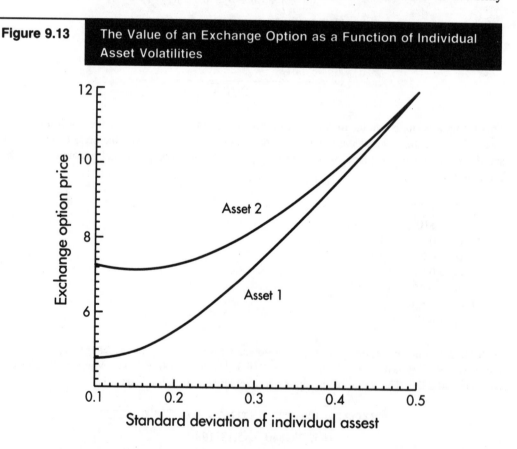

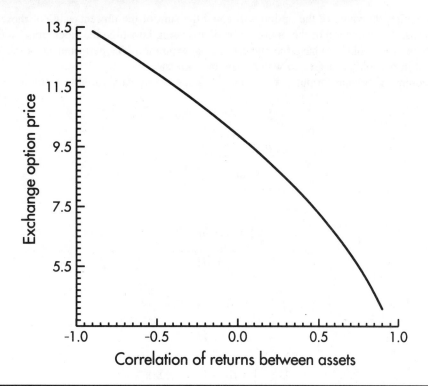

Figure 9.14

The Value of an Exchange Option as a Function of the Correlation Between Assets

assets, and the minimum of two risky assets. We will start with an option on the best of two risky assets and cash. As we will see, the other rainbow options can be understood largely in terms of this first option.

As an example of a two-color rainbow option, consider a zero-coupon bond that pays a stated rate of interest but allows the owner of the bond to choose the currency in which the interest is paid. The value of the bond upon maturity will differ depending on the exchange rate. The right to choose the currency of repayment gives the holder of the bond a call on the maximum of two assets, the repayment in one currency or another. By contrast, consider the same type of bond but assume that the firm may choose the currency of repayment.[14]

Call on the Best of Two Risky Assets and Cash

The owner of this option has a choice among three payoffs at expiration: risky asset 1, risky asset 2, or a fixed cash amount. There is no exercise price. Letting S_{1T} be the terminal value of asset 1, S_{2T} be the terminal value of asset 2, and X be the fixed cash amount, the present value of each payoff is:

Q1. $e^{-r(T-t)}E(S_{1T})$, conditional on $S_{1T} > S_{2T}$ and $S_{1T} > X$

Q2. $e^{-r(T-t)}E(S_{2T})$, conditional on $S_{2T} > S_{1T}$ and $S_{2T} > X$

Q3. $e^{-r(T-t)}X$, conditional on $X > S_{1T}$ and $X > S_{2T}$

Prior to exercise, the value of the option will equal the sum of the present value of these expected payoffs. Thus, the evaluation of the option turns on assessing how high the stock prices are likely to go and which asset is likely to have the highest price at expiration. The performance of the two assets will depend in part on the degree to which they are correlated.

To present the pricing formula, we begin with some preliminary variable definitions:

$$\Sigma^2 = \sigma_1^2 + \sigma_2^2 - 2\rho\sigma_1\sigma_2$$

$$\rho_1 = \frac{\rho\sigma_2 - \sigma_1}{\Sigma}$$

$$\rho_2 = \frac{\rho\sigma_1 - \sigma_2}{\Sigma}$$

$$w_1 = \frac{\ln\left(\frac{S_1}{X}\right) + (r - \delta_1 + 0.5\sigma_1^2)(T - t)}{\sigma_1\sqrt{T - t}}$$

$$w_2 = \frac{\ln\left(\frac{S_2}{X}\right) + (r - \delta_2 + 0.5\sigma_2^2)(T - t)}{\sigma_2\sqrt{T - t}}$$

$$w_3 = \frac{\ln\left(\frac{S_1}{S_2}\right) + (\delta_2 - \delta_1 + 0.5\Sigma^2)(T - t)}{\Sigma\sqrt{T - t}}$$

$$w_4 = \frac{\ln\left(\frac{S_2}{S_1}\right) + (\delta_1 - \delta_2 + 0.5\Sigma^2)(T - t)}{\Sigma\sqrt{T - t}}$$

With these preliminary definitions, the value of each potential payoff is:

Q1. $S_1e^{-\delta_1(T-t)}\{N(w_3) - N_2(-w_1; w_3; \rho_1)\}$

Q2. $S_2e^{-\delta_2(T-t)}\{N(w_4) - N_2(-w_2; w_4; \rho_2)\}$ (9.19)

Q3. $Xe^{-r(T-t)}N_2(-w_1 + \sigma_1\sqrt{T - t}; -w_2 + \sigma_2\sqrt{T - t}; \rho)$

The value of a call on the best of two risky assets and cash, BEST3, equals the sum of these three quantities:

$$BEST3 = Q1 + Q2 + Q3 \tag{9.20}$$

As a computational example, consider the following data:

$$S_1 = \$100$$
$$S_2 = \$95$$
$$X = \$110$$
$$T - t = 1 \text{ year}$$
$$\sigma_1 = 0.2$$
$$\sigma_2 = 0.3$$
$$r = 0.08$$
$$\delta_1 = 0.04$$
$$\delta_2 = 0.03$$
$$\rho = 0.4$$

Since the owner of the option will receive the best of two assets or the cash payment, the value should be at least the present value of the largest quantity, which is the cash payment of $110. However, there is also a chance that one of the two assets will exceed $110 when the option expires in one year, so we must take into account the potential payoff of these other assets.

With our sample data, we have the following intermediate results:

$$\Sigma^2 = 0.082; \quad \rho_1 = -0.279372; \quad \rho_2 = -0.768273$$

$$w_1 = -0.176551; \quad w_2 = -0.172012; \quad w_3 = 0.287381; \quad w_4 = -0.001024$$

$$N(w_3) = 0.613090; \quad N(w_4) = 0.499591$$

$$N_2(-w_1; w_3; \rho_1) = 0.307309; \quad N_2(-w_2; w_4; \rho_2) = 0.147242; \quad N_2(-w_1 + \sigma_1; -w_2 + \sigma_2; \rho) = 0.496938$$

Using these intermediate results, the three partial results for asset 1, asset 2, and the fixed cash payment are:

Q1. $100e^{-0.04}(0.305781) = 29.3787$
Q2. $95e^{-0.03}(0.352349) = 32.4833$
Q3. $110e^{-0.08}(0.496938) = 50.4605$

The value of the option, BEST3, equals the sum these three parts:

$$\text{BEST3} = Q1 + Q2 + Q3 = 29.3787 + 32.4833 + 50.4605 = 112.3224$$

Figure 9.15 shows how the value of this sample option varies inversely with the correlation between the two risky assets.

Call on the Maximum of Two Risky Assets

In this section, we consider calls on the maximum of two risky assets. This is similar to the option on the maximum of two risky assets and cash that we just considered. However, for this option there

Figure 9.15 The Value of a Call on the Best of Two Risky Assets and Cash as a Function of the Correlation Between the Two Risky Assets

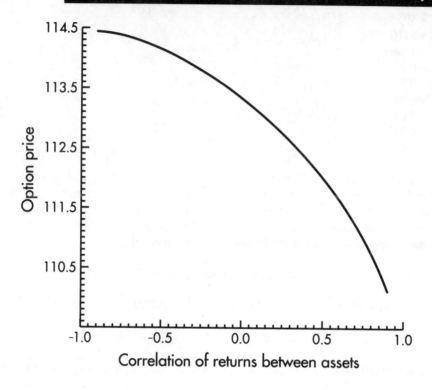

is no potential cash payoff. Further, these options have an exercise price. To exercise the call, the owner pays the exercise price and selects the better of the two risky assets.

The valuation of this option is quite straightforward once we have valued a call on the maximum of two assets and cash. The payoff on a call on the maximum of two assets is the same as that of a call on two risky assets and cash minus the payment of the exercise price:

$$MAX(S_{1T}, S_{2T}, X) - X$$

As we have already seen in the preceding section, the value of an option with payoffs of $MAX(S_{1T}, S_{2T}, X)$ is simply BEST3 $= Q1 + Q2 + Q3$. The future liability X has a present value of $Xe^{-r(T-t)}$. Therefore, the value of a call on the maximum of two risky assets, CMAX, is:

$$CMAX = BEST3 - Xe^{-r(T-t)} = Q1 + Q2 + Q3 - Xe^{-r(T-t)} \qquad (9.21)$$

Using the same data from the previous section, the value of this option will be:

$$BEST3 - Xe^{-r(T-t)} = 112.3224 - 110e^{-0.08(1)} = 10.7796$$

Later in this chapter we will see how to value a put on the maximum of two risky assets.

Figure 9.16 shows that the value of the option on the maximum of two assets varies inversely with the correlation between the two assets. A comparison of Figures 9.15 and 9.16 shows that the value of a call on the best of two risky assets and cash and a call on the maximum of the same two assets have exactly the same sensitivity to the correlation between the two assets.

Call on the Better of Two Risky Assets

A call on the better of two risky assets, CBETTER, is a special case of a call on two risky assets and cash. To form the special case, just specify that the exercise price is zero, $X = 0$. The call on two risky assets and cash is now just a call on two risky assets. With $X = 0$, w_1 and w_2 become arbitrarily large. Therefore,

$$\text{CBETTER} = \text{BEST3, given that } X = 0 \tag{9.22}$$

Using the same inputs as those for a call on two risky assets and cash, the value of this call is CBETTER = 104.9635.

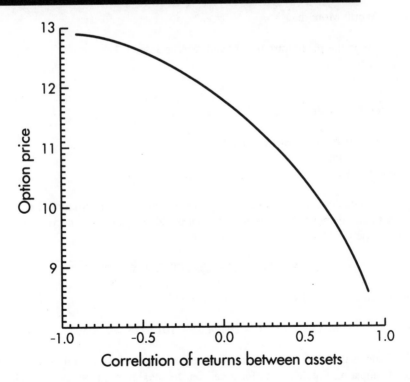

Figure 9.16

The Value of a Call on the Maximum of Two Risky Assets as a Function of the Correlation Between the Two Risky Assets

Put on the Maximum of Two Risky Assets

The valuation of a put on the maximum of two risky assets can be derived as a function of the value of the options we have just been studying. To exercise a put on the maximum of two risky assets, the owner surrenders the more valuable of the two risky assets and receives the exercise price. Thus, the payoff on this put is:

$$MAX[0, X - MAX(S_{1T}, S_{2T})]$$

This payoff can be replicated by the following portfolio:

Replicating Portfolio

Lend the present value of the exercise price
Buy a call on the maximum of the two risky assets with exercise price X
Sell a call on the better of the two risky assets

At Expiration (assume asset 1 is more valuable than asset 2)

Receive X as loan matures

If Asset 1 is Worth More than X

Exercise option on the maximum, pay X, and receive asset 1
Deliver asset 1
  Net Result: 0

If X is Greater Than Value of Asset 1

Let call on the maximum expire worthless
Purchase asset 1 in market
  Net result: $X - S_{1T}$

Thus the payoff from this portfolio will be exactly like the put on the maximum of two risky assets. Therefore, the put and this portfolio must have the same value. Therefore, the value of a put on the maximum of two assets, PMAX, is:

$$PMAX = CMAX - CBETTER + Xe^{-r(T-t)} \tag{9.23}$$

Using the data given above we have:

$$PMAX = 10.7796 - 104.9635 + 101.5428 = 7.3589$$

Figure 9.17 shows that the value of our sample put varies directly with the correlation between the two assets. Comparing Figures 9.16, for a call on the maximum of our two sample assets, and 9.17 shows that calls vary inversely with the correlation, while puts vary directly.

The Value of a Put on the Maximum of Two Risky Assets as a
Function of the Correlation Between the Two Risky Assets

Figure 9.17

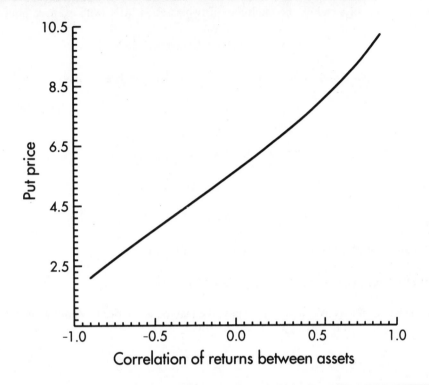

Call on the Minimum of Two Risky Assets

A call on the minimum of two risky assets pays the value of the inferior risky asset upon payment of the exercise price X. This call has the following payoff:

$$\text{Call payoff: MAX}[0, \text{MIN}(S_{1T}, S_{2T}) - X]$$

This call can be replicated by a portfolio of three options we have considered already:

Replicating Portfolio

Buy a plain vanilla option on the first asset with exercise price X
Buy a plain vanilla option on the second asset with exercise price X
Sell a call on the maximum of the two assets with exercise price X

Upon expiration, the portfolio owner exercises the call on the more valuable asset and uses this asset to satisfy the call on the maximum that was sold to form the portfolio. These transactions have a net zero cash flow because the portfolio owner receives X and pays X. The portfolio owner still holds the call on the inferior asset. If the inferior asset is worth X or less, the option expires worthless. If the inferior asset is worth more than X, the portfolio owner exercises for a profit equal to the difference. Therefore, the value of a call on the minimum of two assets, CMIN, with exercise price X equals:

$$CMIN = C_t^M(S_1) + C_t^M(S_2) - CMAX \qquad (9.24)$$

where $C_t^M(S_j)$ indicates a plain vanilla call on asset S_j. Using our data we have:

$$C_t^M(S_1) = 5.4369$$
$$C_t^M(S_2) = 7.4635$$
$$CMAX = 10.7796 \text{ (as solved earlier)}$$

Therefore, the value of a call on the minimum of two assets is:

$$CMIN = 5.4369 + 7.4635 - 10.7796 = 2.1208$$

We show how to price a put on the minimum of two assets later.

Call on the Worse of Two Risky Assets

A call on the worse of two risky assets has a payoff equal to the inferior asset but without the payment of any exercise price. In this case, $X = 0$, so the payoff is:

$$\text{Call payoff: MAX}[0, \text{MIN}(S_{1T}, S_{2T}) - 0] = \text{MIN}(S_{1T}, S_{2T})$$

We have already seen that CBETTER is the same as CMAX, if $X = 0$. Therefore, we can find the value of a call on the worse of two risky assets, CWORSE, by finding the value of plain vanilla calls with $X = 0$ for the two assets and subtracting the value of CBETTER.

$$CWORSE = C_t^M(S_1) + C_t^M(S_2) - CBETTER, \text{ given that } X = 0 \qquad (9.25)$$

Using the same example values:

$$C_t^M(S_1) = 96.0789, \text{ if } X = 0$$
$$C_t^M(S_2) = 92.1923, \text{ if } X = 0$$
$$CBETTER = 104.9635, \text{ as calculated earlier}$$
$$CWORSE = 96.0789 + 92.1923 - 104.9635 = 83.3077$$

Put on the Minimum of Two Risky Assets

A put on the minimum of two risky assets pays X and requires the delivery of the inferior asset. Therefore, the payoff on this put is:

$$\text{Put payoff: } MAX[0, X - MIN(S_{1T}, S_{2T})]$$

To value this put, we create a replicating portfolio:

Replicating Portfolio

Buy call on the minimum of two risky assets with exercise price X
Sell call on the worse of two risky assets
Lend the present value of the exercise price X

At Expiration (assume asset 2 has the lower value)

Receive X

If $S_{2T} \geq X$

Exercise call on minimum, paying X
Deliver inferior asset to complete obligation on sale of call on the worse of two assets
Net Result: 0

If $S_{2T} < X$
Buy inferior asset in market
Deliver inferior asset to complete obligation on sale of call on the worse of two assets
Net Result: $X - S_{2T}$

As this portfolio exactly replicates the payoffs on the put, it must have the same value as the put on the minimum of two risky assets, PMIN. Therefore,

$$PMIN = CMIN - CWORSE + Xe^{-r(T-t)} \tag{9.26}$$

From our previous solutions, we have:

$$CMIN = 2.1201$$
$$CWORSE = 83.3077$$

Therefore:

$$PMIN = 2.1201 - 83.3077 + 101.5428 = 20.3552$$

SUMMARY

In this chapter, we have explored a large variety of exotic options. The analysis focused on European options for which closed-form solutions exist. As we have seen, many of these exotic options can be understood in terms of the familiar plain vanilla options priced in the Merton model.

This chapter considered nine classes of exotic options: forward-start options, compound options, chooser options, barrier options, binary options, lookback options, average price options, exchange options, and rainbow options. For each of these options, the payoffs are more complicated than those of plain vanilla options. We have seen that these specialized payoffs can be used to manage risks or to shape a speculative position more exactly. Many of these options exhibit path dependence.

The **OPTION!** software that accompanies this book can compute the value of all of the exotic options discussed in this chapter and can price all of the example options.

QUESTIONS AND PROBLEMS

For all of the following problems, compute the answers by hand, being sure to show intermediate results. After making the computation, use **OPTION!** to check the accuracy of your computations.

1. Using the following values, find the price of a forward-start put: $S = 100$; $X = 100$; $T - t = 1$ year; $\sigma = 0.2$; $r = 0.1$; $\delta = 0.05$; $tg = 0.5$.
2. Price all four types of compound options assuming the following parameter values: $S = 100$; $\sigma = 0.4$; $r = 0.1$; $\delta = 0.05$; $X = 100$; $x = 8$; $T = 1$ year; $te = 0.25$ years.
3. Price a simple chooser option based on the following parameter values: $S = 100$; $X = 100$; $T = 1$ year; $\sigma = 0.5$; $r = 0.1$; $\delta = 0.05$; $tc = 0.5$ years. By comparing this result with that of the example chooser in the sample text, what can you conclude about the influence of the stock's risk on the value of the chooser?
4. Find the value of a down-and-in put with: $S = 100$; $X = 100$; $T - t = 1$ year; $\sigma = 0.3$; $r = 0.1$; $\delta = 0.05$; BARR = 97; and REBATE = 2.
5. Consider a cash-or-nothing call and put with common parameter values: $S = 100$; $X = 110$; $T - t = 0.5$ years; $\sigma = 0.4$; $r = 0.1$; $\delta = 0.0$; and $Z = 200$. What is the value of each option? What is the value of a long position in both options? Which items of information given above are not needed to value the portfolio of the two options?
6. Consider an asset-or-nothing call and put with common parameter values: $S = 100$; $X = 110$; $T - t = 0.5$ years; $\sigma = 0.4$; $r = 0.1$; and $\delta = 0.0$. What is the value of each option? What is the value of a long position in both options? Which items of information given above are not needed to value the portfolio of the two options?
7. Value a gap call with: $S = 100$; $X = 100$; $T - t = 0.5$ years; $\sigma = 0.5$; $r = 0.1$; $\delta = 0.03$; and $g = 7$.
8. Value a supershare with: $S = 100$; $X_L = 95$; $X_H = 110$; $T - t = 0.5$ years; $\sigma = 0.2$; $r = 0.1$; $\delta = 0.05$. By comparing this calculation with the sample supershare of the text, what can you conclude about the value of supershares and the value $X_H - X_L$?
9. Find the value of a lookback call and put with the common parameters: $S = 110$; $T - t = 1$ year; $\sigma = 0.25$; $r = 0.08$; and $\delta = 0.0$. For the call, MINPRI = 80. For the put, MAXPRI = 130.
10. Find the value of an average price option with these common parameters: $S = 100$; $X = 90$; $\sigma = 0.2$; $r = 0.1$; $\delta = 0.05$; $t_0 = 0.0$; $t_1 = 0.5$; $t_2 = 0.5$; and $A = 95$. Compute the value of the option with observations every two days, $h = 2/365$. Now compute the value of the option assuming continuous observation, that is, $h = 0$. Compare these results with the sample option of the chapter. What does this suggest about the value of the option and the frequency of observation?

11. Consider an exchange option with the following common parameter values: $S_1 = 100$; $S_2 = 100$; $\sigma_1 = 0.3$; $\sigma_2 = 0.2$; $\delta_1 = 0.05$; $\delta_2 = 0.05$; $T - t = 0.5$ years. Compute the value of this exchange option with $\rho = 0.0$ and $\rho = 0.7$. Compare your results with those for the sample exchange option in the chapter. What do these results suggest about the value of exchange options as a function of the correlation between the two assets?

For rainbow options, consider these parameter values: $S_1 = 100$; $S_2 = 100$; $X = 95$; $T - t = 0.5$ years; $\sigma_1 = 0.4$; $\sigma_2 = 0.5$; $r = 0.06$; $\delta_1 = 0.02$; $\delta_2 = 0.03$; and $\rho = 0.2$. (Interpret $X = 95$ as the exercise price or as the cash payment depending on the type of option.) Use this information for problems 12–18.

12. Find the value of an option on the best of two assets and cash.
13. Find the value of an option on the better of two assets.
14. Find the value of a call on the maximum of two assets.
15. Find the value of a put on the maximum of two assets.
16. Find the value of a call on the minimum of two assets.
17. Find the value of a call on the worse of two assets.
18. Find the value of a put on the minimum of two assets.

NOTES

[1] For a good introduction to the idea of path dependence in option pricing, see W. Hunter and D. Stowe, "Path-Dependent Options: Valuation and Applications," *Economic Review*, Federal Reserve Bank of Atlanta, July/August 1992, pp. 30–43.

[2] For more on the pricing and applications of forward-start options, see Mark Rubinstein, "Pay Now, Choose Later," *Risk*, February 1991; Mark Rubinstein and Eric Reiner, "Exotic Options," Working paper, University of California at Berkeley, 1995; and Peter G. Zhang, *Exotic Options: A Guide to the Second-Generation Options*, forthcoming World Scientific Press, 1996.

[3] For the original paper on pricing compound options, see R. Geske, "The Valuation of Compound Options," *Journal of Financial Economics*, 7, March 1979, pp. 63–81. See also Mark Rubinstein, "Double Trouble," *Risk*, December 1991-January 1992; Mark Rubinstein and Eric Reiner, "Exotic Options," Working paper, University of California at Berkeley, 1995; A. Tucker, "Exotic Options," Working paper, Pace University, New York, 1995; and P. G. Zhang, *Exotic Options: A Guide to the Second-Generation Options*, forthcoming World Scientific Press, 1996.

[4] See Mark Rubinstein, "Options for the Undecided," *Risk*, April 1991, and Mark Rubinstein and Eric Reiner, "Exotic Options," Working paper, University of California at Berkeley, 1995.

[5] This peso example is drawn from Peter G. Zhang, *Exotic Options: A Guide to the Second-Generation Options*, forthcoming World Scientific Press, 1996. For pricing of chooser options see also Alan Tucker, "Exotic Options," Working paper, Pace University, New York, 1995.

[6] For more detailed discussion of the pricing of barrier options, see: Mark Rubinstein, "Breaking Down the Barriers," *Risk*, September 1991; Mark Rubinstein and Eric Reiner, "Exotic Options," Working paper, University of California at Berkeley, 1995; Alan Tucker, "Exotic Options," Working paper, Pace University, New York, 1995; and Peter G. Zhang, *Exotic Options: A Guide to the Second-Generation Options*, forthcoming World Scientific Press, 1996.

[7] For a discussion of the pricing of binary options, see Mark Rubinstein, "Unscrambling the Binary Code," *Risk*, October 1991; Mark Rubinstein and Eric Reiner, "Exotic Options," Working paper, University of

California at Berkeley, 1995; Alan Tucker, "Exotic Options," Working paper, Pace University, New York, 1995; Peter G. Zhang, *Exotic Options: A Guide to the Second-Generation Options,* forthcoming World Scientific Press, 1996.

[8] Supershares were created by Nils Hakansson, "The Purchasing Power Fund: A New Kind of Financial Intermediary," *Financial Analysts Journal,* November/December 1976.

[9] The first paper on lookback options appeared in 1979, long before such options actually existed. See Barry Goldman, Howard Sosin, and Mary Ann Gatto, "Path Dependent Options: Buy at the Low, Sell at the High," *Journal of Finance,* 34, December 1979, pp. 1111–27. The results of Goldman, Sosin, and Gatto were generalized to embrace a dividend paying underlying asset analyzed by Mark Garman, in his paper, "Recollection in Tranquility," *Risk,* March 1989, pp. 16–8. For more on the pricing of lookbacks, also see M. Rubinstein and E. Reiner, "Exotic Options," Working paper, University of California at Berkeley, 1995; Alan Tucker, "Exotic Options," Working paper, Pace University, New York, 1995; and Peter G. Zhang, *Exotic Options: A Guide to the Second-Generation Options,* forthcoming World Scientific Press, 1996.

[10] For a discussion of partial lookback options, see Peter G. Zhang, *Exotic Options: A Guide to the Second-Generation Options,* forthcoming World Scientific Press, 1996.

[11] Peter G. Zhang, *Exotic Options: A Guide to the Second-Generation Options,* forthcoming World Scientific Press, 1996.

[12] For a discussion of Asian options, see A. Kemna and A. Vorst, "A Pricing Method for Options Based on Average Asset Values," *Journal of Banking and Finance,* 14, March 1990, pp. 113–29; Mark Rubinstein and E. Reiner, "Exotic Options," Working paper, University of California at Berkeley, 1995; S. Turnbull and L. Wakeman, "A Quick Algorithm for Pricing European Average Options," *Journal of Financial and Quantitative Analysis,* 26, September 1991, pp. 377–89; Alan Tucker, "Exotic Options," Working paper, Pace University, New York, 1995; and Peter G. Zhang, *Exotic Options: A Guide to the Second-Generation Options,* forthcoming World Scientific Press, 1996. Kemna and Vorst give examples of several commodity-linked bonds.

[13] The first paper on exchange options was by William Margrabe, "The Value of an Option to Exchange One Asset for Another," *Journal of Finance,* March 1978. Margrabe distinguished the four applications just mentioned. For additional insights on pricing exchange options, see Mark Rubinstein, "One for Another," *Risk,* July 1991; Mark Rubinstein and Eric Reiner, "Exotic Options," Working paper, University of California at Berkeley, 1995; Alan Tucker, "Exotic Options," Working paper, Pace University, New York, 1995; and Peter G. Zhang, *Exotic Options: A Guide to the Second-Generation Options,* forthcoming World Scientific Press, 1996.

[14] The original paper on rainbow options was by Rene Stulz, "Options on the Minimum or the Maximum of Two Risky Assets," *Journal of Financial Economics,* 10, July 1982, pp. 161–85. Thus, Stulz was pricing two-color rainbow options. Stulz's work was extended to multi-colored rainbow options by Herb Johnson, "Options on the Maximum or the Minimum of Several Assets," *Journal of Financial and Quantitative Analysis,* 22, September 1987, pp. 277–83. The name "rainbow option" was originated by Mark Rubinstein, "Somewhere Over the Rainbow," *Risk,* November 1991. For additional discussion of rainbow options, see Mark Rubinstein, "Return to Oz," *Risk,* November 1994; Mark Rubinstein and Eric Reiner, "Exotic Options," Working paper, University of California at Berkeley, 1995; Alan Tucker, "Exotic Options," Working paper, Pace University, New York, 1995; and Peter G. Zhang, *Exotic Options: A Guide to the Second-Generation Options,* forthcoming World Scientific Press, 1996.

OPTION! INSTALLATION AND QUICK START

INTRODUCTION

OPTION! software is included with each copy of this text. **OPTION!** operates on virtually any IBM PC or compatible and can compute virtually all of the option values and relationships discussed in the text. If the computer has a graphics capability, **OPTION!** can graph many of the option pricing relationships explained in this text. The program can save hundreds of hours of tedious computations and can be used as an effective learning tool to illustrate and explore the option pricing relationships discussed in the text.

The program has been written for easy use. This chapter does not attempt to explain all of the features of **OPTION!**. Instead, it explains the architecture of the program and illustrates how to install and use the software. All of the modules operate similarly, and the text explains the meaning of all the calculations that **OPTION!** can perform.

FEATURES OF OPTION! SOFTWARE

OPTION! can calculate virtually all of the option prices and relationships covered in the text. Figure 1 shows the main menu from the software and the nine modules that constitute the program. This section briefly considers each module.

Module A, Option Values and Profits at Expiration, computes the outcome for various option strategies that are held to expiration of the option. From this module, you can view or print a report summarizing the results of the strategy you are considering. In this module, you can select up to three calls and three puts and the underlying stock. Given your choice of strategies, you can then see how the strategy will perform for various stock prices at expiration. You can also graph these outcomes.

Module B, Option Values and Profits Before Expiration, is similar in structure and spirit to Module A. However, Module B allows you to price the options in your portfolio by using the Black-Scholes and Merton models. You may then see how changing stock prices will affect the current value of your strategy. You may view or print a report and graph the outcomes as a function of the stock price.

Figure 1 The Main Menu for OPTION!

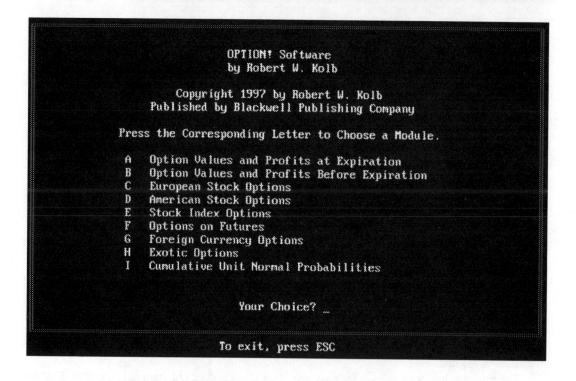

```
                    OPTION! Software
                    by Robert W. Kolb

                Copyright 1997 by Robert W. Kolb
              Published by Blackwell Publishing Company

         Press the Corresponding Letter to Choose a Module.

         A    Option Values and Profits at Expiration
         B    Option Values and Profits Before Expiration
         C    European Stock Options
         D    American Stock Options
         E    Stock Index Options
         F    Options on Futures
         G    Foreign Currency Options
         H    Exotic Options
         I    Cumulative Unit Normal Probabilities


                    Your Choice? _


                To exit, press ESC
```

In Module C, European Stock Options, there are six submodules, identified by the letters A–F. These cover the binomial model with specified price movements (submodule A), the Black-Scholes model (submodule B), Implied Volatility according to the Black-Scholes and Merton models (submodule C), Simulation of Stock and Option Prices consistent with the Black-Scholes model (submodule D), the Binomial Approximation of the Black-Scholes model using stock price movements consistent with a Black-Scholes framework (submodule E), and Dividend Adjustments for European Options (submodule F). Many of these submodules allow extensive graphical analysis of pricing relationships, as we explore later.

Module D, American Stock Options, consists of five submodules that cover virtually all dimensions of pricing American options on individual stocks. Submodule A can compute the exact price of an American call option on a stock with one dividend prior to the expiration of the option. Submodule B uses the analytic approximation devised by Barone-Adesi and Whaley to price American calls and puts written on a stock paying a continuous dividend. Submodule C applies the binomial model to American options on stocks paying proportional dividends. Submodule D applies the binomial model to a stock paying periodic dividend yields, while submodule E applies the binomial model to stocks paying periodic cash dividends. Submodules A and B are accompanied by extensive graphical choices. In submodules C–D, you can specify the number of periods to be used in the binomial model.

Modules E, F, and G cover Stock Index Options, Options on Futures, and Foreign Currency Options, respectively. They are similar in their operation. Each computes the value of call and put options according to the Black-Scholes model, the Merton model, the analytic approximation for American options, the binomial model for a European option, and the binomial model for an American option. Each of these three modules also provides graphical analysis for both the European and American options.

Module H deals with exotic options. As the text explains, there are many different types of exotic options, including forward-start options, compound options, chooser options, binary options, barrier options, lookback options, average price options, exchange options, and rainbow options. For some of these types of exotic options, there are several subspecies. **OPTION!** can price all of these exotic options and graph the price of the option as a function of the key input parameters. The program focuses on European exotic options, as these are the options for which closed-form pricing formulas exist.

The last module, Module I, Cumulative Unit Normal Probabilities, computes univariate and bivariate cumulative probabilities. It is included as a useful utility to avoid tables of these values and interpolations. For example, for computing $N(d_1)$, you can provide the value of d_1, and this module will compute the value of $N(d_1)$ to six decimal place accuracy.

INSTALLATION

The installation of **OPTION!** is extremely easy. The program can operate from a floppy disk drive or can be installed onto a hard drive. We strongly recommend using **OPTION!** from a hard drive to save time.

Installation on a Floppy Drive System

1. Make a back-up copy of the original **OPTION!** diskette.
2. Place the original diskette in a safe location.
3. Place the working copy of **OPTION!** in drive A: and make drive A: the logged drive by giving the following command: ''A:''.
4. Installation is complete. You may run the program by typing ''OPTION!'' and pressing return.

Installation on a Hard Drive System

1. Make a directory to hold the files for **OPTION!**. Assuming that the system hard drive is C: and you want to install the software in a subdirectory called ''OPTION,'' use the Make Directory command as follows:

''MD C:\OPTION''

2. Place the original diskette for **OPTION!** in the A: drive.
3. Copy all the files from the original diskette to the subdirectory on the hard drive created in step 1 by using the following command:

"COPY A:*.* C:\OPTION"

4. To run **OPTION!**, be sure that the logged drive and subdirectory hold the OPTION! files. To do this you can use the following two commands:

"C:" and "CD\OPTION"

5. Installation is complete. Place the original diskette in a safe location. You may start the program with the following command: "OPTION!" and press return.

QUICK START

Great care has been taken to ensure that all of the modules in **OPTION!** function similarly. This section shows how to use the software by going step-by-step through a comprehensive example.

To use **OPTION!**, be sure that the logged drive or subdirectory is the location for all of the **OPTION!** files. To start the program, type "OPTION!" and press ENTER. The program then shows the main menu of Figure 1. The program contains nine modules, lettered A–I. To start a given module from the main menu, press the corresponding letter. To exit a given screen at any time, press ESC. Pressing ESC when the main menu is showing exits the program and returns to DOS. From any screen, pressing ESC repeatedly will exit the program.

In general, the modules allow you to enter data and then press a function key to perform some analysis. For example, the program uses the F1 key to request a solution. F2 is the key for graphics. Watch the bottom line of the screen for special instructions.

For our illustrative problem, we are going to find the value of a European call option according to the Black-Scholes model. (The text examines the mathematics and economics of the Black-Scholes model in detail.) From the main menu shown in Figure 1, we select the module for European Stock Options by pressing "C". Figure 2 shows that there are six submodules for European Stock Option Pricing lettered A–F. Because we want to apply the Black-Scholes model, we now select submodule B by pressing "B."

This brings us to the screen shown in Figure 3. On this screen, we can enter the data necessary to solve our problem. As the text explains, the Black-Scholes model expresses the value of a European option as a function of five underlying variables: the stock price, the exercise price, the time until the option expires, the volatility of the underlying stock, and the risk-free rate of interest. For our problem, we consider a stock that currently trades at $100. The option has an exercise price of $90, and there are 55 days until expiration. The standard deviation of returns for the stock is 0.3, and the risk-free rate of interest is 7 percent.

To enter these values, we navigate from one data entry block to the next by using the up and down arrow keys. If you make a mistake in entering a number, you can delete the last entry by pressing DEL, the delete key. Figure 4 shows these values entered in the screen in the appropriate positions. (We leave the dividend at zero because the stock has no dividend.)

We are now ready to solve the problem. Notice the line of instructions at the bottom of the screen:

Press F1 for option results, F2 to graph, or ESC to exit.

```
                    European Stock Option Pricing

     This module allows the full exploration of the pricing of European
     options on common stocks, with special emphasis on the Binomial Model
     and the Black-Scholes and Merton Option Pricing Models.



           Press the Corresponding Letter to Choose a Module.

      A     The Binomial Model with Specified Price Movements
      B     The Black-Scholes Model and the Merton Model
      C     Implied Volatility in the Black-Scholes and Merton Models
      D     Simulation of Stock and Option Prices
      E     Binomial Approximation of Black-Scholes Model Prices
      F     Dividend Adjustments for European Options

     ESC    Exit this Module




                          Your Choice? _


                       To exit, press ESC
```

Function key F1 is always used to solve a problem, and F2 is always used to bring up the graphics menu. ESC (the escape key) is always used to exit a current screen and return to a previous screen. After we press F1, the screen will appear as in Figure 5, which shows the solution to our problem.

We now decide that we would like to graph some of the option relationships that are explored in the text. Accordingly, we now select F2, which brings up the graphics menu shown in Figure 6. There we have six different options, and we decide to graph the call price as a function of the price of the underlying stock. Therefore, from the graphics menu in Figure 6, we press "A."

This presents another menu, shown in Figure 7. Because we want to graph the price of the call option as a function of the stock price, we now press "A." Figure 8 shows the resulting graph. The curved line in the graph shows the value of the call as a function of the stock price. The lower straight line shows the value of the call at expiration. As we would expect, the price of the call option is an increasing function of the stock price. From the graph, we note that the call price approaches its intrinsic value for higher stock prices. Notice that the graph shows stock prices from $80–$120 on the X-axis. The computer program automatically selects the most appropriate range of X-values based on the particular problem you have specified.

We now assume that you would like to print the graph. With **OPTION!** you can save any graph to a computer file for printing through almost any word processing program. To save the graph, press

| Figure 3 | The Data Screen for the Black-Scholes Model |

```
          Black-Scholes and Merton Option Pricing Models

   Use this screen to find put and call prices according to the Black-Scholes
   and Merton Option Pricing Models.  The program computes put and call values
   with no dividends (Black-Scholes) or with continuous dividends (Merton).

     Stock Price                                                  0.0000
     Exercise Price                                               0.0000
     Days Until Expiration                                        0.0000
     Volatility (standard deviation per year, e.g., 0.30)         0.0000
     Risk-Free Rate per Year (e.g., 0.06)                         0.0000
     Annualized Dividend Yield (e.g., 0.03)                       0.0000

                              OUTPUT AREA




            Press F1 for option results, F2 to graph, or ESC to exit.
```

F7. The screen gives a quick blink and writes the graphics file to the current directory. When you press F7, **OPTION!** creates the graphics file as a PCX file. This is an extremely popular and general graphical format. Most word processing programs (such as Word and WordPerfect) can print these files. The program assigns sequential file names to the graphs that you save. The first PCX file saved to a directory is given the name "KPGRF001.PCX". Subsequent graphs are saved to files with the next unused number in the file name. Figure 8 was saved in this manner and printed through WordPerfect. (To save time and avoid running out of space when saving a graph, it is best to operate **OPTION!** from a hard drive.) If the program is being run under Windows, it is possible to transfer graphs to other programs using the Windows clipboard. Consult the Windows manual for your particular system for instructions on using the clipboard.

At this point, with our graph on screen, we are at the innermost layer of the **OPTION!** program. After viewing the graph, we press ESC, which returns us to the graphics menu for the sensitivity of the option price to the input parameters (Figure 7). We can select another graph choice, or press ESC again. If we press ESC, we return to the graphics menu for the Black-Scholes model (Figure 6). Pressing ESC again returns us to the data entry screen with our data still in place (Figure 5). Here we can enter new values for another problem or press ESC to return to the menu for the European Stock Option submodule (Figure 2). From the menu for the submodule, pressing ESC again returns

The Data for the Sample Problem | **Figure 4**

```
          Black-Scholes and Merton Option Pricing Models

Use this screen to find put and call prices according to the Black-Scholes
and Merton Option Pricing Models.  The program computes put and call values
with no dividends (Black-Scholes) or with continuous dividends (Merton).

   Stock Price                                              100.0000
   Exercise Price                                            90.0000
   Days Until Expiration                                     55.0000
   Volatility (standard deviation per year, e.g., 0.30)      0.3000
   Risk-Free Rate per Year (e.g., 0.06)                      0.0700
   Annualized Dividend Yield (e.g., 0.03)                    0.0000

                         OUTPUT AREA






     Press F1 for option results, F2 to graph, or ESC to exit.
```

us to the main menu (Figure 1). From the main menu, pressing ESC terminates the program and returns us to the operating system.

SUMMARY AND OPERATING TIPS

1. Be sure that you operate **OPTION!** from the logged drive or subdirectory.
2. Use the delete key, DEL, to erase erroneous data entries.
3. Use the escape key, ESC, to leave any screen and return to a previous screen.
   Standard key assignments are:

> F1 = Solve for an option value after data are entered.
> F2 = Proceed to the graphics menu.
> F3 = Choose a report.
> F7 = Save the graph on screen to a file in the current directory with a name of the form
>   KPGRFnnn.PCX.
> ESC = Leave the current screen and return to the previous screen.
> DEL = When entering data, delete the last key stroke.

Figure 5   The Solution to the Sample Problem

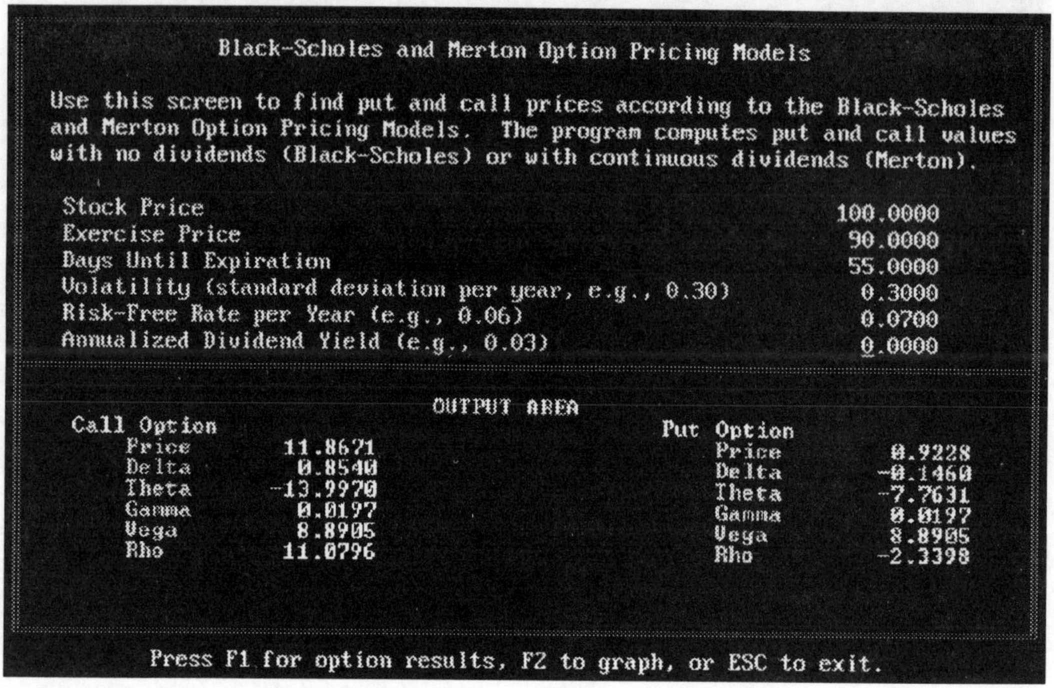

```
              Black-Scholes and Merton Option Pricing Models

 Use this screen to find put and call prices according to the Black-Scholes
 and Merton Option Pricing Models.  The program computes put and call values
 with no dividends (Black-Scholes) or with continuous dividends (Merton).

   Stock Price                                            100.0000
   Exercise Price                                          90.0000
   Days Until Expiration                                   55.0000
   Volatility (standard deviation per year, e.g., 0.30)     0.3000
   Risk-Free Rate per Year (e.g., 0.06)                     0.0700
   Annualized Dividend Yield (e.g., 0.03)                   0.0000

                             OUTPUT AREA
   Call Option                              Put Option
      Price      11.8671                       Price      0.9228
      Delta       0.8540                       Delta     -0.1460
      Theta     -13.9970                       Theta     -7.7631
      Gamma       0.0197                       Gamma      0.0197
      Vega        8.8905                       Vega       8.8905
      Rho        11.0796                       Rho       -2.3398

        Press F1 for option results, F2 to graph, or ESC to exit.
```

The Graphics Menu for the Black-Scholes Model | **Figure 6**

Graphical Analysis of Option Pricing Model Relationships

The program allows you to graph option prices as a function of the
Black-Scholes and Merton model parameters. Alternatively you may graph
option pricing sensitivities (delta, theta, etc.) as a function of the
price of the underlying instrument or the time to expiration.

    A   Graph option prices as a function of input parameters
    B   Graph option sensitivities as a function of price or maturity
    C   Graph sensitivity of a delta neutral portfolio to the cash price
    D   Graph time decay of a delta neutral portfolio
    E   Graph time decay of the call option
    F   Graph time decay of the put option

ESC   Return to the solution screen

                        Your choice?

Figure 7   The Graphics Menu for European Option Prices as a Function of
the Input Parameters

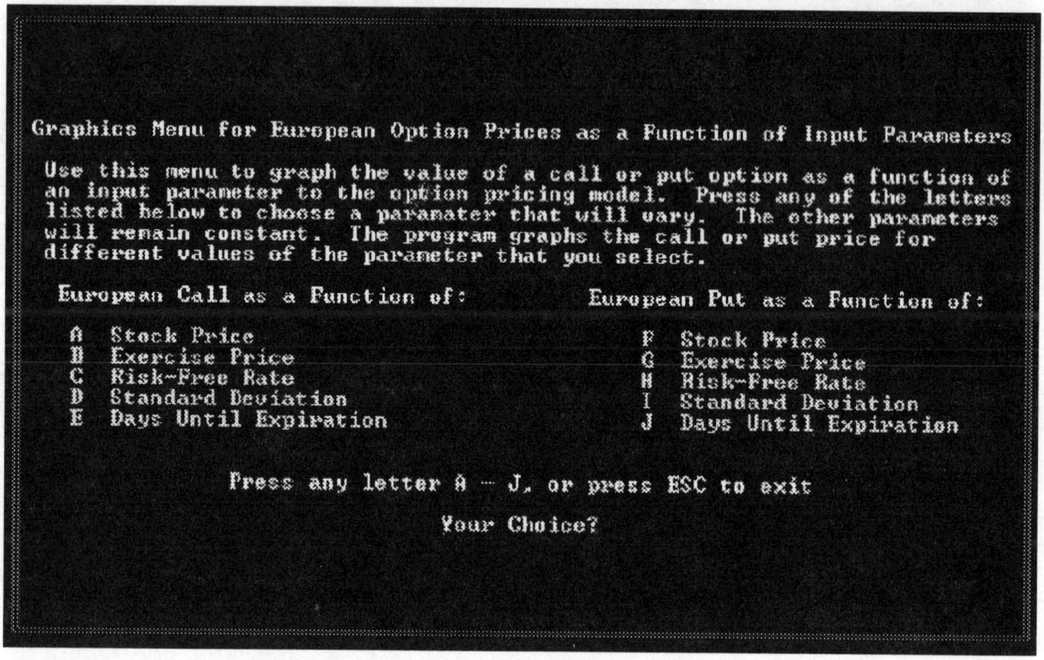

```
Graphics Menu for European Option Prices as a Function of Input Parameters

Use this menu to graph the value of a call or put option as a function of
an input parameter to the option pricing model.  Press any of the letters
listed below to choose a parameter that will vary.  The other parameters
will remain constant.  The program graphs the call or put price for
different values of the parameter that you select.

   European Call as a Function of:        European Put as a Function of:

   A  Stock Price                         F  Stock Price
   B  Exercise Price                      G  Exercise Price
   C  Risk-Free Rate                      H  Risk-Free Rate
   D  Standard Deviation                  I  Standard Deviation
   E  Days Until Expiration               J  Days Until Expiration


           Press any letter A - J, or press ESC to exit

                          Your Choice?
```

The Call Price as a Function of the Stock Price in the Sample Problem   **Figure 8**

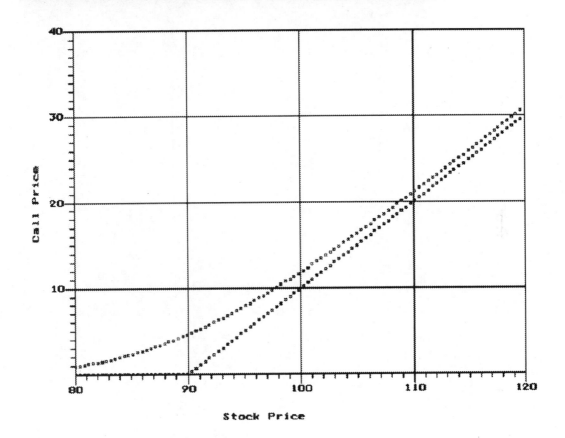

EXERCISES FOR OPTION!

1. Consider a call and a put option on the same underlying stock. Both options have an exercise price of $75. The call costs $5, and the put costs $4. If you buy both the call and the put, what is the position called? Complete the following table showing the value and profits and losses at expiration. Complete an **OPTION!** graph showing both the value of the position at expiration and the profits and losses on the position at expiration.

Stock Price at Expiration	Position Value at Expiration	Position Profit at Expiration
$50		
$65		
$70		
$75		
$80		
$85		
$90		

2. Consider a call and a put on the same underlying stock. Both options have the same exercise price of $50. The stock currently sells for $50. If you buy the stock, sell the put for $3, and buy the call for $4, complete following table showing the value of the entire position and the profits and losses on the position at expiration.

315

Stock Price at Expiration	Position Value at Expiration	Position Profit at Expiration
$35		
$40		
$45		
$50		
$55		
$60		
$65		

3. Consider two calls on the same underlying stock. The calls have the same expiration date and exercise prices of $80 and $90. If the calls cost $12 and $4, respectively, complete the following table showing the value of and profits on a bull spread at expiration using these two calls. Prepare an **OPTION!** graph showing the profits and losses at expiration.

Stock Price at Expiration	Position Value at Expiration	Position Profit at Expiration
$70		
$75		
$80		
$85		
$90		
$95		
$100		
$105		
$110		

4. Consider two puts on the same underlying stock. The puts have the same expiration date and exercise prices of $80 and $90. If the puts cost $4 and $12, respectively, complete the following table showing the value of and profits on a bull spread at expiration using these two puts. Prepare an **OPTION!** graph showing the profits and losses at expiration.

Stock Price at Expiration	Position Value at Expiration	Position Profit at Expiration
$70		
$75		
$80		
$85		
$90		
$95		
$100		
$105		
$110		

5. Consider two calls on the same underlying stock. The calls have the same expiration date and exercise prices of $80 and $90. If the calls cost $12 and $4, respectively, complete the following table showing the value of and profits on a bear spread at expiration using these two calls. Prepare an **OPTION!** graph showing the profits and losses at expiration.

Stock Price at Expiration	Position Value at Expiration	Position Profit at Expiration
$70		
$75		
$80		
$85		
$90		
$95		
$100		
$105		
$110		

6. Consider two puts on the same underlying stock. The puts have the same expiration date and exercise prices of $80 and $90. If the puts cost $4 and $12, respectively, complete the following table showing the value of and profits on a bear spread at expiration using these two puts. Prepare an **OPTION!** graph showing the profits and losses at expiration.

Stock Price at Expiration	Position Value at Expiration	Position Profit at Expiration
$70		
$75		
$80		
$85		
$90		
$95		
$100		
$105		
$110		

7. For the same underlying stock, three calls with the same expiration date have exercise prices of $30, $35, and $40. For a long butterfly spread, complete the following table showing the value of and profits on the position at expiration. Prepare an **OPTION!** graph showing the profits and losses on the position at expiration assuming initial call prices of $11, $8, and $5 for the calls.

Stock Price at Expiration	Position Value at Expiration	Position Profit at Expiration
$20		
$25		
$30		
$35		
$40		
$45		
$50		

8. For the same underlying stock, two calls with the same expiration date have exercise prices of $30 and $40 and cost $11 and $8, respectively. Using these options, create two bull ratio spreads, one with a 2:1 ratio and the other with a 3:1 ratio. Complete the following table for the profits on the two spreads. For each spread, prepare an **OPTION!** graph showing the profits and losses on the positions at expiration.

Stock Price at Expiration	Profits on 2:1 Ratio Spread	Profits on 3:1 Ratio Spread
$20		
$25		
$30		
$35		
$40		
$45		
$50		

9. A stock now sells at $70, and a put on this stock with an exercise price of $70 costs $4. Using these instruments, create an insured portfolio and complete the following table.

Stock Price at Expiration	Profits on Stock Alone	Profits on Insured Portfolio
$50		
$55		
$60		
$65		
$70		
$75		
$80		
$85		
$90		

10. A stock sells at $100, and a call and a put on this stock both expire in one year and have an exercise price of $100. The risk-free rate of interest is 9 percent. For a position that is long the

call, short the stock, and long a bond that pays $100 in one year, complete the following table. What can you infer from the table?

Stock Price at Expiration	Value of Combined Position	Value of Call – Put
$80		
$85		
$90		
$95		
$100		
$105		
$110		
$115		
$120		

11. Consider a call option that expires in one year and has an exercise price of $100. The underlying stock price is $150, and the risk-free rate of interest is 10 percent. From these facts alone, what can you say about the current price of the call option? Using these values in the Black-Scholes model, complete the following table. Draw a graph showing the price of this call as a function of the standard deviation using the values in the table. What does this show about the no-arbitrage bounds for the price of a call option?

Standard Deviation	Call Price
0.9	
0.8	
0.7	
0.6	
0.5	
0.4	
0.3	
0.2	
0.1	
0.01	

12. Consider a put option that expires in one year and has an exercise price of $150. The underlying stock price is $100, and the risk-free rate of interest is 10 percent. From these facts alone, what can you say about the current price of the put option? Using these values in the Black-Scholes model, complete the following table. Draw a graph showing the price of this put as a function of the standard deviation using the values in the table. What does this show about the no-arbitrage bounds for the price of a put option?

Standard Deviation	Put Price
0.9	
0.8	
0.7	
0.6	
0.5	
0.4	
0.3	
0.2	
0.1	
0.01	

13. A put option has an exercise price of $100 and expires in one year. The risk-free rate of interest is 10 percent, and the standard deviation of the underlying stock is .2. Complete the following table. Explain what the table shows about the value of European versus American put options. Prepare a graph showing the put price and the intrinsic value of the put as a function of the stock price using the values in the table below.

Stock Price	Black-Scholes European Put Price	Intrinsic Value of Put
$80		
$85		
$90		
$95		
$100		
$105		
$110		
$115		
$120		

14. A put option has an exercise price of $100 and the underlying stock is worth $80. The risk-free rate of interest is 10 percent, and the standard deviation of the underlying stock is .2. Complete the following table. Explain what the table shows about the value of European versus American put options.

Days Until Expiration	Black-Scholes European Put Price	Intrinsic Value of Put
5		
10		
30		
90		
180		
270		
365		

15. Consider two call options on the same underlying stock. The calls have exercise prices of $80 and $90 and both expire in 150 days. The risk-free rate of interest is 8 percent, and the stock price is $100. Using the Black-Scholes model, complete the following table. What principle does the table illustrate regarding boundary conditions on call options?

Standard Deviation	Call Price $X = \$80$	Call Price $X = \$90$	Price Difference
0.9			
0.8			
0.7			
0.6			
0.5			
0.4			
0.3			
0.2			
0.1			
0.01			

16. Consider a call option with an exercise price of $80 that expires in 150 days. The risk-free rate of interest is 8 percent, and the stock price is $80. Using the Black-Scholes model, complete the following table. What principle does the table illustrate regarding the pricing of call options? Prepare a graph using the data in the table expressing the value of the call option as a function of the standard deviation.

Standard Deviation	Call Price
0.9	
0.8	
0.7	
0.6	
0.5	
0.4	
0.3	
0.2	
0.1	
0.01	

17. Consider two put options on the same underlying stock, with a standard deviation of 0.3. The puts have exercise prices of $80 and $90 and both expire in 150 days. The risk-free rate of interest is 8 percent, and the stock price is $60. Using the Black-Scholes model, complete the following table. What principle does the table illustrate regarding boundary conditions on put options?

Standard Deviation	Put Price X = $80	Put Price X = $90	Price Difference
0.9			
0.8			
0.7			
0.6			
0.5			
0.4			
0.3			
0.2			
0.1			
0.01			

18. Consider two put options on the same underlying stock. The stock trades for $100. One put has an exercise price of $80, while the other has an exercise price of $120. The standard deviation of the stock is 0.3, and the risk-free rate of interest is 11 percent. Complete the following table. What does the completed table indicate about the influence of the time until expiration on the pricing of puts? Explain the difference in the price patterns for the two puts. Would call options exhibit the same kind of price pattern? Explain.

Days Until Expiration	Put Price $X = \$80$	Put Price $X = \$120$
100		
120		
140		
160		
180		
200		
220		
240		
260		

19. A call option expires in one period and has an exercise price of $100. The underlying stock price is also $100. The stock price can rise or fall by 10 percent over the period. Using the one-period binomial model, complete the following table. How is the probability of a stock price increase related to the interest rate? Explain why this relationship makes sense. Explain why the call price varies with the interest rate as it does.

Interest Rate	Call Price	Probability of a Stock Price Increase
0.01		
0.02		
0.03		
0.04		
0.05		
0.06		
0.07		
0.08		
0.09		

20. A stock currently trades at $140, and a call option on the stock has an exercise price of $150 and expires in one year. The standard deviation of the stock price is 0.3, and the risk-free rate of interest is 12 percent. What is the Black-Scholes price for this call option? Complete the following table using the multiperiod binomial model. What is the relationship between prices from the binomial model and the Black-Scholes model? Explain.

Periods	Binomial Model Price
1	
2	
5	
10	
25	
50	
100	
150	
200	

21. A stock currently trades at $140, and a call option on the stock has an exercise price of $150 and expires in one year. The call price is $11.00, and the risk-free rate of interest is 12 percent. What is the standard deviation of the underlying stock? Complete the following table using the Black-Scholes model to find each price and show the price to four decimals. What does the completed table show about the technique necessary to find the volatility when the other parameters are known?

Standard Deviation	Call Price	Error
0.01		
0.2		
0.1		
0.15		
0.125		
0.13		
0.1275		
0.1285		
0.1282		

22. A stock trades for $75 and is expected to pay a dividend of $2 in 30 days. European call and put options on this stock expire in 90 days and have an exercise price of $75. The risk-free rate of interest is 7 percent, and the standard deviation of the stock is 0.3. Find the price of these options according to the Black-Scholes model, ignoring dividends. What are the values of these European options according to the adjustments to the Black-Scholes model for known dividends? Verify your answer by showing your own calculations.

23. A stock trades at $40 and has a standard deviation of 0.4. The risk-free rate is 8 percent. A European call and put on this stock expire in 90 days. The exercise price for the call is $35, and the exercise price for the put is $45. Using the Merton model, complete the following table. What does the completed table show about the influence of dividends on call and put prices?

Continuous Dividend Rate	Call Price	Put Price
0.005		
0.01		
0.02		
0.03		
0.05		
0.075		
0.1		
0.125		
0.15		

24. A stock pays a continuous dividend of 3 percent and currently sells for $80. The risk-free rate of interest is 7 percent, and the standard deviation on the stock is 0.25. A European call and put on this stock both have an exercise price of $75 and expire in 180 days. Find the price of these options according to the Black-Scholes model (i.e., ignoring the dividend) and the Merton model. Find the price of these options according to the binomial model with 5, 25, 50, 100, and 200 periods.

25. A stock pays a proportional dividend equal to 2 percent of its value in 150 days. The current stock price is $120, the risk-free rate is 9 percent, and the standard deviation of the stock is 0.2. A European call and put option on this stock both expire in 270 days and both have an exercise price of $120. Find the price of these options according to the Black-Scholes model (i.e., ignoring the dividend) and the Merton model. Find the price of these options according to the binomial model with 5, 25, 50, 100, and 200 periods.

26. A stock will pay a cash dividend of $1.75 in 150 days. The current stock price is $120, the risk-free rate is 9 percent, and the standard deviation of the stock is 0.2. A European call and put option on this stock both expire in 270 days and both have an exercise price of $120. Find the price of these options according to the Black-Scholes model (i.e., ignoring the dividend) and the Merton model. Find the price of these options according to the binomial model with 5, 25, 50, 100, and 200 periods.

27. A stock trades at $80 and has a standard deviation of 0.4. The risk-free rate of interest is 6 percent. A European call and put both expire in 100 days and have the same exercise price of $80. Complete the following table for the sensitivities of the two options.

Stock	DELTA	THETA	VEGA	RHO	GAMMA
$60					
$65					
$70					
$75					
$80					
$85					
$90					
$95					
$100					

28. A stock trades at $80 and has a standard deviation of 0.4. The stock pays a continuous dividend of 3 percent. The risk-free rate of interest is 6 percent. A European call and put both expire in 100 days and have the same exercise price of $80. Complete the following table for the sensitivities of the two options.

Stock	DELTA	THETA	VEGA	RHO	GAMMA
$60					
$65					
$70					
$75					
$80					
$85					
$90					
$95					
$100					

29. Two stocks have the same standard deviation of 0.4, but Stock A is priced at $110, and Stock B trades for $100. The risk-free rate is 11 percent. Consider two call options written on these two stocks that both expire in 90 days. Call A has an exercise price of $110, while Call B has an exercise price of $100. Find the DELTAs for these two options. What is unusual about the result, and how can it be explained?

30. A stock trades for $50 and has a standard deviation of 0.4. A call on the stock has an exercise price of $40 and expires in 55 days. The risk-free rate is 8 percent. Find the DELTA for the call, and explain how to create a delta-neutral portfolio. (Assume that you are short one call.) Complete the following table.

Stock Price	Call Price	Portfolio Value
$45		
$46		
$47		
$48		
$49		
$50		
$51		
$52		
$53		
$54		
$55		

31. A stock trades for $50 and has a standard deviation of 0.4. A call on the stock has an exercise price of $40 and expires in 55 days. The risk-free rate is 8 percent. Find the DELTA for the call and explain how to create a delta-neutral portfolio. (Assume that you are short one call.) Complete the following table showing how the value of the delta-neutral portfolio changes over time. Assume the stock price does not change. How do you account for the change in the value of the delta-neutral portfolio?

Days Until Expiration	Call Price	Portfolio Value
55		
50		
45		
40		
35		
30		
25		
20		
15		
10		
5		

32. A stock trades for $100 and has a standard deviation of 0.3. A call on the stock has an exercise price of $100 and expires in 77 days. The risk-free rate is 8 percent. Find the DELTA for the call, and form a delta-neutral portfolio assuming that you are short one call. What is the GAMMA for the stock and for the call? Does the portfolio have a positive or negative GAMMA? Complete the following table. How do these values illustrate the GAMMA of the portfolio?

Stock Price	Call Price	Portfolio Value
$80		
$85		
$90		
$95		
$100		
$105		
$110		
$115		
$120		

33. A stock with a standard deviation of 0.5 now trades for $100. Two calls on this stock both expire in 70 days and have exercise prices of $90 and $100. The risk-free rate is 10 percent. Find the

DELTA and GAMMA for both calls. Construct a portfolio that is long one share of stock and that is both delta-neutral and gamma-neutral. For the portfolio, complete the following table.

Standard Deviation	Portfolio Value
0.3	
0.35	
0.45	
0.5	
0.55	
0.6	
0.65	
0.7	

34. A stock sells for $70, has a standard deviation of 0.3, and pays a 2 percent continuous dividend. The risk-free rate is 11 percent. Three calls on this stock all expire in 100 days and have exercise prices of $65, $70, and $75. Using these calls, construct a long position in a butterfly spread. What does the spread cost? Complete the following table for the profitability of the spread as a function of the stock price for the current time and for the expiration date. For the long position, is time decay beneficial or detrimental? Explain.

Stock Price	Profit with $T - t = 100$	Profit at Expiration
$50		
$55		
$60		
$65		
$70		
$75		
$80		
$85		
$90		

35. Consider a long position in a straddle with an exercise price of $50. The stock price is $80, and the standard deviation of the stock is 0.4. The risk-free rate is 6 percent, and the options expire in 180 days. What is the current price of the two options? Prepare a graph of the current value of the straddle as a function of the stock price. On the same axes, graph the value of the straddle at expiration. Let the range of stock prices range from $30 to $70. As a first step to preparing the graph, complete the following table.

Stock Price	Current Straddle Price	Straddle Price at Expiration
$30		
$35		
$40		
$45		
$50		
$55		
$60		
$65		
$70		

36. A stock trades at $50 and has a standard deviation of 0.3. The risk-free rate is 7 percent. An American and a European call on this stock both have an exercise price of $55 and expire in 100 days. The stock will pay a dividend in 50 days, but the amount is uncertain. For the different possible dividend amounts shown in the table below, compute the exact American option price and the Black-Scholes model price with the known dividend adjustment. What kind of systematic difference do you notice in the pricing from the two models, if any?

Dividend Amount	Exact American	Black-Scholes Adjusted for Known Dividends
$0.01		
$0.05		
$0.10		
$0.25		
$0.50		
$1.00		
$1.50		
$2.00		
$3.00		

37. A stock trades for $150 and has a standard deviation of 0.4. The risk-free rate of interest is 7 percent. Two dividends are expected. The first, due in 30 days, is $1.50, while the second, due in 150 days, is $2.00. Find the pseudo-American option price for a call that expires in 200 days with an exercise price of $140. Also, find the option price according to the Black-Scholes model adjusted for known dividends.

38. A stock with a standard deviation of 0.33 trades for $75. The risk-free rate is 6 percent. The stock pays a continuous dividend of 2 percent. An American call and put on this stock have an exercise price of $70 and both expire in 100 days. Find the price of these options using the analytic approximation of the American option price. What are the critical values for the call and the put? Using the Merton model, find the price of both options.

39. A stock has a current price of $80 and a standard deviation of 0.3. The stock pays a continuous dividend of 3 percent. The risk-free rate is 7 percent. An American and a European call on this stock both expire in 200 days, and both have an exercise price of $70. Find the price of the American call according to the analytic approximation formula and the price of the European option according to the Merton model. What is the critical price for the American call? Complete the following table for the two options using the two respective models. Graph the price of the two options as a function of the stock price over the range from $60 to $100. Explain any particularly important features of the graph.

Stock Price	American Call According to the Analytic Approximation	European Call According to the Merton Model
$60		
$65		
$70		
$75		
$80		
$85		
$90		
$95		
$100		

40. A stock has a current price of $70 and a standard deviation of 0.3. The risk-free rate is 7 percent. An American and a European put on this stock both expire in 200 days and both have an exercise price of $80. Find the price of the American put according to the analytic approximation formula and the price of the European option according to the Merton model. What is the critical price for the American put? Complete the following table for the two options using the two respective models. Graph the price of the two options as a function of the stock price over the range from $60 to $100. Explain any particularly important features of the graph.

Stock Price	American Put According to the Analytic Approximation	European Put According to the Merton Model
$60		
$65		
$70		
$75		
$80		
$85		
$90		
$95		
$100		

41. A stock has a current price of $80 and a standard deviation of 0.3. The risk-free rate is 7 percent. An American and a European call on this stock both expire in 200 days and have an exercise price of $70. The stock pays a continuous dividend of 3 percent. Find the price of the American call according to the analytic approximation formula and the price of the European option according to the Merton model. Complete the following table for the two options using the two respective models. How can you explain the price differentials reported in the table?

Stock Price	American Call According to the Analytic Approximation	European Call According to the Merton Model
$60		
$65		
$70		
$75		
$80		
$85		
$90		
$95		
$100		

42. A stock has a current price of $80 and a standard deviation of 0.3. The risk-free rate is 7 percent. An American and a European call on this stock both expire in 200 days and have an exercise price of $70. If the stock is to pay a dividend it will be at a continuous rate, but the rate is uncertain. Alternative dividend rates are given in the table below. Find the price of the American call according to the analytic approximation formula and the price of the European option according to the Merton model for each dividend rate in the table. What do the price differentials in the table indicate about the importance of dividends for call pricing? For any of these dividend rates, should the American option be exercised now? If so, for which dividend rates?

Dividend Rate	American Call According to the Analytic Approximation	European Call According to the Merton Model
0.001		
0.005		
0.01		
0.02		
0.03		
0.04		
0.05		

43. A stock sells for $110 and has a standard deviation of 0.2. The risk-free rate is 7 percent. An American put on this stock has an exercise price of $120 and expires in 200 days. Using the

binomial model for an American put and a European put, complete the following table. Should the American put be exercised now? Explain.

Number of Periods	American Put Price	European Put Price
1		
2		
5		
10		
25		
50		
100		
200		

44. A stock sells for $110 and has a standard deviation of 0.2. The risk-free rate is 7 percent. An American put on this stock has an exercise price of $120 and expires in 200 days. Using the binomial model with 100 periods for an American put and a European put, complete the following table. From the table alone, what can you say about the correct exercise policy for the American put? Using the binomial model with 100 periods, find the exact stock price below which the American put should be exercised. Explain.

Stock Price	American Put Price	European Put Price
$90		
$95		
$100		
$105		
$110		
$115		
$120		
$125		
$130		

45. The HOT100 stock index stands at 4000.00 and has a standard deviation of 0.20. The continuous dividend rate on the HOT100 is 3 percent, and the risk-free rate of interest is 5 percent. Using the Merton model, find the prices for the calls and puts shown in the table below.

Index Value	Call X = 4000.0 $T - t$ = 180 days	Call X = 3750.0 $T - t$ = 90 days	Put X = 4000.0 $T - t$ = 180 days	Put X = 3750.0 $T - t$ = 90 days
3500.0				
3750.0				
4000.0				
4250.0				
4500.0				

46. The HOT100 stock index stands at 4000.00 and has a standard deviation of 0.20. The continuous dividend rate on the HOT100 is 3 percent, and the risk-free rate of interest is 5 percent. Using the Merton model, complete the table below for a call option with 180 days until expiration and an exercise price of $4,000.

Index Value	DELTA	THETA	VEGA	RHO	GAMMA
4500.0					
4250.0					
4000.0					
3750.0					
3500.0					

47. The HOT100 stock index stands at 4000.00 and has a standard deviation of 0.20. The continuous dividend rate on the HOT100 is 3 percent, and the risk-free rate of interest is 5 percent. Using the Merton model, complete the table below for a put option with 180 days until expiration and an exercise price of $4,000.

Index Value	DELTA	THETA	VEGA	RHO	GAMMA
4500.0					
4250.0					
4000.0					
3750.0					
3500.0					

48. The current dollar value of a German mark is $.6100, and the standard deviation of the mark is 0.25. The U.S. risk-free rate is 8 percent, while the German rate is 5 percent. European call and put options on the mark have an exercise price of $.6000 and expire in 250 days. What are these options worth today? If the German interest rate falls from 5 to 4 percent, what happens to the value of the options? Explain.

49. The current dollar value of a German mark is $.6100, and the standard deviation of the mark is 0.25. The U.S. risk-free rate is 8 percent, while the German rate is 5 percent. Consider an American and a European call on the mark with an exercise price of $.6000 that expires in 250 days. What are these options worth today? Should the American option be exercised now? If the

German interest rate falls from 5 to 4 percent, what happens to the value of the options? Does it change the exercise decision? Explain.

50. Options now trade on the well-known widget futures contract. The current widget price is $100 per widget, and the futures price is $107.50. The futures contract expires in two years. The widget market is well-known for its strict adherence to cost-of-carry principles. The standard deviation of the futures price is 0.25. A European and an American call option on this futures have an exercise price of $105.00. What are the two options worth according to the Merton model and the analytic approximation for the American option? What would an American and European put be worth, assuming they have the same contract terms?

51. The text has assumed that the cost-of-carry equals the risk-free rate. Explain how **OPTION!** could be used to value a futures option if the cost-of-carry were less than or greater than the risk-free rate.

52. Using **OPTION!**, complete the following table for forward-start call and put options. $S = 80$; $X = 75$; $T - t = 350$ days; $\sigma = 0.4$; $r = 0.08$; and $\delta = 0.03$. As the table indicates, the day of the grant, tg, varies. Taking the call as an example, what do the values in the table indicate about how the option price varies with tg?

tg in Days	Forward-Start Call	Forward-Start Put
50		
100		
150		
200		
250		
300		
349		

53. Complete the following table for the compound options shown below. Common parameters are: $S = 100$; $\sigma = 0.3$; $r = 0.01$; $\delta = 0.04$; $X = 100$; $te = 100$ days; and $T - t = 365$ days. As the table indicates, the exercise price of the compound option varies.

Exercise Price of Compound Option	Call-on-Call	Call-on-Put	Put-on-Call	Put-on-Put
$5				
$10				
$15				
$20				
$25				
$30				
$35				

54. Complete the following table for the compound options shown below. Common parameters are: $S = 100$; $\sigma = 0.3$; $r = 0.01$; $\delta = 0.04$; $X = 100$; $x = 10$; and $T - t = 365$ days. As the table indicates, the expiration date of the compound option varies.

Expiration Date of Compound Option in days	Call-on-Call	Call-on-Put	Put-on-Call	Put-on-Put
50				
100				
150				
200				
250				
300				
350				

55. Consider a European straddle with the following parameters: $S = 50$; $X = 50$; $T - t = 365$ days; $\sigma = 0.5$; $r = 0.06$; and $\delta = 0.03$. What is the value of the straddle? Now consider a chooser option with the same parameters but a varying choice date. Complete the table shown below. What does the table illustrate about the relationship between chooser prices and straddle prices?

Choice Date, tc, in Days	Chooser Value
0	
1	
50	
100	
150	
200	
250	
300	
350	
355	
360	
364	

56. Consider a European call and a European put with parameter values of: $X = 70$; $T - t = 180$ days; $\sigma = 0.25$; $r = 0.1$; and $\delta = 0.0$. What is the value of the call and put if $S = 80$? Now consider a down-and-in call and a down-and-in put, with BARR = 80 and REBATE = 0.0. Using these data, complete the following table. What do these results suggest about the value of barrier options relative to plain vanilla options?

Stock Price	Down-and-In Call	Down-and-In Put
$120		
$100		
$90		
$85		
$83		
$82		
$81		
$80.10		
$80.01		

57. Consider an up-and-out call and an up-and-out put with the following common parameter values: $T - t = 180$ days; $\sigma = 0.2$; $r = 0.1$; $\delta = 0.03$; BARR = 100; and REBATE = 0. Complete the following table. What can you conclude from the completed table?

Stock Price	Up-and-Out Call $X = 80$	Up-and-Out Put $X = 100$
$99		
$95		
$90		
$85		
$80		
$75		
$70		

58. Consider an up-and-out call and an up-and-out put with the following common parameter values: $S = 98$; $\sigma = 0.2$; $r = 0.1$; $\delta = 0.03$; BARR = 100; and REBATE = 0. Complete the following table, and interpret the results.

$T - t$ in Days	Up-and-Out Call $X = 80$	Up-and-Out Put $X = 100$
1		
2		
5		
10		
20		
50		
100		
300		

59. A supershare is written with the following parameters: $S = 100$; $T - t = 365$ days; $\sigma = 0.4$; $r = 0.1$; and $\delta = 0.06$. Complete the following table for this supershare, assuming the varying upper and lower bounds in the table. What does the table illustrate about the influence of the bounds on the prices of supershares?

X_L	X_H	Supershare
70	80	
80	90	
90	100	
95	105	
100	110	
110	120	
120	130	

60. Consider two lookback calls with the following common parameters: $S = 100$; $T - t = 90$ days; $r = 0.06$; and $\delta = 0.0$. As the table indicates, the two calls are the same except one has MINPRI = $50, while the other has MINPRI = $95. Complete the following table and explain the differences in the prices of the two options.

Standard Deviation	Lookback Call MINPRI = 50	Lookback Call MINPRI = 95
0.1		
0.2		
0.3		
0.4		
0.5		
0.6		
0.9		

61. Consider an option to exchange one asset for another with $S_1 = 100$; $S_2 = 200$; $\delta_1 = 0.01$; $\delta_2 = 0.01$; $T - t = 90$ days; and $\rho = 0.0$. Complete the following table and interpret your results.

$\sigma_1 = \sigma_2$	Price of Exchange Option
0.5	
0.4	
0.3	
0.2	
0.1	
0.05	

62. A call on the maximum of two assets has the following parameters: $S_1 = 100$; $S_2 = 100$; $T - t = 365$ days; $r = 0.08$; $\delta_1 = 0.0$; $\delta_2 = 0.0$; $\rho = 0.0$. Complete the following table and interpret your results.

$\sigma_1 = \sigma_2$	Call Price	Put Price
0.5		
0.4		
0.3		
0.2		
0.1		
0.05		
0.01		
0.001		
0.0001		

APPENDIX

**Cumulative Distribution Function
for the Standard Normal Random Variable**

	.00	.01	.02	.03	.04	.05	.06	.07	.08	.09
0.0	.5000	.5040	.5080	.5120	.5160	.5199	.5239	.5279	.5319	.5359
0.1	.5398	.5438	.5478	.5517	.5557	.5596	.5636	.5675	.5714	.5753
0.2	.5793	.5832	.5871	.5910	.5948	.5987	.6026	.6064	.6103	.6141
0.3	.6179	.6217	.6255	.6293	.6331	.6368	.6406	.6443	.6480	.6517
0.4	.6554	.6591	.6628	.6664	.6700	.6736	.6772	.6808	.6844	.6879
0.5	.6915	.6950	.6985	.7019	.7054	.7088	.7123	.7157	.7190	.7224
0.6	.7257	.7291	.7324	.7357	.7389	.7422	.7454	.7486	.7517	.7549
0.7	.7580	.7611	.7642	.7673	.7704	.7734	.7764	.7794	.7823	.7852
0.8	.7881	.7910	.7939	.7967	.7995	.8023	.8051	.8078	.8106	.8133
0.9	.8159	.8186	.8212	.8238	.8264	.8289	.8315	.8340	.8365	.8389
1.0	.8413	.8438	.8461	.8485	.8508	.8531	.8554	.8577	.8599	.8621
1.1	.8643	.8665	.8686	.8708	.8729	.8749	.8770	.8790	.8810	.8830
1.2	.8849	.8869	.8888	.8907	.8925	.8944	.8962	.8980	.8997	.9015
1.3	.9032	.9049	.9066	.9082	.9099	.9115	.9131	.9147	.9162	.9177
1.4	.9192	.9207	.9222	.9236	.9251	.9265	.9279	.9292	.9306	.9319
1.5	.9332	.9345	.9357	.9370	.9382	.9394	.9406	.9418	.9429	.9441
1.6	.9452	.9463	.9474	.9484	.9495	.9505	.9515	.9525	.9535	.9545
1.7	.9554	.9564	.9573	.9582	.9591	.9599	.9608	.9616	.9625	.9633
1.8	.9641	.9649	.9656	.9664	.9671	.9678	.9686	.9693	.9699	.9706
1.9	.9713	.9719	.9726	.9732	.9738	.9744	.9750	.9756	.9761	.9767
2.0	.9772	.9778	.9783	.9788	.9793	.9798	.9803	.9808	.9812	.9817
2.1	.9821	.9826	.9830	.9834	.9838	.9842	.9846	.9850	.9854	.9857
2.2	.9861	.9864	.9868	.9871	.9875	.9878	.9881	.9884	.9887	.9890
2.3	.9893	.9896	.9898	.9901	.9904	.9906	.9909	.9911	.9913	.9916
2.4	.9918	.9920	.9922	.9925	.9927	.9929	.9931	.9932	.9934	.9936
2.5	.9938	.9940	.9941	.9943	.9945	.9946	.9948	.9949	.9951	.9952
2.6	.9953	.9955	.9956	.9957	.9959	.9960	.9961	.9962	.9963	.9964
2.7	.9965	.9966	.9967	.9968	.9969	.9970	.9971	.9972	.9973	.9974
2.8	.9974	.9975	.9976	.9977	.9977	.9978	.9979	.9979	.9980	.9981
2.9	.9981	.9982	.9982	.9983	.9984	.9984	.9985	.9985	.9986	.9986
3.0	.9987	.9987	.9987	.9988	.9988	.9989	.9989	.9989	.9990	.9990
3.1	.9990	.9991	.9991	.9991	.9992	.9992	.9992	.9992	.9993	.9993
3.2	.9993	.9993	.9994	.9994	.9994	.9994	.9994	.9995	.9995	.9995
3.3	.9995	.9995	.9995	.9996	.9996	.9996	.9996	.9996	.9996	.9997
3.4	.9997	.9997	.9997	.9997	.9997	.9997	.9997	.9997	.9997	.9998

INDEX